PERSPECTIVES OF INDIAN THOUGHT

DR N. C. PANDA

BHARATIYA KALA PRAKASHAN
DELHI (INDIA)

First Edition : 2007

Published by **C.P. Gautam**
BHARATIYA KALA PRAKASHAN
3421-A, IInd Floor, Narang Colony, Tri Nagar,
Delhi-110035. Phone : 27393083, 32967505
E-mail: bkp3421@yahoo.co.in

ISBN : 978-81-8090-167-6

Laser Type Setting by :
A-ONE GRAPHICS
Pitampura, New Delhi-110088

Printed by
BDH Printers at Salasar Imaging Systems, Delhi.

॥ श्रीः ॥

सच्छास्त्राम्भोधिमन्थोदितसरससुधाशेमुषीसेवितास्या
भट्टाचार्या दिविस्था गुरुगणगुणिता गोपिकामोहनाख्याः ।
विद्याजीवावताराः प्रथत इह यशः प्राक्प्रतीच्योस्तु येषां
तेषूपास्त्या निबद्धाञ्जलिरुपहरणं किञ्चिदेतत्तनोमि ॥

Dedicated with profound respects
To
my revered teacher
Late Prof. Dr Gopikamohan Bhattacharya

Former Prof. and Head Dept. of Sanskrit, Pāli & Prakrit, Dean, Faculty of I
Studies and Founder-Director, Institute of Sanskrit & Indological Studie.
Kurukshetra University, Kurukshetra

Contents

प्रो० वाचस्पति उपाध्याय
कुलपति
Prof. Vachaspati Upadhyaya
Vice Chancellor
श्री लालबहादुरशास्त्री राष्ट्रिय संस्कृत विद्यापीठ
नई दिल्ली-११००१६
Shri Lal Bahadur Shastri
Rashtriya Sanskrit Vidyapeetha
(Deemed to be University)
New Delhi-110016

सचिव
महर्षि सान्दीपनि
राष्ट्रीय वेदविद्या प्रतिष्ठान
(मानव संसाधन विकास मंत्रालय, भारत सरकार का स्वायतशासी संस्थान) प्रधिकरण भवन, द्वितीय तल, भरतपुरी, उज्जैन-४५६०१० (म.प्र.)
SECRETARY
Maharshi Sandipani
Rashtriya Vedavidya Pratishthan
(An autonomous organisation of the Ministry of HRD, Govt. of India) Pradhikaran Bhavan, II Floor, Bharatpuri, Ujjain-456010 (M.P.)

शुभाशंसा

डॉ० नरसिंहचरणपण्डामहोदयस्य **Perspectives of Indian Thought** इत्याख्यं प्रकाश्यं पुस्तकं पठित्वा मोदामृतपायीव मोमुद्यते मे मनः। पुस्तकेऽस्मिन् कतिपयानि वैदिकानि चिन्तनानि, वेदानुगामिषु महाभारतकूर्मवामनादिपुराणेषु उपनिबद्धानि विविधानि मौलिकानि तत्त्वानि, बौद्धसाहित्यनिष्ठम् अनेकसिद्धान्तजातं, कश्मीरशैवदर्शनरहस्यानि, मेघदूतादिविशिष्टग्रन्थान्तर्भूतानि सारतत्त्वानि ग्रन्थकारेण सम्यग् विमृश्यसमुपन्यस्तानीति समकालमेव तस्य वैदुष्यं विविधविषयस्थापनक्षमता च स्फुटीभवतः।

विविधेषु पुराणेषु रामायणे महाभारते नानाविधदर्शनशास्त्रेषु वेदानाम् उपबृंहणं समजायतेति मतं विद्वद्भिः सप्रमाणम् आकलितमस्ति। पुराणेषु विविधदेवानां देवोपासकानां च बलवीर्योत्साहादिजन्यसकलकल्याणसिद्ध्या सहितं यत् तीर्थानां माहात्म्यं वर्णितमस्ति, तत्र वैदिकमन्त्राणाम् उपयुक्ततात्पर्यनिर्णयस्तानावच्छिन्नतया दर्शितं प्रयोगवैशिष्ट्यमेव कारणमिति तर्कयितुं शक्यते। तद्वत् पुराणेषु अवतारवर्णनादिरुपक्रमो वैदिकवाङ्मये इन्द्रादिदेवानाम् अलौकिकवृत्तेः प्रभावेण दृश्यमानोऽस्ति। अतः पुराणेतिहासादिग्रन्थेषु आख्यानोपाख्यानादिसहायतया तद्गतं वर्णनं सिद्धान्तं न दिदृक्षुभिः जनैस्तेषां समेषां सूत्रात्मकस्रोतोरूपेण वैदिकसाहित्यमवश्ययमेव विमर्शेयुरिति पुस्तकप्रणेता विवक्षति ।

डॉ० पण्डामहोदयो युवा भूत्वाऽपि तथाविधान् विविधान् प्रौढचिन्तनसंवलितान् विषयान् विविच्य लिङ्गवयसोः अपेक्षया गुणानामेव महत्त्वं पोषयतो महाकवेः भवभूतेः एतामेवोक्तिं संपोषयति--

"गुणाः पूजास्थानं गुणिषु न च लिङ्गं न च वयः" इति।

विषयाणां भाषा प्राञ्जला स्पष्टार्थसञ्चारिका चाऽस्ति। विषया अपि प्राचीनजीवनदर्शनस्य विविधचिन्तनपद्धत्यनुसारिणः सन्तो वर्तमानकाले प्रासङ्गिका विद्यते इतीदं वैशिष्ट्यं समुल्लसति पुस्तकेऽस्मिन्।

सुधियः पाठकाः पुस्तकगतं विमर्शरसं संग्रहीतुं प्रवर्तन्ताम्, तेन प्रोत्साहितः पुस्तकलेखकः डॉ० पण्डामहोदयः पुस्तकान्तरलेखनाय समीहताम्, तदर्थम् अतितरां समेधतां चेति कामयमानो वर्ते।

उपाध्यायः

–प्रो० वाचस्पति उपाध्यायः
कुलपतिः
श्री लालबहादुरशास्त्रीराष्ट्रियसंस्कृतविद्यापीठ, नई दिल्ली

Blessings

It gives me immense pleasure to introduce Dr N.C. Panda, a young scholar whom I know since 1986, when he was working as a Research Scholar in the Dayanand Chair of Vedic Studies at Panjab University, Chandigarh, and awarded Ph.D. degree in Sanskrit (Vedic Studies) in 1990. He has qualified himself with Acharya in Buddhism (1998), Acharya in Darśana Śāstra (2001), Certificate course in German Language (1985) and Āyurveda-ratna (1989). Since 1987 I found him continuously contributing research papers to the standard Journals of country published in Hindi, Sanskrit and English. He has been attending Seminars and Conferences organized by various Universities and Academic Institutions and presenting papers on different topics on Indology. I found him enthusiastically taking part in discussions.

Dr Panda has got a good experience of research methodology and editing of Sanskrit and Buddhist texts, Journals and articles by associating himself with various research project works under Kalātattvakośa, and Kalāmūlaśāstra undertaken by the Indira Gandhi National Centre for the Arts, New Delhi.

It is a matter of great pleasure that a collection of 17 research papers (both published and unpublished) in English, contributed by Dr Panda from time to time, is being published in a book-form with the title '**Perspectives of Indian Thought**.'

I hope Dr Panda will keep his pursuit of knowledge continued and he will contribute more work in his field of specialization. May God bless him, so that he may prove his ability in form of bringing more work from his pen.

Prof. Braj Bihari Chaubey

Former Director,
V.V.B.I.S. & I.S.
Panjab University, Hoshiarpur
Chairman & Director,
Sangyan Vedic Studies & Research Centre
Hoshiarpur

Grams : Vidyapeetha

PROF. HAREKRISHNA SATAPATHY
Vice-Chancellor

RASHTRIYA SANSKRIT VIDYAPEETHA
(Deemed University)
Tirupati-517 507 (A.P.)
Accredited with A+ Grade by NAAC
Tel./Fax : 0877-2287680
(O) 2287836
(R) 2287826
E-mail : hks_vc@yahoo.com

Foreword

It is a unique pleasure on my part to compliment Dr Narasingha Charan Panda, Sr. Research Officer in Indira Gandhi National Center for Arts, Varanasi, on the occasion of the publication of his book entitled **"Perspectives of Indian Thought"**. This is a collection of his research papers presented before the intellectual audience on various occasions and highly appreciated because of their originality and deep alacrity on the subject. The papers deal with entire canvas of topics including Vedas, Epics, Purāṇas, Buddhism, Kashmir Śaivism and some other renowned works of classical Sanskrit literature, which are very much useful for the researchers as well as the seekers of knowledge in Indian system of philosophical thoughts and ethical principles.

So many seers, saints, savants and prophets have appeared in this sacred land of knowledge and wisdom with definite mission at various points of time to save the mankind from imminent danger. The purpose is made clear from the beginning of their life and career as promoters of human values and profounder of philosophical theories. Keeping in view this noble mission, those prophets and rishis have given a message to the mankind that constantly assures the world of everlasting place, supreme bliss and unending joy. The sacred scriptures, like Vedas, Upaniṣadas, Epics, Purāṇas so on and so forth, are there to guide the human race in its proper direction for all times to come. Dr Panda, the author of the present book, with his extraordinary craftsmanship to grasp the things and uncommon quality to penetrate deep into the matter, has made serious and sincere efforts to revisit, renew and refurbish these messages in his inimitable style of presentation, for which he deserves the appreciation of one and all.

Dr Panda is an erudite scholar and a well-known researcher. He has written so many research papers and edited some valuable works to his credit. His unquenched thirsts for knowledge, uncommon inclination towards Indian systems of philosophy and incessant labour to analyze the traditional thoughts with modern outlook have brought immense laurels for him. He has got a long way to traverse; a long future to conquer and a long area to explore to enrich the limitless world of Sanskrit literature. May his journey for exploring the new vistas of knowledge and wisdom be happy and prosperous with the divine blessings of Almighty and good wishes of his friends, philosophers and mentors.

May this publication be also crowned with resounding success as his earlier ones.

16/8/06

—Prof. H.K. Satapathy
Vice-Chancellor
Rashtriya Sanskrit Vidyapeeth
(Deemed University), Tirupati, A.P.

Preface

It affords me immense pleasure to know that Dr Narasingha Charan Panda (M.A., M.Phil., Ph.D., Darshanacharya, Bauddhadarshanacharya), Senior Research Officer, Indira Gandhi National Centre for the Arts, Varanasi, is bringing out a book entitled "**Perspectives of Indian Thought**", a brilliant collection of his Papers on different aspects of Indology: Papers 1-3 deal with the Vedic literature: 1. ***The Veda: A Moral Code for Humanity***; 2. ***Ornaments in the Vedic Literature***, 3. ***Maharshi Dayananda Sarasvati as an Interpreter of the Vedas*** ; Papers 4-5 treat of the Vedic concepts in the Mahābhārata; 4. ***Reflection of the Vedas in the Mahābhārata***; Papers 6-8 discuss problems of the Purāṇas; 6. ***Naimisāraṇya Tīrtha as depicted in the Epics and the Purāṇas*** ; 7. ***Concept of Avatāra in the Kūrma-Purāṇa***; 8. ***Socio-religious aspect in the Vāmana-Purāṇa***; Papers 9-12 have Buddhism and the Buddhist literature as their subject; 9. ***Buddhist Concept of Basic Material Element: A Scientific Critique***; 10. ***Concept of Indriya in Buddhism***; 11. ***Concept of Bhūmi in the Buddhist Literature with special reference to the Daśabhūmika-sūtra***; 12. ***Māra in the Buddhist Literature***; Papers 13-15 touch upon concepts of Kashmir Śaivism; 14. ***Abhinavagupta on Mystical Experience***; 15. ***Symbols and Śakti Worship***, while papers 16-17 relate themselves to the classical Sanskrit Literature; 16. ***Geographical Data in the Meghadūta***; 17. ***Socio-economic Thoughts in the Śukranītisāra***. The book is also equipped with Bibliography, a Glossary, an Index and illustrations.

I congratulate Dr Panda, a serious scholar gifted with an unassuming nature, on this publication. It will certainly create interest in both indologists as well as the general readers. I trust Indology, especially Sanskrit studies shall be further enriched by other works from his pen.

May goddess Sarasvati shower her blessings on him.

—**Prof. Maan Singh**
Recipient of the President's Certificate of Honour
Former Professor & Head, Dept. of Sanskrit,
Gurukula Kangri University, Haridwar; Himachal Pradesh
University, Shimla; Kurukshetra University, Kurukshetra.
Director, Institute of Sanskrit and Indological Studies;
Maharshi Dayananda Centre for Vedic Studies,
Kurukshetra University, Kurukshetra.

आमुखम्

विचित्रहारो व्यरचि प्रकामं
विद्याविलासोपवनप्रसूनैः ।
शास्त्रौघनिर्मन्थविदग्धबुद्ध्या
सारस्वते वर्त्मनि यन्नृसिंहः ॥ १ ॥

वाराणसीं प्राप्य कलालिकेन्द्रं
गान्धीन्दिरानामयुतं गरिष्ठम् ।
श्रीविश्वनाथस्य सुसन्निधाने
सुसन्निधौ संकटमोचनस्य ॥ २ ॥

वेदेषु काश्मीरशिवस्वतन्त्र-
त्रिकाख्यशास्त्रे विशदं विवेकी ।
पुराणबौद्धादिविशिष्टवादे
सत्तथ्यतर्कैः कलिता निबन्धाः ॥ ३ ॥

वेदेषु जुष्टां मनुजस्य नीती-
राचारशास्त्रं त्वपि तत्र भूषाः ।
विवेचिता अंगविशेषरम्याः
श्रुतिप्रसिद्धाः सुखदाः समस्ताः ॥ ४ ॥

श्रुतिर्महाभारतदृष्टकीर्ति-
र्गीता त्वथो यज्ञवदातरूपम् ।
श्रीनैमिषं सर्वपुराणभूमिः
कूर्मावतारोऽपि पुराणदृष्ट्या॥ ५ ॥

श्रीवामने धर्मसमाजबोधो
बौद्धेषु द्रव्येष्वथ मूलभूतम् ।
वैज्ञानिकं तत्त्वमथेन्द्रियाणां
भूमेश्च सूत्रे दशभूमिकाख्ये ॥ ६ ॥

तत्सौगते मारकथां विवक्षुः
सद्दर्शनप्रेरितदृष्टिमृष्टाम् ।
काश्मीरशैवाद्वयशास्त्रभासि
शिवस्वरूपं किल विश्वतीर्णम्॥ ७ ॥

अथाभिनूत्नाभिनवोदिता सा
गूढा परा संविदनन्यभूमिः ।
उक्ता च अंकेतदलञ्च शक्ते-
र्नीराजनायां कथितं रहस्यैः ॥ ८ ॥

भौगोलिकं मेघनिसर्गकाव्ये
वृत्तान्तमुक्त्वाप्यथ शुक्रनीतौ ।
समाज इत्यर्थ इति प्रसिद्धं
पक्षद्वयं सारयुतं व्यचारि ॥ ९ ॥

अत्र स्थिता सप्तदश प्रबन्धा
विद्वन्मनीषां च विशिष्टदृष्टिम् ।
संलक्षयन्तीति न संशयो मे
प्रत्नस्य नूत्नो विहितो विचारः ॥ १० ॥

पान्थोऽयं कुरुक्षेत्रे पण्डितमेधाविच्छात्रमित्रममुम्
सारस्वतश्रेयसे जिहीर्षति शुभाशयान् शतशः ॥ ११ ॥

–डॉ० सुरेन्द्रमोहनमिश्रः
संस्कृतपालिप्राकृतविभागः
कुरुक्षेत्र विश्वविद्यालयः, कुरुक्षेत्रम्

Acknowledgements

At the very outset, I must express my deep sense of gratitude and sincere thanks to esteemed Sir **Prof. Vacaspati Upadhyaya**, Hon'ble Vice-Chancellor, Sri Lal Bahadur Shastri Rashtriya Sanskrit Vidyapeetha, New Delhi, a great scholar of Indology and an ideal promoter of Sanskrit teaching and learning, for writing a few words as '**Blessings**' of this book.

I am also extremely grateful to revered **Prof. H.K. Satapathy**, Hon'ble Vice-Chancellor, Sri Venkateswara Sanskrit University, Tirupati, for contributing a scholarly '**Foreword**' to this work. My thanks are due to him.

It is also a matter of great satisfaction for me to extend my sincere obligation and due thanks to those erudite scholars of Sanskrit, from whose heart a token of appreciation came out as '**Blessings**' to this volume. Their best wishes are remaining as a source of inspiration for my future academic perspectives. Hence, I am greatly beholden to respected **Prof. A.C. Sarangi**, Vice-Chancellor, Sri Jagannath Sanskrit University, Puri, **Prof. D.B. Sen Sharma**, Kolkatta, **Prof. Bhawanilal Bhartiya**, Jodhpur, **Prof. Sivji Upadhyaya**, Varanasi, **Prof. Biswanath Bhattacharya**, Varanasi, **Prof. B.B. Chaubey**, Hoshiarpur, **Prof. Siniruddha Dash**, Chennai, **Prof. Rai Anand Krishna,** Varanasi, **Prof. Ranvir Singh**, Kurukshetra, **Prof. G.C. Tripathi**, New Delhi, **Prof. Vikram Kumar**, Chandigarh, **Prof. Sri Narayana Mishra,** Varanasi, **Prof. Bhim Singh**, Kurukshetra, **Prof. Ram Shankar Tripathi** (Sarnath), Varanasi, **Prof. M.L. Wadekar**, Baroda, and **Prof. Amar Nath Pandey**, Varanasi.

I am also extending my sincere regards and gratefulness to **Prof. Maan Singh**, whose illuminating guidance and timely encouragement facilitated my work immensely.

I beg to express my sincere thankfulness to **Mahāmahopādhyāya Prof. Rewaprasada Dwivedi**,Varanasi, **Prof. Gangadhar Panda**, Varanasi, **Dr Arvind Kumar,** Kurukshetra, **Prof. Virendra Kumar Mishra,** Shimla, and **Dr Ravindra Kumar Panda,** Baroda, for their rendering valuable suggestions from time to time.

I acknowledge my heartfelt gratitude to **Dr Surendra Mohan Mishra**, Kurukshetra and **Dr Gopabandhu Mishra**, B.H.U., Varanasi, for their enlightening inspiration and scholarly suggestions to complete this work successfully.

I am really thankful to my sincere friend **Dr Sukumar Chattopadhyaya,** I.G.N.C.A., for his ingenuous help, constant cooperation and invaluable suggestions, whenever I needed.

I am also deeply grateful to all my respected teachers, friends, colleagues of V.V.B.I.S. & I.S., Panjab University, Hoshiarpur; my wife Shradhanjali and lovely daughter Prajñā, who directly or indirectly have helped me a lot by their varied activities.

I feel highly delighted in dedicating the book to my esteemed teacher late **Prof. Gopikamohan Bhattacharya** for his ingenuous affection and kind blessings. So, for me personally this is an occasion to pay a great tribute to the noble soul.

Sri C.P. Gautam, publisher of **Bharatiya Kala Prakashan**, Delhi, deserves special mention here. Due to his personal interest and sincere effort the book came out in a stipulated period. Hence, I extend my heartiest thanks and obligations to him. I am also equally thankful to **Sri Raman Chaudhary** for his useful suggestions and timely cooperation.

Lastly, I owe an enormous debt of gratitude to all those scholars/individuals and institutions that have made the illustrations accompanying the book possible. I thank them for permitting me to illustrate the art objects from their collections and for generously supplying photographs with the permission to reproduce them. Special mention may be made of National Museum of India, New Delhi, Bharat Kala Bhavan, B.H.U., Varanasi, Sarnath Museum, Varanasi, Indira Gandhi National Centre for the Arts, New Delhi/Varanasi, Jñāna Pravāha, Varanasi, Archaeological Survey of India, New Delhi, Patna Museum, Ptana and C.I.H.T.S., Sarnath. I am also highly thankful to the Directors/Heads of the above institutions for their kind cooperation.

—N. C. Panda
Reader in Sanskrit

27 June, 2007
Panjab University
V.V.B.I.S. & I.S.
Sadhu Ashram
Hoshiarpur (Punjab)

Abbreviations

AV	:	Atharvaveda
BhG/Gītā	:	Bhagavad Gītā
BORI	:	Bhandarkar Oriental Research Institute
Ch.	:	Chapter
ChāUp	:	Chāndogya Upaniṣad
Comm.	:	Commentary
DBhūSū	:	Daśabhūmika Sūtra
Ed./ed.	:	Editor / edited
edn.	:	Edition
Fig.	:	Figure
JBORS	:	Journal of the Bihar and Orissa Research Society
K.S.T.S.	:	Kashmir Śaiva Text Series
Lit.	:	Literally
Mbh	:	Mahābhārata
MSūAl	:	Mahāyāna Sūtrālaṅkāra
Nir	:	Nirukta
p.	:	page
Pl.	:	Plate
P.T.S.	:	Pāli Text Society
ṚV	:	Ṛgveda
Vol.	:	Volume

List of Transliteration

अ	आ	इ	ई	उ	ऊ	
a	ā	i	ī	u	ū	
ए	ऐ	ओ	औ	अं	अ:	ऋ
e	ai	o	au	ṁ	ḥ	ṛ
क	ख	ग	घ	ङ		
ka	kha	ga	gha	ṅa		
च	छ	ज	झ	ञ		
ca	cha	ja	jha	ña		
ट	ठ	ड	ढ	ण	ळ	
ṭa	ṭha	ḍa	ḍha	ṇa	ḷ	
त	थ	द	ध	न		
ta	tha	da	dha	na		
प	फ	ब	भ	म		
pa	pha	ba	bha	ma		
य	र	ल	व	श	ष	स
ya	ra	la	va	śa	ṣa	sa
ह	क्ष	त्र	ज्ञ			
ha	kṣa	tra	jña			

List of Illustrations/Plates

Chapter XII

Chapter XV

Opinion of Eminent Scholars on the Work

In English

1. **Prof. G.C. Tripathi**
Professor & Head (Kalakosha Division)
Indira Gandhi National Centre for the Arts
New Delhi.

2. **Prof. Biswanath Battacharya**
Former Head,Dept. of Sanskrit,
Banaras Hindu University,Varanasi.

3. **Mahāmahopādhyāya Prof. Rewaprasada Dwivedi**
Former Dean,
Faculty of Sanskrit,
B.H.U., Varanasi

4. **Prof. Devavrata Sen Sharma**
Research Professor, Sri Rama-krishna Mission,
Golpark, Kolkata
Recipient of President's Certificate of Honour
Former Chairman, Dept. of Sanskrit, Pali & Prakrit
Ex-Director, Institute of Sanskrit & Indological Studies
Ex-Dean, Faculty of Indic Studies, Kurukshetra University
Former M.M Gopinath Kaviraj Senior Research Professor,
Asiatic Society, Kolkata

5. **Prof. A.C. Sarangi**
Vice-Chancellor
Shri Jagannath Sanskrit Vishvavidyalaya, Shri Vihar,
Puri, Orissa

6. **Prof. M.L. Wadekar**
Offg. Director, Oriental Institute
M.S. University of Baroda, Vadodara

7. **Prof. Sriniruddha Dash**
Professor and Head,
Deptt. of Sanskrit
University of Madras, Madras

8. **Prof. Bhawani Lal Bhartiya**
Editor, Paropkārī Journal
Former Professor & Head
Dayanand Chair for Vedic Studies
Panjab University, Chandigarh.

9. **Prof. Amar Nath Pandey**
Former Professor & Head
Dept. of Sanskrit
Mahatma Gandhi Kashi Vidyapith
Varanasi.

10. **Prof. Rai Anand Krishna**
Former Dean, Faculty of Arts
& Director,
Bharat Kaḷa Bhawan, Banaras Hindu University
Varanasi.

11. **Prof. Dr Ranvir Singh**
Director
Institute of Sanskrit & Indological Studies
Kurukshetra University
Kurukshetra.

In Sanskrit

1. **प्रो० श्रीनारायण मिश्रः**
पूर्वकलासंकायप्रमुखः,
आचार्यः संस्कृतविभागाध्यक्षचरश्च
काशीहिन्दूविश्वविद्यालयः, वाराणसी

2. **प्रो० शिवजी उपाध्याय**
उपकुलपतिचर: एवम् विभागाध्यक्षश्च
साहित्य संगीत कला विभाग
सम्पूर्णानन्द संस्कृत विश्वविद्यालय,
वाराणसी

3. **प्रो० गंगाधरपण्डाः**
आचार्योऽध्यक्षश्च
पुराण-इतिहास विभाग
सम्पूर्णानन्द संस्कृत विश्वविद्यालय,
वाराणसी

4. **प्रो० डॉ० भीमसिंहः**
आचार्योऽध्यक्षश्च
संस्कृत-पालि-प्राकृतविभागे
कुरुक्षेत्र-विश्वविद्यालयः
कुरुक्षेत्रम्

5. **प्रोफेसरः डॉ० विक्रम कुमारः**
संस्कृतविभागः,
अध्यक्ष, दयानन्द वैदिक अनुसन्धान पीठ,
पंजाब विश्वविद्यालयः

6. **प्रो० रामशंकरः त्रिपाठी**
शोधाचार्यः
केन्द्रयोच्चतिब्बतीशिक्षासंस्थानम्
सारनाथः, वाराणसी।
पूर्व आचार्य एवं अध्यक्ष, बौद्धदर्शन विभाग
सम्पूर्णानन्द संस्कृत विश्वविद्यालय

Introduction

Realizing the truth or reality through intuition, ancient seers of India present us their treasure of profound knowledge. Their deep intuitive insight gives birth to all the systems of Indian thought. This store-house of sagacity is an eternal source of inspiration to all the researchers in the multidisciplinary fields of Indian thought. There is no other means in the world as capable of sanctifying as knowledge (*na hi jñānena sadṛśaṁ pavitram iha vidyate—Gītā* IV.38).

Vedic hymns are revealed and handed down from generation to generation by oral tradition and hence these should be studied with great care. But due to the lack of proper knowledge later philosophers have tried to misinterpret the Vedas. Still the modern scholars are trying to find out the nearest ideas of fundamental concepts. Keeping this view in mind an attempt has been made here to represent some thoughts of Indian cultural tradition. In this collective composition seventeen articles have been taken as a symbol of wholeness in Indian cultural tradition. Sixteen *kalās* or parts of moon symbolize an aspect of parted concept but beyond that a stage remains which symbolizes the Brahman as a whole.

Vedas play a significant role in the field of moral and spiritual teachings. As a moral code of entire humanity and purifier of speech, mind and breath, the Vedas lead to move in a proper direction to get the liberation. Besides the attitude of Vedic people towards spiritual knowledge, it is very interesting to note that they try to understand the basic approach to practical life even through the beautification of body by the fashion of wearing ornaments starting from the head down to the feet. Hence, a large variety of ornaments are used during the Vedic period as head ornaments, ear ornaments, necklace or chains, chest or breast ornaments, armlets, wristlets, waist ornaments and ornaments even for feet.

Next, the author of this collection focus on the methods of interpretation of the Vedic hymns by Dayānanda where the basic principles of interpretation is based on the *Nirukta* of Yāska. Dayānanda also believes in the threefold approach of interpretation as *ādhyātmika, ādhidaivika* and *ādhiyājñika*. Yogi Aurobindo also appreciates Dayānanda's approach towards the interpretation of the Vedas on 'capital importance for understanding the peculiar method of the Vedic Ṛṣis.'

Next, to show the origin of epical thoughts and ideas in the Vedas the author presents the reflection of the Vedas in the *Mahābhārata* where the Vedic subjects like *yajña, karma, dharma, darśana*, etc. are crystallized. The *Mahābhārata* serves as a nucleus of Hinduism as worldly wisdom and Vedic knowledge are interlinked with various religious attitudes. In the Śāntiparva of the *Mahābhārata* this epic is called as *Mahopaniṣad*: *idaṁ mahopaniṣadaṁ caturvedasamanvitam* (Mbh XII.339.11). Different Vedic subjects like Vedic deities and seers, Vedic *saṁskāras, āśramas, yajñas, karmas*, etc. are highlighted in this part.

Yajña or sacrificial ritual is actually an active performance of reciprocal balance, based on the policy of giving and taking, the way for harmony between the human being and Divine. As a symbol of Vedic knowledge and cultural tradition, the concept of Vedic *yajñas* is also inherited in later generation of great epics and as a result several *yajñas* are described in the *Mahābhārata* in a modified way like *dravya-yajña, tapoyajña, yoga-yajña* and *svādhyāya jñāna-yajña*. The sacrifices are the centre of cultural tradition of ancient India, leading to *dharma* and finally to reach the Supreme goal, Brahman or liberation.

Relating with the Vedic literature and Epics, the author also deals with an important *tīrtha*—Naimiṣāraṇya as depicted in the Epics and Purāṇas, treating the same as holy and famous place of Northern India. For establishing the religious upliftment and final attainment of the highest goal of the people of different ages in this *tīrtharāja,* the author has tried to support this from Vedic literature and Epics and Purāṇas.

Similarly, incarnation or *avatāra* is also an important concept of the Purāṇas. Describing the source and necessity of *avatāras*, number and types of various *avatāras* of Epics and Purāṇas are also described here. Theory of evolution is also related with this *avatāravāda* which unlocks the mysteries of nature. In this article an attempt has been made to represent the various *avatāras* of Lord Viṣṇu and Lord Śiva, depicted in the *Kūrma Purāṇa.*

In this Purāṇic order the author also adds the socio-religious aspects in the *Vāmana Purāṇa* where ancient caste-system, *āśrama vyavasthā, brahmacarya*, etc. are described along with the religious concepts like *yajña, pūjā, vrata, tīrtha, śrāddha & dāna,* etc.

After completing this Purāṇic journey, the author peeps into the Buddhism where four articles are presented. The first of which deals with the Buddhist concept of basic material element where an attempt has been made to discuss matter, the collective organism, consisting of the fourfold substratum of colour, smell, taste and contact, relating with modern Scientific outlook. In Buddhism four principal characteristics of matter are referred—earth element, water element, fire element and air element, which are also almost same as in the modern scientific concept of existing three forms of matter—solid, liquid and gas. *Pṛthivī* is a solid form, water is a liquid form and the rest two: *tejas* and *vāyu* are gaseous form of matter.

Next, the Buddhist concept of *indriyas* or twenty-two bodily faculties are discussed in detail. Six sense organs—eye, ear, nose, tongue, body and mind act as eternal self-hood. Femininity and masculinity indicate the two faculties of differentiating sex. Faculties of bodily pleasure, pain, joy, grief and equanimity are sufferings of worldly life. But the five ethical faculties—faith, energy, mindfulness, concentration and wisdom help to stop the suffering. The rest three faculties of enlightenment—initial intermediate help a person to reach the supreme goal pertain to the super mundane.

In the same (Buddhist) philosophy, *bhūmi* is treated as a multidimensional concept. Here the ten *bhūmis* or spiritual stages on *bhūmis* of a Bodhisattva are elaborately described. These are actually the stages of spiritual progress for the attainment of perfect and highest knowledge (*tattva-jñāna*). The last article of this category focuses on Māra, a weak state of mind. To achieve emancipation, one should struggle against the fetters and hindrances and man only he or she should be able to reach the destination, i.e. Nirvāṇa.

Next two articles discuss the enriched Tantra and Āgama—"Nature of the Absolute in Kashmir Śaivism" and "Abhinavagupta on Mystical Experience." Relating the basic concept with other Tāntric texts, the author also deals with the symbols and Śakti worship.

Geographical data in the *Meghadūta* fills our heart with joy and pleasure. It is surmised that Kālidāsa's description of cloud-route is a symbol of contemporary topography or geography of India. The last or seventeenth article is a full-offering to the scholars and it deals with Socio-economic thoughts as reflected in the *Śukranītisāra*.

The author has done his best in these articles. Finally, this work is actually a mental sacrifice (*mānasa-yajña*) of auspicious number seventeen to get the *prasāda* from the Supreme Being.

The work is also enriched with a number of Illustrations / plates including various *yantras* of ten Mahāvidyās, incarnations of god, sacrificial utensils used in the Vedic rituals, etc. Besides an Index and a General Bibliography, an addition of a Glossary of technical terms is also a notable feature of this volume.

However, despite of the author's best endeavour, the presence of some mistakes and blemishes in this work could not be avoided for which he craves the indulgence of the intelligent readers.

The Veda : A Moral Code for Humanity

The Veda is the fountain head or repository of all knowledge and wisdom, an outline of the whole universe covering all the matters relating to animate and in-animate. It is so called, because of every matter contained therein, in forms of a man of human life called the law of righteousness to understand which there is no other valid means or the proof. The Veda inspires the law giver, as it is called the code of laws. It teaches all kinds of laws to the entire humanity for their prosperity in various fields. Hence, it is called a code book of all laws.

But, it is specially called a moral code for humanity; because, the moral law, which reminds man of his position in nature, is given in the unparalleled code of universal ethics of the hoary Veda, whose melodious music indelibly impresses it on the mind. Its study for a sufficiently long time habituates the mind to it in dealing with the concerns of daily life. Man then does not act like dumb and driven cattle, but goes about as a responsible member of society.

The Veda is a big ocean of treasure of moral and spiritual teachings. It teaches ethical values and moral obligations towards gods, seers, Brahmins/teachers, mother and motherland. The human being should always follow the moral and spiritual advices of the Veda for his well being as well as for the true prosperity of the mankind.

In the *Yajurveda* it is said that the Supreme Lord or *Īśa* is the Creator and ruler of this universe and hence the Supreme self is the controller of the individual self. One should feel obliged towards God for this multifarious and unique creation. He has created everything for the enjoyment as well as sustenance of human beings. So every universal being has the proper right to live better and enjoy the great creation of the Lord. But being the Supreme ruler, He puts some moral restrictions in the way of living as well as enjoyment of life of the human beings. It is obvious that we are social beings and should live amicably in the society. The religious duties and obligations of every man should be well maintained It is advised that the human beings should be helpful, merciful towards others. Hence, the *mantra* says:

ईशा वास्यमिदं सर्वं यत्किञ्च जगत्यां जगत् ।
तेन त्यक्तेन भुञ्जीथा मा गृधः कस्यस्विद्धनम्।।[1]

All this-whatsoever moves in this ephemeral world are enveloped by the God—*Īśa*, the Supreme Lord of this universe. Enjoy the good things of life as gifts of God. Do not covet the wealth of any one, i.e. what belongs to others.

It is a clear indication to the human being that his existence is due to the Grace of God. And for his smoothly maintenance He has provided everything, i.e. food, cloth and other valuable things. But the question arises, whatever he is enjoying being thought that it is his thing or property but in reality it is not true. It means all the enjoyable things, i.e. house, food, ornaments, property, etc. do not belong to him permanently. Hence, these (movable and immovable) enjoyable things (*dhanam*) belong to God; although, it is being created for us to enjoy, but we have no right to misuse the wealth of God. So it is said '*tena tyaktena bhuñjithā*'. After '*tyāga*'-renouncing for others one should enjoy. Moreover one should not have any attachment towards this unreal wealth. Whatever one has gathered or earned out of that a major portion should be given to poors, needy persons or helpless persons and the rest wealth would be enjoyed by him. Hence, it is the moral as well as religious duty of a wealthy man to extend support to the poors and pay gifts to the desired persons. However, after performing these moral obligations towards financially backward persons of the society one should live his life in a better order.

Further, the Veda advises that only by accomplishing religious *karmas* like performance of various sacrifices, render free service to the desired people, pay gifts to see the happiness of others, etc. one should wish to live a hundred years in the society. *Karma* should be the main basis of our existence without which life has no value:

कुर्वन्नेवेह कर्माणि जिजीविषेच्छतं समाः ।
एवं त्वयि नान्यथेतोऽस्ति न कर्म लिप्यते नरेः॥[2]

In this world, one should desire to live a hundred years, a life, by performing energetic actions. For a man, this is the way to be freed from the attachment to actions, because there is no other way to this consummation.

Therefore, one should desire to live by doing only such deeds or *karmas* as Agnihotra, five great sacrifices (*pañca-mahā-yajña*), etc., which are enjoined by scriptures. The Vedic advices are: one should not hanker after his life or death, and should go to the forest to maintain '*sannyāsa dhrama*' in proper period of his life. This should be the real aim of his life. The human beings are advised to follow the seven rules of conduct established by the Vedic seers and wise persons. The verse says:

सप्त मर्यादाः कवयस्ततक्षुस्तासामेकामिदभ्यंहुरो गात्।
आयोर्ह स्कम्भ उपमस्य नीळे पथां विसर्गे धरुणेषु तस्थौ॥[3]

The seven pathways fixed by the great wise men are really help a person to get all prosperity in the world. He is a sinner who deviates from any one of them. Agni is the protector of life from serious sin or moral offence. Hence, a man should follow the cosmic law as well as rules of conduct established by our ancient seers.

The Veda further advises to keep distance from passion / lust (*kāma*), anger (*krodha*), covetousness (*lobha*), delusion / infatuation (*moha*), pride (*mada*), and enviousness/ hostility (*matsara*). Because these six disorders (*vikāras*) must provoke a being to commit any sin or to behave abnormally, this is harmful for him. The six wicked elements should be elevated from mind and heart, otherwise the life of a person would move towards hell. This thing is nicely exemplified in the *Ṛgveda* as:

उलूकयातुं शुशुलूकयातुं जहि श्वयातुमुत कोकयातुम्।
सुपर्णयातुमुत गृध्रयातुं दृषदेव प्र मृण रक्ष इन्द्र ॥[4]

The nature and special quality of different animals/beasts are mentioned in this *mantra*. Owl is a lustful or amorous bird while the owlet is an angry animal. The nature of owl and owlet, viz. *moha* and *krodha* should be totally destroyed and ignored by the human beings. Secondly, the nature of dog and cuckoo, viz. *matsara* and *kāma* should also be properly destroyed Thirdly, the nature of eagle and vulture, viz. *mada* & *lobha* is not even favourable for human being. Hence, all ill-minded spirits and thoughts of these animals and birds must be fully destroyed Otherwise, the smooth spiritual journey of the human being would be hampered and finally stopped

Desire for a good and auspicious life has always and everywhere been a human aspiration. The Vedic seers always seek and pray for receiving auspicious powers and thoughts from the God. The *Ṛgveda* rightly says:

आ नो भद्राः क्रतवो यन्तु विश्वतोऽदब्धासो अपरीतास उद्भिदः।
देवा नो यथा सदमिद् वृधे असन्नप्रायुवो रक्षितारो दिवेदिवे॥[5]

May the auspicious powers and thoughts come to us from every quarter, which are unmolested, unhindered and always victorious? The gods ever may stay with us to protect us from day to day problems and help us to achieve prosperity.

Here it is advised to the human beings that God is the bestower of all things and hence pray Him to receive all materialistic pleasures as well as eternal happiness.

The Vedic moral teachings are essential for the sanctification of *vāk, manas*, heart and other senses of every human being. The man may listen good and sacred speeches and see excellent things. He should enjoy his life by worshipping gods with purity and serving to the great scholars with true devotion. In the words of Veda:

भद्रं कर्णेभिः शृणुयाम देवा भद्रं पश्येमाक्षभिर्यजत्राः।
स्थिरैरङ्गैस्तुष्टुवांसस्तनूभिर्व्यशेम देवहितं यदायुः॥[6]

A man should think better, hear better and do better for himself and for others. His speech should be soft and sweet, because, Goddess Lakṣmī lives in lofty and purified speech. Secondly, sweet speech is a bond of unity and friendship. It is a medium of expression of (our) thoughts and feelings to the gods, *pitṛs* and men, through worship, *śrāddha*, and general conversation, respectively. The word is represented as the product of meditation, love and common concern.

Regarding the merits of smooth expression of views, the Veda advises :

सक्तुमिव तितउना पुनन्तो यत्र धीरा मनसा वाचमक्रत ।
अत्रा सखायः सख्यानि जानते भद्रैषां लक्ष्मीर्निहिताधि वाचि॥[7]

The wise persons always express their speeches or words through wisdom, like men cleansing corn in a cribble. Thus, friends know and recognize each other's friendship and good fortune (Śrī) lives in their speech for ever.

Hence, it is obvious to speak sweet words or to be soft spoken for receiving good fortune and prosperity.

As the universe is created by God, so the whole world should be treated as a family (*vasudhaiva kuṭumbakam*). So in this God's creation all the human beings should be one and united (*saṁgha śaktau kaliyuge*). Let us meet together, talk together and work together for the well-being of our society.

सं गच्छध्वं सं वदध्वं सं वो मनांसि जानताम्॥[8]

Besides, for universal friendship, equality & brotherhood, Veda rightly teaches us as:

समानो मन्त्रः समितिः समानी समानं मनः सह चित्तमेषाम्।
समानं मन्त्रमभि मन्त्रये वः समानेन वो हविषा जुहोमि॥
समानी व आकूतिः समाना हृदयानि वः।
समानमस्तु वो मनो यथा वः सुसहासति॥[9]

Being the words of God Veda teaches all to maintain a healthy, peaceful and spiritual life in the society.

Like Vedas, the words of Upaniṣads are also very useful in our day to day activities. One cannot negate their teachings as the seers of Upaniṣads had a right approach to educate people in a proper direction in a way of their spiritual journey, i.e. towards liberation. The *Bṛhadāraṇyaka Upaniṣad* preaches self-restraint, generosity and compassion. It is said that the gods, demons and men all had gone for enlightenment to their common father Prajāpati (Creator of the Universe), and he honestly instructed them with one single syllable, '*da*'. The gods understood it as self control (*dama*), the demons as compassion (*dayā*), and men as charity or gift (*dāna*). In the words of Upaniṣad:

दाम्यत दत्त दयध्वमिति तदेतत् त्र्यं शिक्षेद्दमं दानं दयामिति॥[10]

For the human beings Prajāpati advises to offer gifts to the poor and desired persons. Thus, gift (*dāna)* is essentially a human virtue, because man being a social being must think of others around him and come to their aid by curtailing his own enjoyment. Hence, man transgresses his own *dharma* or rather, goes against the inherent law of his nature if he hoards everything for his own enjoyment and is not charitable in his disposition.[11]

The *Bṛhadāraṇyaka Upaniṣad* also teaches to perform pious deeds for getting good results:

पुण्यो वै पुण्येन कर्मणा भवति पापः पापेनेति॥[12]

The commentator Śaṅkarācārya explains the nature of pious act (*puṇya-karma*) and sinful act (*pāpa karma*) as:

तस्मात् पुण्यो वै शास्त्रविहितेन पुण्येन कर्मणा भवति,
तद्विपरीतेन विपरीतो भवति पापः पापेन॥[13]

The *Chāndogya Upaniṣad,* expresses the ethical basis of the Upaniṣadic doctrine through a simile, as water does not stick to the leaf of a lotus-flower, so evil actions do not stick to him who knows this self.

यथा पुष्करपलाश आपो न श्लिष्यन्त एवमेवंविदि पापं कर्म न श्लिष्यत इति॥[14]

After completion of the Gurukula education some moral advices are given by the teacher to the disciples as an essential part of their daily duty. These moral as well as spiritual teachings are nicely presented in the *Taittirīya Upaniṣad* as:

सत्यं वद। धर्मं चर। स्वाध्यायान्मा प्रमदः। आचार्याय प्रियं धनमाहृत्य प्रजातन्तुं मा व्यवच्छेत्सीः। सत्यान्न प्रमदितव्यम्। धर्मान्न प्रमदितव्यम्। कुशलान्न प्रमदितव्यम्। भूत्यै न प्रमदितव्यम्। स्वाध्यायप्रवचनाभ्यां न प्रमदितव्यम्।

देवपितृकार्याभ्यां न प्रमदितव्यम्। मातृदेवो भव। पितृदेवो भव। आचार्यदेवो भव। अतिथिदेवो भव। यान्यनवद्यानि कर्माणि तानि सेवितव्यानि। नो इतराणि। ....॥[15]

It means, always speak the truth. Practise virtuous deeds (*dharma*). Don't neglect to study the Vedas. Having properly offered the desirable wealth or intended gifts to the teacher, do not stop the line of progeny. There should be no carelessness or negligence about truth. One should not deviate from religious activities. No one should be careless about his self protection. One should not be careless to perform the auspicious acts. Never be negligent about the study and teaching (of the *śāstras*).

The duties towards gods and manes must be performed In no way they are to be ignored The mother should be worshipped as goddess. Similarly, the father, teacher and guests are also to be honoured and duly worshipped as gods. Besides, perform those acts which are not blameable, but pious and praiseworthy. The actions of ours should be commendable one which is prescribed by the *śāstras* and scriptures.

It is to be noted that these moral teachings of the Upaniṣads are not only meant for students but for all. Human beings are rightly advised by the seers of the scriptures to follow the glorious spiritual and moral teachings of the Vedas and Upaniṣads for attaining eternal peace, happiness and healthy life. Hence, obviously Veda, the word of God is a moral code for the entire humanity.

REFERENCES

1. *Yajurveda*, XL. 1; cf. *Īśopaniṣad*, 1.
2. *ibid.*, XL. 2; cf. *Īśopaniṣad*, 2.
3. *Ṛgveda*, X.5.6.
4. *ibid.*, VII.104.22.
5. *ibid.*, I.89.1; cf. *Yajurveda*, XXV.14.
6. *ibid.*, I.89.8; cf. *Yajurveda,* XXV.21.
7. *ibid.*, X.71.2.
8. *ibid.*, X.191.2.
9. *ibid.*, X.191.3-4.
10. *Bṛhadāraṇyaka Upaniṣad*, V.2.3.
11. *Studies in the Upaniṣads*, Govindagopal Mukhopadhyaya, Pilgrims Book Pvt. Ltd., Delhi, 1st edition, p. 141.
12. *Bṛhadāraṇyaka Upaniṣad*, III.2.13.
13. *ibid.*, commentary of Śaṅkarācārya.
14. *Chāndogya Upaniṣad*, IV.14.3.
15. *Taittirīya Upaniṣad*, I.11.

Ornaments in the Vedic Literature

The use of ornaments in the Vedic period is very interesting to study. Though the term '*alaṁkāra*' in the sense of ornaments is noted in the Post-Saṁhitā period, but there are various types of ornament mentioned in the Saṁhitās. The term '*alaṁkāra*' is derived from the root *kṛ*-with the indeclinable *alaṃ* or *araṃ*, which means 'ornament', 'decoration' 'beautification' and 'ornamentation', etc. The word '*alaṁkāra*' is also defined by different lexicographers.

The *Amarakośa* counts five names of ornaments, viz., **"अलङ्कारस्त्वाभरणं परिष्कारो विभूषणम्। मण्डनं च।"**[1] The *Vaijayantī-kośa* also gives the five synonyms of '*alaṁkāra*' as :

अलङ्कारस्त्वाभरणं भूषणं मण्डनं पुनः। विभूषणं परिष्कारः[2]**...।**

It further elaborates these synonymous terms in the following way :

विभूषणं परिष्कारः कर्णिका कर्णभूषणम्॥[3]

Alaṁkāra means *ābharaṇa,* 'ornament', while *bhūṣaṇa* (**भूष्यतेऽनेन, भूष्-करणे ल्युट्**) means *maṇḍana,* 'adoration'; *vibhūṣaṇa* means embellishment and finally *karṇikā* stands for *karṇabhūṣaṇa*—any type of 'ear ornament'. Besides, the *Medinī-kośa*[4] too elucidates the term *'alaṁkāra'*—**अलंकारस्तु हारादावुपमादावलङ्कृतौ**, i.e., *alaṁkāra* states ornaments like necklace etc., figure of speech, like simile (*upamā*) etc.; and decoration or beautification (*alaṁkṛti*).

The word '*alaṁkāra*'/'*araṁkṛta*' is found in the *Atharvaveda* (II.12.7), *Āpastamba-Dharma-Sūtra* (II.149, XXVI. 18), *Gautama-Dharma-Sūtra* (XVIII.21), *Kātyāyana-Śrauta-Sūtra* (VIII.9.26, IX.7.4), *Chāndogya-Upaniṣad* (VIII.8.2,5; 9.1) and also in the *Kauṣītaki-Upaniṣad* (I.4).

Now we will study on the ornaments used by both men and women in the Vedic period, found in different Vedic texts. Probably there were some differences in the shape of the ornaments mentioned for both sexes. But it is difficult to identify the forms and designs of ornaments used by both male and female in that period.

The ornaments for the body starts from the head down to the feet, i.e. head-ornaments, ear-ornaments, neck and chest-ornaments, waist-ornaments and feet-ornaments.

A. Head Ornaments:

There were a number of head ornaments mentioned in the Vedic texts. The name of these ornaments are : *stukā (stūpa), kumba, kurīra, opaśa, śṛṅga* and *tirīṭa*, etc. *Stukā* denotes a 'tuft of hair' or wool in the *Ṛgveda*[5], *Atharvaveda*[6] and other later texts[7]. R.T.H. Griffith translates it as 'locks of hair'[8]. *Stūpa*[9] means 'tuft of hair' and *stūpa*[10] also denotes the 'top-knot' of hair as designating the upper part of the head. *Kumba* is mentioned with *opaśa* and *kurīra* as an ornament of women's hair in the *Atharvaveda.*[11]

"क्लीबं क्लीबं त्वाकरं वध्रे वध्रिं त्वाकरमरसारसं त्वाकरम्।
कुरीरमस्य शीर्षणि कुम्बं चाधिनिदध्मसि॥ (AV 6.138.3)

यस्माद् एवं तस्माद् अस्य द्वेषस्य नपुंसकीभूतस्य शीर्षणि शिरसि कुरीरं केशजालं कुम्बं तदाभरणं च स्त्रीणाम् असाधारणम् अधिनिदध्मसि उपरि निक्षिपामः। यद् आह आपस्तम्बः। अत्र पत्नीशिरसि कुम्बकुरीरम् अध्यूहते। इति (आपस्तम्ब-श्रौतसूत्रम्, X.9.5)

Sāyaṇa explains *kurīra* as 'a net of hair' and *kumba* as 'its ornament (*ābharaṇam*), and he also quotes from *Āpastamba-Śrauta-Sūtra* (X.9.5) the sentence, *'atra patnīśirasi kumba kurīram adhyūhate'*. Both words plainly signify some distinctively womanish head-dress or ornament. The word *kurīra*[12] denotes some sort of head ornaments used by women in the descriptions of the *Ṛgveda*[13] and in the *Atharvaveda*[14]. According to the *Yajurveda-Saṁhitā*[15] the goddess Sinīvālī is described by the epithets *su-kapardā, su-kurīra, svopaśā,* as wearing a beautiful head-dress.

Geldner[16] translates *kurīra* as 'horn' and *kurīrin* as 'a crested animal'. But according to Macdonell and Keith[17] *kurīrin* (having a *kurīra*) is a word occuring in an ambiguous passage of the *Atharvaveda,* in which it may be taken either as a noun meaning a 'crested animal', perhaps as Zimmer[18] suggests the 'peacock', or as an epithet of the word *aja,* 'goat' in which case it might mean 'horned'. But even in the latter alternative a metaphorical application of the word seems sufficient, just as in the *Pañcaviṁśa-Brāhmaṇa* (XIII.4.3) *opaśa* is used for the horns of cattle, and thus renders unnecessary the adoption of Geldner's[19] view that the original meaning of *kurīra* is 'horn'. Sūryakānta[20] translates the word *kurīra* as **शिरवेष्टन** -'head-dress for women'. He quotes a line from the *Gopatha-Brāhmaṇa* (III.21) as :**'कुरीरं धारयेत् 'जटावान् स्यात्'।** According to Monier Williams[21] *'kurīra'* is a kind of head-dress for women but according to Ray Govind Chand[22] it was a head ornament with which the head of a bride was adorned He has identified *kurīra* with *śṛṅga* or *mukuṭa*. Finally A.C. Das[23] is of the opinion that the word *kurīra*, probably meant a form of coiffure in which the hair was braided into erect crests. *Tirīṭa* has also been described as a head ornament, or head-dress or diadem[24]. It is found in the *Atharvaveda* in the adjectival derivative *tirīṭin* used of a demon, and presumably meaning 'adorned with a tiara'. This way, *ātakā*[25], *pratisara*[26] and other hand ornaments are also found in the Vedic Saṁhitās.

B. Ear Ornaments:

Like head ornaments, the description of ear ornaments are also found in the Vedic literature. Among the major ear ornaments of the Vedic period special mention may be made of *karṇaśobhana, pravarta, hiraṇyakarṇa, vṛṣa-khādi,* etc.

Karṇaśobhāna[27] denotes an 'ornaments for the ear'. It was most probably the name of *kuṇḍala,* worn by both men and women. Some deity is also called 'gold-eared' as mentioned in the *Ṛgveda*[28]. *Pravarta* means a round ornament, i.e. an ear-ring[29], as it is derived from the root *vṛt,* which means to encircle. Hence, it seems probable that the ear-ornament called *pravarta* might have been circular, similar to the present day, *kuṇḍala.* In the *Atharvaveda* the word *pravarta* also occurs in the sense of circular ornament, as :

विज्ञानं वासोऽहरुष्णीषं रात्री केशा हरितौ प्रवर्तौ कल्मलिर्मणिः॥[30]

Macdonell after the Mahīdhara's commentary on the *Taittirīya-Saṁhitā* interpreted the term as round-shaped-ear-ornament. Probably, *hiraṇyakarṇa*[31] was an ear-ornament made of gold. *Vṛṣakhādi* is also a type of ear-ornament mentioned in the *Ṛgveda*[32]. Macdonell after following Bollensen's reference[33] suggested the meaning of the term *vṛṣakhādi* as 'strong ring', while R.T.H. Griffith translates this (term) as 'strong men's ring'. M. Williams renderes it as 'having large bracelets or rings.'

C. Neck and Chest Ornaments:

Neck and chest ornaments were too popular ornaments used by both men and women in Vedic times, mentioned in the Vedic texts. In the neck and chest ornaments special mention may be made of *rukma, niṣka, hiraṇya-srak, sraj* and *maṇi*. *Rukma* (in the *Ṛgveda*[34]) denotes golden ornament for the neck, which came down to the chest or breast. In the Brāhmaṇas[35] it designates a gold plate. Sāyaṇa, while commenting '**रुक्म वक्षसः**' of *Atharvaveda* (VI.22.2), writes "**रुक्मः स्वर्णमयम् आभरणं वक्षःस्थले येषां (तादृशाः सन्तः)**". 'Griffith translates '*rukmavakṣasa*' as wearing ornaments of gold on their breasts'. It was an ornament circular in shape and worn round the neck or on the breasts, may be a sort necklace. Similarly, *niṣka* is frequently mentioned in the Vedic texts as a golden ornament worn on the neck. The *Ṛgveda*[36] states - '**शतं राज्ञो नाधमानस्य निष्का**'— 'a hundred necklets from the king beseeching'. Other examples from the *Atharvaveda* (V.17.14, XX.127.3), *Śatapatha Brāhmaṇa* (XIII.4.1, 7.11), *Aitareya Brāhmaṇa* (VIII.22), *Kātyāyana Śrauta Sūtra* (XIV.2.28)[37], *Chāndogya Upaniṣad* (IV.2.1), etc. are also found in this respect. As *niṣkas* were used as coins, we may guess that they were either of round or square shape and strung together as neck-ornaments. Even today, gold coins are strung together and worn on the neck both by men and women in our country. *Hiraṇya-srak* is also described as a neck ornament in the *Atharvaveda* (X.6.4) as :

हिरण्यस्त्रगयं मणिः श्रद्धां यज्ञं महो दधत्। गृहे वसतु नोऽतिथिः।

W.D. Whitney translates this as 'golden-garlanded amulet' and R.T.H. Griffith translates this as 'amulet decked with chain of gold'. Similarly, *sraj*[38] was also a garland, ordinarily worn by men, and made either of flowers or golden lace wrought into flowers. The Aśvins are described as *puṣkara-sraj,* 'lotus-wreathed'. The *maṇi* also worn round the neck, as in the *Ṛgveda* (I.122.14) we find the epithet *maṇigrīva,* 'having a jewel on the neck'. The 'jeweller', (*maṇi-kāra*) is mentioned in the list of victims at the *puruṣamedha* in the *Yajurveda.*[39]

D. Wrist Ornaments:

The ornaments which were worn on the wrist like a *kaṅkaṇa,* mentioned in the Vedic texts were, *khādi, parihasta, śaṅkha*, etc. *Khādi* was an ornament for arms. It was either a golden 'anklet' worn both by male and female or an 'armlet' worn on the arm or wrist like a bangle. It also sometimes signified a ring on the hands, known as: *'Khādihasta',* mentioned in the *Ṛgveda*[40]. *Parihasta*[41] was also an ornament for the wrist. Monier Williams writes "*parihasta,* an amulet put round the hand to secure the birth of a child"[42]. Sāyaṇa renders it **"परिहस्तं हस्तं परिवेष्ट्य वर्तमानं कंकणादिरूपं....."**[43] Hence, it is now clear that *parihasta* was a wrist ornament but; about its shape it is still doubtful, without any evidence. *Śaṅkha* in the *Atharvaveda*[44], with the epithet Kṛśaṇa denotes a pearl-shell used as an amulet. In the later literature it denotes a 'shell' or 'conch' used for blowing as a wind instrument, viz., **"यथा शङ्खस्य ध्मायमानस्य न बाह्याञ्शब्दाञ्शक्नुयाद् ग्रहणाय, शङ्खस्य तु ग्रहणेन शङ्खध्मस्य वा शब्दो गृहीतः।"**[45]

E. Waist Ornaments:

Among the waist ornaments *mekhalā* and *muñja* were most popular girdles in the Vedic period. *Mekhalā* denotes 'girdle' in the later Saṁhitās and the Brāhmaṇas. A discussion on *mekhalā* is found in the *Atharvaveda,* VI.133. This *sūkta* is only meant for *'mekhalābandhanam'*. *'Mekhalābandhana'* is also popular these days both by men and women. In the *Āśvalāyana-Gṛhya-Sūtra* it is said that the 'girdle' of the Brāhmaṇa (*brahmacārin*) should be made of *muñja* grass, that of a Kṣatriya of a bow-string and that of a Vaiśya woolen (**तेषां मेखला–मौञ्जी ब्राह्मणस्य धनुर्ज्या क्षत्रियस्य आवी वैश्यस्य**).[46]

F. Feet Ornaments:

Khādi and *hiraṇyapāvā* were the best ornaments, which were worn on the feet. The word *'khādaya'* occurs in the *Ṛgveda* (V.54.11), which is translated by R.T.H. Griffith as 'anklets on feet'. According to M. Monier Williams this means 'a ring worn on the hands or feet (by the Maruts)' (*Ṛgveda,* V.54.11). Probably *khādi* was a bangle for feet, which was quite thick and about its actual shape it is still doubtful.

Hiraṇyapāvā[47] was a feet ornament made of gold, as it seems from its name. Griffith translates the word *hiraṇyapāvā* as 'gold-ringed fingers'.

In addition to these ornaments some other ornaments are also mentioned in the Vedic texts, viz., *añji, nṛmṇa, ṛṣṭi, stāgara, phaṇa, vimukta, ātakā, yoktra, raśanā, mauli, prāvepa, prākāśa*, etc.

Out of these above mentioned ornaments some were used on a regular basis and some were on different occasions. So it is now clear from this study that men and women were used to wear the ornaments of high qualities in the Vedic period.

REFERENCES

1. *Amarakośa,* II.6.101-102.
2. *Vaijayantī-kośa*, IV.3.133, cf. V.4.41.
3. *ibid.*, IV.3.133.
4. XVIII.242a.
5. IX.97.17.
6. VII.74.2 (Vide, W.D. Whitney's English translation on AV)
7. *Kāṭhaka-Saṁhitā,* II.2, XXV.2, *Śatapatha-Brāhmaṇa,* III.2.1.13, etc.
8. *Hymns of the Ṛgveda,* vol. II, p. 360.
9. *Vājasaneyi-Saṁhitā,* II.2; XXV.2, *Śatapatha-Brāhmaṇa*, I.3.3.5; III.5.3.4.
10. *Ṛgveda,* I.24.7, VII.2.1; *Taittirīya-Saṁhitā,* III.3.6.5; *Pañcaviṁśa-Brāhmaṇa,* XIII.4.4.
11. Sāyaṇa's *Bhāṣya* on *Atharvaveda,* VI.138.3.
12. 'Decorated with the head-dress called *kurīra*', Monier Williams, *Sanskrit English Dictionary,* p.294.
13. X.85.8.
14. VI.138.3.
15. *Taittirīya Saṁhitā,* IV.1.5.3; *Maitrāyaṇī-Saṁhitā,* II.7.5; *Vājasaneyi-Saṁhitā,* XI.56.
16. *Vedische Studien,* I, pp. 131-132.
17. *Vedic Index of Names and Subjects,* vol. I, p. 164.
18. *Altindisches Leben,* 91.
19. *Vedische Studien*, I.130.
20. *A Practical Vedic Dictionary,* p.251.
21. *Sanskrit English Dictionary,* p.294.
22. *Vaidika-Kālīna-Ābhūṣaṇa.*
23. *Ṛgvedic Culture,* ch. V, p.218, (Bharatiya Publishing House, Varanasi, Reprint edition).
24. M.M. Williams, *Sanskrit English Dictionary.* P.448, R.T.H. Griffith, *Hymns of the Atharvaveda* (VIII.6.7), vol. I, p. 337; W.D. Whitney, *Hymns of the Atharvaveda* (VII.6.7), vol. II, p.495.
25. *Ṛgveda,* V.55.6.
26. *Atharvaveda,* VIII.5.1.
27. **उत नः कर्णशोभना पुरूणि धृष्णवा भर**–*Ṛgveda,* VIII.78.3.
28. I.122.14, cf. *Ṛgveda,* I.64.10.
29. M.M. Williams, *Sanskrit English Dictionary,* p. 693; and Suryakanta, *A Practical Vedic Dictionary,* p. 470.
30. *Atharvaveda,* XV.2.5; cf. XV.2;13,19,25.

31. *Ṛgveda,* I.122.14.
32. अस्तार इषुं दधिरे गभस्त्योरनन्तशुष्मा वृषखादयो नरः (I.64.10cd).
33. Bollensen, *Orient and Occident,* II.461.
34. I.64.4, 166.10; V.56.1, 57.5; VII.56.13; VIII.20.11; X.78.2, cf.*Atharvaveda,* V.12.6; VI.22.2, IX.5.25; *Taittirīya-Saṁhitā,* II.3.2.3; V.I.10.3; *Vājasaneyi-Saṁhitā,* XIII.40,etc.
35. *Śatapatha-Brāhmaṇa,* III.5.1.20; V.2.1.21; *Taittirīya-Brāhmaṇa*, I.8.2.3; 9.1, etc.
36. I.126.2; cf. II.83.10, V.19.3; VII.56.11.
37. सप्तदश वृषल्यो निष्ककण्ठाः—means the *śūdra* women (or unmarried girls) wearing golden necklaces should also be given as seventeen (hundred) gifts. This indicates that in ancient times the women were fond of ornaments.
38. *Vājasaneyi-Saṁhitā,* XXX.7; *Taittirīya-Brāhmaṇa,* III.4.3.1.
39. *Ṛgveda,* IV.38.6; V.53.4, VIII.47. 15; 56.3, *Atharvaveda,* I.14.1 (where it means a 'cluster of flowers' from a tree); *Śatapatha-Brāhmaṇa*, XIII.5.4.2, etc.
40. I.168.3, V.58.2, VII.56.13.
41. *Atharvaveda,* VI.81.1-3.
42. *Sanskrit English Dictionary,* p.604, cf. A *Practical Vedic Dict.,* Suryakanta, p.416.
43. Vide, Sāyaṇa's commentary on *Atharvaveda,* VI.81.3.
44. IV.10.1 (शङ्खः कृशनः पात्वंहसः–IV.10.4 (शङ्ख आयुष्प्रतरणो मणिः)।
45. *Bṛhadāraṇyaka-Upaniṣad,* II.4.8.
46. *Āśvalāyana-Gṛhya-Sūtra*, I.19.10-11.
47. *Ṛgveda,* IX.86.43.

Maharṣi Dayānanda Sarasvatī as an Interpreter of the Vedas

According to our ancient concept, when God created men, He revealed the Vedas for their proper guidance. The Vedas radiate light that illumine the world.

Ancient Indian scholars, who had faith in the Vedas, have gone through the Brāhmaṇas, Āraṇyakas, Upaniṣads and commentaries on the Vedas, interpreted the Vedas in their own way. Among the commentators on the Vedas, the commentaries of Skandasvāmī, Durga, Udgītha, Harisvāmī, Uvaṭa, Bhaṭṭa-Bhāskara, Venkaṭa-Mādhava, Ātmānanda, Ānanda-Tīrtha, Mādhava, Mahīdhara, Bharatasvāmī, Sāyaṇa and others are available.

Although many commentaries and interpretations by different scholars on Vedas were available during the period of Maharṣi Dayānanda, but they failed to emphasize the sublimity of thoughts found in them. Svāmī knew that Sāyaṇa and his predecessors, in their interpretation of the Vedas, deviated from thc rules laid down by Yāska and some of their interpretations are meaningless and irrelevent. That is why he thought it essential to write a commentary on the Vedas. But, unfortunately, he could not write the commentaries on all the four Vedas owing to his premature death. Only he wrote a full commentary on the *Yajurveda* and up to the 2nd hymn of sixty-first Sūkta of the seventh book (VII.61.2) of the *Ṛgveda*.

(A) Methods of Interpretation of the Vedas by Dayānanda:

The *Ādhyātmika* (Metaphysical), *Ādhidaivika* (Super Natural) *Ādhibhautika* (Supra-physical) and *Ādhiyājñika* (Ritualistic) methods of the interpretation of the Vedas have been in Vogue in the Vedic literature since earliest times. But Svāmī Dayānanda approved of only two kinds of interpretations, viz., metaphysical and practical. According to him, subjects such as God's form, characteristics, nature, work, worship, prayer, praise, adoration, *yoga*, *mokṣa* or salvation, etc. are metaphysical (*Ādhyātmika*). All other subjects, except mentioned under metaphysical subjects, including *varṇa* (caste), *āśramas* (stages of life), *rājadharma* (polity), physics, architecture, economics, medical science commerce, agriculture, etc. come under practical (*Vyāvahārika*) subjects. Thus, according to Dayānanda, the method of interpreting the Vedas on metaphysical lines can be called the metaphysical method, while that which interprets the hymns from the practical point of view is called practical method. These two methods, as accepted by Dayānanda, incorporate within themselves, all the methods of interpretation of the Vedas used by his predecessors, such as metaphysical, naturalistic, ritualistic and practical.

Dayānanda, in his *Ṛgvedādi-Bhāṣya-Bhūmikā* under the heading of "Pratijñā-viṣaya", writes that he would give both the metaphysical and practical interpretations of the hymns which can be interpreted so because of the figures of the speech like '*Śleṣa*' etc. Hence, in his *Vedabhāṣya*, he has interpreted a number of Vedic hymns in both the ways. In other words, we can say that no other scholar before Dayānanda has given so many types of interpretations of the Vedic hymns as Dayānanda. The practical interpretation of the Vedas, given by him in his *Bhāṣya*, makes us realize that the Vedas have depicted the social system very elaborately. From the point of view of the treatment of various subjects in the Vedas, we can say that it is an original contribution of Dayānanda.

(B) Peculiarities of Dayānanda's Vedic Interpretation (*Veda-Bhāṣya*):

The main basic principles of the interpretation of the Vedas as understood by Dayānanda, are the following:

(1) The background of his *bhāṣya* is the sincere conception that the Vedas are the words of God. Hence, they contain pure and absolute knowledge.

(2) The words used in the classical Sanskrit are greatly differ, as regards to their meaning, from the words used in the Vedic language. It is difficult to interpret the Vedas taking in view of the current sense of the words in ordinary language.

(3) The words of the Vedas are *yaugika* and are in a fluid state; they are not *rūḍha* (static) in meaning, i.e., all Vedic words have derivative or etymological sense. The Vedas have no *rūḍhi* words (words with conventional sense). All words denote derivative and general sense. They are derived from the roots, hence they can be interpreted variously. It is not proper to locate the popular meaning of a word in the Vedas everywhere; that is to say, the meaning of a word in the Vedas may be different from the meaning in vogue at present. For instance, the word '*ahi*' generally means a serpent, but in the Veda it signifies 'a cloud'.[1]

(4) Following the footsteps of Yāska, Dayānanda also believes that the Vedic words are used in the Vedas to denote triple significance of the *mantras*, i.e., *ādhyātmika*, *ādhidaivika* and *ādhiyājñika*.

(5) The *pada* text of the *mantras* have not always been adhered to. The Vedic sense is more important than the man-made *pada-pāṭha*. Even Yāska has not adhered to the *pada* text. In the *Nirukta* (V. 21), he derives the word "*māsakṛt*" (in Ṛv I. 105.18) in two ways—(i) *māsa+kṛt*, and (ii) *mā+sakṛt*. Yāska attaches importance to

the sense and not to the grammatical formations; so does Dayānanda believe. Yāska says:

arthanityaḥ na saṁskāramādriyeta parīkṣeta.[2]

Patañjali, the author of the *Mahābhāṣya*, also says :—

na lakṣaṇena padakārā anuvartyāḥ,
padakāraiḥ nāmalakṣaṇamanuvartyam.[3] **(III.1.103)**

(6) Dayānanda follows the schools of etymologists, i.e., the Nairuktas. Hence, he does not believe that the Veda contains narratives or references to historical personages. Undoubtedly all descriptions are symbolic and figurative, as Yāska says:

"tat ko vṛtraḥ? megha iti nairuktāḥ/tvāṣṭro'sura ityaithihāsikāḥ/apāñca jyotiṣaśca miśribhāvakarmaṇo varṣakarma jāyate/tatropamārthena yuddhavarṇā bhavanti."[4]

(7) According to Dayānanda, *devatā* means the subject matter of the *mantra*, or hymn. All words signifying a *devatā*, e.g., Agni, Varuṇa and Indra, are the names of One Supreme Lord. There is only One Supreme Being described in the Vedas and Agni, Vāyu, etc. are merely His different names, indicating His most important attributes.

This matter is really set at rest by the well-known *mantra* of the *Ṛgveda* :—

"indraṁ mitraṁ varuṇamagnimāhuratho divyaḥ sa suparṇo garutmān/ekaṁ sad viprā bahudhā vadantyagniṁ yamaṁ mātariśvānamāhuḥ."[5]

It means, He is One; sages call Him by many names, e.g., Agni, Yama and Mātariśvan.

(8) The feminine words, such as Aditi, Uṣā, Iḍā, Sarasvatī, Bhāratī, Pṛthivī, etc., used in the Vedas, portray the motherly form of God as well as are connotative of woman, wife, lady-teacher, housewife, electricity, voice, energy, etc.

(9) While interpreting the Vedas, it is not necessary to follow the traditional *viniyogas*. The Vedic hymns can be commented upon independent of such meanings.

(10) In the Vedas, there is no proper description of the history of *ṛṣis*, kings, countries, towns, rivers, etc. The names seem to be historical but have their contextual meaning. Hence, the *Ārya-Dasyu* battle referred to in the Vedas does not mean any war between the Āryans and the Dravidians, that is said to have taken place in history.

(11) In the Vedas, there is no description of human actions such as the animal or human sacrifice, killing of cows, eating of meat, use of liquor, obscenity, adultery, etc. Those who find or support these as approved or confirmed by the Vedas are confused and are not clear about its true meanings.

(12) While giving suitable interpretations—metaphysical or practical or both of the Vedas, metaphysical, physical, social, national and other various elements can be discovered in them.

(C) Excellence of Svāmī Dayānanda's Vedic Commentary:

Svāmī Dayānanda wrote his *Vedabhāṣya* keeping the above basic principles in mind. He has employed the scientific method of interpretation, based on Nirukta school, throughout his Vedic exegesis. It has many advantages. A few Indian scholars and all Europoan scholars have offered bitter criticism against the Vedic teachings. These are very easily removed through the medium of this interpretation. Agni, Varuṇa, Āditya, Mātariśvā and Indra may mean anything in different contexts, but they also mean Supreme Being (Brahman) described under different names. These are different names of God (One Lord). The discovery of this method, which was vogue in Yāska's age, is quite new in modern times and it has brought about a new revolution in understanding the Vedic theme. In order that no doubt may be left concerning the monotheistic worship of the ancient Āryans, we may quote here from the *Nirukta* :

"māhābhāgyād devatāyā eka ātmā bahudhā stūyate/ekasyātmano'nye devāḥ pratyaṅgāni bhavanti.[6]"

It means, One Supreme Soul is variously praised on account of his Omnipotence. Other *devatās* are but *pratyaṅgas* (i.e., various manifestations) of this One Supreme Soul.

From these points it is now quite clear that Dayānanda's interpretation of the Vedas, based on etymological method, has a sound support in Yāska's *Nirukta* and the Brāhmaṇas too.

It will be reasonable if a few citations from the Vedas themselves are given below in support of the theory that there was monotheism, i.e., worship of One God. It will clearly justify Dayānanda's stand:

(A) ***"ekaṁ sad viprā bahudhā vadanti."***[7]

(He is one; sages call him by many names.)

(B) ***"agne bhūriṇi tava jātavedo deva svadhāvo'mṛtasya nāma"***[8].

(Many are thy names O Agni—Immortal, God, Divine, Jātavedas.)

(C) ***"indro māyābhiḥ pururūpa īyate."***[9]

(Indra moves multiform, in his wonderful creation.)

(D) ***"tadevāgnistadādityastad vāyustadu candramāḥ/tadeva śukraṁ tad brahma tā āpa sa prajāpatiḥ."***[10]

(Even He is Agni, He is Āditya, He is Vāyu, He is Candramā, He is Śukra, He is Brahma, He is Āpa, He is Prajāpati.)

(E) ***"so'ryamā sa varuṇaḥ sa rudraḥ sa mahādevaḥ."***[11]

"so'gniḥ sa eva mahāyamaḥ."[12]

(He is Aryamā, He is Varuṇa, He is Rudra, He is Mahādeva.)

(He is Agni, He is Sūrya, He is verily Mahā-Yama.)

(F) ***"na dvitīyo na tṛtīyaścaturtho nāpyucyate,......***
na pañcamo na ṣaṣṭhaḥ saptamo nāpyucyate,.......
nāṣṭamo na navamo daśamo nāpyucyate,.......
sa eṣa eka ekavṛd eka eva,.......
sarve asmin devā ekavṛto bhavanti."

It means, neither second, nor third, nor yet fourth is He called He is called neither fifth, nor sixth, nor yet seventh. He is called neither eighth, nor ninth, nor yet tenth. He is the Sole, the Absolute One, the One alone. In Him all gods become simple and One.

Nothing can be clearer than this. All these quotations will convince the reader that the ancient Āryans had worshipped only One God. So, Dayānanda's interpretaton, which establishes this fact before the scholars, must be admitted as a very good attempt for understanding the purport of the Vedic teachings.

This way Svāmī Dayānanda brought a great change in the concept of the Veda and its true meaning. One of the chief characteristics of his *Vedabhāṣya* is that it establishes harmony between Religion and Science. He was possibly the first great religious leader who taught that Religion and Science are one and that the Science in elementary form can be found in the greatest religious books of the world, i.e. the Vedas. To him goes the credit for demolishing the supposed insuperable barrier between Religion and Science. That Dayānanda's line changed the mode of thinking of the celebrated Vedic Scholars as of the common masses can be seen from many examples. Prof Max Müller, who in 1873 called the Vedas pastoral songs, later wrote, after reading Dayānanda's commentary, as :

"In the study of the history of human mind, in the study of ourself, India occupies a place second to no other country, whatever sphere of human mind you may select for your study, whether it be religion, mythology or philosophy, or whether it be laws or customs, primitive art or science, you have to go to India."

The Westerners had always regarded the Vedas as the collection of the songs of primitive shepherds and hunters and farmers. Svāmī Dayānanda showed them to be (among other things) the greatest repositories of knowledge. This has encouraged the scholars and researchers to work in such fields as Mathematics, Astronomy, Metereology, Botany, Chemistry, Aeronautics and other sciences and locate their sources in the Vedas.

All such work is a tribute to the pioneering inspiration, initiated by Dayānanda in his *Veda-bhāṣya*.

Yogi Aurobindo, in his book '*Secrets of the Veda*' appreciates Dayānanda's approach towards the interpretation of the Vedas, as:

"It is remarkable attempt by Svāmī Dayānanda, the founder of Ārya Samāj, to reestablish the Veda as a living religious Scripture, Dayānanda took as his basis a free use of the old Indian philosophy which is found in the *Nirukta*. Himself a great Sanskrit scholar, he handled his materials with remarkable power and independence. Specially creative was his use of that peculiar feature of the old Sanskrit tongue which is best expressed by a phrase of Sāyaṇa as: *dhātūnām anekārthatvāt'*—the multisignificance of roots'. We shall see that the right following of this clue is of capital importance for understanding the peculiar method of the Vedic Ṛṣis."[14]

Again, he states on the method of Dayānanda's interpretation on Vedic hymn:

"Dayānanda's interpretation of the hymns is governed by the idea that the Vedas are a plenary revelation of religious, ethical and scientific truth. Its religious teaching is monotheistic and the Vedic gods are different descriptive names of One Deity; they are at the same time indication of his powers as we see them working in Nature and by a true understanding of the sense of the Vedas we could arrive at all the scientific truths which have been discovered by modern research.....Dayānanda has given the clue to the linguistic search of the Ṛṣi and re-emphasised one central idea of the Vedic religion, the idea of the One Being with the *devas* expressing in numerous names and persons the many-sidedness of his unity."[15]

He (Aurobindo) further adds : "In the matter of Vedic interpretation, I am convinced that whatever may be the final complete interpretation, Dayānanda will be honoured as the first discoverer of right clues. Amidst chaos and obscurity of old ignorance and age-long misunderstanding, his was the eye of direct vision that pierced to the truth and fastened on that which was essential. He has found the keys of the doors that time had closed and rent as under the seals of the imprisioned fountains.".[16]

Max Müler also calls Dayānanda's interpretation of the Vedic hymns as the most revealing.

This way, it is now clear that the method of Dayānanda's Vedic interpretation is totally different from other interpretations available till today. Really his style of interpretation was a unique one, from which we got some positive informations and also a new direction to read and to understand the Vedas in a proper manner for the welfare of our society.

REFERENCES

1. *Nirukta*, II.17.
2. *ibid.*, II.1.
3. *Mahābhāṣya*, III.1.103.
4. *Nirukta*, II.16.
5. *Ṛgveda*, I.164.46.
6. *Nirukta,* VII.4.
7. *Ṛgveda*, I.164.46.
8. *ibid.*, III.20.3.

9. *ibid.*, VI. 47.18.
10. *Yajurveda*, XXXII.1.
11. *Atharvaveda*, XIII.4.4.
12. *ibid.*, XIII.4.5.
13. *ibid.*, XIII.5.16-21.
14. *Secrets of the Veda*, part I, Chapter 1, p. 29.
15. *ibid.*, pp. 29-31.
16. *Aurobindo: Bankim, Tilak and Dayānanda*, p. 44.

Reflection of the Vedas in the *Mahābhārata*

The *Mahābhārata* is a great epic depicting the foundations of all Indian culture and civilization. It is the nucleus of all religious thoughts of the men and women in India specially who are devoted to Hinduism. It is not only a mere *kāvya* but a *mahākāvya*. The sages and the seers used to praise it from the innermost corner of their heart. As consonants and vowels interlinked with the words, as worldly wisdom and Vedic knowledge interlinked with all religious attitudes, so the *Mahābhārata* is interconnected with all auspicious thoughts and intuitions.

The *Mahābhārata* is called the fifth Veda, viz. the Kārṣṇa Veda[1], i.e., the Veda of Kṛṣṇa Dvaipāyana Vyāsa, and the essence of other Vedas.[2] One should study the Vedas with its help. Because, one who does not have a knowledge of this highly sacred and authentic work, is not a learned man even though one may be a profound scholar of the Vedas and Upaniṣads. Vedavyāsa, the compiler of the Vedas, desired to make them easy and profitable to mankind. So he composed this great epic with the extended thoughts of the Vedas. In that sense this great epic *Mahābhārata* is called the fifth Veda[3], containing illustrated and glorified ideas of the Vedas.

The *Mahābhārata* is an *ārṣa kāvya* (*grantha*), because it is composed in the light of the (four) Vedas. The Vedas are also mentioned throughout the *Mahābhārata* in hundreds of passages.[4] They are usually referred in the plural as the Vedas, but the terms like *śruti* (Mbh XII.268.10; 297.33, etc.), *āmnāya* (Mbh XII.268.33), *chandas* (Mbh XII.339.69) and *traividyā* (Mbh XII.123.20) are also employed They are also referred to by name as the *Ṛk* (Mbh XII.342.97; 348.22, etc.), *Yajus* (Mbh XII.244.26; 342.99, etc.), *Sāman* (Mbh XII.342.97; 348.10 etc.), and *Atharva* (Mbh XII.342.100, etc). The name of *Śatapatha Brāhmaṇa* (Mbh XII.318.11, 16-17; 342.13), *Āraṇyaka* (Mbh XII.343.13; 349.1), *Upaniṣad* (Mbh XII.318.34, 112; 339.111, etc.) and *Vedāṅgas* (XII.37.11; 69.31, etc.) are also mentioned in this epic. In the Śāntiparvan it is clearly stated by Lord Nārāyaṇa that perfectly following the four Vedas, the *Yajurveda*, the *Ṛgveda*, the *Sāmaveda* and the *Atharvaveda*, this epic *Mahābhārata* will be an authority in the world with regard to both work and renuciation:

प्रवृत्तौ च निवृत्तौ च यस्मादेतद् भविष्यति।
यजुर्ऋक्सामभिर्जुष्टमथर्वांगिरसोस्तथा॥[5]

Further this epic is treated as an Upaniṣad, which contains Vedic teachings, i.e. eternal knowledge of the four Vedas. As said:

इदं महोपनिषदं चतुर्वेदसमन्वितम्।[6]

Hence, different Vedic subjects like the importance of Vedas and Vedic scholars, Vedic *devatās* and *ṛṣis*, Vedic *saṁskāras*, Vedic *āśramas*, Vedic *yajñas*, Vedic *karmas*, etc. have been discussed in the *Mahābhārata*. In this paper an attempt is made to highlight these subjects in brief, which are reflected in the *Mahābhārata* (i.e. in the Śāntiparvan).

I.1 Glorification of the Vedas and Vedic Scholars:

The Vedas are regarded as authentic by all. People never disregard them. For the welfare of the humanity Vedas, Vedāṅgas and other scriptures were created by the God. So, it is said:

धर्मशास्त्राणि वेदाश्च षडङ्गानि नराधिप।
श्रेयसोऽर्थे विधीयन्ते नरस्याक्लिष्टकर्मणः॥[7]

The *Mahābhārata* clearly defines the nature, characteristic of a *vedavit*, or *vedajña puruṣa*. It says that one who behaves all creatures like his own relatives and one who is acquainted with *brahmatattva*, is said to be a master of all the Vedas.[8] It further adds that he is said to be a qualified knower of the Vedas, who is conversant with that which gratifies one, whose stomach is empty, which pleases one who is angry, and which invigorates one whose bodies are feeble. Besides, one who is well-versed in the Vedas, knows everything, for everthing is established in the Vedas. Verily, the present, past and future all exist in the Vedas. Hence, it is said:

येन तृप्यत्यभुञ्जानो येन तृप्यत्यवित्तवान्।
येनास्नेहो बलं धत्ते यस्तं वेद स वेदवित्॥[9]

And :

सर्वं विदुर्वेदविदो वेदे सर्वं प्रतिष्ठितम्।
वेदे हि निष्ठा सर्वस्य यद् यदस्ति च नास्ति च॥[10]

I.2 *Nāstika-puruṣa* and Vedas:

In the *Mahābhārata*, the term '*nāstika*' is found in several passages. The word '*nāstika*' generally means 'atheist'. Those who reject the traditional Vedic system are designated as *nāstikas*. Severe punishment is given to the atheist persons during *Mahābhārata* period. Unbelievers (of the Vedas), with their hands bound, are send to the dense forests, full of lions, elephants, snakes and robbers.[11] In another chapter Pitāmaha Bhīṣma explains that due to *'vedanindaka karma'* Indra took birth in the form of a jackal in his previous birth. In the words of Indra he has rejected the Vedas and stopped the recitation of the Vedas and also told arrogantly to the Brahmins. So due to this sin he took birth as a jackal, which is said as under:

अहमासं पण्डितको हैतुको वेदनिन्दकः।
आन्वीक्षिकीं तर्कविद्यामनुरक्तो निरर्थिकाम्॥
नास्तिकः सर्वशङ्की च मूर्खः पण्डितमानिकः।
तस्येयं फलनिर्वृत्तिः शृगालत्वं मम द्विज॥[12]

No man acquires any blessedness or good result by disregarding the Vedas. Therefore, disregard of the Vedas, disobedience to the dictates of the traditional scriptures, and violation of all wholesome restraints, are productive of self-destruction.

अप्रामाण्यं च वेदानां शास्त्राणां चाभिलङ्घनम्।
अव्यवस्था च सर्वत्र तद् वै नाशनमात्मनः॥[13]

So in no way, the Vedas and other scriptures are disregarded by the author of *Mahābhārata*.

2.1 Vedas and Seers/Sages (*ṛṣi/muni*):

The *Mahābhārata* records a number of seers and sages. Marīcī, Aṅgiras, Atri, Pulastya, Pulaha, Kratu and Vasiṣṭha—these seven seers have created by Brahmā. They are famous and foremost of all the seers, well-versed in the Vedas. These seven seers are known as *citraśikhaṇḍin* in the Śāntiparvan:

मरीचिरत्र्यङ्गिरसौ पुलस्त्यः पुलहः क्रतुः।
वसिष्ठश्च महातेजास्ते हि चित्रशिखण्डिनः॥[14]

एते वेदविदो मुख्या वेदाचार्याश्च कल्पिताः।[15]

Elsewhere of the Śāntiparva these above said seven *ṛṣis* including Manu are known as eight elements. The world depends upon these elements. Brahmā created these for the welfare of all creatures. From these eight elements has originated this vast universe.[16] Beside these *ṛṣis*, the Śāntiparvan also records other prominent sages, namely, Asita, Devala, Nārada, Parvata, Kakṣīvān, Parśurāma Vasiṣṭha, Jamadagni, Viśvāmitra, Atri, Bharadvāja, Harismaśru, Kuṇḍadhāra, and Śrutaśravās. The eminent sages by worshipping Lord Viṣṇu with concentrated minds with the help of *mantras* (*ṛcās*), and by penances, succeeded in attaining to success through the grace of that great God endued with intelligence.[17]

2.2 Vedavyāsa and Veda (rules of Study of Vedas):

It is known that Vedavyāsa has compiled the (four) Vedas. According to the Śāntiparvan, Vedavyāsa has four prominent disciple, namely, Sumanta, Vaiśaṁpāyana, Jaimini, and Paila. These four disciples have perfectly mastered of the Vedas with their six branches. For the propagation of Vedic learning Vedavyāsa has properly advised to his disciples that the Vedas should always be imparted to him, who is a

Brahmin or to him who is highly desirous of listening and knowing to Vedic teachings. He further adds that the Vedas should never be imparted to one who has not formally become a true disciple, nor should they be given to one who is not observant of right vows. These should be known as the proper qualifications of persons who can be accepted as disciples for the communication of Vedic knowledge. No *vedavidyā* should be imparted to one without a proper examination of one's character. Let all desciples conquer all difficulties, and let all of them meet with auspicious success. The Brahmins should be given top priority for learning of the Vedas, but at the same time other castes should not be ignored These are the rules of study of the Vedas as explained by Vedavyāsa in the *Mahābhārata*:

वेदस्याध्ययनं हीदं तच्च कार्यं महत् स्मृतम्।[18]

2.3 Śukadeva and Veda:

According to Śāntiparva, Vedavyāsa's son Śukadeva was also a great sage. He has studied Vedas[19] from his own father. Once Vedavyāsa with his son Śuka, started to recite the Vedas in a loud sweet voice, observing all the rules of accent and, as it were, filling the three worlds with that sound.

शुकेन सह पुत्रेण वेदाभ्यासमथाकरोत्।
स्वरेणोच्चैः स शैक्ष्येण लोकानापूरयन्निव।।[20]

Śukadeva was also an extraordinary sage, because just after his birth, the Vedas, with all their mysteries and all their abstracts, came for living in him, even as they live in his father, Vedavyāsa:

उत्पन्नमात्रं तं वेदाः सरहस्याः ससंग्रहाः।।
उपतस्थुर्महाराज यथास्य पितरं तथा।[21]

2.4 Yājñavalkya and Veda:

It is started in Śāntiparva of the *Mahābhārata* that *ṛṣi* Yājñavalkya had worshipped the Sun God and learnt *śukla yajus* from him. The appelation '*śukla*' (white) owes its origin in all probability to the connection with the Sun—the white sacrificial utterances were revealed by the Sun. In contrast with this the older *Yajurveda* was called the black one, i.e. *Kṛṣṇa Yajurveda*. The Sun God also blessed him to edit entire *Śatapatha Brāhmaṇa* and which was also gladly accepted by Yājñavalkya.

कृत्स्नं शतपथं चैव प्रणेष्यसि द्विजर्षभ।....

And :

ततः शतपथं कृत्स्नं सरहस्यं ससंग्रहम्।
चक्रे सपरिशेषं च हर्षेण परमेण ह।।[22]

It is also known from the *Mahābhārata* that Yājñavalkya has received fifteen *śākhās* of the *Śukla Yajurveda* from the Sun.[23]

2.5 Nārada and Veda:

Devarṣi Nārada is well-versed in the *Śrutis* and Upaniṣads.[24] His knowledge and wisdom are great. He always tries to conquer all earthly desires by listening to Vedic recitations and attending to the Purāṇas. He is endued with great learning in the scriptures. So he never disregards or hates any kind of *śāstras*. He is a great renouncer and he never dis-respects any one. He is free from cupidity and deception. In a true sense he is an eminent *ṛṣi*. Therefore, he is everywhere adored with respect. In chapter 335 of the Śāntiparva, Nārada clearly justifies himself as a real Vedic seer by stating the following verse:

पूजां गुरूणां सततं करोमि परस्य गुह्यं न तु भिन्नपूर्वम्।
वेदाः स्वधीता मम लोकनाथ तप्तं तपो नानृतमुक्तपूर्वम्।।[25]

3. *Devatās* and Veda:

The *Mahābhārata* records a number of *devatās* and nature and functions. The prominent among them are: Agni, Brahmā and Nārāyaṇa (Viṣṇu).

3.1 Agni and Veda:

The most important and famous of the Vedic gods is Agni, the fire-god. In the first *mantra* of the *Ṛgveda* (*agnimīiḷe purohitaṁ yajñasya devam ṛtvijam; hotāraṁ ratna dhātamam*—ṚV I.1.1). Agni is designated as the *hotā* and *purohita* of the Vedic sacrifice. In the *Mahābhārata* Agni is also called as the *hotā* of the Vedic *yajña*.

अग्निर्हि यज्ञानां होता कर्ता स चाग्निर्ब्रह्म।।[26]

So Agni is truly the *hotṛ* and performer of sacrifices. He is also known as the Brahmā of the sacrifice. No libation can be poured into sacrificial fire without uttering *mantras*; there can be no penances without a person to perform them; the worship of deities and men and the seers is accomplished by the libations poured with *mantras*. Therefore, Agni has been regarded as the *hotṛ* of the universe and of sacrifices. Moreover, he is the instrument through which the gods and men do good to the universe. Agni is also known as Viṣṇu. Because entering in all creatures, he upholds their vital airs. In the words of *Mahābhārata*:

अग्निर्विष्णुः सर्वभूतान्यनुप्रविश्य प्राणान् धारयति।[27]

3.2 Brahmā and Veda:

At the very outset the Brahman caused (created) those excellent Vedic sounds (*vedavidyā*) that are embodiment of true knowledge and that have neither beginning nor end to flow on. The names of seers, all things that have been created, the varieties of form seen in things, and the course of all actions, have all originated from the Vedas. As it is described in the epic:

अनादिनिधना विद्या वागुत्सृष्टा स्वयम्भुवा।।
ऋषीणां नामधेयानि याश्च वेदेषु सृष्टयः।

नानारूपं च भूतानां कर्मणां च प्रवर्तनम्॥
वेदशब्देभ्य एवादौ निर्मिमीते स ईश्वरः।
नामधेयानि चर्षीणां याश्च वेदेषु सृष्टयः॥[28]

Indeed, in the beginning Brahman created all things from the words of the Vedas. Truly, the names of the seers and sages, and all else that has been created, are found in the Vedas. When the Vedas were seized or stolen forcibly by two powerful Asuras, Brahman became stricken with grief and prayed Nārāyaṇa to restore the Vedas. In the words of Brahman the importance of the Vedas cannot be ignored at any cost. Thus he presented the significance of the eternal knowledge as:

वेदा मे परमं चक्षुर्वेदा मे परमं बलम्।
वेदा मे परमं धाम वेदा मे ब्रह्म चोत्तरम्॥
मम वेदा हृताः सर्वे दानवाभ्यां बलादितः।
अन्धकारा हि मे लोका जाता वेदैर्विनाकृताः॥
वेदानृते हि कुर्यां लोकानां सृष्टिमुत्तमाम्।
अहो बत महद् दुःखं वेदनाशनजं मम॥[29]

Hence, from the above informative verses it is clear that without the Vedas, i.e. *vedavidyās*, the creation has no meaning and the whole world have become covered with darkness. This way, the Vedas can not be separated from Brahman and hence it has no existence without Brahman and his entire creation.

3.3 Nārāyaṇa and Veda:

The Supreme Puruṣa is identified at same places, with Lord Kṛṣṇa, Viṣṇu and Nārāyaṇa as the creator of this Universe. The importance of Cosmic Puruṣa is wisely noticed in the Puruṣa-sūkta of the *Ṛgveda* (X.90). According to the *Mahābhārata* this Puruṣa (Sūkta) occurs in all the Vedas and it is well-known to be at one with *ṛta* and *satya*. The author of *Mahābhārata*, Vedavyāsa has thought upon it in a proper way:

इदं पुरुषसूक्तं हि सर्ववेदेषु पार्थिव।
ऋतं सत्यं च विख्यातमृषिसिंहेन चिन्तितम्॥[30]

Like the form and features of Puruṣa in the Puruṣa Sūkta of the *Ṛgveda*, the Lord Nārāyaṇa has also thousand heads, thousand feets, thousand eyes, thousand stomaches and thousand hands. With one of his mouths He utters the syllable '*om*' and then the *gāyatrī* following '*om*'. His other mouths utters *mantras* from the four Vedas. The Lord of all the *devas*, the Divine God who is adored in sacrifices (*yajñas*), held in His hands a sacrificial altar, a *kamaṇḍalu*, a *daṇḍakāṣtha*, a bundle of *kuśa* grass, and a little blazing fire.[31]

The Vedas, *yajñas*, plants and herbs have created by Lord Nārāyaṇa to appease the Vedic gods, which is stated as under:

इत्यर्थं निर्मिता वेदा यज्ञाश्चौषधिभिः सह॥
एभिः सम्यक् प्रयुक्तैर्हि प्रीयन्ते देवताः क्षितौ।[32]

Lord Nārāyaṇa is called by His devotees in different names, namely Adhokṣaja[33], Ghṛtāci[34] and Hiraṇyagarbha[35]. These names of Nārāyaṇa have also been cited in the *kośas* and other *śāstras*. It is very interesting to note that Lord Nārāyaṇa is regarded as the embodied form of the *Ṛgveda*, containing of twentyone thousand *mantras*. Individuals conversant with the Vedas also call him the embodiment of the Sāmans, i.e. *Sāmaveda* of thousand *mantras*. So the learned Brahmins, who are devoted worshippers of Nārāyaṇa sing (pray) Him in the Āraṇyakas as:

एकविंशतिसाहस्त्रं ऋग्वेदं मां प्रचक्षते।
सहस्त्रशाखं यत् साम ये वै वेदविदो जनाः॥
गायन्त्यारण्यके विप्रा मद्भक्तास्ते हि दुर्लभाः।[36]

The *adhvaryuṣ* sing Nārāyaṇa in the *Yajurveda*, which consists of one hundred and one branches.[37] He is also regarded by the wise Brahmins of the *Atharvaveda* as identical with the Atharvans, consisting of five *kalpas* and all the *kṛtyas*.[38] Thus, all the sub-divisions of different Vedas with their *śākhās*, and all the *mantras* that compose these branches (*śākhās*) and all the vowels that occur in those *mantras*, and all the rules in respect of pronunciation, are considered as the real creation of Nārāyaṇa,[39] the Supreme Lord of this universe.

4. Kings and Veda:

The learned scholars have suggested that the king should live, reciting everyday the Vedas.[40] In the *Mahābhārata* regarding the study of kings it is noted that a king should be conservant with the Vedas and their *aṅgas* (branches), possessed of wisdom, engaged in penances, and devoted to the performance of *yajñas*. All these qualities should permanently reside in a king. Hence, it is rightly said:

वेदवेदाङ्गवित् प्राज्ञः सुतपस्वी नृपो भवेत्।
दानशीलश्च सततं यज्ञशीलश्च भारत॥[41]

The three kinds of fire, the three Vedas and *yajñas* with *dakṣiṇā*, all disappear when the king becomes careless.[42] *Traividyā* here means the three Vedas. The king should not oppress Vedic priests, all of whom are respected and held high esteem. By suppressing these holy priests he incurs blame and sin.

ऋत्विक्पुरोहिताचार्यान् सत्कृतानभिसत्कृतान्।
न ब्राह्मणान् घातयीत दोषान् प्राप्नोति घातयन्॥[43]

Hence, the *ṛtrik*, *purohita* and *ācārya* should not be given any type of pain by the king. It also indicates that the Vedic priests deserved every respect in the society. King Yudhiṣṭhira has worshipped the well-versed Vedic Brahmins at the time of his royal coronation (वेदाध्ययनसम्पन्नान् धृतिशीलसमन्वितान्-Mbh XII.40.19). Bhīṣma has advised king Yudhiṣṭhira to protect Brahmins of pious deeds and devoted to the study of the Vedas as also all other men in his kingdom.

It is known from the *Mahābhārata* that king Yudhiṣṭhira[44] has read the *Ṛgveda*, the *Yajurveda*, the *Sāmaveda*, the *Chandas*, astronomy, *Nirukta*, *Vyākaraṇa* and *Śikṣā*. *Chandas* here means *Atharvaveda*. Bhīṣma[45] has learned Veda and Vedāṅgas from *ṛṣi* Cyavana and Maharshi Vasiṣṭha. King Janaka[46] was also well versed in the Vedas and other *śāstras*. Most of the kings of the *Mahābhārata* age were conversant of the Vedas and other scriptures and so they have a good respect for the Vedas and Vedic scholars in their mind. They used to follow the guide lines of the Vedas in their day to day life. Besides, it is important to note that in the palace (*rājabhavana*) of king Dilipa, the sound of Vedic recitations never ceased[47] Hence, it is clear from the above references that the kings of the epical age were admirer of the Vedas and Vedic culture.

5. Caste (*varṇa*) system and Veda:

The *Ṛgveda* gives an account of the origin of the castes (*varṇas*) from different organs of the Cosmic Puruṣa—the *brāhmaṇas* from the mouth, the *rājanyas* (*kṣatriyas*) from his arms, the *vaiśyas* from his thigh and the *śūdras* from his feet.[48] The *Mahābhārata* accepts this account and mentions in many places, for an example:

ब्राह्मणो मुखतः सृष्टो ब्रह्मणो राजसत्तम।
बाहुभ्यां क्षत्रियः सृष्ट ऊरुभ्यां वैश्य एव च॥
वर्णश्चतुर्थः पश्चात् तु पद्भ्यां शूद्रो विनिर्मितः॥[49]

It is clear from the above verses that the Vedic *varṇa vyavasthā* (caste system) was reflected in the society of the *Mahābhārata* age. In addition to this, the epical age was the age of brahmanism. So brahmanism has become the subject matter of the *Mahābhārata*. The glory of brahmanism has been heralded everywhere in it. The *brāhmaṇa* class was in great supremacy—they used to be respected and revered by other classes in the society. They are like Agni, who uphold sacrifices. The sacrifices, which the *brāhmaṇas* perform, strengthen the dities.[50] Brahman, in creating the universe, first created the *brāhmaṇas* (Mbh XII.188.1). The *brāhmaṇas* become immortal by studying the Vedas, and go to heaven through the aid of such study.

The Vedic knowledge was highly essential for a true Brahmin in the epical age. Hence, Vedavyāsa clarifies that he who has mastered over all the Vedas and observed the vow of *brahmacarya*, he who knows *ṛk*, *yajus* and *sāman mantras*, is called a real Brahmin.[51] Vedavyāsa further adds that a *kṣatriya* should give charity (*dāna*) to the best Brahmins. No gift should be offered to a Brahmin destitude of knowledge of the Vedas. Gifts should be offered to him, who is a *śrotriya*, i.e. one who possessed of knowledge of the Vedas. So, there is no doubt that a gift offered to a Brahmin bereft of the Vedic knowledge becomes fruitless, in consequence of the fault of the recipient.[52] Therefore, the duty of a Brahmin is to read and teach the Vedas throughout his life.[53]

In the *Mahābhārata*, the Brahmin is known as "*mantradarśinaḥ*", because he is well-versed in the *mantras*, i.e. Vedas. Like Brahmin the *kṣatriya* and *vaiśya* also have every right to study the Vedas. As said in the Śāntiparva:

क्षेत्रजं सेवते कर्म वेदाध्ययनसंगतः। ...क्षत्रिय उच्यते॥

And :

...वेदाध्ययनसंपन्नः स वैश्य इति संज्ञितः॥[54]

But the *śūdra* does not study the Vedas due to his impurity and bad conduct.

सर्वभक्षरतिर्नित्यं सर्वकर्मकरोऽशुचिः।
त्यक्तवेदस्त्वनाचारः स वै शूद्र इति स्मृतः॥[55]

So, due to *nindita karma* and unrighteous conduct, the *śūdra* is being deprived for studying the Vedas.[56] He is responsible for this only for his ill deeds, but no *śāstra*, i.e. *Mahābhārata* has not banned him to study the Vedas. The *Mahābhārata* emphatically says that one should do his ordained duties properly and sincerely, because it earns glory, which leads to heaven.

6. *Āśrama-dharma* and Veda:

The life of the individual was divided into four stages of *āśramas*, viz. *brahmacaryāśrama*, *gṛhasthāśrama*, *vānaprasthāśrama* and *sannyāsāśama*. The duties of the individual, determined by different stages are very elaborately discussed in this epic. This *āśramavyavasthā* is fully *Vaidik* and the individual used to follow this since his birth till death. The *brahmacaryāśrama* is a period of learning and discipline. After proper initiation, the *brahmacārī* goes to a teacher's house, known as *gurukula*, and stays their till the completion of his education. Here a strict moral education is given to the *brahmacārin*. Sage Bhṛgu explains the duties of the *brahmacārin* in chapter CXCI of the Śāntiparvan. According to him the main task of this stage is to study the Vedas and to know the nature of God, and world. Because without studying Vedas no one can judge actions as right or wrong and even cannot choose the right path of life. In the *gṛhasthāśrama* the *gṛhastha* engages himself in ritual sacrifices. Besides *vedādhyayana*, the house holder should perform his *gṛhasthadharma* properly. In this *āśrama* he should always worship and receive such guests (*atithi*)[57], those are presenters of sacrificial offerings and cleansed by Vedic lore and devoted to excellent vows and penances. In rest two *āśramas* the individual has to perform religious rites and regular study of the Vedas. However, in these four *āśramas* the individual maintained a religious and sacred life as prescribed in the Vedas and other scriptures.

7. *Yajña* and Veda:

According to the Vedic tradition, performance of *yajña* is essential for every human being as a part of life. It also played an important role in the spreading of knowledge as on the occasion of their performance, learned Brahmins were invited The traditional Brahmins chant Vedic *mantras* in the *yajña*. Because without *mantras*, the *vaidika yajña* has no value. The *devatās* can be invoked through sacred *mantras*.

Henceforth, the *ṛtvik* or *purohita* of the *yajña* should be conversant of the Vedas. In the Śāntiparva the word *ṛtvik* is clearly explained as: "those Brahmins who are competent to officiate as priests, i.e. *ṛtvik*, should know the *chandas* including the *sāmans* and the rites which are laid down in the Śrauta literature".

प्रतिकर्म पराचार ऋत्विजां स्म विधीयते।
छन्दः सामादि विज्ञाय द्विजानां श्रुतमेव च॥[58]

Thus, it is suggested that a Brahmin should perform various kinds *yajñas* and *iṣṭis* (sacrificial rites):

इष्टीश्च विविधाः प्राप्य क्रतूंश्चैवाप्तदक्षिणान्[59]॥

The main purpose of *yajña* is to please the gods: "**यज्ञः प्रीणाति देवताः**"[60]. Regarding the shares of sacrificial offering (*yajña bhāga*) it is mentioned that through the *devatās*, Lord Nārāyaṇa receives his share and this has been mentioned in the Vedic Sūtras.[61]

In the Vedic sacrifice a number of things should not be entertained by the priests. Because, wine, fish, honey, meat, alcohol and preparations of rice and seasame seeds have introduced by the knaves. The use of these things in *yajñas* is not prescribed in the Vedas. As rightly said in the *Mahābhārata*:

सुरा मत्स्या मधु मांसमासवं कृसरौदनम्।
धूर्तैः प्रवर्तितं ह्येतन्नैतद् वेदेषु कल्पितम्॥[62]

Regarding the use of trees (woods of trees) in *yajñas*, the *Mahābhārata* states that those trees should be used in the *yajñas*, whose names have mentioned in the Vedas:

यज्ञियाश्चैव ये वृक्षा वेदेषु परिकल्पिताः॥[63]

In the epical age kings used to perform different types of *yajñas* and *iṣṭis*. So in the *Mahābhārata* several *yajñas*[64] and *iṣṭis*[65] are mentioned Only names can be mentioned in this brief paper. Aśvamedha *yajña* performed by several kings like Sagar (Mbh XII.29.132), Pṛthu (Mbh XII.29.143), Rāma (Mbh XII.29.59) and others. Vājapeya *yajña* was performed by king Yajāti (Mbh XII.29.96). However, Rājasūya and Aśvamedha sacrifices were performed to raise political status, and also to help the performer to get the heaven. Subjects related to *yajña*, like *vedi*[66], *kuṇḍa*[67] and *yūpa*[68] have also been discussed in the *Mahābhārata* in several places. In a true sense, the Vedic *yajñas* and their applications have nicely refelected in *Mahābhārata* age.

8. *Yugas* and Veda:

It is known from the *Mahābhārata* that the people of *treatā*, *dvāpara* and *kali* ages are inspired with doubts, i.e. with reference to the declarations of the *śruitis*. The people, however, of the *satya-yuga* are sincerely devoted to penances, vows, and observant of righteousness. In fact, in that age all people highly regard the *Ṛgveda*, the *Yajurveda* and the *Sāmaveda* as identical notwithstanding their apparent diversity.

This means the people of *satyayuga* paid respect to all the Vedas equally. They have not seen any difference among these Vedas. In the beginning of *treatāyuga*, the Vedas, Vedic *yajñas* and divisions of caste and the several modes of life existed in their entirety.[69] On account of the duration of life of persons being decreased in the *dvāpara* age, those suffer decline. In the *dvāpara* age as well as in the *kali* age, the Vedas are overtaken by perplexity.[70]

In the *kali* age, the Vedas become so scarce that they may not be seen even by men. Afflicted by inequity they suffer extermination along with the rites and sacrifices laid down in them. As truly said in the *Mahābhārata*:

दृश्यन्ते न च दृश्यन्ते वेदाः कलियुगेऽखिलाः।
उत्सीदन्ते सयज्ञाश्च केवला धर्मपीडिताः॥[71]

Therefore, in the *kaliyuga* through universal sin (*pāpa*) the Vedas disappear (Mbh XII.238.17). As the rain from the sky causes all products of the earth to grow, likewise the Vedas, in every age, develops all its auxiliaries (*aṅgas*):

सृजते सर्वतोऽङ्गानि तथा वेदा युगे युगे।[72]

Here, '*aṅgāni*' means the observances necessary for the practice of *yoga* as also all kinds of rites and vows. The Vedas cause these to grow, and they, in their turn, add all students of the Vedas in achieving their purposes.

9. Philosophical thoughts and Veda:

In the *Mahābhārata* we find discussions of philosophical views of different religious institutions. The Vedic and Upaniṣadic philosophy are the main subject matter of philosophy of the *Mahābhārata*. Yoga philosophy has been preached in the Śāntiparvan by *ṛṣi* Yājñavalkya. Sāṁkhya philosophy of Maharshi Kapila has also been discussed in the same *parvan*. Similarly, the theme of Vedānta, Yoga, Mīmāṁsā philosophy are also found in the *Mahābhārata*. However, a detailed discussion has also been made in various philosophical concepts like: *Īśvara*, *Ātman, jīva, Prakṛti, Puruṣa, dharma-adharma, karma, mokṣa, mahābhūta, vidyā-avidyā*, etc. The names of sage Kapila, Gautama and Jaimini are also mentioned in the Śāntiparvan. Even the reference to *puruṣa sūkta*, one of the philosophical *sūktas* of the Vedas, is also occurred in the Śāntiparva of *Mahābhārata*. So from the philosophical point of view, *Mahābhārata* records the main theme and concept of Vedic and Upaniṣadic thoughts.

10. Conclusion:

In the conclusion, it may be said that the Vedic thoughts have been reflected as well as echoed in the *Mahābhārata*. The Vedic subjects like *yajña, karma, dharma, darśana*, etc. are crystallized and concentrated, but these subjects are more extensively discussed & elaborated in this great epic. There is no doubt that the Vedic subjects are more simplified and flourished in the *Mahābhārata*. Some changes of thoughts as we observe in it, are due to the changing condition of human attitudes and social orders.

The doctrines formulated in Vedic time under the then circumstances might loose their essence in the epical age are conditioned by the change of time and angles of visions for proper perspective. Hence, the epical thoughts and ideas though have their origin in the Vedas are found with a little difference in principles and ethics. Vedavyāsa has also stated that the subjects contained in the *Mahābhārata* are the theme of Vedic ideas. Therefore, it is aptly said by him:

इतिहासपुराणाभ्यां वेदं समुपबृंहयेत्।[73]

REFERENCES

1. कार्ष्णं वेदमिमं विद्वाञ्छ्रावयित्वार्थमश्नुते। महाभारत (गीता प्रेस संस्करण) I. 62.18.
2. चतुर्भ्यः सरहस्येभ्यो वेदेभ्यो ह्यधिकं यदा।।
   महत्त्वे च गुरुत्वे च ध्रियमाणं यतोऽधिकम्।। *ibid.*, I.1.272cd and 273cd.
   Cf. इदं हि वेदैः समितं पवित्रमपि चोत्तमम् ।। *ibid.*, I.62.16 and 49.
3. कृष्णद्वैपायनव्यासो वेदव्यासो महानृषिः।
   वेदानध्यापयामास महाभारतपञ्चमान्।। महाभारत, शान्तिपर्व, 340.19-21.
   Cf. इतिहासपुराणं पञ्चमं वेदानां वेदम्। Chā Up VII.1.2.
4. *Mahābhārata* (Mbh) Śāntiparva, 39.20 (*Veda viduṣām*); 39.32; 29.12; 25.4; 121.51; 53.54; 122.47; 128.10; 180.47; 182.15; 193.10; 201.1; 220.17; 224.46; 225.19,25; 228.74; 241.1,6; 242.3; 226.14; 265.7; 268.8, 10, 33; 297.33; 299.24; 29; 301.46; 302.3; 318.10; 328.22; 339.22; 340.22; 341.45; 342.120; 343.12-13, 61;344.12; 345.9; 348.10, 22; 349.1, 9-11, 13, 15, 41, 64, 66, 69, 73; 350.19; 354.14, etc.
5. *ibid.*, XII.335.40.
6. *ibid.*, XII.339.111.
7. *ibid.*, XII.297.40; cf. XII.227.60.
8. ज्ञानवित् सर्वभूतानां सर्ववित् सर्ववेदवित्।। *ibid.*, XII.251.3.
9. *ibid.*, XII.251.18.
10. *ibid.*, XII.270.43, cf. Mbh XII.270.42.
11. व्यालकुञ्जरदुर्गेषु सर्पचोरभयेषु च।
    हस्तावापेन गच्छन्ति नास्तिकाः किमतः परम्।। *ibid.*, XII.181.5.
12. *ibid.*, XII.180.47 and 49.
13. *ibid.*, XII.79.19, cf. XII.79.10.
14. *ibid.*, XII.335.29, cf. XII.335.27-28.
15. *ibid.*, XII.340.70 ab.
16. मरीचिरङ्गिराश्चात्रिः पुलस्त्यः पुलहः क्रतुः।
    वसिष्ठश्च महात्मा वै मनुः स्वायम्भुवस्तथा।।
    ज्ञेयाः प्रकृतयोऽष्टौ ता यासु लोकाः प्रतिष्ठिताः।
    वेदवेदाङ्गसंयुक्तान् यज्ञान् यज्ञाङ्गसंयुतान्।।

निर्ममे लोकसिद्ध्यर्थं ब्रह्मा लोकपितामहः।
अष्टाभ्य प्रकृतिभ्यश्च जातं विश्वमिदं जगत्।। *ibid.*, XII.340.34-36.

17. *ibid.*, XII.192.16-17.
18. *ibid.*, XII.327.49.
19. सोऽधीत्य निखिलान् वेदान् सरहस्यान् ससंग्रहान्। *ibid.*, XII.324.24.
20. *ibid.*, XII.328.23.
21. *ibid.*, XII.324.22-23.
22. *ibid.*, XII.318.11ab and 16.
23. दश पञ्च च प्राप्तानि यजूंष्यर्कान्मयानघ। *ibid.*, XII.318.21ab.
24. वेदश्रुतिभिराख्यानैरर्थानभिजिगीषति।
    तितिक्षुरनवज्ञाता तस्मात् सर्वत्र पूजितः।।
    ibid., XII.230.12, cf. XII.230.13-20.
25. *ibid.*, XII.335.3.
26. *ibid.*, XII.342.12.
27. *ibid.*, XII.342.15.
28. *ibid.*, XII.232.24cd-26; cf. XII.232.28.
29. *ibid.*, XII.347.32-34.
30. *ibid.*, XII.350.5.
31. सहस्रनयनः श्रीमाञ्छतशीर्षः सहस्रपात्।।
    सहस्रोदरबाहुश्च अव्यक्त इति च क्वचित्।
    ओङ्कारमुद्गिरन् वक्त्रात् सावित्रीं च तदन्वयाम्।।
    शेषेभ्यश्चैव वक्त्रेभ्यश्चतुर्वेदान् गिरन् बहून्।
    आरण्यकं जगौ देवो हरिर्नारायणो वशी।।
    वेदिं कमण्डलुं..... ज्वलितं च हुताशनम्।।
    धारयामास देवेशो हस्तैर्यज्ञपतिस्तदा। *ibid.*, XII.339.6cd-10ab.
32. *ibid.*, XII.340.66cd-67ab.
33. निरुक्तं वेदविदुषो वेदशब्दार्थचिन्तकाः।
    ते मां गायन्ति प्राग्वंशे अधोक्षज इति स्थितिः।। *ibid.*, XII.342.83.
34. घृतं ममार्चिषो लोके जन्तूनां प्राणधारणम्।
    घृतार्चिरहमव्यग्रैर्वेदज्ञैः परिकीर्तितः।। *ibid.*, XII.342.85.
35. हिरण्यगर्भो द्युतिमान् य.एष च्छन्दसि स्तुतः।
    योगैः सम्पूज्यते नित्यं स एवाहं भुवि स्मृतः।। *ibid.*, 342.96.
36. *ibid.*, XII.342.97-98ab.
37. षट्पञ्चाशतमष्टौ च सप्तत्रिंशतमित्युत।।
    यस्मिंशाखा यजुर्वेदे सोऽहमाध्वर्यवे स्मृतः।
    ibid., XII.342.98-99ab.
38. पञ्चकल्पमथर्वाणं कृत्याभिः परिबृंहितम्।।
    कल्पयन्ति हि मां विप्रा अथर्वाणविदस्तथा। *ibid.*, XII.342.99cd-100ab.

39. शाखाभेदाश्च.... क्रमाक्षरविभागवित्। *ibid.*, XII.342.100cd-102ab.
40. अध्येतव्या त्रयी नित्यं भवितव्यं विपश्चिता।। *ibid.*, XII.8.27cd.
41. *ibid.*, XII.69.31.
42. अग्निस्त्रेता त्रयी विद्या यज्ञाश्च सहदक्षिणाः।
सर्व एव प्रमाद्यन्ति यदा राजा प्रमाद्यति।। *ibid.*, XII.91.8; cf. Mbh XII.91.7.
43. *ibid.*, XII.132.9.
44. ऋक्सामसंघाश्च यजूंषि चापि च्छन्दांसि नक्षत्रगतिं निरुक्तम्।
अधीत्य च व्याकरणं संकल्पं शिक्षां च.....।। *ibid.*, XII.201.8; cf. XII.19.2.
45. भार्गवाच्च्यवनाच्चापि वेदानाङ्गोपबृंहितान्।
प्रतिपेदे महाबाहुर्वसिष्ठाच्चरितव्रतः।। *ibid.*, XII.37.11.
46. *ibid.*, XII.320.5-6.
47. त्रयः शब्दा न जीर्यन्ते.... स्वाध्यायघोषो.....।। *ibid.*, XII.29.79.
48. ब्राह्मणोऽस्यमुख.... अजायत। *Ṛgveda*, X.90.12.
49. *Mahābhārata*, XII.72.4-5; cf. XII.72.5-10,
also cf. XII.342.20.
50. *ibid.*, XII.342.14-15.
51. सर्वान् वेदानधीयीत शुश्रूषुर्ब्रह्मचर्यवान्।
ऋचो यजूंषि सामानि न तेन न स वै द्विजः।। *ibid.*, XII.251.2.
52. यथा दारुमयो हस्ती यथा चर्ममयो मृगः।
ब्राह्मणश्चानधीयानस्त्रयस्ते नाम बिभ्रति।।
ibid., XII.36.46; cf. *Manusmṛti*, II.157.
53. *ibid.*, (Mbh) XII.297.30.
54. *ibid.*, 189.5-6.
55. *ibid.*, XII.189.7.
56. *ibid.*, XII.188.15.
57. *ibid.*, XII.243.8.
58. *ibid.*, XII.79.2.
59. *ibid.*, XII.251.4ab.
60. *ibid.*, XII.121.37d.
61. यज्ञैर्ये चापि यक्ष्यन्ति सर्वलोकेषु वै सुराः।।
कल्पयिष्यन्ति वो भागांस्ते नरा वेदकल्पितान्।
यो मे यथा कल्पितवान् भागमस्मिन् महाक्रतौ।।
स तथा यज्ञभागार्हो वेदसूत्रे मया कृतः। *ibid.*, XII.340.61cd-63ab.
62. *ibid.*, XII.265.9.
63. *ibid.*, XII.265.11.
64. *ibid.*, XII.29.114; 24.7; 12.17; 129.11; 284.183; 323.9, etc.
65. दर्शपूर्णमास-Mbh XII.29.114; 269.2; चातुर्मास्य-Mbh XII.29.114; 269.20; अग्न्याधान, सोमयाग, चातुर्मास्य-Mbh XII.268.38; 29.114; 269.20; इष्टि-Mbh XII.297.39; 244.25.

66. *ibid.*, XII.40.12; 339.9; 343.60.
67. *ibid.*, XII.320.180-181.
68. *ibid.*, XII.29.74; 265.8.
69. त्रेतादौ केवला वेदा यज्ञा वर्णाश्रमास्तथा।
....*ibid.*, XII.238.14ab.
70. द्वापरे विप्लवं यान्ति वेदाः कलियुगे तथा।
....*ibid.*, XII.238.15ab.
71. *ibid.*, XII.232.36.
72. *ibid.*, XII.238.18.
73. *ibid.*, I.1.267.

Concept of *Yajña* in the *Mahābhārata*

Yajña is the principal institution and symbol of Vedic tradition and knowledge. It is an act of worship, symbolizing inner submission, consecration and surrender to higher powers, gods and the Supreme *Brahman*. The word *yajña* is derived from the root *yaj-*, which means to worship, to offer, to adore, etc. According to the *Nighaṇṭu*, *yajña* has fifteen synonyms, viz. *yajña, vena, adhvara, medha, vidatha, nārya, savana, hotrā, iṣṭi, devatātā, makha, viṣṇu, indu, prajāpati* and *gharma*[1]. But in the *Amarakośa* only seven synonyms of *yajña* are recorded, viz. *yajña, sava, yāga, adhvara, saptatantu, makha* and *kratu*[2]. So, *yajña* or sacrifice is a well-known act of worship as say the etymologists.

In the *Mahābhārata,* the true nature and the very concept of Vedic *yajñas* are also found. This paper very precisely deals about the different features of *yajñas* as described in the great epic *Mahābhārata*. According to it Prajāpati, the Lord of all creatures, of righteous soul, created creatures with the purpose that they would worship Him by sacrifices with profuse presents. As said in the epic:

असृजद्धि प्रजा राजन् प्रजापतिरकल्मषः।
मां यक्ष्यन्तीति धर्मात्मा यज्ञैर्विविधदक्षिणैः॥[3]

For this purpose the creator has created creepers, trees, herbs (*auṣadhi*), clean animals, and clarified butter (*havīṁṣī*) as main material of sacrifice.[4] In order to gratify Lord Nārāyaṇa the creator He has created Vedas, *yajñas,* plants and herbs.[5] The human-beings would satisfy Lord Nārāyaṇa and other gods by performing various *iṣṭis* and *yajñas*. Secondly, in the *Bhagavadgītā*, which is part of the *Mahābhārata,* the broader concept of *yajña* is elucidated as:

सहयज्ञाः प्रजाः सृष्ट्वा पुरोवाच प्रजापतिः।
अनेन प्रसविष्यध्वमेष वोऽस्त्विष्टकामधुक्॥[6]

In the beginning of the creation the creator Brahmā has created mankind along with *yajña* and asked to gain prosperity with it, for *yajña,* like *Kāmadhenu* which is the bestower of all desires. Because the simultaneous creation of (mankind) human being and *yajña* must have been for meeting man's both inner and outer needs. Prajāpati here stands for the scheme and principle of both human and social growth. According to Prajāpati, the creator, propitiating the gods with *yajña* is the best way to get *mokṣa* or *svarga* or the attainment of knowledge of *Brahman*. Hence, it is rightly said:

देवान्भावयतानेन ते देवा भावयन्तु वः।
परस्परं भावयन्तः श्रेयः परमवाप्स्यथ॥
इष्टान्भोगान् हि वो देवा दास्यन्ते यज्ञभाविताः॥[7]

Besides, those who after performing sacrifices to gods, etc. eat the remains of the food, which is called *amṛta* are freed from all sins committed at the five places[8] of animal-slaughter as well as from those sins which result from voluntary acts of injury and other causes.

Vedas and *Yajñas* :

The Vedic people mostly thought of *yajñas* as acts of pleasing *devatās* the means for getting the favour of God—welfare and material prosperity along the path of *ṛta*. They paid offerings for favours without any consciousness of sin. A sacrificer must be an upholder of truth (*satyadhṛt*); *yajñas* are a binding force between men and gods; they are for the good of all, hence it is a social duty.[9] Not to perform sacrifice is, therefore, a social evil, an inhuman thing. Hymns, oblations, fire-praise and laudation of the deity, offering something to Him to express one's submission and veneration and destroying of this gift by casting it into fire—such is the essence of Vedic *yajñas*. According to Puruṣa Sūkta of the *Ṛgveda*, the *devatās* accomplished their *yajña* by means of *yajña*, these were the primeval ordinances (***yajñena yajñamayajanta devāḥ*......**)[10]. The complete symbolism of *yajña-vidyā* may be invoked for grasping the implications of this *mantra*. The most perfect example of *yajña* performed by *yajña* is that of the two parents creating new life, each being a form of *prāṇāgni* as explained by the *Aitareya Brāhmaṇa*: ***"yajño vai tad devā yajñam ayajanta yad agnināgnim ayajanta"***.[11] Fire is produced from fire—this is the great law of cause and effect which is the foundation of all Purāṇic and material working (***agnināgniḥ samidhyate*... ...**).[12] As a popular saying goes on "***yathā piṇḍe tathā brahmāṇḍe***"—there is complete correspondence between the individual and the universal, or between the bodily cell and the cosmic consciousness, or between the small atom and the big solar system; everywhere it is the law of '*yajñena yajñam*'. Sāyaṇa, the commentator of the Vedas says that the gods perfomed this *yajña* mentally (*mānasena saṁkalpena*) with *puruṣa* as the victim. This means that they meditated upon the whole world as being made from the body of the great *puruṣa*. If everything is *puruṣa*, anything sacrificed becomes the *pruruṣa*. Interpreting this *mantra* on the analogy of a somewhat similar verse in the *Bhagavadgītā* (IV.24), it may be understood to say that everything depends upon

Brahman (puruṣa) for its existence that is also their end, all the *Brahman*—whether the oblation, the fire, or the sacrificer.

ब्रह्मार्पणं ब्रह्म हविर्ब्रह्माग्नौ ब्रह्मणा हुतम्।
ब्रह्मैव तेन गन्तव्यं ब्रह्मकर्मसमाधिना॥[13]

Life itself is the great sacrifice, where *Brahman* Himself is at the same time the *yajamāna* or sacrificer, the fire where sacrifice is offered, the material of the sacrifice (*havi*), the God to whom sacrifice is offered, Whom one attains by living his life as if it is *Brahmakarma* or an offering of all its fruits to *Brahman* is total absence of desire. Everything belongs to Brahman (*puruṣa*), the One Supreme Being, and is an effect of him; so in offering anything we offer Him what is His Own.

In the *Ṛgveda*, *yajña* is said to be the centre (*nābhi*) of the Universe. It signifies a creative act of all levels; on the biological plane it is the creation of new life matter that is *yajña,* a union of Agni and Soma; whenever there is such a creative process, there is the centre of the universe, the meaning being that the entire mystery or potentiality of the cosmic process becomes inherent in the centre of that *yajña*. Hence, whatever is created by *yajña* is the true image of Prajāpati or all the gods. The word *nābhi* stands for the centre in Vedic symbolism. It is the seat of the highest Divine principle—'ईश्वरः सर्वभूतानां हृद्देशेऽर्जुन तिष्ठति।' (BhG XVII.61). In fact it is essential that a *nābhi* or *hṛddeśa* should come into existence to reflect the glory of Divine Splendour and such a centre is created only as *yajña*. There are two conceptions of the father and the mother whose union becomes a *yajña*. The father is like the centre (*nābhi*) of the circle and mother the circumference (*paramanta*)[14]. Hence, the creation of the world itself was even regarded as the fruit of sacrifice performed by the Supreme Being.

There are four principal priests (*ṛtviks*) connected with the four Vedas. The principle of this division rests on that of division of duties among the different classes of priests, cooperating in the performance of worship of *yajña* or sacrifice. It is well-explained by the great etymologist Yāska in his *Nirukta*[15] as: 'ऋचां त्वः पोषमास्ते...यज्ञस्य मात्रां विमिमीत उ त्वः'[16] This *Ṛgvedic mantra* specifically says the application of the duties of *ṛtviks*. The duty of the priest *hotā,* at the time of sacrifice is to make ready his collection of *ṛks* gathered from different places, and fix it as his *śastra*. This duty of another priest is to measure out the whole structure of the sacrifice. This priest is called *adhvaryu,* who belongs to the *Yajurveda*. Apart from *adhvaryu,* there is also *udgātā* in a sacrifice, who sings certain *mantras*. The collection of *mantras* meant for *udgātā* has been called the *Sāmaveda*. The fourth priest is called *brahmā,* who is supposed to be a specialist of all the four Vedas, including the *Atharvaveda*.

In the *Mahābhārata* also the words like *ṛtvik, hotā* (Mbh XII.272.8) and *adhvaryu* occur in different contexts. The word *ṛtvik* is explained in the Śāntiparva as:

प्रतिकर्म पराचार ऋत्विजां स्म विधीयते।
छन्दः सामादि विज्ञाय द्विजानां श्रुतमेव च।।[17]

This means "those Brahmins who are competent to officiate as priests, i.e. *ṛtviks,* should know the *chandas* including the *sāman* and the rites which are laid down in the *Śrauta* literature. At another place it is said that the *ṛtviks, purohitas* and *ācāryas* should not be given any type of pain by the kings.[18] So, it is clear that the position of *ṛtviks* and *ācāryas* was very high in the epic age, because they were performing various *yajñas* and other traditional rituals. It is also stated that *ṛtvik, purohita* and *ācārya,* when well versed in the Vedas, behave mildly towards others. Due to the influence of Vedic *mantras,* the priests were more humble, soft spoken and well-cultured during Mahābhārata age.[19] Each of these four priests has three assistants and thus the total number of priests goes to sixteen (*ṣoḍaśārtvik kratuśca*......Mbh XII.280.27). Agni is known as the *hotā* and the performer of sacrifices. He is again designated as the Brahmā of the sacrifice. As the *Mahābhārata* states:

अग्निर्हि यज्ञानां होता कर्ता स चाग्निर्ब्रह्म।[20]

The *Mahābhārata* is still famous for its *dharma-yuddha,* fought between Kauravas and Pāṇḍavas. The Pāṇḍavas were supported by the *devatās* as they promoted *dharma* in their kingdom. The *Mahābhārata* war too was considered as a *karma-yajña*. So, in this war-sacrifice (*raṇa-yajña*) the *hotā*, *adhvaryu* and *yajña* materials are described by Indra as under:

ऋत्विजः कुञ्जरास्तत्र वाजिनोऽध्वर्यवस्तथा।
हवींषि परमांसानि रुधिरं त्वाज्यमुच्यते।।[21]

It means, elephants are the *ṛtviks* of that sacrifice, and horses are its *adhvaryus.* The flesh of enemies is its libations and blood is its liquid offerings (*ghee*). Hence, the nature and functions of priests are clearly depicted in the *Mahābhārata.*

The connection of *yajña* with the Veda can be known from the following convictions of the great epic *Mahābhārata:*

(i) The Vedas were spoken out by Brahmā for *yajñas* or they were created by Him along with *yajña.*[22]

(ii) One Veda was divided into four so that *yajñas* can be performed successively.

(iii) The *yajñas* came out from the Vedas and these satisfied the *devatās:*

वेदैर्यज्ञाः समुत्पन्ना यज्ञैर्देवाः प्रतिष्ठिताः।[23]

(iv) Four principal sacrificial acts are connected with the four Vedas.

(v) Persons following the Vedas usually worship *devatās* by performing *yajñas*.

(vi) There will be no *yajñas* if the Vedas are destroyed, i.e. if the *mantras* will not be chanted in the *yajñas,* it is useless and fruitless. Because, *devatās* can be invoked through sacred *mantras*. Hence, a *mantra draṣṭā-puruṣa* or *vedapāṭhi-puruṣa* (a person who knows Vedic *mantras* properly) is treated as an ideal one in the society of epic age.[24]

(vii) Regarding the use of trees in the Vedic sacrifices, the *Mahābhārata* states that those trees should be used in the *yajñas* whose names are mentioned in the Vedas:

यज्ञियाश्चैव ये वृक्षा वेदेषु परिकल्पिताः।।[25]

So, in place of Vedic trees, ordinary trees can not be used in the Vedic *yajñas.*

(viii) In the Vedic *yajñas* a number of things should not be entertained by the priests. Because, wine, fish, honey, meat, alcohol, etc. have been introduced by the knaves. Hence, the use of these things in *yajñas* is not prescribed in the Vedas. The *Mahābhārata* clearly states this as:

सुरा मत्स्या मधु मांसमासवं कृसरौदनम्।
धूर्तैः प्रवर्तितं ह्येतन्नैतद् वेदेषु कल्पितम्।।[26]

However, the sacrifice was believed to have existed from the eternity like the Vedas.

Types of *Yajñas* :

According to Mahātmā Vidura, when *satya* (truth) is covered with ignorance, the performance of *yajñas* takes place in the society. Śaṅkarācārya says "*brahma satyaṁ jaganmithyā*" and *satyaṁ jñānam anantaṁ brahma,* etc. So, *Brahman* is only *satya* and the rest *brahmāṇḍa* world is treated as *asatya* or unreal. When *Brahman* covers itself with *māyā (āvaraṇa)* the real nature and form of the *Brahman* is not at all understandable by the ordinary people. Then it becomes essential for the *jīvas* to perform various types of *yajñas*. It is a means to know the true nature and form of *satya* or *Brahman*. Hence, *yajña* is perfect medium to know the real nature of *satya* or *Brahman*. This *yajña* or sacrifice is of three types, viz. *mānasika - yajña, vācika-yajña* and *kārmika-yajña,* as Mahātmā Vidura describes it:

यतो यज्ञाः प्रवर्धन्ते सत्यस्यैवावरोधनात्।
मनसान्यस्य भवति वाचान्यस्याथ कर्मणा।।[27]

It means, owing to having understood the nature of truth to which are directed all *yajñas*, a certain class of men perform *yajñas* (sacrifices) by mind (meditation), another by words (recitation of *mantras*) and rest by actions, i.e. ritualistic performance.

Besides, the above types of *yajñas* , the Bhīṣmaparva of *Mahābhārata* speaks of five kinds of *yajñas* as:

द्रव्ययज्ञास्तपोयज्ञा योगयज्ञास्तथापरे।
स्वाध्यायज्ञानयज्ञाश्च यतयः संशितव्रताः।।[28]

Yajñas are of different kinds: viz. (a) *dravya-yajña*—where material objects are offered as oblations, objects which appeal to and indulge the senses; (b) *tapoyajña*—

where all desires and out going activities are offered to be consumed in the fire of asceticism and penance; (c) *yoga-yajñas*—where senses are sacrificed at the fire of *saṁyama* or self-control, the practice of detachment; and (d) *svādhyāya-jñāna-yajña—a yajña* in the form of study of the sacred texts (Vedas) and pursuit of knowledge by *brahmacarya.* The *Ṛgveda* (I.84.2) mentions the *yajña* of *ṛṣis* by means of *śruti* or prayer and of mortals by sacrifice, where I.18.7 of the *Ṛgveda* refers to the *yajñas* of sages in their pursuit of knowledge.

In addition to these, the Śāntiparva of *Mahābhārata* records three types of *yajñas,* viz. *svādhyāya yajña* (study of the Vedas to be a sacrifice), *jñāna yajña* (learning to be a sacrifice) and *dhyāna* (*manana*) *yajña* (contemplation in mind to be a great sacrifice).[29]

The *Bhagavadgītā* (Mbh, Bhīṣmaparva, 28.24) speaks about *jñāna yajña.* Right knowledge is represented as a sacrifice in the *Gītā* (IV.24). The sacrifice performed with material objects produces material effects, whereas wisdom sacrifice does not produce any material effects. So, *jñānayajña* is superior to the sacrifice perfomed with material objects (Mbh, Bhīṣmaparva, 28.33). For, wisdom which is the means of liberation (*mokṣa*), comprehend all actions. Besides *jñānayajña,* the *Mahābhārata* also speaks about *karmayajña.* The entire Mahābhārata war or the *dharmayuddha* was practically a *karma (pradhāna) yajña,* as it is clearly known from the *karma yoga* chapter of the *Bhagavadgītā.* The place Kurukshetra was a *raṇabhūmi* or *karmabhūmi* for both the Pāṇḍavas and Kauravas. Very interestingly Duryodhana has described the *raṇayajña* or *karmayajña* in the following way:

अहं च तात कर्णश्च रणयज्ञं वितत्य वै।
युधिष्ठिरं पशुं कृत्वा दीक्षितौ भरतर्षभ॥
रथो वेदी स्रुवः खड्गो गदा स्रुक् कवचोऽजिनम्
चातुर्होत्रं च धुर्या मे शरा दर्भा हविर्यशः॥[30]

It means, Duryodhana said: "I and Karṇa will perform the sacrifice of war after preparing ourselves, making Yudhiṣṭhira the beast for sacrifice. In this sacrifice, my *ratha* will be substitute for the platform (*vedi*); my *khaḍga* (scimitar), the ladle; my *gadā* (mace), the large ladle; and my coat of mail, the witness; my horses will answer the purpose of the four priests (*caturhotram*); my hafts will stand for the *kuśa* grass; and my fame for the clarified butter (*haviṣya*)".

He also stated that having performed this (*raṇa*) *yajña* in the field of battle, in the great honour of the god of death (Yama), and having won a victory and slain our enimies, we shall come back surrounded by a halo of glory. This way, the *raṇayajña* in the form of a *karmayajña* has been nicely described in the *Mahābhārata.* This is the importance of (*bhāvanātmaka*-ornamental) *karmayajña.*

Accessories of *Yajña (yajñāṅgas):*

The Creator Prajāpati has created the *yajñāṅgas* along with *yajña.* The Lord of all creatures made the gods to celebrate sacrifices with their help.[31] The inferior animals, human beings, trees and herbs, all desire for the attainment of heaven. There is no means, however, except *yajña* by which they can acquire the fruition of that desire. The *Mahābhārata* clearly mentions about the seventeen *yajñāṅgas,* i.e. accessories or limbs of sacrifices. These accessories or the limbs have a special importance in the sacrifices. Without these *yajñāṅgas,* a sacrifice can not be performed So to perform any Vedic sacrifice the priest must take help of the following *yajñāṅgas:*

औषध्यः पशवो वृक्षा वीरुदाज्यं पयोदधि।
हविर्भूमिर्दिशः श्रद्धा कालश्चैतानि द्वादश।।
ऋचो यजूंषि सामानि यजमानश्च षोडश।
अग्निर्ज्ञेयो गृहपतिः स सप्तदश उच्यते।।[32]

The herbs (*auṣadhī*), animals, trees, creepers, clarified butter, milk, curds, other *yajña havis, bhūmi,* different *diśas,* faith (*śraddhā*), and *kāla* (time), form the twelfth *yajñāṅga,* the *ṛks,* the *yajus,* the *sāmans* and the sacrificer himself forming the sixteenth *aṅgas* and the fire which should be known as the householder–these seventeen are said to be the limbs of the *yajña* and it is the root (cause) of the universe and its movements. As these *yajñāṅgas* are highly essential in the sacrifices, so by collecting these things people celebrate sacrifices. However, following to the lines of *śruti,* the *Mahābhārata* records this as under:

अङ्गान्येतानि यज्ञस्य यज्ञो मूलमिति श्रुतिः।[33]
यज्ञार्थानि हि सृष्टानि यथार्था श्रूयते श्रुतिः।[34]

Besides, these above mentioned *yajñāṅgas, ṛtviks* and *dakṣiṇā* are also treated as the *aṅgas* of sacrifice. Regarding the importance and function of the four priests it has already been discussed earlier in this paper. The *dakṣiṇā* has a great significance in the Vedic *yajñas*. *Dakṣiṇā* means fees paid to the priest for sacrifical acts. Though it is not mentioned in the above list as an *aṅga* of the *yajña,* but elsewhere in the text it is known as an essential accessory of sacrifice, without which the sacrifice would be treated as fruitless and incomplete. Therefore, the epic adds:

यज्ञाङ्गंदक्षिणा तात वेदानां परिबृंहणम्।
न यज्ञा दक्षिणाहीनास्तारयन्ति कथंचन।।[35]

It is wisely advised by Bhīṣma to Yudhiṣṭhira that *dakṣiṇā* is one of the *aṅgas* of sacrifice and conduces to the nourshment of the Vedas. A *yajña* without proper fee can never provide any prosperity to its *yajamāna.* At several places in the text[36] it is told to the king for performing *yajña* and then provide huge *dakṣiṇā* to the priests. Therefore, it is always advised that *dakṣiṇā* should invariably be paid to the priests in order to achieve prosperity and desired results from the sacrifice.

***Ahiṁsā* and *Yajñas* :**

The bloody sacrificing of animals by violence is not supported by the Vedic religion. As the *Śatapatha Brāhmaṇa* says: "***adhvaro vai yajñaḥ,***"[37] so there should be no violence in the sacrifice. The epic *Mahābhārata* also stressed for the prevention of *hiṁsā* in the sacrifical acts, so it aptly explains:

सर्वकर्मस्वहिंसा हि धर्मात्मा मनुरब्रवीत्।
कामकाराद् विहिंसन्ति बहिर्वेद्यां पशून् नराः॥[38]

The Dhrmātmā Manu has spoken highly of harmlessness in all acts. Indeed, men kill animals in sacrifices, actuated only by the desire of fruits. In fact (*vaidika*) *dharma* never permits or allows killing animals in the sacrifices. Hence, harmlessness (*ahiṁsā*) to all creatures is the highest of acts (duties), as it is well said in the *Mahābhārata*: "अहिंसा सर्वभूतेभ्यो धर्मेभ्यो ज्यायसी मता।"[39]—Abstention from injury (*hiṁsā*) is the true religion, which is perfect about its rewards. The religion of cruelty is not at all beneficial and auspicious.[40] The *Mahābhārata* condemns '*hiṁsā* and advises that the sacrifices should remain far from any type of injury or violence "तस्माद्धिंसा न यज्ञिया"[41]. This way, the *Mahābhārata* praises *ahiṁsā*[42] and disallows as well as discards violence (*hiṁsā*) in the sacrifices and other rituals.

Varṇas* and *Yajñas:

The Hindu society consisted of four castes or classes, known as *varṇa,* down from the Vedic times (*Ṛgveda*, X.90). The four *varṇas* are: *brāhmaṇa, kṣatriya, vaiśya* and *śūdra*. In the *Mahābhārata,* Vidura advises Dhṛtarāṣṭra that regular bathing, performance of *yajña,* study of the Vedas, speaking the truth and working to serve one's teacher ensure that a *brāhmaṇa* never falls from the domain of *brāhmaṇa*.[43] Having studied the Vedas, kindled sacred fires and worshipped them with *yajñas*, protected his subjects and made himself pure by taking up arms on behalf of cows and Brahmins, a *kṣatriya* who falls in battle goes to heaven.[44] Having studies the Vedas, divided his wealth between the *brāhmaṇas*, *kṣatriyas,* and his dependents at proper times, and having smelled the aroma of the smoke of three kinds of sacred fire, a *vaiśya* enjoys the delights of *svarga-loka*.[45] Venerating the three higher *varṇas* as is proper for each, a *śūdra* has his sins destroyed by their satisfaction and after giving up his body goes to heaven.[46]

A *brāhmaṇa* fulfils his duty by self-control, recitation of Vedas, giving charity and performing *yajñas*. So a Brahmin has every right to perform any *yajña* for the welfare of the society.[47] A *kṣatriya* should give but never receive charity and execute *yajñas* though not as the priest: "यजेत न च याजयेत्।".[48]He should learn and read the Vedas but not teach them to others. Learned rulers who have performed *yajñas* and conquered in battle are the best of those who reach heaven.[49] A *vaiśya* should pay gifts, study the Vedas, celebrate *yajñas* and acquire wealth by honest means.[50] Prajāpati created the *śūdras* as the helper of the other *varṇas*. If a *śūdra* approaches anyone from the higher *varṇas* and offers his service, he should be engaged; *piṇḍa* should be offered on his behalf by his employer and he should be maintained when he grows old, frail or sonless. So, a *śūdra* has proper right to offer *śrāddha* or *piṇḍadāna* for his old or sonless owner.[51] The epic says that a *śūdra* has right to perform *yajña,* like other three *varṇas*, but he is not competent to utter *svāhā* and *svadhā* or any other Vedic *mantra.* It is rightly mentioned in the text as:

उक्तस्त्रयाणां वर्णानां यज्ञस्तस्य च भारत।
स्वाहाकारवषट्कारौ मन्त्रः शूद्रे न विद्यते॥[52]

Therefore, *śūdra,* without observing the *vratas* laid down in the Vedas, should adore the gods in minor sacrifices, called *pākayajñas*: "तस्माच्छूद्रः पाकयज्ञैर्यजेताव्रतवान् स्वयम्।"[53]. It is now clear that every *varṇa* (caste) has right to perform *yajñas*[54] with certain rules, prescribed for the particular caste. Besides, the sacrifice of devotion (*śraddhā-yajña*) is also laid down for all *varṇas.*[55] The *Mahābhārata* also specified to perform *yajñas* for different *varṇas* as:

आलम्भयज्ञाः क्षत्राश्च हविर्यज्ञा विशः स्मृताः।
परिचारयज्ञाः शूद्रीश्च जपयज्ञा द्विजातयः॥[56]

The above verse denotes that the sacrifice ordained for *brāhmaṇas* consists in recitation of *mantras,* that for *kṣatriyas* consists in the destruction of animals for the satisfaction of gods, that for *vaiśya* consists in the rearing of crops, etc. and that for *śūdras* mental and physcial service of the three other *varṇas*. This way, in the epic age all the four *varṇas* were performing *yajñas* and other rituals.

In the epic age people/kings used to perform various types of *yajñas* and *iṣṭis.* So, in the *Mahābhārata,* several (Vedic) *yajñas* and *iṣṭis* are mentioned, viz. *pañca-mahā-yajña, Aśvamedha, Rājasūya, Vājapeya, Sarpayajña, Agnihotra & Darśa-paurṇamāsa,* etc.

Pañca-mahā-yajña (Five Great Sacrifices):

Like the *Śatapatha Brāhmaṇa* (XI.5.7), the *Mahābhārata* also advised to perform five great sacrifices, viz. *brahmayajña, devayajña, pitṛyajña, bhūtayajña* and *nṛ* or *manuṣya-yajña*. These great *yajñas* are to be performed every day by all householders for prosperity, mental peace and other religious merits. Hence, great epic states:

पञ्चै पूजयँल्लोके यशः प्राप्नोति केवलम्।
देवान् पितॄन् मनुष्यांश्च भिक्षूनतिथिपञ्चमान्॥[57]

स्वाध्यायेन महर्षिभ्यो देवेभ्यो यज्ञकर्मणा।
पितृभ्यः श्राद्धदानेन नृणामभ्यर्चनेन च॥[58]

By worshipping these five, viz. the gods, the ancestors, men, *sannyāsins* and guests, a man obtains fame in this world. In this verse the word *bhikṣu* or *bhikṣu-yajña* replaces or comes instead of *brahma* or *brahma-yajña. Bhikṣu* here means a *sannyāsī* or *ṛṣi*. The idea is the same either for performing *bhikṣuyajña* or *ṛṣiyajña. Brahmayajña* is a sacrifice to satisfy *Brahman,* i.e. the study and teaching of the Vedas. This is a *yajña* to satisfy Brahmadeva, the creator of Vedas or to please *ṛṣis* or *draṣṭās* of the

Vedas. The epic also refers to offer *havana* to the *devatās* and *tarpaṇa* to the ancestors, for relieving from their debts.

देवतानां पितृणां चाप्यनृणो ह्यनसूयकः।[59]
श्राद्धं पितृभ्यो न ददाति दैवतानि न चार्चति।
सुहृन्मित्रं न लभते तमाहुर्मूढचेतसम्।।[60]

The epic also stresses for *atithi-yajña*[61] (*ātithyaṁ hi prayatnataḥ*) and *bhūta yajña* (*pañcabhūtamayo yajñaḥ*).[62] Hospitality should be shown to even one's enemy when the latter comes to his house. One should, with deligence do the duties of hospitality towards a person who seeks shelter. Indeed, one is particularly bound to do so if he leads the life of a house-holder that consists of the five sacrifices. If one, while like a house-holder, fails to perform these five sacrifices, he loses, as laid down in the scriptures, both this and the next world. As it is said:

पञ्च यज्ञास्तु यो मोहान्न करोति गृहाश्रमे।
तस्य नायं न च परो लोको भवति धर्मतः।।[63]

Therefore, it is advised that a man must perform continuously these *pañca mahāyajñas* throughout his life for all round prosperity and spiritual merits.

Aśvamedha-*yajña*—This sacrifice is said to be based on the *Ṛgveda*, I.162 and the *Yajurveda*, chapters 22-25. The *Mahābhārata* records a number of kings who have performed this sacrifice to strengthen their kingdom. King Bharata has performed *Aśvamedha* sacrifice in Kurukshetra (*hayamedhena yajñena....*)[64]. Besides, king Sagara (Mbh XII.29.132), Pṛthu (Mbh XII.29.143), Rāma (Mbh XII.29.59) and Rājā Janamejaya (Mbh XII.152.38) have also celebrated this *yajña* with traditional fervour and spirit.

Vājapeya-*yajña*—This is an animal sacrifice offered to Prajāpati. It is to be performed in the rainy season. Besides, it is also noted that this *yajña* was performed for the attainment of victory and power not only by kings, but also by any well-to-do member of the three higher castes. According to the *Mahābhārata* several kings like Pratardana, Vasumanā, Śivi, Auśīnara and Aṣṭaka had performed the *Vājapeya* for gratifying Lord Viṣṇu.[65] In different contexts this sacrifice is described in the *Mahābhārata*. According to Śāntiparva, *Vājapeya* was also performed by king Yayāti (29.96).

Rājasūya-*yajña*—This *yajña* could be performed only by a *kṣatriya, (rājā rājasūyena yajeta).*[66] In the *Śatapatha Brāhmaṇa* (IX.3.4.8) it is said that 'by performing the *Rājasūya* one becomes a king *(rājan)* and by *Vājapeya* an emperor (*samrāṭ*).King Hariścandra and Yudhiṣṭhira have performed this sacrifice to gratify their ancestors. In the Sabhāparva it is said that king Yudhiṣṭhira was advised by Nārada to perform this *yajña*. Due to the merits of this *yajña* his forefathers, especially Pāṇḍu enjoyed *indraloka,* like Hariścandra and other kings. Hence, it is truly said:

ये चान्ये च महीपाला राजसूयं महाक्रतुम्।
यजन्ते ते सहेन्द्रेण मोदन्ते भरतर्षभ॥[67]

King Yudhiṣṭhira was called *'sarvajit'* (*sarvajit tena cocyate*)[68], when he celebrated this sacrifice with great success. So it was essential for a king ιo perform this *yajña* for obtaining all kinds of sacred merits.

Agnihotra-*yajña*—*Agnihotra* is generally offered twice in the morning and in the evening. For this, the daily *homa* is to be performed and maintained by a *brāhmaṇa,* throughout his life.

According to the *Mahābhārata,* those persons will not attain the *yamaloka,* who honour and perform *agnihotra* with its prescribed rules.[69] Further, this epic adds that through *agnihotra* sacrifice, the performer goes to the heaven.[70]

Sarpa-*yajña*—The *Mahābhārata* describes this *yajña* as the destruction of snakes in the *yajñavedi*. Due to the curse on Kadrū, mother of snakes, the snakes were destroyed in this sacrifice, performed by king Janamejaya of Pāṇḍava dynasty. Sage Āstika has praised this sacrifice and extended his blessings to the king for its fruitful completion. Vedavyāsa was one of the priests of this unique sacrifice.[71]

In addition to these *yajñas,* the *Mahābhārata* advises to perform *Darśapūrṇamāsa* and *Cātrumāsa* sacrifices.[72] This epic also records other sacrifices like *Sarvamedha*[73], *Agnyādhāna, Somayāga*[74] and various *sattras*. Subjects related to *yajña* like (*vedi* and) *kuṇḍa*[75], *puroḍāśa*[76], *yūpa*[77], *paśu*[78], *haviṣ*[79] etc. have also been discussed in this great epic. In a true sense, the Vedic *yajña* and their applications have nicely reflected the society of this epic age.

Kings and *Yajñas:*

In the Śāntiparva, king Yudhiṣṭhira has requested Bhīṣma to advise him regarding the conduct of a king by which the king succeeds in advancing his subjects and earning regions of happiness in the other world. In reply Pitāmaha Bhīṣma said: "the king should be more liberal and perform sacrifices and he should observe vows and penances. Moreover, the king should be efficiently devoted to the duty of protecting his subjects":

दानशीलो भवेद् राजा यज्ञशीलश्च भारत।[80]

King Yudhiṣṭhira was also advised to perform various sacrifices for remaining free from tensions and sorrows, like Indra (Mbh XII.22.13). Because, sacrifice, gift, mercy, the Vedas, truth and penance—these are highly purifier things for kings. As rightly said:

यज्ञो दानं दया वेदाः सत्यं च पृथिवीपते।
पञ्चैतानि पवित्राणि षष्ठं सुचरितं तपः॥[81]

By following these above six things, a king will definitely acquire great merit and blessedness. He is even advised to perform *Rājasūya; Aśvamedha, Devayajña, Pitṛ-*

yajña, Ṛṣi-yajña and other *yajñas* for attaining great success, wealth and fame in life. Hence, it is truly mentioned in the text as:

विजितात्मा मनुष्येन्द्र यज्ञदानपरो भव॥[82]
पालयित्वा प्रजाः सर्वाः धर्मेण वदतां वर।
राजसूयाश्वमेधादीन् मखानन्यांस्तथैव च॥[83]
अर्चयित्वा पितॄन् सम्यक् पितृयज्ञैर्यथाविधि।
देवान् यज्ञैर्ऋषीन् वेदैरर्चयित्वा तु यत्नतः॥[84]

The sacrifice (*yajña*) is really a pious deed In the performance of *yajña* the money should not be collected from the subjects under the circumstances of fear and cruelty. This is not at all praiseworthy by the saints (Mbh XIII.61.21-22). On the other hand, the king should perform sacrifice with such money as is willingly paid to his treasury by prosperous subjects. Sacrifices should never be performed with money earned with severity and exhortation. So it is said in the Anuśāsana Parva of the great epic as:

अपीडिताः सुसंवृद्धा ये ददत्यनुकूलतः।
तादृशेनाप्युपायेन यष्टव्यं नोद्यमाहृतैः॥[85]

It is advised that the king should then perform great sacrifices with large gifts in the form of *dakṣiṇā*, when on account of his being devoted to the benefit of his subjects, the latter bathe him with copious showers of riches brought willingly by them for the purpose. So it is rightly advised in the *Mahābhārata* as:

यदा परिनिषिच्येत निहितो वै यथाविधि।
तदा राजा महायज्ञैर्यजेत बहुदक्षिणैः॥[86]

The kings were highly influenced by the advice of great *ṛṣis, ṛtviks, purohitas,* sages and other elderly religious personalities. As it is told in the epic that by suppressing Vedic priests (*ṛtviks*), and the *ācāryas* the kings are blamed in the society (..... *ṛtvikpurohitācāryān*...Mbh XII.132.9). Apart from this, three kinds of fire, the three Vedas and *yajñas* with *dakṣiṇās* (fees), all disappear when the king becomes careless:

अग्नित्रेता त्रयी विद्या यज्ञाश्च सहदक्षिणाः।
सर्व एव प्रमाद्यन्ति यदा राजा प्रमाद्यति॥[87]

However, the role of the kings was very important and equally impressive in the performance of *yajñas* and *iṣṭis* in the epic age. The *Mahābhārata* records the names of different kings and various *yajñas* in several occasions. The names of some important kings, who have performed different *yajñas* in their kingdom, are: Janaka, Hariścandra, Sagar, Śivi, Yajāti, Rāma, Pṛthu, Janamejaya, Bharata, Pāṇḍu, Yudhiṣṭhira and others.

The *yajña*, which is the centre of the Vedic system (life) may be thus understood as the law of being and the only foundation of the human religion. It takes the individual through a course of self-realization in progressive stages by which he becomes more and more universal and his outlook and interests remain perfect until he is emancipated and merged in the Absolute. It is *yajña* which leads to *dharma* and it is *dharma* which leads to *Brahman*. Hence, the performance of Vedic *yajña* purifies the deeds of the human beings and finally, it leads the sacrificer (*yajamāna*) towards the Supreme Bliss. However, one should perform *yajña* according to his ability and desire with highest devotion and perfection. Thus, by praising *yajña* the *Mahābhārata* expressively says:

न हि यज्ञसमं किञ्चित् त्रिषु लोकेषु विद्यते।
तस्माद् यष्टव्यमित्याहुः पुरुषेणानसूयता॥[88]

NOTES & REFERENCES

1. *Nighaṇṭu*, III.17.
2. *Amarakośa*, II.7.13. It is very interesting to note that the term *kratu* is not mentioned in the *Nighaṇṭu*. Perhaps it is a later development. In the *Mahābhārata* the word *kratu* is also used in the sense of *yajña (rājasūyaṁ kratuśreṣṭham...Mahābhārata,* Sabhāparva, 12.25; *iṣṭiśca... kratūmścaivāptadakṣiṇām*–Mbh XII.251.4, etc.). The Soma juice forms the oblation in the *kratus*. The *kratus* are further sub-divided into those called *ahīna*, which are Soma *yāgas* lasting from one to eleven days, and *sattra* which continued from twelve days to a hundred or a thousand years, the *dvādaśāha* being regarded as both an *ahīna* and a *sattra*. *Kratus* governed by fix time duration as *ekāha, daśāha,* etc. *Agniṣṭoma*, *Vājapeya* and *Rājasūya* are *kartus* not *satras*.
3. *Mahābhārata,* (Śāntiparva), XII.12.20.
4. *ibid.,* XII.12.21.
5. इत्यर्थं निर्मिता वेदा यज्ञाश्चौषधिभिः सह॥
   एभिः सम्यक् प्रयुक्तैर्हि प्रीयन्ते देवताः क्षितौ। –*ibid.,* XII.340.66-67ab.
6. *ibid.,* Bhīṣmaparva, 27.11-12 (cf. *Gītā,* III.10).
7. *ibid.,* Bhīṣmaparva, 27.10 (cf. *Gītā*, III.11-12 ab).
8. The five places referred to are the fire-place, the water-pot, the cutting, grinding and sweeping apparatus. These are the five places where injury to life is daily committed The sins committed here are said to be washed away by the five *mahāyajñas,* which every *brāhmaṇa* ought to perform, are intended to satisfy the *bhūtas,* the *ṛṣis,* men, the gods, and the *pitṛs* (cf. *Manusmṛti,* II.67-73).
9. *Ṛgveda,* X.63.12; VIII.70.11.
10. *ibid*; X.90.16, cf. *Ṛgveda*, I.164.50.
11. *Aitareya Brāhmaṇa*, I.16.
12. *Ṛgveda,* I.12.6; cf. *Sāmaveda,* 844 (II.194); *Taittirīya Saṁhitā*, I.4.46; and *Taittirīya Brāhmaṇa,* II.7.12.3.
13. *Mahābhārata*, Bhīṣma-parva, 28.24 (*Gītā*, IV.24).

14. Agrawala, V.S., *The Thousand Syllabled Speech,* Vol. I, 1963, pp. 126-27.
15. ऋचामेकः पोषमास्त पुपुष्वान्। होता। *Nirukta*, I.8.
16. *Ṛgveda,* X.71.11.
17. *Mahābhārata,* XII. 79.2.
18. ऋत्विक् पुरोहिताचार्यान्...न घातयीत...। *ibid.*, XII.132.9.
19. ऋत्विक्पुरोहिताचार्या मृदुब्रह्मधरा हि ते। *ibid.*, XIII.59.24.
20. *ibid.*, XII.342.12; cf. XII.342.10.
21. *ibid.*, XII.98.15.
22. *ibid.*, XII.340.35-36; Bhīṣmaparva, 27.10, etc.
23. *ibid.*, Vanaparva, 150.28.
24. सर्वेषामेव भूतानां पुरुषः श्रेष्ठ उच्यते।
    पुरुषेभ्यो द्विजानाहुर्द्विजेभ्यो मन्त्रदर्शिनः।। *ibid.*, XII.214.2.
25. *ibid.*, XII. 265.11.
26. *ibid.*, XII. 265.9.
27. *ibid.*, V.45.16.
28. *ibid.*, Bhīṣmaparva, 28.28; cf. *Gītā*, IV.28.
29. स्वाध्याययज्ञा ऋषयो ज्ञानयज्ञास्तथापरे।
    अथापरे महायज्ञान् मनस्येव वितन्वते।। Mbh XII.12.24.
30. *ibid.*, Uddyogaparva, 58.12-13.
31. *ibid.*, XII. 268.21; cf. XII.340.35-36.
32. *ibid.*, XII. 268.25-26.
33. *ibid.*, XII. 268.27ab.
34. *ibid.*, XII. 268.30ab.
35. *ibid.*, XII. 79.11.
36. स त्वं यज्ञैर्महाराज यजस्व बहुदक्षिणैः। *ibid.*, XII.22.13;
    Cf.XII.20.5; XII.51.8; XII.61.24.XII.25.1.4, etc.
37. *Śatapatha Brāhmaṇa,* III.9.2.1.
38. *Mahābhārata,* XII. 265.5.
39. *ibid.*, XII.265.6.
40. अहिंसा सकलो धर्मो हिंसाधर्मस्तथाहितः। *ibid.*, XII.272.20ab.
41. *ibid.*, XII.272.18; cf. XII 12.272.17, 19, 5.
42. *ibid.*, XII.245.20; 215.6; 265.4-6; 109.12, etc.
43. *ibid.*, Uddyogaparva, 40.25.
44. *ibid.*, 40.26.
45. *ibid.*, 40.27.
46. *ibid.*, 40.28.
47. *ibid.*, XII.60.10-12.
48. *ibid.*, XII.60.13.
49. *ibid.*, XII.60.14.
50. वैश्यस्यापि............दानमध्ययनं यज्ञः शौचेन धनसंचयः। *ibid.*, XII.60.21.

51. देय: पिण्डोऽनपत्याय भर्तव्यौ वृद्धदुर्बलौ।। *ibid.*, XII.60.35.
52. *ibid.*, XII.60.37.
53. *ibid.*, XII.60.38.
54. *ibid.*, XII.60.44.
55. ततः सर्वेषु वर्णेषु श्रद्धायज्ञो विधीयते। *ibid.*, XII.60.45.
56. *ibid.*, XII.238.12.
57. *ibid.*, Uddyogaparva, 33.75.
58. *ibid.*, XII.292.10.
59. *ibid.*, XII.326.15.
60. *ibid.*, XIII.33.35; cf. XIII.60.17-18.
61. *ibid.*, XII.146.5-6; cf. XII.235.25.
62. *ibid.*, X.18.5.
63. *ibid.*, XII.146.7.
64. *ibid.*, Vanaparva, 129.15.
65. वाजपेयेन यज्ञेन तर्पयन्ति सुरेश्वरम्।। *ibid.*, Uddyogaparva, 121.11cd.
66. *Lāṭyāyana Śrauta Sūtra,* IX.1.1.
67. *Mahābhārata*, II.12.20; cf. II.12.25-26.
68. *ibid.*, II.13.24.
69. *ibid.*, Vanaparva, 62.76.
70. *ibid.*, Uddyogaparva, 40.26. (cf. *Viduranīti*, VIII.26); cf. XIII.58.32.
71. *ibid.*, 1.55.8-9; cf. I.54.7, etc.
72. *ibid.*, XII.269.20; cf. XII.29.114.
73. *ibid.*, XII.24.7; cf. XII.12.27.
74. *ibid.*, 268.38.
75. *ibid.*, XII.40.12; 339.9; 343.60 (for *vedi*); Mbh XII.320.180 181 (for *kuṇḍa*).
76. *purodāśo hi sarveṣāṁ paśūnāṁ medhya ucyate, ibid.*, XII.263.42 ab.
77. *ibid.*, XII.29.74; 265.8; 130.46; 98.25.
78. *ibid.*, XII.269.18; 12.21; 268.20; 268.24.
79. *ibid.*, XII.98.15; 268.25.
80. *ibid.*, XII.75.2.
81. *ibid.*, XII.152.7.
82. *ibid.*, XII.22.10.
83. *ibid.*, XII.63.17.
84. *ibid.*, XII.63.20.
85. *ibid.*, XIII.61.23.
86. *ibid.*, XIII.61.24.
87. *ibid.*, XII.91.8.
88. *ibid.*, XII.60.54.

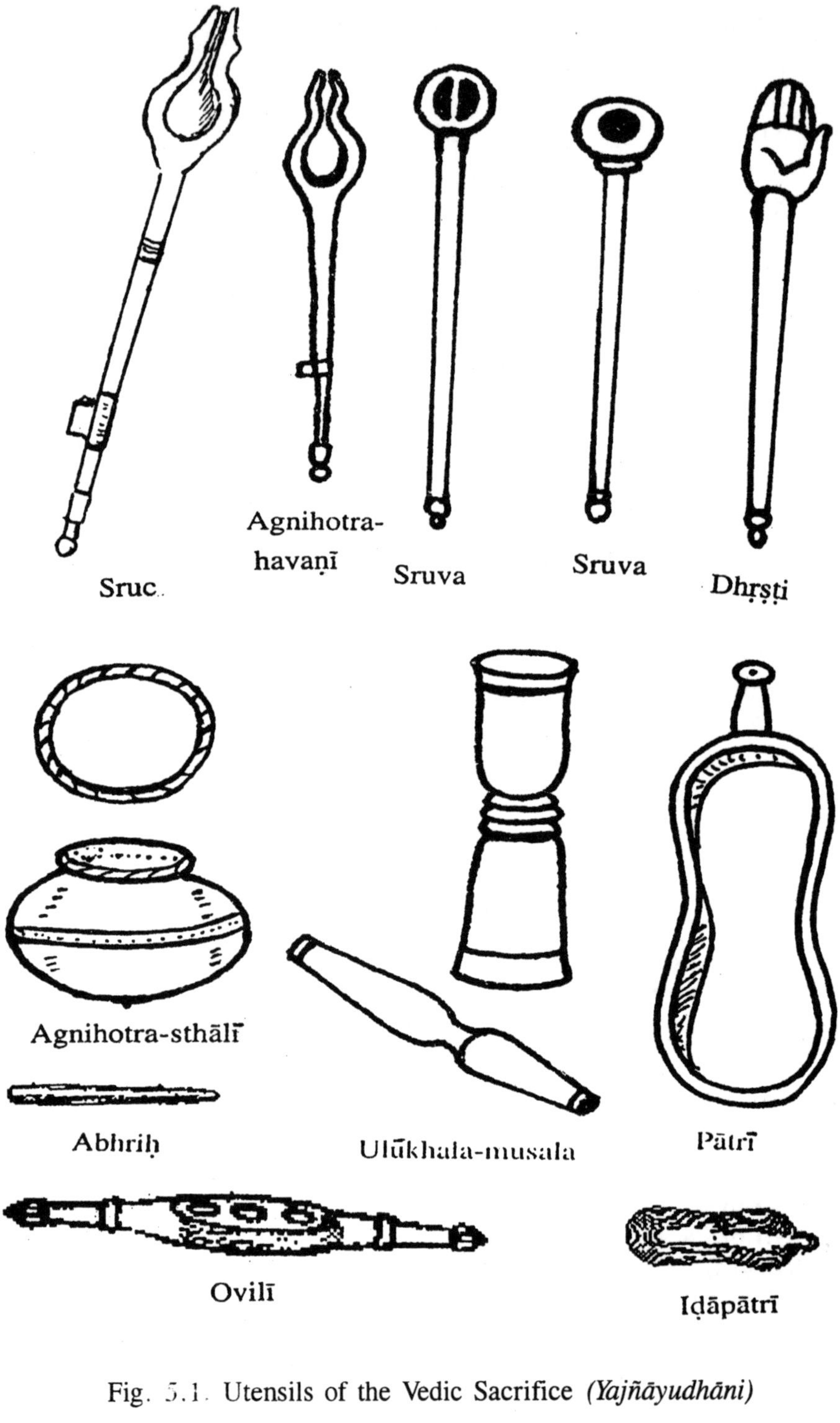

Fig. 5.1. Utensils of the Vedic Sacrifice *(Yajñāyudhāni)*

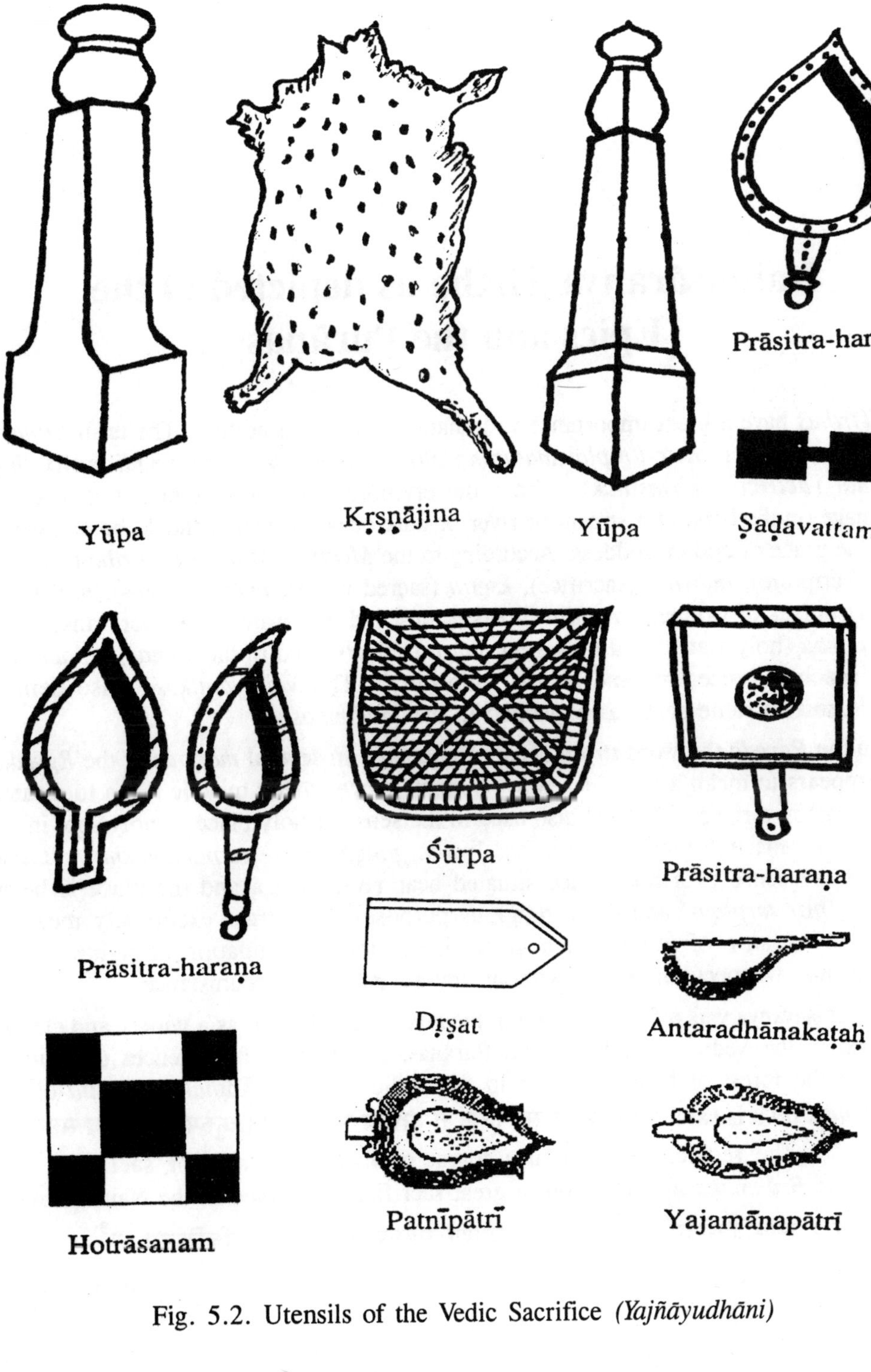

Fig. 5.2. Utensils of the Vedic Sacrifice *(Yajñāyudhāni)*

Naimiṣāraṇya Tīrtha as depicted in the Epics and the Purāṇas

Tīrthas have a great importance in Indian culture and tradition. The term *tīrtha* is derived from the root *tṛ-(tṛ plavanataraṇayoḥ)* 'to cross' with the *uṇādi* suffix *thak* (*pātṛtudi vaciricisicibhyasthak*).[1] From the etymological sense it means a place of pilgrimage on the bank of a stream or river or tank or pond, which should be crossed to attain the grace of god or goddess. According to the *Medinīkośa* the term *tīrtha* means 'a *śāstra* (scripture), *adhvara* (sacrifice), *kṣetra* (sacred place), *upāya* (means), *nārī-rajaḥ* (timely courses of women), *avatāra* (stairs to descend into water of a river, tank, etc.), *ṛṣi-juṣṭāmbu* (holy water used by sages), *pātra* (objects used in the *yajñas*), *upādhyāya* (*guru,* teacher, preceptor) and *mantrī* (minister)'.[2] The *Vaijayantīkośa*[3] also defines *tīrtha* almost in same sense as explained in the *Medinīkośa*.

In the *Ṛgveda* the word *tīrtha* occurs frequently. In several *mantras* of the *Ṛgveda*, *tīrtha* appears to mean a road or a way.[4] In some places *tīrtha* may be taken to mean a ford (*ghāṭa*) in a river.[5] *Tīrtha* is also used in the sense of holy place or holy spot in the *Ṛgveda*.[6] Sāyaṇa interprets the term as: '*yathā gaṅgāditīrthe tarpaṇamukhe*'.[7] It also indicates the sense of a holy place situated near river Gaṅgā and the place is being used for '*pitṛ tarpaṇa*' and other religious purposes. So, *tīrtha* exclusively means a locality or expanse of water which gives rise to the accumulation of righteousness owing to its own peculiar nature without any adventitious circumstance.

Naimiṣāraṇya was a famous *tīrtha* in the post-Vedic period, as a widely and clearly described in the Vedic texts, Epics and Purāṇas. A number of references to Naimiṣāraṇya or the forest of Naimiṣa occur in the Vedic texts. In *Kāṭhaka Saṁhitā* of the *Śukla Yajurveda* it is said: **"नैमिष्या वै सत्रमासत त उत्थाय सप्तविंशति कुरुपञ्चालेषु वत्सतरान्वत तान्वको..."** —the residents of Naimiṣa forest performed a *satra* or sacrifice. The *Śāṅkhāyana Brāhmaṇa* also mentions a great sacrifice performed in the Naimiṣāraṇya:

"अथ ह स्माह दैवोदासिः प्रतर्दनो नैमिषीयाणां सत्रमुपगम्योपासद्य विचिकित्सां..."[9]

Besides, the *Jaiminīya Brāhmaṇa* states that a *satra* (sacrifice) was performed in Naimiṣa forest by the sages:

"अथा ह वै नैमिशीया इति सत्रिणस् सोमशुष्मगृहपतयस् सत्रं निषेदुः।"[10]

The people of this forest called Nimiśīya or Naimiṣya which is also mentioned in the *Tāṇḍya Mahā Bhāhmaṇa* of the *Sāmaveda* as:

एतेन वै नैमिशीयाः सर्व्वामृद्धिमाध्र्नवन् सर्व्वामृद्धिमृन्धुवन्ति य एतदुपयन्ति (नैमिशीया नैमिशाख्यवासिनः)।[11]

From these Vedic passages it is clear that Naimiṣāraṇya was a sacred place or *tīrtha* where seers were performing different Vedic sacrifices as a part of their religious duties.

The importance of this holy *tīrtha* is also known from the description of the *Rāmāyaṇa*. The Aśvamedha sacrifice was performed by Śrī Rāma in the Naimiṣāraṇya to show his prowess and sovereignty. He met with the Brahmins and discussed with them regarding the preparation of this sacrifice. However, he was extremely pleased after being known the sacred knowledge of the Brahmins,[12] residing in the forest. Then he ordered his administrative people[13] to prepare the vast sacrificial place at Naimiṣa forest, situated near Gomatī river.

यज्ञवाटश्च सुमहान् गोमत्या नैमिषे वने।[14]

It is also noted that the great king of Ayodhyā Lord Rāma was staying in this *tīrtha* with his brother Lakṣmaṇa.[15] He asked Lakṣmaṇa to invite Sugrīva and other princes for the sacrifice and to put up a large number of tents in the Naimiṣa forest on the bank of the river Gomatī for their grand reception. At this invitation the sage Vālmīki also came to the Naimiṣāraṇya to attend the sacrifice, accompanied by his disciples including Lava and Kuśa. A few huts were put up in a part of the forest for their residence.[16] During Rāma's stay in the Naimiṣāraṇya, all other kings brought presentations for him and he also returned their hospitality by honouring them in true spirit.

नैमिषे वसतस्तस्य सर्व एव नराधिपाः।
आनिन्युरुपहारांश्च तान् रामः प्रत्यपूजयत्॥[17]

It is clear from the above verse that the Ayodhyā-*pati* Rāma, being an incarnation of Lord Nārāyaṇa, was successively performing *yajñas* in the Naimiṣa *tīrtha* and even reciprocating due honour to the sages, Brahmins and kings for their active participation in the Aśvamedha sacrifice.

The importance of Naimiṣa *tīrtha* was also glorified in the *Mahābhārata*. It describes and even clarifies the reasons why one should visit and stay in this holy place. The epic further elaborates that Naimiṣa *tīrtha* is frequented by the *siddhas*, where Brahmā with the celestials always dwells. The sages perform their daily religious duties as well as great traditional Vedic sacrifices in this forest and the gods are coming and residing there for receiving their *yajña-bhāgas* from the *yajamānas* or sacrificers. The following verse clarifies it as:

ततस्तु नैमिष्यं गच्छेत् पुण्यं सिद्धनिषेवितम्।
तत्र नित्यं निवसति ब्रह्मा देवगणैः सह॥[18]

The Naimiṣa *tīrtha* is even able to destroy the sins (*pāpas*) of the human beings. Only by wishing to go to Naimiṣa, half of one's sins is destroyed As soon as a man enters it, he is cleansed of all his sins. As it is rightly said in the *Mahābhārata*:

नैमिषं मृगयानस्य पापस्यार्धं प्रणश्यति।
प्रविष्टमात्रस्तु नरः सर्वपापैः प्रमुच्यते॥[19]

The Naimiṣa (*tīrtha*) is identified as one of the best *tīrthas* of India. As it is mentioned that all the *tīrthas* rest in Naimiṣa, so one should stay here at least for a month.[20] Besides, by performing regular holy bath and preferring good *sāttvika* diet in Naimiṣāraṇya, one would obtain the fruits of many sacrifices.[21] According to the *Mahābhārata* this forest *tīrtha* is an auspicious place for the *sādhakas,* sages and religious minded persons or devotees. Anybody who gives up his life in Naimiṣa by fasting, he definitely sanctifies his race (*kula*) for seven generations upwards and downwards. Hence, the great epic *Mahābhārata* specifically adds:

पुनात्यासप्तमं चैव कुलं भरतसत्तम।
यस्त्यजेन्नैमिषे प्राणानुपवासपरायणः॥[22]

The Naimiṣa *tīrtha* is really a sacred and holy region or a religious place of pilgrimage. The wise men have advised that "a person who remains in this *tīrtha*, feels that as if he is in the heaven."[23]

The Purāṇas too have elaborately discussed the real significance of Naimiṣa *tīrtha.* The name of the forest is said to have been derived from the fact that the *nemi* (circumference) of the *dharmacakra* was shattered there. According to the description of the *Varāha Purāṇa*, the entire army of the demon king Durjaya was destroyed completely and reduced to ashes by the discus (*cakra*) of Lord Hari. Having performed it, the Supreme Lord said to the sage Gauramukha : "I have killed the army of the demon in a twinkle of the eye (*nimeṣa*). Hence, this forest would be named as 'Naimiṣ a' and would be the abode of Brahmins."

उवाच निमिषेणेदं निहितं दानवं बलम्।
अरण्येऽस्मिंस्मस्ततस्त्वेवं नैमिषारण्यसंज्ञितम्।
भविष्यति यथार्थं वै ब्राह्मणानां विशेषतः॥[24]

The *Varāha Purāṇa* also prescribed for performing *śrāddha-karmas* for the *pitaras* in this sacred *tīrtha.* All the evils are warded off if some one devotedly worships the Manes after taking a holy bath in the Gomatī river in Naimiṣāraṇya.[25] Definitely, the *pitaras* get satisfied by receiving *śrāddha-annas* and *tarpaṇas* from their relatives in this *tīrtha.* Besides, the Purāṇa adds that by taking a bath in the Naimiṣa *tīrtha* on the thirteenth day (*trayodaśī tithi*) a man would shake of all his sins.[26]

According to *Śiva Mahā Purāṇa*, Lord Brahmā has advised to Brahmins the means of salvation. He said : "I will release this mentally created wheel. The place where its rim (*remi*) gets shattered will be auspicious for your *sādhanā* or meditation." The Purāṇa nicely describes the words of Brahmā as:

एतन्मनोमयं चक्रं मया सृष्टं विसृज्यते।
यत्रास्य शीर्यते नेमिः स देशस्तपसः शुभः।।[27]

Hence, after advising this to the devoted Brahmins Lord Brahmā created a mental wheel as bright as sun. Then, after properly bowing Lord Śiva he released the wheel. Those delighted pious Brahmin devotees bowed to the Lord and pursued the wheel to the place where its rim got shattered The sacred wheel thus hurled fell on a smooth charming rock in a certain forest where the water was sweet and clear. That forest became famous as Naimiṣa *tīrtha*. It is a *pavitra bhūmi* and known as a place of *tapas* and *sādhanā*. The *devas, yakṣas, gandharvas, vidyādharas,* sages and even pious human beings will reside here for their religious duties and ceremonies. Hence, this forest of Naimiṣa will be renowned as a *puṇya kṣetra* (sacred worship place) for the liberated souls and *mumukṣu* beings.

तद्वनं तेन विख्यातं नैमिष्यं मुनिपूजितम्।
अनेकयक्षगन्धर्वविद्याधरसमाकुलम्।।[28]

The *Devī Bhāgavata Purāṇa* also goes with the *Śiva Purāṇa* by adding that the Naimiṣa *tīrtha* is a famous and holy place, as the *cakra* or *nemi* of Brahmā has stopped there for the seekers of truth. As said:

नेमि संशीर्यते यत्र स देशः पावनः स्मृतः।[29]

The speciality of this Naimiṣa *tīrtha* is that the impact of Kali would not be seen here. It means Kali (*yuga*) will not be able to enter into the *tīrtha* due to its religious sanctity and all the residents of Naimiṣāraṇya will remain there until the *satyayuga* comes back. The text clarifies this as:

कलेस्तत्र प्रवेशो न कदाचित्संभविष्यति।
तावत्तिष्ठन्तु तत्रैव यावत्सत्ययुगं पुनः।।[30]

Hence, Naimiṣa *tīrtha* will never come under the worse impact of Kali. This is really the main speciality of this *tīrtha*, as blessed by the Highest Lord.

According to the *Kūrma Purāṇa*, Naimiṣa *tīrtha* is well known in the universe. Being more liked by Lord Mahādeva than any other *tīrthas*, it is remission of great sins. As aptly said in the text:

इदं त्रैलोक्यविख्यातं तीर्थं नैमिषमुत्तमम्।
महादेवप्रियतरं महापातकनाशनम्।।[31]

So, due to the Grace of Lord Śiva Naimiṣāraṇya is known as a *puṇya-sthāna* (or *puṇya kṣetra*). It is created by the Highest Deity, Lord Brahmā for the performance of *sādhanā* (penance) by the *ṛṣis* (sages), desirous of seeing Mahādeva.[32] Once the six outstanding Brahmin families, viz. the Maricis, the Atris, the Vasiṣṭhas, the Kratus, the Bhṛgus and the Aṅgirasa, formely approached the Brahmā, how to see the Lord Īśāna (*Īśānam... kenopāyena paśyāmo brūhi deva*).[33] In the reply, the Creator Brahmā advised them to perform a *sastra* (sacrifice) of the duration of one thousand years, free from all the defects. Regarding the place of the sacrifice He said I will tell you the place where you will perform the same. Then He touched the mind-wheel and desired it to leave. Thereafter, the Lord told the sages : "this wheel has been discharged by me. You follow it without any delay."[34] Where the rim of this wheel gets shattered will be the auspicious place for the purpose of *tapas* and sacrifices (*yatrāsya nemiḥ śīryeta sa deśastapasaḥ śubhaḥ*).[35] As it rolled on, its rim got shattered at a place which came to be remembered by the name Naimiṣa. It is very holy and is honoured everywhere by all the sages and devotees of god. In the words of *Kūrma Purāṇa*:

तस्य वै व्रजतः क्षिप्रं यत्र नेमिरशीर्यत।
नैमिषं तत् स्मृतं नाम्ना पुण्यं सर्वत्र पूजितम्।।

सिद्धचारणसंपूर्णं यक्षगन्धर्वसेवितम्।
स्थानं भगवतः शंभोरेतन्नैमिषमुत्तमम्।।[36]

So, undoubtedly, Naimiṣāraṇya is a sacred place and a famous *tīrtha*, where anyone can perform sacrifice and even continue *tapas* for seeking liberation. As described, it is a place full of *siddhas, cāraṇas* and other *dharmātmās*. It is resorted to by *yakṣas* and *gandharvas*. This excellent holy place Naimiṣa is the pleasant abode of Lord Śambhu or Śiva. Formerly, *devas,* along with *gandharvas, yakṣas,* serpents and the demons performed their penance (*tapas*) here and finally attained excellent boons.[37] Resorting to this holy *tīrtha,* the six old Brahmin families, viz. Maricis, Atris, etc. propitiated the Lord Mahādeva with great concentration, by means of sacrifices and finally perceived Maheśvara. Therefore, it is clear now that every religious ceremonies being performed here must provide some positive result or intended things to its performers, in time. As it is mentioned that each of the following holy rites performed here shall destroy the sins committed in the course of seven births.

अन्नदानं तपस्तप्तं श्राद्धयामादिकञ्च यत्।
एकैकं नाशयेत्पापं सप्तजन्मकृतं तथा।।[38]

Therefore, it is advised that one should offer *dāna* to the poor beings and perform *śrāddha* for the satisfaction of Manes (*pitaras*). Besides, he should properly perform austerities (*tapas*) and *sādhanās,* along with regular rites and other sacrifices for the destruction of *pāpas* and for attaining the final goal of life. The foremost significance of this holy *tīrtha* is, even till today, Lord Maheśvara of universal vision sports about along with His spouse Rudrāṇī (Pārvatī), while the Pramathas surround Him as attendants. As said:

अत्र देवो महादेवो रुद्राण्यो किल विश्वदृक्।
रमतेऽद्यापि भगवान्प्रमथैः परिवारितः।।[39]

Another significance of this *tīrtha* as mentioned in the *Kūrma Purāṇa* is that "by giving up their lives here in this Naimiṣāraṇya, the *dvijas* etc. will go to the *brahmaloka,* after which they are not born again."

अत्र प्राणान् परित्यज्य नियमेन द्विजातयः।
ब्रह्मलोकं गमिष्यन्ति यत्र गत्वा न जायते।।[40]

Henceforth, the final intension of each human being is to get *mokṣa* or *nirvāṇa* or liberation. A sage, a *sādhaka* or a true devotee always seek to attain salvation through various religious performances. At the end, he obtains emancipation and never returns to this world in the form of a being. This has been properly said in the *Bhagavad Gītā*: "neither the sun nor the moon nor even the fire can illumine that Supreme Self-effulgent state, attaining to which they never return to this world. This is My Supreme Abode."

न तद्भासयते सूर्यो न शशाङ्को न पावकः।
यद् गत्वा न निवर्तन्ते तद्धाम परमं मम।।[41]

Hence, due to the good impact of great *tīrtha*, like Naimiṣāraṇya and performance of *puṇya karmas* the human being attains liberation.

However, in the conclusion it can be said that Naimiṣāraṇya is really a holy and famous *tīrtha* of the Brahmāvarta or Bhāratavarṣa. This has been nicely depicted in the Vedic texts, Epics, and Purāṇas. Both Lord Viṣṇu and Brahmā have created or introduced this holy *tīrtha* for the religious upliftment and final attainment of the highest goal or liberation of the people of different ages. This has also been the pleasant abode of Lord Śiva and Devī Pārvatī and a *yajña bhūmi* (place of sacrifice) of Bhagavān Rāma and other great seers. Hence, this *puṇya bhūmi* of Naimiṣāraṇya is really known as a king of all the sacred *tīrthas*, i.e. *tīrtharāja* of this great country since time immemorial.

REFERENCES

1. *Uṇādi Sūtra*, 164 (II.7)
2. तीर्थं शास्त्राध्वरक्षेत्रोपाय नारीरजःसु च।
   अवतारर्षिजुष्टाम्बुपात्रोपाध्यायमन्त्रिषु।। *Medinīkośa*, XVII.7.
3. तीर्थं मन्त्राद्युपाध्यायशास्त्रेष्वम्भसि पावने।।
   पात्रोपायावतारेषु स्त्रीपुष्पे योनियज्ञयोः। *Vaijayantīkośa*, VI.3.13cd-14ab.
4. तीर्थे नार्यः पौंस्यानि तस्थुः।। *Ṛgveda*, I.169.6
5. अरित्रं वां दिवस्पृथु तीर्थे सिन्धूनां रथः।। *Ṛgveda*, I.46.8

6. धीतिरससृग्रमंशास्तीर्थे न दस्ममुप यन्त्यूमाः।। *Ṛgveda*, X.31.3.
7. Sāyaṇa Bhāṣya on *Ṛgveda*, X.31.3.
8. *Kāṭhaka Saṁhitā*, X.6.
9. *Śāṅkhāyana Brāhmaṇa*, XXVI.5.
10. *Jaiminīya Brāhmaṇa*, I.363.
11. *Tāṇḍya Mahā Brāhmaṇa*, XXV.6.4; cf. *Kauṣītaki Brāhmaṇa*, XXVI.5.
12. स तेषां द्विजमुख्यानां वाक्यमद्भुतदर्शनम्।
    अश्वमेधाश्रितं श्रुत्वा भृशं प्रीतोऽभवत् तदा।। रामायण, उत्तरकाण्ड 91.8.
13. आज्ञाप्यतां महाबाहो तद्धि पुण्यमनुत्तमम्। *ibid.*, Uttarakāṇḍa 91.16ab.
14. *ibid.*, 91.15cd.
15. विज्ञाय कर्म तत् तेषां रामो लक्ष्मणमब्रवीत्। *ibid.*, Uttarakāṇḍa 91.9.
16. वर्त्तमाने तथाभूते यज्ञे च परमाद्भुते।
    सशिष्य आजगामाशु वाल्मीकिर्भगवानृषिः।।
    स दृष्ट्वा दिव्यसंकाशं यज्ञमद्भुतदर्शनम्।
    एकान्त ऋषिसंघातश्चकार उटजाञ्शुभान्।। रामायण, उत्तरकाण्ड 93.1-2.
17. *ibid.*, Uttarakāṇda 92.4.
18. *Mahābhārata,* Vanaparva 84.59.
19. *ibid.*, Vanaparva 84.60.
20. तत्र मासं वसेद् धीरो नैमिषे तीर्थतत्परः।
    पृथिव्यां यानि तीर्थानि तानि तीर्थानि नैमिषे।। *ibid.*, Vanaparva 84.61.
21. कृताभिषेकस्तत्रैष नियतो नियताशनः।
    गवां मेधस्य यज्ञस्य फलं प्राप्नोति भारत।। *ibid.*, Vanaparva 84.62.
22. *ibid.*, Vanaparva 84.63.
23. स मोदेत् सर्वलोकेषु एवमाहुर्मनीषिणः।
    नित्यं मेध्यं च पुण्यं च नैमिषं नृपसत्तम ।। *ibid.*, Vanaparva 84.64.
24. *Varāha Purāṇa*, XI.108-109.
25. गङ्गा सरयूमथवा विपाशां सरस्वतीं नैमिषगोमतीं वा।
    ततोऽवगाह्यार्चनमादरेण कृत्वा पितृणामहितानि हन्ति।। *ibid.*, XIII.48.
26. त्रयोदश्यां नैमिषे च प्रयागे च चतुर्दशीम्।....
    कालेष्वेषु नरः स्नात्वा सर्वपापं व्यपोहति।। *ibid.*, 174.56-57.
27. *Śiva Purāṇa*, Vāyavīya Saṁhitā, Ch. 3.53.
28. *ibid.*, 3.57.
29. *Devī Bhāgavata Purāṇa*, I.2.29.
30. *ibid.*, I.2.30.
31. *Kūrma Purāṇa*, Uttarārdha (2nd part), Ch. 43.1.
32. महादेवं दिदृक्षूणामृषीणां परमेष्ठिना।
    ब्रह्मणा निर्मितं स्थानं तपस्तप्तुं द्विजोत्तम।। *ibid.*, Ch. 43.2.
33. *ibid.*, Chapter 43.5.

34. मुक्त्वा मनोमयं चक्रं संस्पृष्ट्वा तानुवाच ह।
क्षिप्तमेतन्मया चक्रमनुव्रजत मा चिरम्।। *ibid.*, Ch. 43.7.
35. *ibid.*, Chapter 43.8.
36. *ibid.*, Chapter 43.9-10.
37. अत्र देवाः सगन्धर्वाः सयक्षोरगराक्षसाः।
तपस्तप्त्वा पुरा देवा लेभिरे प्रवरान्वरान्।। *ibid.*, Ch. 43.11.
38. *ibid.*, Ch. 43.13.
39. *ibid.*, Chapter 43.15.
40. *ibid.*, Chapter 43.16.
41. *Bhagavad Gītā*, Chapter XV.6.

Concept of *Avatāra* in the *Kūrma Purāṇa*

The incarnation of God on the earth is called *avatāra*. *Avatāra* (from the √*tṛ* - to cross over, to attain, to save, with the prefix *ava*-down; and so, *ava* + √*tṛ*- to descend in, to appear, to become incarnate) means 'descending' and the term is applied to the act of a Divine or Supernatural Being in assuming the form of a man or animal, and continuing to live in that form till the purpose for which that form was assumed or carried out. So *avatāra* is an appearance of any deity on earth, or descent from heaven, and it bears a great importance as a religious concept in the Indian tradition and culture.

Source of *Avatāras* (incarnations):

The term *avatāra* is relatively late, and an older word for the phenomenon is 'manifestation' (*āvirbhāva*[1] & *prādurbhāva*). The word *avatāra* does not occur in the classical Upaniṣads, though there are a few references in later Upaniṣads.[2] It is listed in Pāṇini's *Aṣṭādhyāyī*[3] (4th cent. B.C.) and occurs in many standard works after the Epic literature. But there are faint glimmerings of the theory of *avatāras* and of these forms even in the earliest Vedic literature.[4] In the *Ṛgveda*[5] it is said that Indra was the grandson of the sage Śṛṅgavṛṣa. This may be interpreted as meaning that Indra was supposed to have descended on the earth in a human form. Again, in the *Ṛgveda* the sage Vāmadeva explains 'I was Manu and I was also the Sun.'[6] This is referred to in the *Bṛhadāraṇyaka Upaniṣad*[7] and often relied upon in support of the doctrine of the transmigration of souls. It may be capable of that interpretation, but if that is not accepted it will at least tend to support the proposition that the Vedic sage thought that the Sun could be born on the earth as a human being. It clearly indicates that there was an *avatāra* of Sun. Besides, according to the *Śrīmad Bhāgavata*, the first incarnation of God is *Puruṣa*[8], as it is mentioned in the famous Puruṣasūkta of the *Ṛgveda*. Some scholars have definitely observed in the following Ṛgvedic verse (*mantra*), the germ of the doctrine of the *avatāra,* viz.

"पादोऽस्य विश्वा भूतानि त्रिपादस्यामृतं दिवि।"[9]

Prof. S.N. Dasgupta in his *History of Indian Philosophy,* says that here there is the starting-point of the theism of the *Bhagavad Gītā*, the idea of God as not only immanent but transcendent, a universe which is no illusion, and the doctrine of incarnation.[10] Certainly this hymn is important, and it is quoted in the theistic *Śvetāśvatara Upaniṣad* and in the *Gītā.*[11] Hence, *Bhāgavata* clearly states that this *Puruṣa* form (*rūpa*) is the original source of different *avatāras,* as well as the real base of creation of *devatās*, human beings, animals and other creatures.[12] However, the beginnings of the doctrine of *avatāra* and some of the well known *avatāras* of Viṣṇu may also be traced to the Vedic literature. In the Vedic idea of Lord Viṣṇu, as a solar divinity, coming down to the earth from the highest abode, and so in the frequent allusions in the Vedic literature, it is clear that gods assumed different forms in order to accomplish their several exploits. In the Vedic literature[13], we actually come across of the early indications of the *Matsya, Kūrma, Varāha, Vāmana* and other incarnations.

Necessity of *Avatāras:*

The theory of *avatāras* brings to mankind a new spiritual message and it presupposes the recognition of Viṣṇu as a Supreme God, the creator and ruler of the universe, the upholder not only of the cosmic, but, also of the moral order of the world. When the enemies endanger the order of the world, the Lord incarnates Himself for the purpose of defending it. It is a comforting belief for the ordinary man to hold that when the affairs of the world are in a mess, God comes down to the earth to set matters right[14], i.e. when the world is in serious trouble, people believe that deliverance will come by the grace of God and they are often justified in their belief by their appearance of godly men who appear with some noble mission and masterly idea suited to the particular time and place when they appear.

Another purpose of the Supreme God assuming the worldly form is to educate the mortals[15] (because the people, in general follow the footsteps of the great men). The Supreme Power appears in human form as the *guru,* the teacher, to lead them beyond the delusion of ignorance, to where there is no difference between the *guru* and the disciple.

In addition to these, the manifestation of the Lord is intended only for bestowing the boon of the final beatitude or liberation on the human beings. As it is said in the *Śrīmad Bhāgavata:*

नृणां निःश्रेयसार्थाय व्यक्तिर्भगवतो नृप।[16]

Number & Types of *Avatāras:*

In the *Mahābhārata,* the *Rāmāyaṇa* and the Purāṇas it is frequently stated that Lord Viṣṇu comes down to the earth often for punishing the wicked, for the protection of good and the establishment of *dharma*. *Śrīmad Bhāgavata*, the most popular Purāṇa, states that the *avatāras* of Viṣṇu are innumerable, like the rivulets flowing from an inexhaustible lake.[17] In the *Mahābhārata,* the *avatāras* are stated to be ten and they are the same as now generally accepted except that Haṁsa which is mentioned instead of Buddha and Kṛṣṇa is called Sātvata.[18] Among the Purāṇas also, several Purāṇas do not mention Buddha as an *avatāra*. The *Matsya Purāṇa* mentions the well-known ten *avatāras*[19] including Buddha as the 9th *avatāra*[20] of Viṣṇu. Besides, the *Agni Purāṇa*[21], the *Padma Purāṇa*[22] and the *Varāha Purāṇa*[23] enumerate the well-known ten *avatāras* of Viṣṇu. The names of the ten *avatāras* are thus: (1) *Matsya*-the fish, (2) Kūrma-the tortoise, (3) Varāha-the boar, (4) *Narasiṁha*-the man-lion, (5) Vāman-the dwarf, (6) Paraśurāma (7) Śrī Rāma, (8) Śrī Kṛṣṇa, (9) Buddha, and (10) Kalkī. The *Bhāgavata Purāṇa* makes the number of *avatāras* twenty-two[24] including the minor ones. These are: (1) Puruṣa, (2) Varāha (3) Nārada, (4) Nara &Nārāyaṇa, (5) Kapila, (6) Dattātreya, (7) Yajña, (8) Ṛṣabha, (9) Pṛthu, (10) Matsya, (11) Kūrma, (12) Dhanvantarī, (13) Mohinī, (14) Narasiṁha, (15) Vāmana, (16) Paraśurāma, (17) Vedavyāsa, (18) Rāmacandra, (19) Balarāma, (20) Śrī Kṛṣṇa, (21) Buddha, and (22) Kalkī (yet to come). The *Gītagovinda* of Śrī Jayadeva speaks of ten *avatāras* of Lord Viṣṇu. Jayadeva[25] takes Balarāma as an *avatāra,* instead of Kṛṣṇa and explains Kṛṣṇa as the Supreme Lord, the Puruṣottama in his *Gītagovinda*.

The God takes three kinds of *avatāras* (incarnations), such as:

(a) *Pūrṇāvatāra* (full incarnation): When the God manifests Himself in the form of a human being for the full span of life, this is known as *pūrṇāvatāra.* The examples of this kind are: Śrī Rāma, Śrī Kṛṣṇa, Vedavyāsa, etc.

(b) *Aṁśāvatāra* (partial incarnation): When the incarnation is only partial, i.e. the activity of such manifestation is limited to a particular time, place or incident, it is called *aṁśāvatāra.* The most famous and common manifestations of Lord Viṣṇu under this category are in the form of animals of semi-human beings, such as Vāmana, Varāha, Narasiṁha, Kūrma, Matsya, etc.

(c) *Āveśāvatāra*:*Āveśa* means overshadowing. The example of this kind is Paraśurāma *avatāra.*[26] When Śrī Rāma had married Sītā and was returning from Mithilā, he was accosted by Paraśurāma and challenged to a duel, where it is said that after bending Viṣṇu's bow, Viṣṇu's influence in Paraśurāma, passed on to Śrī Rāma. Thereafter, Paraśurāma is said to be no longer an *avatāra.* In this case, Viṣṇu's influence that overshadowed the soul of Paraśurāma, passed on to Śrī Rāma, leaving Paraśurāma a mere *ṛṣi* (sage). This is clearly a case of *āveśa* or overshadowing.

Avatāravāda **and Theory of Evolution:**

The *avatāras* give us the keys which will make us unlock the mysteries of nature. They represent the different stages of evolution in the different departments of nature. Even if we take into consideration the ten *avatāras* (of Lord Viṣṇu) as they stand, the different stages of evolution are there. The circumstances which necessitated these *avatāras* and the mighty deeds accomplished by Viṣṇu on these occasions are most graphically and exhaustively described Attempts have been made to rationalize the different forms assumed by Viṣṇu in different incarnations. In the beginning of the creation there were waters everywhere, and, to suit this condition of the world, the first incarnation of Viṣṇu was, appropriately enough, in the form of a fish—the animal to be found in water. Then the earth began gradually to take shape among those waters, and therefore in His second incarnation, Viṣṇu appeared as a tortoise, which can easily move both in water and land. The later stages of evolution are of animal life in the forests. Then comes the boar (Varāha) incarnation. The Boar lives on land alone. Next we have the transition between the animal and the human worlds in the man-lion (Narasiṁha) incarnation. The development is not completely fulfilled when we come to the dwarf (Vāmana) incarnation. The first stage of man is that of the brutish, violent, uncivilized Rāma with axe (Paraśurāma), who devastates the rest of humanity; later we get the divine spiritual Śrī Rāma, who consecrates family life and affections, and Śrī Kṛṣṇa, who exhorts us to enter into the warfare of the world; and after him Buddha, who, full of compassion for all living beings, works for the redemption of mankind. Last of all we have the incarnation yet to come, the Kalkī, who will fight against evil and injustice with the sword in hand.

(Major) *Avatāras* in the Kūrma Purāṇa:

(A) *Avatāras* of Lord Viṣṇu—In the *Kūrma Purāṇa*, various *avatāras* of Lord Viṣṇu as well as Lord Śiva are mentioned According to the *Śrīmad Bhāgavata* (I.3.1ff.), Vedavyāsa is accepted as one of the twenty-two *avatāras* of Lord Viṣṇu. The *Kūrma Purāṇa* also counts Vyāsa as an *avatāra* of Viṣṇu. However, different *avatāras* of Lord Viṣṇu recorded in the *Kūrma Purāṇa* are: (1) Kūrma, (2) Varāha, (3) Narasiṁha, (4) Vāmana, (5) Śrī Rāma, (6) Śrī Kṛṣṇa, (7) Balarāma, and (8) Vedavyāsa. A brief discussion on the above mentioned *avatāras* of Viṣṇu is as follows.

(1) *Kūrmāvatāra* (Tortoise incarnation):

The Kūrma *avatāra* of Lord Viṣṇu is one of the most popular legends of ancient India. It is interesting to note that the origin of the Kūrma legend is found in the *Śatapatha Brāhmaṇa*, where it is not connected with Viṣṇu but with Prajāpati.[27] During the churning of the milky ocean, Lord Janārdana took the form of a tortoise and supported the churning rod of Mount Mandara on His back to enable gods and demons to extract *amṛta* from the ocean.[28] On seeing the imperishable Viṣṇu, the cosmic witness assuming the form of a tortoise, Nārada and other great sages along with the *devas* eulogized the Lord. In the words of the *Kūrma Purāṇa:*

देवाश्च तुष्टुवुर्देवं नारदाद्या महर्षयः।
कूर्मरूपधरं दृष्ट्वा साक्षिणं विष्णुमव्ययम्।।[29]

Surpirisingly, this story of Kūrma *avatāra* of Lord Viṣṇu is described in the *Kūrma Purāṇa* in three verses only.

(2) *Varāhāvatāra* (Boar incarnation):

The Varāha *avatāra* is much more popular and is mentioned a number of times in the Epic and Purāṇas. First of all, in the *Śatapatha Brāhmaṇa,* the earth was very small, the size of a span, but it was torn up by a boar called Emūṣa, who was her Lord Prajāpati.[30] In the *Taittirīya Saṁhitā,* Prajāpati became a boar and seized the wind or the ocean.[31] The *Kūrma Purāṇa*[32] explains the story thus: "In the beginning there was nothing but one single vast sheet of water, a terrible ocean full of darkness, without any division and devoid of wind. Nothing was known at that time. Then appeared Brahmā, who was also called Nārāyaṇa as He lays asleep on the Cosmic Waters. This means, when Brahmā like Viṣṇu slept over the Cosmic Waters, he came to be designated as 'Nārāyaṇa'. Then Nārāyaṇa, taking the form of a Boar, uplifts the earth out of waters by means of His tusks."[33]

But the *Kūrma Purāṇa* records another version in which Viṣṇu assumed the Boar incarnation to kill the demon Hiraṇyākṣa.[34]

(3)*Narasiṁhāvatāra* or *Nṛsiṁhāvatāra* (Man-lion incarnation):

The *Kūrma Purāṇa* records a detailed discussion on Narasiṁha or Nṛsiṁha *avatāra*. The story of Man-lion incarnation of Viṣṇu is different from all Vaiṣṇava Purāṇas, wherein He manifests Himself out of a column (*stambha*) to protect his devotee Prahlāda from his cruel father Hiraṇyakaśipu. Here, Prahlāda, at the behest of his father, fights against the great Man-lion *avatāra*. When he was discomfited and found that the Pāśupata *astra* discharged by Hiraṇyakaśipu had no effect on the furious *avatāra,* then he came to know that He was Viṣṇu and hence prevented his father and other people to desist from fighting against Viṣṇu. The qualities or attributes of Lord Viṣṇu are uttered by Prahlāda:

अयं नारायणोऽनन्तः शाश्वतो भगवानजः।
पुराणः पुरुषो देवो महायोगी जगन्मयः।
अयं धाता विधाता च स्वयंज्योतिर्निरञ्जनः॥
ईश्वरः सर्वभूतानामन्तर्यामी गुणातिगः॥
गच्छध्वमेनं शरणं विष्णुमव्यक्तमव्ययम्।[35]

When this was spoken by Prahlāda, the evil minded Hiraṇyakaśipu deluded much by Viṣṇu's *māyā,* spoke to his son:

अयं सर्वात्मना वध्यो नृसिंहोऽल्पपराक्रमः॥
समागतोऽस्मद्भवनमिदानीं कालचोदितः।[36]

Then Prahlāda laughed at this and spoke to his father thus:

मा निन्दस्वैनमीशानं भूतानामेकमव्ययम्।
कथं देवो महादेवः शाश्वतः कालवर्ज्जितः॥
कालेन हन्यते विष्णुः कालात्मा कालरूपधृक्॥[37]

However, in spite of Prahlāda's repeated prevention to discontinue war against Viṣṇu, the evil minded demon king Hiraṇyakaśipu faught with the infinite Lord Narasiṁha and finally the Lord killed the demon by the means of his claws.

(4) *Vāmanāvatāra* (Dwarf incarnation):

In the *Taittirīya Saṁhitā,* it is said that when the gods and demons were struggling for the world, Viṣṇu sacrificed to himself in the shape of a dwarf and so conquered; therefore, those who desire victory should offer a dwarf beast to Lord Viṣṇu.[38] According to the *Kūrma Purāṇa,* Viṣṇu was born as a dwarf (Vāmana) incarnation from Aditi, the features of which are as follows:

चतुर्भुजं विशालाक्षं श्रीवत्साङ्कितवक्षसम्।
नीलमेघप्रतीकाशं भ्राजमानं श्रिया वृतम्।।[39]

This means (Aditi gave birth to Lord Viṣṇu) who had four arms and large eyes, whose chest is marked by *śrīvatsa* emblem, who resembless the blue cloud in complexion, who was resplendent and surrounded by glorious halos (*Śrī*).

Then, in the course of time, Bali, son of Vairocana and grandson of Prahlāda, worshipped Viṣṇu, the all-pervading Lord of *yajñas*, by performance of *yajña.* He also worshipped *brāhmaṇas* after giving them abundant wealth. The Brahmin sages came to the sacrificial hall of king Bali. At the same time, Lord Viṣṇu came to know about this and finally He came to the place of *yajña* assuming the form of a Vāmana (dwarf).[40] Then coming near to the king Bali, Vāmana Brahmin begged him for the space traversed by three steps of his own feet. The demon king granted Him the desired land and after getting this *dāna*, he Lord Viṣṇu spoke to *daitya: "pātālamūlaṁ praviśeti bhūyaḥ"*[41]—"enter the root (the downmost part) of the nether world". The Lord Vāmana, further advised to the demon king Bali as:

ध्यायस्व मां सततं भक्तियोगात्प्रवेक्षसे कल्पदाहे पुनर्माम्।[42]

By the path of devotion, meditate on me continuously. At the end of the Kalpa, you will enter me once again.

However, this story slightly differs from other Purāṇic[43] legends.

(5) *Śrī Rāmāvatāra:*

The story of Rāma is one of the most popular of all Indian historical legends and religious myths. In the *Rāmāyaṇa,* Rāma is seen most clearly as the *avatāra* of Lord Viṣṇu. The chapter twentyone of the *Kūrma Purāṇa* records mainly the story of Śrī Rāma, the hero of the *Rāmāyaṇa*. The introductory verses (1-15) mention some important kings preceding Rāma like Bhagīratha and their exploits. Probably Rāma alone was originally considered as an incarnation, and his brothers were only later, through their connection with him, regarded as partial incarnations. His wife Sītā, came to be regarded as incarnation of Lakṣmī, the consort of Viṣṇu. Rāma is one of the greatest *avatāras,* a being of pure character, both human and divine.[44] As the *Kūrma Purāṇa* adds:

रामो दाशरथिर्वीरो धर्मज्ञो लोकविश्रुतः।।...
जज्ञे रावणनाशार्थं विष्णुरंशेन विश्वभुक्।...
रामः परमधर्मात्मा सेनामिव च षण्मुखः। ...[45]

However, the purpose of this incarnation of Viṣṇu is the killing of the ten-headed demon king Rāvaṇa, whose evil power threatens the world. The perfect sage, perfect king, perfect warrior and perfect family man Śrī Rāma is considered the very embodiment of *dharma*. The story of Rāma as an incarnation stated in the *Kūrma Purāṇa* is almost same as noted in other Purāṇas.

(6) *Kṛṣṇāvatāra:*

The greatest among Viṣṇu's incarnations, the speaker of *Bhagavad Gītā,* the quintessential Godhead, Śrī Kṛṣṇa surpasses all other divine manifestations in popularity, sweetness, beauty and splendour. He is the most adored of all incarnations.[46]

Kṛṣṇa's name occurs first in the *Chāndogya Upaniṣad,* where it is said that Ghora Aṅgirasa imparted a particular piece of secret knowledge to Kṛṣṇa, the son of Devakī.[47] Description of Kṛṣṇa's life is a favourite topic in the Purāṇas.[48] In the *Kūrma Purāṇa,* Kṛṣṇa, an incarnation of Viṣṇu, is shown to have performed penance and propitiated Śiva for getting a son[49] from Jāmbavatī. After strenuous austerity Lord Śiva accompanied with Devī Pārvatī appeared before Kṛṣṇa and politely spoke Him the following words:

किमर्थं पुण्डरीकाक्ष तप्यते भवता तपः।
त्वमेव दाता सर्वेषां कामानां कर्मणामिह॥

त्वं हि सा परमा मूर्त्तिर्मम नारायणाह्वया।
न विना त्वां जगत्सर्वं विद्यते पुरुषोत्तम॥[50]

It means, Kṛṣṇa, the Supreme Lord of this universe, the bestower of all desires and holy rites, is not required to perform any penance for obtaining any material things.

Devī Pārvatī identifies Herself with Lord Kṛṣṇa as it is disclosed by Pārvatī, while singing the attributes of Śrī Kṛṣṇa. In the words of *Kūrma Purāṇa:*

त्वं हि नारायणः साक्षात्सर्वात्मा पुरुषोत्तमः।
प्रार्थितो दैवतैः पूर्वं सञ्जातो देवकीसुतः॥

पश्य त्वमात्मनात्मानमात्मनां मम सम्प्रति।
नावयोर्विद्यते भेद एकं पश्यन्ति सूरयः॥[51]

In the above verses Devī Pārvatī tries to show the identification of Gods, i.e. in reality there is no difference (*bheda*) among Gods and Goddesses (*ekaṁ sad viprā…*). However, the story of Śrī Kṛṣṇa, as an incarnation, stated in the *Kūrma Purāṇa* is almost same as noted in other Purāṇas.

(7) *Balarāmāvatāra:*

Balarāma was the elder brother of Śrī Kṛṣṇa. According to the *Kūrma Purāṇa,* Balarāma, who was known as Halāyudha and Saṁkarṣaṇa, the wielder of the plough as his weapon, was *Śeṣa* himself:

हलायुधः स्वयं साक्षाच्छेषः सङ्कर्षणः प्रभुः॥[52]

Lord Balarāma's wife was Revatī by name. She begot two sons: Niśita and Ulmuka.[53] No more description on Balarāma is available in the *Kūrma Purāṇa*.

(8) *Vyāsāvatāra:*

The Purāṇas declare that Vyāsa was the son of Parāśara, an incarnation of Lord Viṣṇu.[54] He was called Kṛṣṇa Dvaipāyana because he was born on an island (*dvīpa*) in the Yamunā river and Kṛṣṇa because he was of dark complexion. His mother was Satyavatī (*vyāsaṁ satyavatī sutam*).[55]

According to the *Kūrma Purāṇa*, Lord Hari, the all pervading Viṣṇu, out of His free will, incarnated Himself as Kṛṣṇa Dvaipāyana Vyāsa, the compiler and arranger of Vedas in present form.

कृष्णद्वैपायनो व्यासो विष्णुर्नारायणः स्वयम्।
अवातरत्स सम्पूर्णस्वेच्छया भगवान् हरिः॥[56]
तत्प्रसादादसौ व्यासं वेदानामकरोत् प्रभुः॥[57]

So, Vedavyāsa specifically divides the *mantras* into four Vedas at the end of every Dvāpara *yuga*. The *Viṣṇu Purāṇa*[58], the *Vāyu Purāṇa*[59] and the *Bhaviṣya Purāṇa*[60] give a list of twenty-eight *avatāras* (incarnations) of Vedavyāsa. Similarly, the *Kūrma Purāṇa* also furnished a list of 28 sages who carried out the job of Vyāsas and came to be considered as the incarnations of Vyāsa. The names of 28 Vyāsas[61] are as under:—

(1) Svāyambhuva Manu, (2) Prajāpati, (3) Uśanas, (4) Bṛhaspati, (5) Savitā, (6) Mṛtyu, (7) Indra, (8) Vasiṣṭha, (9) Sārasvata, (10) Tridhāmā, (11) Tṛvṛṣa, (12) Śatatejā, (13) Dharma, (14) Sucakṣu, (15) Trayyāruṇi, (16) Dhanañjaya, (17) Kṛtañjaya, (18) Ṛtañjaya, (19) Bharadvāja, (20) Gautama, (21) Vācaśravā, (22) Śuṣmāyaṇā, (23) Tṛṇabindu, (24) Vālmīki, (25) Śakti, (26)Parāśara, (27) Jātukarṇa, and (28) Kṛṣṇa Dvaipāyana.

Vedavyāsa instructed four great disciples in the four Vedas, viz. Paila, Vaiśampāyana, Jaimini and Sumantu respectively, in *Ṛgveda, Yajurveda, Sāmaveda* and *Atharvaveda*.[62] It is believed that whenever *dharma* and Veda declined Vyāsas were born for the benefit of human beings.

(B) *Avatāras* of Lord Śiva:

The *Kūrma Purāṇa* gives a list of twentyeight incarnations[63] of Lord Mahādeva in Kaliyuga, which is as follows:

(1) Śveta, (2) Sutāra, (3) Madana, (4) Suhotra, (5) Kaṅkaṇa, (6) Lokākṣi, (7) Yogīndra, (8) Dadhīvāha, (9)Ṛṣabha, (10) Bhṛgu, (11) Ugra, (12) Atisamākhyāta (Atri), (13) Bali (Vāli), (14) Gautama, (15) Vedadarśī, (16) Gokarṇa, (17) Guhāvāsī, (18) Śikhaṇḍa-dhṛk, (19) Yajamālin (Jaṭāmātya), (20) Aṭṭahāsa, (21) Dāruka, (22) Lāṅgalī, (23) Mahāyāma, (24) Śūli, (25) Diṇḍamuṇḍīśvara, (26) Sahiṣṇu, (27) Soma-Śarmā, and (28) Nakulīśa.

However, it is worth noting that in the list of Śiva's incarnations and their disciples included the names of some ancient Śaivite teachers, like Nakulīśvara, etc.

Conclusion:

Though some *avatāras* of Lord Viṣṇu are absent in the *Kūrma Purāṇa*, still from the above study it may be safely concluded that the tendency of showing oneness to many form, i.e. henotheism to polytheism and finally go back to the oneness indicating the Vedic theory of monotheism, e.g. *'ekaṁ sad viprā bahudhā vadanti...'* Secondly, it is also clear that an *avatāra* or incarnation is a descent of God[64] into man and not an ascent of man into God. Although we accept a number of *avatāras* of either Viṣṇu or Śiva, but in reality both are conceived as one and these *avatāras* are treated as the essence or part of one God or Absolute, appear in the world for the protection of *dharma* as well as for the welfare of beings in time.

REFERENCES

1. तस्य तच्चेतसो देवः स्तुतिमित्थं प्रकुर्वतः।
   आविर्बभूव भगवान् पीताम्बरधरो हरिः।। विष्णुपुराण, I.20.14.
2. Vide, Jacob, G.A., *Concordance to the Principal Upaniṣads and Bhagavadgītā,* 1963 edition, p. 117.
3. *ave tṛstrorghañ, Aṣṭādhyāyī,* III.3.120.
4. Upadhyaya, Baladev, *Purāṇa Vimarśa,* Ch.V, p. 170 (3rd edition).
5. यस्ते शृङ्गवृषो नपात् प्रणपात्कुण्डपाय्यः। न्यस्मिन्दध्र आ मनः।। ऋग्वेद, VIII.17.13. *Nirukta,* VIII.2 explains that "Sāyaṇa, the great commentator takes *'napāt'* to mean *'putra'* here.
6. अहं मनुरभवं सूर्यश्चाहं कक्षीवाँ ऋषिरस्मि विप्रः। ऋग्वेद, IV.26.1
7. अहं ब्रह्मास्मीति। ... प्रतिपेदेऽहं मनुरभवं सूर्यश्चेति। बृहदारण्यक उपनिषद्, I.4.10; cf, शास्त्रदृष्ट्या तूपदेशो वामदेववत्। ब्रह्मसूत्र, I.1.30.
8. जगृहे पौरुषं रूपं भगवान् महदादिभिः।
   सम्भूतं षोडशकलमादौ लोकसिसृक्षया।। श्रीमद्भागवत, I.3.1.
9. *Ṛgveda*, X.90.3 (*puruṣasūkta*).
10. Dasgupta, S.N., *A History of Indian Philosophy,* Part II, p. 523ff., 1991, Reprint.
11. *Śvetāśvatara Upaniṣad,* III.12ff.; *Bhagavad Gītā*, XIII.13.
12. एतन्नानावताराणां निधानं बीजमव्ययम्।
    यस्यांशांशेन सृज्यन्ते देवतिर्यङ्नरादयः।। श्रीमद्भागवत, I.3.5.
13. *Śatapatha Brāhmaṇa*, I.8.1.1-6 (Matsya *avatāra*); VII.5.1.5 (Kūrma); XIV. 1.2.11 (Varāha); I.2.5.1ff. (Vāmana); and *Chāndogya Upaniṣad*, III.17.6 (Kṛṣṇa), etc.

14. यदा यदा हि धर्मस्य ... धर्मसंस्थापनार्थाय सम्भवामि युगे युगे।। गीता, IV.7-8.
 Cf. असतां निग्रहार्थाय धर्मसंरक्षणाय च।
 अवतीर्णो मनुष्याणामजायत यदुक्षये।
 स एवं भगवान् विष्णु:कृष्णेति परिकीर्त्यते।। महाभारत, वनपर्व, 272.71-72. Also cf. *Mahābhārata,* Āśvamedhika Parva, 54.13; *Vāyu Purāṇa,* 98.69; *Devī Bhāgavata,* VII.39; *Brahma Purāṇa* 180.26-27 and 181.2-4, etc.
15. मर्त्यावतारस्त्विह मर्त्यशिक्षणं रक्षोवधायैव न केवलं विभो:। श्रीमद्भागवत, V.19.5.
16. *Śrīmad Bhāgavata*, X.26.14; cf. *Bhāgavata*, III.24.36 & III.25.1.
17. अवतारा ह्यसंख्येया हरे: सत्त्वनिधेर्द्विजा:।
 यथाऽविदासिन: कुल्या: सरस: स्यु: सहस्रश:।। श्रीमद्भागवत (पुराण), I.3.26; cf. हरिवंश, I.41.41; महाभारत, शान्तिपर्व, 339.106.
18. हंस: कूर्मश्च मत्स्यश्च प्रादुर्भावा द्विजोत्तम।
 वराहो नरसिंहश्च वामनो राम एव च ।।
 रामो दाशरथिश्चैव सात्वत: कल्किरेव च। महाभारत, शान्तिपर्व, 339.103-104.
19. *Matysa Purāṇa,* 285.6-7.
20. *ibid.,* 47.247.
21. *Agni Purāṇa,* Chapters 2-16.
22. *Padma Purāṇa,* II.257.40-41.
23. मत्स्य: कूर्मो वराहश्च नरसिंहोऽथ वामन:।
 रामो रामश्च कृष्णश्च बुद्ध: कल्की च ते दश।। वराह पुराण, IV.2;
 cf. *Padma Purāṇa,* VI.229.90; *Liṅga Purāṇa,* II,48.31-32; *Matsya Purāṇa* 285.6-7; *Garuḍa Purāṇa,* I.86-10-11 and II.20.31-32.
24. *Śrīmad Bhāgavata,* I.3.1-25.
25. वेदानुद्धरते जगन्निवहते भूगोलमुद्बिभ्रते।
 दैत्यं दारयते बलिं छलयते क्षत्रक्षयं कुर्वते।
 पौलस्त्यं जयते हलं कलयते कारुण्यमातन्वते।
 म्लेच्छान्मूर्च्छयते दशाकृतिकृते कृष्णाय तुभ्यं नम:। गीतगोविन्द, I.1.16.
26. Vide, *Mahābhārata*, II.49; III.98; 116-117, etc.; *Matsya Purāṇa*, Ch. 47; *Viṣṇu Purāṇa*, IV.7; IV.11; *Śrīmad Bhāgavata,* I.3.20; II.7.22.
27. स यत् कूर्मो नाम स तद् वै रूपं कृत्वा प्रजापति: प्रजा असृजत। शतपथ ब्राह्मण, VII.5.1.5.
28. पुरामृतार्थं दैतेयदानवै: सह देवता:।
 मन्थानं मन्दरं कृत्वा ममन्थु: क्षीरसागरम्।।
 मध्यमाने तदा तस्मिन्कूर्मरूपी जनादर्दन:।
 वभार मन्दरं देवो देवानां हितकाम्यया।। कूर्मपुराण, I.1.27-28.
29. *ibid.,* I.1.29.

30. *Śatapatha Brāhmaṇa,* XIV.1.2.11.
31. आपो वा इदमग्रे सलिलमासीत्। तस्मिन् प्रजापतिर्वायुर्भूत्वाऽचरत्। स इमामपश्यत्। तं वाराहो भूत्वाऽहरत्। तैत्तिरीय संहिता, VII.1.5.1.
32. I.6.1-21; cf. *Viṣṇu Purāṇa*, I.4.32-36; *Vāyu Purāṇa,* VI.16-23, etc.
33. जलक्रीडासु रुचिरं वाराहं रूपमास्थितः। कूर्मपुराण, I.6.8.
34. *ibid.,* I.16.81-83.
35. *Kūrma Purāṇa,* I.16.65cd-66, 67cd-68ab.
36. *ibid.,* I.16.69cd-70ab.
37. *ibid.*, I.16.71-72ab.
38. *Taittirīya Saṁhitā,* II.1.3; cf. *Śatapatha Brāhmaṇa,* XIV.1.1; I.2.5.
39. *Kūrma Purāṇa*, I.17.42.
40. विज्ञाय विष्णुर्भगवान् भरद्वाजप्रचोदितः।
    आस्थाय वामनं रूपं यज्ञदेशमथागमत्।। कूर्मपुराण, I.17.48.
41. *ibid.,* I.17.61.
42. *ibid.,* I.17.62.
43. *Mahābhārata,* Vana Parva, 272.61-70; *Vāyu Purāṇa,* 98. 74-88; *Padma Purāṇa,* II.239-240; *Agni Purāṇa*, IV.5-11, *Śrīmad Bhāgavata,* VIII.15-23, etc.
44. Bulke, Kamil, *Rāmakathā,* pp. 1-29.
45. *Kūrma Purāṇa*, I.21.16cd, 18ab & 25ab.
46. वेदानुद्धरते...कृष्णाय तुभ्यं नमः।। गीतगोविन्द, I.1.16.
47. तद्वैतद्घोर आंगिरसः कृष्णाय देवकीपुत्रायोक्त्वोवाचापिपास एव स बभूव...।। छान्दोग्य उपनिषद्, III. 17.6; cf. *Kūrma Purāṇa,* I. 24.70
48. *Kūrma Purāṇa,* I.24.70-86 & I.25.1-92; cf. *Agni Purāṇa,* 12.1-56; *Matsya Purāṇa,* 47.1.27; *Viṣṇu Purāṇa,* V.1.1-38; *Garuḍa Purāṇa,* I.144.1-11; *Śrīmad Bhāgavata,* X.1.1-90; *Harivaṁśa,* I.35.1-22; III.73.1-90, etc.
49. *Kūrma Purāṇa*, I.25.1.
50. *ibid.,* I.25.80-81.
51. *ibid.,* I.25.88-89.
52. *ibid.,* I.24.72.
53. रेवती नाम रामस्य भार्यासीत्सुगुणान्विता।
    तस्यामुत्पादयामास पुत्रौ द्वौ निशितोल्मुकौ।। *ibid.*, I.24.79.
54. *Kūrma Purāṇa*, I.52.1-26; *Devī Bhāgavata,* I.3.26-33; *Bhāgavata Purāṇa,* I.4.14-25, etc.
55. *Kūrma Purāṇa*, II.11.137.
56. *ibid.,* I.51.48-49.
57. *ibid.,* I.52.11.
58. अष्टाविंशतिकृत्वो वै वेदो व्यस्तो महर्षिभिः।
    वैवस्वतेऽन्तरे तस्मिन्द्वापरेषु पुनः पुनः।। विष्णुपुराण, III.3.9.
59. I.23.109-207.

60. I.4.14-25.
61. *Kūrma Purāṇa*, I.52.1-11 (Varanasi edition only).
62. *ibid.*, I.52.12-15.
63. वेदव्यासावताराणि द्वापरे कथितानि तु।
    महादेवावताराणि कलौ शृणुत सुव्रताः।। —*ibid.*, I.53.1; also cf. I.53.2-53.
64. एका मूर्तिस्त्रयो देवा ब्रह्मविष्णुमहेश्वराः।
    रजः सत्त्वतमोभिश्च संयुताः कार्यकारकाः।। –श्रीदेवीभागवतपुराणम्, I. 8.4.

Socio-religious Aspects in the *Vāmana Purāṇa*

The *Vāmana Purāṇa* reserves a significant place in the list of Vaiṣṇava Purāṇas, attributed to Vāmana, the first human incarnation of Lord Viṣṇu. It describes a detail account of Vāmana incarnation and deals with a number of important, interesting and common Purāṇic topics, like: *Varṇāśrama-vyavasthā*, creation, worship of Lord Viṣṇu, Śiva and Devī Durgā, wars between gods and demons, description of *tīrthas*, performance of *yajña, śrāddha, vrata, upacāra,* offering of *dāna*, description of *ākhyānas, upākhyānas, stotras* and *mokṣa*. In this paper the socio-religious aspects of *Vāmana Purāṇa* will be discussed.

Social Aspect:

The social aspect mainly covers the *varṇa-vyavasthā, āśrama-vyavasthā*, the natural duties and conduct of four castes, etc.

Varṇa System (*Varṇa Vyavasthā*):

The terms like *varṇa, jāti*, etc. are used to denote 'caste' in the Sanskrit literature. The word *varṇa* means colour or complexion or light. The four *varṇas* or castes, viz. *brāhmaṇa, kṣatriya, vaiśya* and *śūdra* are mentioned in the Puruṣasūkta of the *Ṛgveda*. It states that the origin of *brāhmaṇa* is from the mouth of Puruṣa, *kṣatriya* from his arms, *vaiśya* from his thighs and *śūdra* from his feet.[1] According to the *Vāmana Purāṇa* Lord Śiva is the founder of four castes (*cāturvarṇyaka-rasthathā*).[2] He is the combination of these four castes.[3]

***Brāhmaṇa*:**

The Brahmins belong to the priest class. They not only claim almost divine honour as their birth right, but also in general the other three *varṇas* submit readily to their authority, and hence the Brahmin claims superiority over all castes. According to the *Manu Smṛti*, the natural duties of Brahmin are: teaching, studying of the Vedas, performing sacrifices, worship for others and giving (*dāna*) and accepting of gifts (*pratigraha*).[4] The *Vāmana Purāṇa* prescribes that the Brahmins should practise austerity, perform their religious duties and undertake journeys to the places of pilgrimage. So it is said:

ब्राह्मणाश्च तपो धर्मं तीर्थयात्राश्च कुर्वते।[5]

The Brahmins always deserve respect in the society. If the earth is always adorned with *brāhmaṇas*, in association with the *kṣatriyas*, then the great kings prosper in the world.[6] The text further adds that the Brahmins are always considered as highly respectable persons in the society. The *Vāmana Purāṇa* says 'when the noble Brahmins are worshipped, Lord Viṣṇu is worshipped' Those ignorants certainly go to *naraka* (hell), who are hostile towards them.[7] The devotees of Lord Viṣṇu should not ignore Brahmins, rather they should worship them with great devotion. As the Lord Himself has said: 'Brahmins are my body.'

तानर्चयेन्नरो भक्त्या ब्राह्मणान् विष्णुतत्परः।
एवमाह हरिः पूर्वं ब्राह्मणा मामकी तनुः॥[8]

Hence, a Viṣṇu *bhakta* should pay high regards to the Brahmins. In no way, they are to be ignored, insulted and hatred by the true devotees of Viṣṇu. So, no Brahmins, learned or otherwise, should be despised As he is the divine body of Viṣṇu, a man should worship him.[9] Besides, the Brahmins should be offered gifts (*dāna*) to please Lord Viṣṇu. In the month of Caitra, the things like printed cloths, beds and seats (*āsana*) should be bestowed upon Brahmins to seek pleasure of Lord Viṣṇu.[10] Similarly, sandal-wood paste and garlands of good scent should be given to great Brahmins to afford pleasure Madhusūdana in the month of Vaiśākha.[11] This way, teaching of the Vedas, officiating as priests at sacrifices and receiving the *dāna* (gifts) are the special privileges of the Brahmins. In addition to these, the *Vāmana Purāṇa* emphasises the importance of not only on the Vedic studies but also on *snāna, japa-dhyāna*, performance of important rituals, worship of deities, *saṁdhyā, tarpaṇa* and *śrāddha*. As these are also daily duties of a true Brahmin.

Kṣatriya:

The *kṣatriyas* belong to the warrior class. The natural duties of a *kṣatriya* have been prescribed by Manu[12] as: capacity in protection of subjects, to offer charity, to perform sacrifices, to study the Vedas and to abstain from attaching himself to sensual pleasures, i.e. music, dance, etc. Besides, heroism, vigour, firmness, resourcefulness, not fleeting from battle, generosity and lordliness are also some qualities of a *kṣatriya*. The *Vāmana Purāṇa* defines the normal duties of a *kṣatriya* as:

स्वाध्याययज्ञनिरता दातारः शस्त्रजीविनः।
क्षत्रियाः सन्तु दैत्येन्द्र प्रजापालनधर्मिणः॥[13]

A king should always be associated with efficient Brahmins. He should take care of the people of his state like his own son. Besides, the king is advised to respect all other *varṇas* and even to their respective duties. When the king fails to perform his duties properly then his prosperity definitely stops.[14] The *Vāmana Purāṇa* further adds that during the rule of Prahlāda, who was an adorer of Gods and Brahmins, kings performed sacrifices on this earth in strict observance of the laws.

तस्मिञ्शासति दैत्येन्द्रे देवब्राह्मणपूजके।
मखानि भुवि राजानो यजन्ते विधिवत्तदा।।[15]

The demon kings, like Prahlāda, Balī, etc. were the true devotees of Viṣṇu and properly performing their religious as well as administrative duties for the pleasure of (their) subjects.

Vaiśya:

The *vaiśyas* are belonging to the trading class. Their natural duties have been allotted by Manu as: to tend cattle, to bestow gifts, to perform sacrifices, to study the Vedas, to trade, to lend money, and to cultivate land.[16] According to the *Bhagavad Gītā*: agriculture, rearing of cows and honest exchange of merchandise—those constitute the usual duty of a *vaiśya* (कृषिगौरक्ष्यवाणिज्यं वैश्यकर्म स्वभावजम्).[17] The *Vāmana Purāṇa* defines the functions of a *vaiśya* as:

यज्ञाध्ययनसंपन्ना दातारः कृषिकारिणः।
पाशुपाल्यं प्रकुर्वन्तु वैश्या विपणिजीविनः।।[18]

Hence, trade, agriculture, study of the Vedic texts, performance of sacrifice and cattle rearing are the main duties of *vaiśyas*. At another place the text exclusively states the major *vṛttis* of the *vaiśyas* as: '*vaiśyāśca paśuvṛttisthā*'—the livelihood of *vaiśyas* are based on cattle rearing (*paśupālana*).[19]

Śūdra:

The *śūdras* are recognised as labouring class of the society. According to Manu: 'one occupation only the Lord prescribed to the *śūdra* to serve properly to other three castes.'[20] This is also supported by the *Bhagavad Gītā*, when it says:

परिचर्यात्मक कर्म शूद्रस्यापि स्वभावजम्।।[21]

It means, service of the other class is the usual duty of a *śūdra*. In the *Vāmana Purāṇa,* Prahlāda defines the normal functions of a *śūdra* as:

ब्राह्मणक्षत्रियविशां सदा सुश्रूषणे रताः।
शूद्राः सन्त्वसुरश्रेष्ठ तवाज्ञाकारिणः सदा।।[22]

The *śūdras* should always serve the *brāhmaṇas, kṣatriyas* and *vaiśyas* devotedly. Besides, he should also follow the orders of kings and others. At another place the text writes that '*śūdrāḥ śuśrūṣaṇe ratāḥ*'[23]—the *śūdras* are devoted to service.

However, a king is advised to respect all the *varṇas*. Rather he should help them in their needs, i.e. while they are performing their respective duties. This way, the *dharma* will flourish and when *dharma* is in full flourish, a king prospers. As rightly said:

यदा वर्णाः स्वधर्मस्था भवन्ति दितिजेश्वर।
धर्मवृद्धिस्तदा स्याद्वै धर्मवृद्धौ नृपोदयः।।[24]

There should be a good coordination among all the castes. Besides, they would be more honest and sincere in achieving their respective duties. Prahlāda advises the demon king Bali to see that all castes stick to their own duties. When that thrives, you will prosper; when that is at a discount your loss is said to occur.[25]

***Āśrama-dharma*:**

The *āśrama-dharma* is associated with all the *āśramas*. The word *āśrama* is derived from the root *śram-* to exert oneself and hence it may mean a place where exertions are performed and the action of performing such exertion. Literally, the word *āśrama* is meant a halting or resting place. Therefore, it denotes a halt, a stoppage or a stage in the journey of life, just for the sake of rest, just for preparing oneself for further journey. The *āśramas* are four in number, viz. *brahmacarya, gārhasthya, vānaprashtha* and *sannyāsa*. Each of the *āśramas* constitute a stage of life in which the individual has to train himself for a certain period, and exert himself within the circuit of the same to qualify himself for the next. The Dharmaśāstra writers like Manu, Yājñavalkya, etc. have accepted four *āśrama-dharmas*, viz. *brahmacarya* (stage of student hood), *gārhasthya* (house holder), *vānaprastha* (stage of forest hermit), and *sannyāsa* (stage of ascetic life).

***Brahmacarya Āśrama*:**

The word *brahmacārī* occurs in the *Ṛgveda*[26] *(brahmacārī carati veviṣadviṣaḥ sa devānāṁ bhavatyekamaṅgam)* and the *Taittirīya Saṁhitā*[27] (*brahmacārivāsī tadavadānai-revāva dayate*....). Besides, the word *brahmacarya* occurs in the *Taittirīya Saṁhitā*[28] (*brahmacaryeṇa ṛṣibhyo*) and the *Taittirīya Brāhmaṇa*[29] (*brahmacarya-mevānena careyamiti*....).

Following Vedic tradition, the *Vāmana Purāṇa* mentions that this *brahmacarya āśrama* is only meant for the *brāhmaṇas* and *kṣatriyas*. The Purāṇa clarifies this as:

गार्हस्थ्यं ब्रह्मचर्यं च वानप्रस्थं त्रयाश्रमाः।
क्षत्रियस्यापि कथिता ये चाचारा द्विजस्य हि।।[30]

It means, the rules of conduct of the householder, the student and the forest dweller (*araṇya-vāsī*) prescribed for the *brāhmaṇa* have also been indicated for the *kṣatriya*.

In the *brahmacaryāśrama*, the *brahmacārī* used to stay in the *Gurukula*. Here in the *Gurukula, guru* is treated as the God or Brahmā for the students. Before starting any work one should pray to his teacher (*guru*) as the teacher is more respectable than any deity. The *Vāmana Purāṇa* specified in details the rules and regulations governing the life of a *brahmacārin*. After the investiture of the sacred thread (*upanayana saṁskāra*) the student will enter into the first stage of life, i.e. *brahmacarya āśrama*. This sacred thread ceremony marked the beginning of his Vedic studies at the teacher's home where he had to lead quite a disciplined and regulated life, engaging himself in attendance on fire, bathing and wandering about for alms and always eating food after obtaining his permission. As the text clarifies this as:

स्वाध्यायोऽथाग्निशुश्रूषा स्नानं भिक्षाटनं तथा।
गुरोर्निवेद्य तच्चाद्यमनुज्ञातेन सर्वदा।।[31]

Besides, the *guru's* personal work should be performed by the disciple with full effort, devotion and great pleasure. On being called for by the *guru* he should study with true devotion and undiverted attention.[32] The disciple should read one, two or all the Vedas[33] and other *śāstras* from his *guru* in proper way. In this *āśrama* the student maintains one's celibacy. Finally, after completing the period of studentship and giving or offering fees (*dakṣiṇā*) to the teacher, he should leave the *Gurukula* with his due permission.[34]

Gārhasthya Āśrama:

The word *gṛhapati* (lord of house) occurs in the *Ṛgveda*[35] nearing the same meaning as *gṛhastha*. After completing the period of *brahmacarya* in the *Gurukula*, the student enters the next stage of life, i.e. *gṛhastha*. The *Vāmana Purāṇa* states that the man should enter the householder's stage with the desire of leading the life of a householder.

गार्हस्थ्याश्रमकामस्तु गार्हस्थ्याश्रममावसेत्।[36]

This Purāṇa allows all the castes including *śūdra*[37], to enter into this *āśrama* and to maintain *gṛhastha* life in the society. Following Vedic tradition the text further adds that among four *āśramas*, the *gṛhasthāśrama* is the best, as this stage combines all the stages of life and it is the only means to acquire *dharma*[38], one of the *puruṣārthas* of life. A man should be first a householder and then a forest hermit, because a *gṛhastha* gets fame, wealth and religious merit. The *Mahābhārata* states the superiority of the *gṛhasthāśrama* over all.[39] The Smṛtis also bestow the highest praise upon this *āśrama* and mentions that all the *āśramas* subsist by receiving support from the householder and since men in the three other *āśramas* are daily supported by the householder with gifts of sacred knowledge and food. Therefore, householder is the most excellent order.

Sadācāra (obligatory code of conduct) is a part of *gṛhasthāśrama* as stated in the *Vāmana Purāṇa*. The text presents *sadācāra*, with the imagery of tree with *dharma* (law) as its root, *artha* (objective) as branches, *kāma* (impelling desires) as flowers and *mokṣa* (fulfilment) as fruit.[40] It strictly advises to follow the rules of *sadācāra* and said: 'the householder should ever be devoted to the observance of good conduct or behaviour, for there is no prosperity here or hereafter for him who transgresses good conduct.'

गृहस्थेन सदा कार्यमाचारपरिपालनम्।
न ह्याचारविहीनस्य भद्रमत्र परत्र च।।[41]

It further states that sacrifice, charity and austerity do not conduce here to the prosperity of one who transgresses good conduct.[42] A man of bad conduct can not be happy here (in this *loka*) or hereafter. So positive effort should be made to preserve good conduct. As good conduct always destroys evils and other difficulties in life.[43] The true nature or the characteristics of *sadācāra* is *dharma*[44], i.e. the daily routine of a householder. One should rise early in the morning and after that he should remember the great deities (Brahmā etc.), sages and recite the *maṅgala-stotra*, told by Mahādeva.[45] In this long *stotra*, Lord Śiva advises to a householder to recall (*smaraṇa*), at the time of waking to the three principal deties (Brahmā etc), twelve ancient seers (Bṛgu, Vasiṣṭha, Kratu, Aṅgirasa, Manu, Pulastya, Pulaha, Gautama, Raibhya, Marīci, Cyavana and Ṛbhu), four (Bhāgavata) incarnations (Sanatkumar, Sanaka, Sanandana, Sanātana), seven *svaras* (musical notes), seven *rasātalas* (nether worlds), five great elements, seven oceans, seven Kulaparvatas, seven seers (*saptarṣis*), seven large continents (*dvipas*), seven spheres Bhū and others for conferring an auspicious morning.[46] So, if a man recites, recalls and hears with devotion in the morning the *suprabhāta* benediction, surely will then the evil effect of bad dreams be destoyed by the grace of God. Socondly, it is desirable for a householder to go out (in the morning) only after he has bathed his body and offer water to the *pitṛs* and *devas*, performed *homa* and touched some auspicious objects or things like: *dūrvā*-grass, curd, ghee, a pitcher of water, a cow and her calf, a bull, gold, cowdung, the *svastika* (*yantra*), *akṣata* (white rice), fried rice, honey, and a Brahmin girl, white and auspicious flowers, fire, sandal, the rays of the sun and, the *Aśvattha vṛkṣa*.[47]

In addition to these, some other moral and ethical advises are also given to the householder to perform better duty and receive good results in his day to day life. For example, the *Vāmana Purāṇa* advises:

वृथाऽटनं वृथा दानं वृथा च पशुमारणम्।
न कर्त्तव्यं गृहस्थेन वृथा दार परिग्रहम्।।[48]

It means, aimless wandering, purposeless gift or contribution, killing animals on occasions other than *śrāddha* and *yajña*, and improper marriage should not be indulged in by a householder. Because, aimless moving brings about interruption in the performance of the daily and compusory religious duties, purposeless *dāna* (offering) causes loss of money, unnecessary killing of animals produce severe sin and leads to hell (*naraka*).[49]

However, on account of *ācāra* or *sadācāra* this Purāṇa includes a complete routine to be followed from rising in the early morning until retiring in the night, after the day's labour. Most of it is based on the *Manu Smṛti*, where it touches hundred of miscellancous items involved in the daily routine of a householder, such as: rules of health and hygiene, purification, food, dress, ethical and social conduct, worship of gods, performance of sacrifices, daily *saṁdhyās* and *pitṛtarpaṇas*.

This way, the *Vāmana Purāṇa* gives much emphasis on the *gārhasthyāśrama* or *gṛhasthadharma* through which a householder has to follow the advises of the *śāstras* and elderly religious persons to live a better life in the society.

Vānaprastha Āśrama:

The *Vāmana Purāṇa* states that the *brāhmaṇa*, *kṣatriya* and *vaiśya*—these three castes are allowed to enter into this *āśrama*.[50] It further describes the real purpose, status, conditions and importance of this stage. The intelligent man who sees the grandsons and observes the decline of his body should enter the stage of *vānaprastha* or *vānaprasthāśrama* for the purification of his *ātman* (self).

अपत्यसंततिं दृष्ट्वा प्राज्ञो देहस्य चानतिम्।
वानप्रस्थाश्रमं गच्छेदात्मनः शुद्धिकारणम्॥[51]

The man enters upon the stage of a forest hermit for securing the liberation of his soul after having seen the offsprings of his sons and the decaying of his body. Being followed the rules of the Dharmaśāstras, the *Vāmana Purāṇa* also fix some rules and conditions of the daily life style of the person entering into this third stage of life. It prescribes that in the forest the man should live by using the forest things or products and practising austerities (*tapa*) and self-mortification, sleeping on the ground, practising celibacy, worshipping the gods, manes and special care for guests. Besides these, regular offering in fire, bathing three times in a day, performing *saṁdhyā*, wearing matted hair and bark garment, and using oily things produced in the forest, this is the *vānaprastha* way of life.[52] Hence, it is obvious that a man enters into this stage may follow the prescribed religious duties with true sincerity and devotion for the purification of self as well as to obtain liberation, the highest goal of life.

Sannyāsa Āśrama:

This is the last religious stage of a man who so desires to lead or maintain a systematic life for the purification of his body and mind and soul. This *āśrama* completes the cycle of the four *āśramas* (starting from *brahmacarya* to *sannyāsa*), prescribed by the Dharmaśāstras. The *Vāmana Purāṇa* specifically states that the man enters upon the last stage, i.e. the stage of an ascetic, must have disconnect relations from his relatives, friends, etc. He should maintain celibacy by controlling over his sense organs and not residing for a long period in one place.[53] Besides, he should have to lead a celibate life and practise abstinence from anger and pleasures of senses. He must have an equal mental attitude towards all beings. The Purāṇa further mentions that a *sannyāsī* would maintain his livelihood through begging (*bhikṣā-vṛtti*). However, he should have a strong desire to attain the true knowledge of self and self-realisation. Though the life of this stage is too critical but highly disciplined one, which leads him to obtain final emancipation. The text clarifies this as:

अनारम्भस्तथाहारो भैक्षान्नं नातिकोपिता।
आत्मज्ञानावबोधेच्छा तथा चात्मावबोधनम्॥[54]

Hence, a clear picture of all those four *āśramas* of different castes elaborately depicted in the *Vāmana Purāṇa*. While giving general view on this *varṇāśrama* system P.V. Kane says:

"The *varṇa* system classified the whole community and was addressed to people in the mass; the *āśrama* theory addresses itself to the individuals in a community and maps out for them how they should order their lives and what preparation are required for the several goals of human life."[55]

Religious Aspect:

Man, being a social creature always tries to perform various religious practices. This is the only way for him to maintain (his) identity or existence. Because without any virtuous activity, religious exchange and belief, a man is counted as a beast in the society. Hence, in the religious aspects of the *Vāmana Purāṇa* we will deal with some of the terms like: *dharma, yajña, pūjā, vrata, tīrtha, śrāddha* and *dāna*.

Dharma:

Dharma is the actualization of truth and the backbone of our society. Etymologically, the word *dharma* is derived from the root *dhṛ*-with the suffix *man*, meaning 'to uphold, to support, to nourish.' Therefore, connotatively, it means that which holds, bears or sustains, and in the compound sense that is called *dharma* which holds, bears or sustains the world and its people. In most cases the meaning of *dharma* is 'religious ordinances or rites.'[56]

The *Vāmana Purāṇa* discusses various *dharmas*, firstly the rules of morality, universally to be followed by all man, called *sāmānya-dharma*. Besides, the different *āśrama dharmas* have also been explained including *sadācāra*, i.e. obligatory code of conduct for the householders. The great demon king is being advised by the sage to accept the ten limbed *dharma* for prosperity. These *dharmas* are to be followed by all castes in different stages (*āśramas*) of life. These widely accepted ten *dharmas* are as follows: *ahiṁsā* (non-violence), *satya* (truth), *asteya* (non-stealing), *dāna* (charity), *kṣānti* (forbearance), *dama* (self-restraint), *śama* (tranquillity), *akārpaṇya* (non-miserliness), *śauca* (purity) and *tapa* (austerity).[57] Earlier, in the same sense, *dharma* was defined by Manu.[58] However, undoubtedly the Purāṇakāra has taken this idea from the Dharmaśāstras. While talking about *dharma* the Purāṇa writers give much stress on the Vedas, Upaniṣads and Dharmaśāstras. So being followed the line of *śrutis* and *smṛtis*, the *Vāmana Purāṇa* presents a clear picture of *dharma* to be accepted by all castes. Regarding *dharma* it is advised to both demons and human beings that *dharma* is the supreme goal. Men devoid of *dharma* go to the great hell of *Raurava*. So, *dharma* is not to be shunned in any circumstances. It is then told:

तस्माद् धर्मो न संत्याज्यो धर्मो हि परमा गतिः।
धर्महीना नरा यान्ति रौरवं नरकं महत्॥[59]

According to the pious sages *dharma* enables a safe passage in heaven and even here in this world, and *adharma* always leads to downfall from this world and the next *loka*.[60] Prahlāda, was widely known as a true devotee of Lord Nārāyaṇa and also recognised as a religious one. Therefore, Andhaka, a demon king, while praising Prahlāda as a virtuous personality said: 'you are the only person, devoted to *dharma*, but I do not practise *dharma*' (*bhavān dharmaparastveko nāhaṁ dharma samācare*).[61]

It is noted in the *Vāmana Purāṇa* that Bali was a virtuous king who ruled according to *dharma*. Goddess Lakṣmī was pleased with him and came to reside in his kingdom. Along with *devī* Lakṣmī came other goddesses and Divine Graces, such as: Hrī, Kīrti, Dyuti, Prabhā, Dhṛti, Kṣamā, Bhūti, Ṛddhi, Mahāmati, Śruti, Smṛti, Iḍā, Śānti, Puṣṭi and Kriyā. The heavenly Apsarases, well versed in dance and music, submitted to Bali, the entire universe and incomparable prosperity were acquired by Bali, the defender of the doctrine of Brahman.[62] Further it is mentioned that when the different castes sincerely perform their respective duties, then the *dharma* flourishes, and when the *dharma* is in full flourish, a king prospers. Hence, without *dharma*, *abhyudaya* or prosperity is not possible. That is why, it is rightly said that '*dharmo rakṣati rakṣitaḥ*.'

The four *puruṣārthas*, i.e. *dharma, artha, kāma* and *mokṣa* remain in and around of the *āśramas* in four different *yugas*. The *mokṣa* occupies the hermitage at the end of *Satyayuga*, where the *dharma* occupies the hermitage in the beginning of *Kali-yuga*.[63] Hence, *dharma* has a great importance specially in the *Kaliyuga*. The gods, men and *sādhyas* attain *dharma*, etc. by the praise (*saṅkīrtana*), remembrance (*smaraṇa*), sight (*darśana*) and touching (*saṁsparśana*) of the Supreme God. By the Grace of it, gods, men and *sādhyas* attain *dharma, artha, kāma* and *mokṣa*.

संकीर्तनात् स्मरणाद् दर्शनाच्च संस्पर्शनादेव च देवतायाः।
धर्मार्थकामाद्यपवर्गमेव लभन्ति देवा मनुजाःससाध्याः॥[64]

This way, in the *Kaliyuga*, *dharma* and other *puruṣārthas* can be attained by the human beings and others. The *dharma* along with other *puruṣārthas* lay on the forehead of the Vāmana.[65]

King Bali, being a true devotee of Lord Viṣṇu, had built a temple. The great sculptor of Indra then constructed a fine image of Keśava (Viṣṇu). The king himself and his wife did cleaning, smearing and such other work in the temple.[66] The beautiful Vindhyāvalī herself lighted the lamp in the temple of Viṣṇu and wise king got *kīrtana* and recitation of sacred texts (*dharma-śravaṇa*) done by exalted Brahmins well-versed in the *Paurāṇika Śāstras*.[67]

The Purāṇa also advises that remaining firmly on the path of righteousness one should earn money (*dharmato dhanamāhāryam*).[68]

Yajña:

Yajña generally means sacrifice or the offering of the self. It is a part of *dharma*. As the *Chāndogya Upaniṣad* explicitly mentions three constituent elements of *dharma*, viz. *yajña, adhyayana* and *dāna:*

त्रयो धर्मस्कन्धा यज्ञोऽध्ययनं दानमिति प्रथमः[69]

The sacrifice purifies everything and thus it symbolizes the sense of purification.[70] *Yajña* is a part of life. Hence, the *Vāmana Purāṇa* advises that 'one should perform sacrifices to the best of his ability' (*yaṣṭavyaṁ cāpi śaktitaḥ*).[71] According to the *Vāmana Purāṇa* Lord Viṣṇu is associated with *yajña,* as He is known as the Soul, Lord and Creator of sacrifices. The Brahmins worship Him with sacrifices.

यज्ञैर्यजन्ति यं विप्रा यज्ञेशं यज्ञभावनम्।
तं यज्ञपुरुषं विष्णुं प्रणतोऽस्मि सनातनम्।।[72]

Lord Viṣṇu is also known as '*yajña-varāha*'[73] and '*sarvayajñamayadeva.*'[74] Every useful and essential accessories (*yajñāṅgas*) of a *yajña* are known as Viṣṇu, as He is the *hotā* (sacrificer), *homa* (sacrifice), *havya* (oblation to the gods), *hūyamāna* (being offered as an oblation) and *havyavāṭ* (fire) of any great sacrificial rite[75] (*yajñakarma*). The utensils of *yajña*, i.e. *sruk, sruva, kapāla, ulūkhala, araṇi,* etc. are also known as Viṣṇu.[76] Besides, the *Vāmana Purāṇa* (60.40) repeatedly and exclusively identified Lord Viṣṇu with *yajña, yajamāna, iḍya, yājaka, jñātā, jñeya, dhyeya, dhyātṛ* and *īśvara*. Hence, Viṣṇu is not at all separate from *yajña* and its essential accessories (*yajñāṅgas*).

यज्ञस्त्वं यजमानस्त्वमीड्यस्त्वमसि याजकः।
ज्ञाता ज्ञेयस्तथा ज्ञानं ध्येयो ध्याताऽसि चेश्वरः।।

The human beings would satisfy Lord Viṣṇu and other gods by performing various sacrifices. When the gods are pleased the rain falls on the earth and the production of food (*anna*) is possible only through the rain. Therefore, the beings are depend upon food and food on rain and rain on holy sacrifice. This way, sacrifice is the medium to please the gods for the existence of human life in the earth. It is aptly said:

यज्ञैर्विना नो प्रीयन्ते देवाः स्वर्गनिवासिनः।
अप्रीता न प्रयच्छन्ति वृष्टिं सस्यस्य वृद्धये।।
तस्माद् यज्ञैश्च देवैश्च धार्यते सचराचरम्।[77]

Therefore, the universe is sustained by the sacrifices and gods.

The *Vāmana Purāṇa* further adds that in the old age Indra had performed one hundred Aśvamedha sacrifices and due to its outcome he went to *brahmaloka*.[78] The story of Dakṣa's *yajña* to which Śiva and Satī were not invited are also described in this Purāṇa. King Bali too performed the great Aśvamedha sacrifice, where he had offered everything including three *pada* (steps) *bhūmi* to the *Vāmana* (*avatāra* of Lord Viṣṇu). So, various kings performed different sacrifices to please Viṣṇu, Śiva and other deities for the welfare of their states.

Pūjā:

The word *pūjā* is a common term for worship in Sanskrit literature. It has a number of synonyms, such as: *arcanā, vandanā, saparyyā, arhaṇā, namasyā, arcā,* etc.*Pūjā* is done everyday to the *iṣṭa-devatā* or any other god, worshipped by the man.

It is also an essential part of path of devotion, and is included as important subject in the nine disciplines of *bhakti* (*navadhābhakti*) in the *Bhāgavata Purāṇa*. For people, who can not actually commune with the Divine God within themselves through meditation, external worship of Him offers the next best form of Communion. Backed by true faith, external worship gives the devotee a positive feeling of having some real service to the Lord and this goes a great way in enhancing his devotional fervour.[79]

The *Vāmana Purāṇa* has stressed for the worship of Lord Viṣṇu, because by doing so one is freed from sin.[80] Worship to Hari or Nārāyaṇa may provide the highest and everlasting perfection (*paraṁ siddhim*).[81] Even he, who is devoted to other gods, worship Keśava deceitfully, attains the lofty position of the holy saints. The merit or fruits that is acquired by the continuous worship of Viṣṇu is never attained even by men who have practised austerity properly. On the other hand, he who does not worship Lord Viṣṇu with external and internal fearlessness and offers not flowers, leaves, water, blossoms, etc. to Him, indeed is robbed by the robber fixed by destiny. It is wisely said:

वाह्यैस्तथान्तःकरणैरविक्लवैर्यो नार्चयेत् केशवमीशितारम् ।
पुष्पैश्च पत्रैर्जलपल्लवादिभिर्नूनं स मुष्टो विधितस्करेण॥[82]

Therefore, the Nakṣatrapuruṣa Viṣṇu is being worshipped and gives sweetness of speech, splendour and other desire objects.[83]

***Vrata*:**

The term *vrata* is derived from the root *vṛ*-'to choose.' The other meanings of *vrata* are: law, order, command, domain, customary activities, religious duty, worship, ascetic performance, vow, sacred work, etc. In the *Vāmana Purāṇa* the word *vrata* is used in the sense of religious observance, penance and voluntary *karma*. Those men in whose family there in neither *Veda* nor *Śāstra*, and no *vrata* is kept, are called *nagna* by the sages. Their food is prohibited[84] Any rarest things and intended objects can be obtained through the performance of *vrata* or vow.[85] The *Vāmana Purāṇa* deals with religious observances prescribed for the rainy season beginning from the 11th day of the bright half of *Āṣāḍha* when Viṣṇu goes to sleep in calm repose (*Hariśayana*) along with the *devas* up to the 11th day of the bright half of *Kārtika* when the Lord awakens (*devaprabodhini-ekādaśī*). This *vrata* is called *aśūnya-śayanā*, and any one observes it is rewarded with perpetual union with his wife as Lord Viṣṇu does not become separated from Goddess Lakṣmī.[86] The *vrata* is observed by imposing a strict regimen and discipline of life on one's ownself. Another *vrata* named '*Kālāṣṭamī*'[87] begins from *aṣṭami tithi* (dark) of *Bhādrapada* to same *tithi* in the month of *Māgha* for a period of six months, but it is continued for another six months from *Phālguna* to *Śrāvaṇa*. This *vrata* claims especial association with the cult of Śiva. The text also explains other *vratas*, like *akhaṇḍa-dvādaśīvratam*[88], *taptakṛcchra-vratam*[89], *śrāvaṇa-dvādaśī-vratam*[90] and *nakṣatrapuruṣa-vratam*[91]. Lord Maheśvara even performed a great vow for acquiring energy.[92] However, the *Vāmana Purāṇa* elaborately discussed a number of important *vratas* for obtaining eternal peace and happiness.

Tīrtha:

Tīrthas show the cultural importance of our country. The word *tīrtha* means a place of pilgrimage on the bank of a stream or river or tank, which should be crossed to attain the grace of god or goddess. There is a good deal of discussion in the Purāṇas about those who are entitled or have the eligibility for pilgrimage or *tīrtha-yātrā*. The *Mahābhārata* exclusively states that the *brāhmaṇas*, *kṣatriyas*, *vaiśyas* and *śūdras*, when they have bathed in holy places, are not born again.[93] It was believed that going on a pilgrimage and bathing in the holy rivers and ponds a man may be freed from sins. The *Vāmana Purāṇa* has discussed various *tīrthas* and its great significance very extensively. It deals almost all the important *tīrthas* of ancient India.

Regarding the importance of *tīrtha* it is said that those who remember *tīrthas* and propitiate the gods, and bath with faith, attain final beatitude or liberation:

ये स्मरन्ति च तीर्थानि देवताः प्रीणयन्ति च।
स्नान्ति च श्रद्दधानाश्च ते यान्ति परमां गतिम्।।[94]

Prahlāda, a true devotee of Lord Viṣṇu has expressed his keen interest to go for a long pilgrimage to holy places for the expiration of sin.[95] It is observed that most of the *tīrthas* are known for its sacred power to free men and manes from the sins. For example, the *Vāmana Purāṇa* says: 'I shall go to Kurukshetra and live there'—he who repeats this, gets rid of all sins.[96] Besides, knowledge of the Supreme Being, *śrāddha* in Gayā, death in Gograha and residence in Kurukshetra—these have been declared to be the four varieties of salvation of man.[97] The *Vāmana Purāṇa* elaborately discussed the importance of various *tīrthas*. It is not possible to deal with all the *tirthas* here. So, the name of some famous *tirthas* are as follows: 1. Kurukshetra (XXII.20; Saro Māhātmya, I.13, XI.24, etc.); 2. Kanakhala (IV.19, XXV.52); 3. Gayā (Saro Māhātmya XII.8, XV.48, XXIII.19, etc.); 4. Godāvarī (XXXIX.128,154); 5. Gokarṇa (LXII.5, LXIII.28, etc.); 6. Puṣkara (VII.37, Saro Māhātmya XIII.41, XVI.19,21, 23, etc.); 7. Prayāga (III.26; XXV.51, etc.); 8. Varanasi (III.42, XXV.49, LVII.30, etc.); 9. Virajākṣetra (XXIII.19); 10. Daṇḍaka (Saro Māhātmya XIV.45); 11. Prabhāsa (XXI.91); 12. Śukratīrtha (Saro Māhātmya XIV.23, XXV.1); 13. Sthāṇutīrtha (Saro Māhātmya I.12, XIX.13); 14. Vadarikāśrama (VI.4,21,23, XXI.96, etc); 15. Naimiṣāraṇya (VII.37-39); 16. Daśāsvamedha (III.41,53, etc.); 17. Kedāra (XXI.97; XXIV.10,11,17); 18. Kāmarūpa (LVII.54, LXIII.33); 19. Pṛthūdaka (XII.45 etc.); 20. Soma *tīrtha* (XXI.91, LVII.12, 43).

This Purāṇa specifically describes Sthāṇu *tīrtha* in the Saro Māhātmya. In this Māhātmya the other associate *tīrthas* of Sthāṇu *tīrtha* of Sthāṇveśvara or Kurukshetra have been glorified Another speciality of this *tīrtha* is that both Vāmana and Bali are associated with this sacred place. Hence, through some additional chapters (Saro Māhātmya) the significance of Bali, Vāmana and Sthāṇveśvara Mahādeva are discussed

Śrāddha:

Śrāddha is meant for some offerings with faith to the departed souls, i.e. manes.

Whatever is given with *śraddhā* to the Brahmins intending it to be for the well-being of *pitṛ-puruṣas* (manes) at a proper day (*tithi*) and time, in a proper place, to deserving persons and in accordance with the prescribed procedure is called *śrāddha* in our Indian tradition. Through the description of various *tīrthas*, the *Vāmana Purāṇa* has prescribed to offer *tarpaṇas* and *śrāddhas* for the manes. It is not even forget to mention the specific day (*tithi*), month and place, where this *śrāddha-karma* would be performed for the emancipation of the departed souls. The *Vāmana Purāṇa* advises to all the castes for performing *śrāddha* ceremony in the usual manner and according to their own practices.[98] The person who offers *śrāddha* or *piṇḍa* to the manes definitely he attains *mokṣa* or *paramapada* or *mukti* or liberation. In the Kapisthala *tīrtha* (Kaithal) the man who performs *śrāddha* on the *caturdaśī* of the bright fortnight of *Caitra* month, attains the most exalted position (*paramapada*).[99] In the Nāgahrada *tīrtha* specially on the *daśamī tithi,* the *śukla pakṣa* of the month of *Caitra*, a holy bath, muttering of *mantra* and *śrāddha* lead to the path of liberation.[100] Offering of *śrāddha* at Gayā *tīrtha* eternally pleases the manes.

गयायां च यथा श्राद्धं पितॄन् प्रीणाति नित्यशः।[101]

A famous river Apagā is situated near the eastern side of Mānuṣa *tīrtha*. Anybody who will perform *śrāddha* near that river on fourteenth (dark) of *Bhādra* month, he attains liberation (*piṇḍado muktimāpnuyāt*).[102]

However, it is a strong belief of the Hindu people that by performing *śrāddha* and *tarpaṇa* in various *tīrthas* may provide peace and liberation to the departed souls.

Dāna:

Dāna or gift is a constituent of *dharma*. The *Vāmana Purāṇa* is famous for the *dāna* given by Bali to Vāmana, the Lord Viṣṇu. Śukra, the *guru* of the demons warned Bali that he should not design to accept even the smallest request from anyone for gift of any kind. To this advice Bali reacted in the most maganimous manner by saying that within the *yājñic* field if anyone asked even his head he would not hesitate to part with it. Secondly, Lord Nārāyaṇa, who is pleased with vows (*vratas*) and fasts of various kind, comes and says give me (*dehi*). What else is greater than this great event. In the words of Bali:

यज्ञोऽस्मिन्यदि यज्ञेशो याचते मां जनार्दनः।
निजमूर्द्धानमप्यस्मै दास्याम्येवाविचारितम्॥
स मे वक्ष्यति देहीति गोविन्दः किमतोऽधिकम्।
नास्तीति यन्मया नोक्तमन्येषामपि याचताम्॥[103]

King Bali here expatiates on the virtues of *dāna* and considers that the piety prevailing in his kingdom was the fruit of the seed sown by him in the form of *dāna*, i.e. *dāna-bīja-phala*. *Dāna* is a great religious act. Due to its outcome everybody in

3. ब्राह्मणाः क्षत्रिया वैश्याः शूद्रा वर्णावराश्च ये।
ibid., XXVI.110.
4. अध्यापनमध्ययनं यजनं याजनं तथा।
दानं प्रतिग्रहं चैव ब्राह्मणानामकल्पयत्।।
मनुस्मृति, I.88.
5. *Vāmana Purāṇa*, VII.24ab.
6. भूम्यां सदा ब्राह्मणभूषितायां क्षत्रान्वितायां. . ऋद्धिं प्रयान्तीह नराधिपेन्द्राः।।
वामनपुराण, XLVIII.42.
7. पूजितेषु द्विजेन्द्रेषु पूजितः स्याज्जनार्दनः।
एतान् द्विषन्ति ये मूढास्ते यान्ति नरकं ध्रुवम्।।
ibid., LXVIII.7
8. *ibid.*, LXVIII. 8.
9. ब्राह्मणो नावमन्तव्यो बुधो वाप्यबुधोऽपि वा।
सोऽपि दिव्या तनुर्विष्णोस्तस्मात् तामर्चयेन्नरः।।
ibid., LXVIII.9.
10. चैत्रे चित्राणि वस्त्राणि शयनान्यासनानि च।
विष्णोः प्रीप्यर्थमेतानि देयानि ब्राह्मणेष्वथ।।
ibid., LXVIII.25.
11. गन्धमाल्यानि देयानि वैशाखे सुरभीणि वै।
देयानि द्विजमुख्येभ्यो मधुसूदनतुष्टये।।
ibid., LXVIII.26.
12. प्रजानां रक्षणं दानमिज्याध्ययनमेव च।
विषयेष्वप्रसक्तिश्च क्षत्रियस्य समासतः।।
मनुस्मृति, I.89.
13. *Vāmana Purāṇa*, XLVIII, 45.
14. *ibid.*, XLVIII.49.
15. *ibid.*, VII.23.
16. पशूनां रक्षणं दानमिज्याध्ययनमेव च।
वणिक्पथं कुसीदं च वैश्यस्य कृषिमेव च।।
मनुस्मृति, I.90.
17. *Bhagavad Gītā*, XVIII.44.
18. *Vāmana Purāṇa*, XLVIII.46.
19. *ibid.*, VII.24.
20. एकमेव तु शूद्रस्य प्रभुः कर्म समादिशत्।
एतेषामेव वर्णानां शुश्रूषामनसूयया।।
मनुस्मृति, I.91.

21. *Bhagavad Gītā*, XVIII.49.
22. *Vāmana Purāṇa*, XLVIII.47.
23. *ibid.*, VII.24.
24. *ibid.*, 48.48.
25. तस्माद् वर्णाः स्वधर्मस्थास्त्वया कार्याः सदा बले।
    तद्वृद्धौ भवतो वृद्धिस्तद्धानौ हानिरुच्यते।।
    ibid., XLVIII.49.
26. X.109.5.
27. VI.3.10.5.
28. *ibid.*
29. III.10.11
30. *Vāmana Purāṇa*, XV.62.
31. *ibid.*, XIV.5.
32. गुरोः कर्मणि सोद्योगः सम्यक् प्रीत्युपपादनम्।
    तेनाहूतः पठेच्चैव तत्परो नान्यमानसः।।
    ibid., XIV.6.
33. According to Manu one has to devote 36 years to get maturity over the Vedas. The text says: '*traivedikaṁ vratam*' (*Manusmṛti*, III.1). According to the Commentator Kulluka (*trayo veda ṛgjajuḥsāmākhyāstesām*) the three Vedas meant are the *Ṛgveda*, *Yajurveda* and *Sāmaveda*. The *Atharvaveda* is here, as in most of the ancient Dharmasūtras, left out together. Baudhāyana, alone, states that the term of studentship extends over forty-eight years and that rule includes the *Atharvaveda*.
34. एकं द्वौ सकलान् वापि वेदान् प्राप्य गुरोर्मुखात्।
    अनुज्ञातो वरं दत्त्वा गुरवे दक्षिणां ततः।।
    Vāmana Purāṇa, XIV.7.
35. *vāmaṁ gṛhapatiṁ naya—Ṛgveda*, VI.53.2.
36. *Vāmana Purāṇa*, XIV.8ab.
37. गार्हस्थ्यमुत्तमं त्वेकं शूद्रस्य क्षणदाचर।।
    ibid., XV.63.
38. आश्रमांस्तुलया सर्वान् धृतानाहुर्मनीषिणः।
    एकतश्च त्रयो राजन् गृहस्थाश्रम एकतः।।
    तपः श्रेष्ठं प्रजानां. . . . कुटुम्बविधिनानेन यस्मिन् सर्वं प्रतिष्ठितम्।
    Mbh XII. 12.12 & XII. 11.21.
39. अत्याश्रमानयं सर्वानित्याहुर्वेदनिश्चयाः।
    ब्राह्मणाः श्रुतिसम्पन्नास्तान् . . . . . ।। *ibid.*, XII.12.6-7.
40. *Vāmana Purāṇa*—A Study by V.S. Agrawala, Ch. 47, p. 47.
41. *Vāmana Purāṇa*, XIV.15.
42. यज्ञदानतपांसीह पुरुषस्य न भूतये।

भवन्ति यः समुल्लङ्घ्य सदाचारं प्रवर्तते।
ibid., XIV.16.

43. दुराचारो हि पुरुषो नेह नामुत्र नन्दते।
कार्यो यत्नः सदाचारे आचारो हन्त्यलक्षणम्।। *ibid.*,XIV.17.
Cf. आचारो भूतिजननः आचारः कीर्तिवर्धनः।
आचाराद् वर्धते ह्यायुराचारो हन्त्यलक्षणम्।। महाभारत, XIII.104.154.

44. आचार लक्षणो धर्मः . . . .आचारः श्रेष्ठ उच्यते।। महाभारत, XIII.104.155; आचारो परमो धर्मः । मनुस्मृति, I.108.

45. ब्रह्मा मुरारिस्त्रिपुरान्तकारी भानुः शशी भूमिसुतो बुधश्च।
गुरुश्च शुक्रः सह भानुजेन कुर्वन्तु सर्वे मम सुप्रभातम्।।
Vāmana Purāṇa, XIV.23.

46. *ibid.*, XIV.24-27.

47. *ibid.*, XIV.34-37.

48. *ibid.*, XIV.41

49. वृथाऽटनान्नित्यहानिर्वृथादानाद्धनक्षयः।
वृथा पशुघ्नः प्राप्नोति पातकं नरकप्रदम्।। *ibid.*, XIV.42.

50. *ibid.*, XV.62-63.

51. *ibid.*, XV.56.

52. तत्रारण्योपभोगैश्च तपोभिश्चात्मकर्षणम्।
भूमौ शय्या ब्रह्मचर्यं पितृदेवातिथिक्रिया।।
होमस्त्रिषवणं स्नानं जटावल्कलधारणम्।
वन्यस्नेहनिषेवित्वं वानप्रस्थविधिस्त्वयम्।। *ibid.*,XV.57-58.

53. सर्वसङ्गपरित्यागो ब्रह्मचर्यममानिता।
जितेन्द्रियत्वमावासे नैकस्मिन् वसतिश्चिरम्।। *ibid.*, XV.59.

54. *ibid.*,XV.60.

55. *History of Dharmaśāstra*, Vol. V, part II, p. 1645.

56. अतो धर्माणि धारयन्–ऋग्वेद, I.22.18; धर्माणि पुष्यसि–ऋग्वेद, V.26.6;धर्माणामिमम्–ṚV VIII.43.24, etc.

57. अकार्पण्यं च शौचं च तपश्च रजनीचर।।
दशाङ्गो राक्षसश्रेष्ठ धर्मोऽसौ सार्ववर्णिकः। वामनपुराण, XIV.1-2.

58. धृतिः क्षमा दमोऽस्तेयं शौचमिन्द्रियनिग्रहः।
धीर्विद्या सत्यमक्रोधो दशकं धर्मलक्षणम्।। मनुस्मृति, VI.92.

59. *Vāmana Purāṇa*, XL.35.

60. धर्मस्तु गदितः पुंभिस्तारणे दिवि चेह च।
पतनाय तथाऽधर्म इह लोके परत्र च।। *ibid.*, XL.36.

61. *ibid.*, XL.41 cd.

62. *ibid.*, Saro Māhātmya, II.14-20.

63. *ibid.*, LXII.19.
64. *ibid.*, LXIII.46.
65. *ibid.*, LXV.26.
66. *ibid.*, LXVIII.58.
67. गेयं स धर्म्यश्रवणं च धीमान् पौराणिकैर्विप्रवरैरकारयत्। *ibid.*, LXVIII.59.
68. *ibid.*, XV.52.
69. *Chāndogya Upaniṣad*, II.23.I.
70. एष ह वै यज्ञो योऽयं पवते। एष ह यन्निदं सर्वं पुनाति।
    यदेष यन्निदं सर्वं पुनाति। तस्मादेष एव यज्ञः। *ibid.*, IV.16.1
71. *Vāmana Purāṇa*, XV.52.
72. *ibid.*, LIX.83.
73. *ibid.*, LX.22.
74. *ibid.*, LX.32.
75. होता होमश्च हव्यं च हूयमानश्च हव्यवाट्। *ibid.*, LX.37.
76. स्रुकस्रुवौ परधामासि कपालोलूखलोऽरणिः. . . . । *ibid.*,LX.39.
77. *ibid.*, Saro Māhātmya,XXVI.14-15.
    Cf. अन्नाद्भवन्ति भूतानि पर्जन्यादन्नसम्भवः।
    यज्ञाद्भवति पर्जन्यो यज्ञः कर्मसमुद्भवः।।
    BhG III.14-15.
78. *Vāmana Purāṇa*,LII.32.
79. *Worship of Sri Ramakrishna* (Ramakrishna Math, Madras), preface, p. iv.
80. संपूजयन् यः प्रणतश्च विष्णुम्। ....फलंसमग्रं परिहीनपापः।
    Vāmana Purāṇa, LXIX.4.
81. *ibid.*, LXVII.68.
82. *ibid.*, LXVII.76.
83. *ibid.*, LIV.34.
84. येषां कुले न वेदोऽस्ति न शास्त्रं नैव च व्रतम्।
    ते नग्नाः कीर्तिताः सद्भिस् तेषामन्नं विगर्हितम्।। *ibid.*, XV.35.
85. *ibid.*, L.40.
86. *ibid.*, XVI.21-23.
87. *ibid.*, XVI.24-25.
88. *ibid.*, XVI.26.
89. *ibid.*, XXXVI.9-10.
90. *ibid.*, LIII.60-75.
91. *ibid.*, LIII.81, LIV.39.
92. स महाव्रतमुत्पाद्य . . .।। *ibid.*, XXXIV.4.
93. ब्राह्मणाः क्षत्रिया वैश्याः शूद्रा वा राजसत्तम।।
    न वै योनौ प्रयायन्ते स्नातास्तीर्थे महात्मनः।।
    महाभारत, वनपर्व, 82.30-31.

94. *Vāmana Purāṇa*, Saro Māhātmya, XII.5.
95. अहं च पापोपशमार्थमीशमाराध्य यास्ये
प्रतितीर्थयात्राम्। *ibid.*, LI.56.
96. *ibid.*, Saro Māhātmya, XII.12.10.
97. *ibid.*, Saro Māhātmya, XII.8.
98. स्वाः स्वाः कर्मक्रियाः कुर्युः सर्ववर्णा यथाक्रमम्। *ibid.*, XV.47.
99. यस्तत्र कुरुते श्राद्धं. . . . . प्राप्नोति परपंपदम्।। *ibid.*, Saro Māhātmya, XC.17
100. श्राद्धं मुक्तिमार्गप्रदायकम् । *ibid.*, Saro Māhātmya, XV.40.
101. *ibid*; Saro Māhātmya, XV.48.
102. *ibid.*, Saro Māhātmya, XV.6.
103. *ibid.*, XXXI.23-24 (Venkateswara Press Edition, Bombay).
104. *ibid.*, Saro Māhātmya, X.24-25.
105. *ibid.*, Saro Māhātmya, X.28.
106. *ibid.*, Saro Māhātmya, X.44.
107. *ibid.*, LXV.17.

Buddhist Concept of Basic Material Element : A Scientific Critique

The structural exposition of the beings has been made with two reals, viz. *nāma* and *rūpa*. The term *nāma* (*namati iti nāmam, cintanaṁ vā*) stands for the inner personality, expressing itself through the *citta* (consciousness) and *cetasika* (psychic factors). *Rūpa* (matter) refers to the physical personality, within and without, gross in nature and material in character with all its varieties of manifestations. Matter is that which appears or manifests itself to the senses (*rūpati iti rūpam*) without ever suggesting reality or stability, substance or substratum. So matter is what materializes. Different meanings are given of this materializing as pressure, pain, disappearance or change. Thus matter is something that disappears. In Modern science matter is anything that has mass (heaviness) and occupies space. To understand this material world knowledge of matter is most essential. An element consists of only one type of atoms.

The elaborate discussion of the *Dhammasaṅgaṇi* begins by defining *rūpa* or matter as: **"चत्वारो च महाभूता चतुन्नञ्च महाभूतानम् उपादाय रूपम्**[1]—the four *mahābhūtas* or great basic elements that proceeding from the grasping of that is called *rūpa*. Buddhaghosa explains it by saying that *rūpa* means the four *mahābhūtas* and those which arise depending on them as a modification of them. In the *rūpa* the six senses including their affections are also included In the *Saṁyutta Nikāya* the Buddha says "O Bhikkhus it is called *rūpam*, because it manifests (*rūpayati*); how does it manifests? It manifests as cold, and as heat, as hunger and as thirst, it manifests as the touch of gnats, mosquitos, wind, the sun and the snake; it manifests, therefore it is called *rūpa*"[2]. This *rūpa* or matter is atomic.

Matter is regarded as the collective organism or collocation, consisting of the fourfold substratum of colour, smell, taste and contact. The unit possessing this fourfold substratum is known as *paramāṇu*, which is the subtlest form of *rūpa*. It cannot be pierced through or picked up or thrown away. It is indivisible, unanalysable, invisible, inaudible, untastable and intangible. It is not permanent, but is like a momentary flash into being. The simple atoms are called *dravya- paramāṇu* and the compound atoms *saṁghāta-paramāṇu*.[3] A *dravya-paramāṇu* never arises or exists in isolation. It always arises and exists in combination with other *dravya-paramāṇus*. A collection of them, forming a unity and having a simultaneous origination and a simultaneous cessation, is called *saṁghāta-paramāṇu*, 'aggregate-atom', i.e. molecule[4] (*na vai paramāṇurūpa-mekaṁ pṛthagbhūtam asti / saṁghātasthaṁ tu tad rūpyate eva*[5]). The smallest *saṁghāta-paramāṇu* is an octad consisting of the four primary elements and four of the secondary elements, viz. *rūpa, rasa, gandha* and *sparśa*. That the four primary elements always arise simultaneously and that the secondary elements cannot arise independently of the primary, are the two fundamental principles involved in the conception of the *saṁghāta-paramāṇu*. This is a brief note of the two kinds of *paramāṇu* postulated by the Vaibhāṣikas. According to Prof. Th. Stcherbatsky "the combined atmos (*saṁghāta-paramāṇu)* alone appear in phenomenal reality, the simple ones, or infra-atomic elements, presumably, were relegated to transcendental reality, in accordance with the general character of a Buddhist element."[6] The organs of sense are also regarded as modifications of atomic matter. Seven such *paramāṇus* combine together to form an '*aṇu*', and it is in this combined form only that they become perceptible. The combination takes place in the form of a cluster having one atom at the centre and others around it. The point which must be remembered in connection with the conception of matter is this, that the qualities of all the *mahābhūtas* or primary elements are inherent in the *paramāṇus*.

The ultimate units of matter elements are known as *paramāṇu* or the properties. These properties are of four different kinds, viz. *pṛthivī* (earth particles), *ap* (water particles), *vāyu* (air particles), and *tejas* (fire particles). These are known as four *mahābhūtas* or great elements.[7] Most of the schools of Indian thought, notably the Sāṁkhya, the Vedānta and the medical tradition as represented by Caraka and Suśruta, recognizes five great elements, such as: *pṛthivī, ap, tejas, vāyu* and *ākāśa*. That *ākāśa* (ether or space) is the fifth, is admitted by the Nyāya-Vaiśeṣika too.

In Buddhism, although hypothetically these *mahābhūtas* are said to be of different types, they are seldom found in isolation[8]; each type remains in a mixed up condition with the remaining types. Each particular class of *mahābhūtas* contains its one characteristic feature, e.g. the earth particle (*pṛthivī paramāṇu*) as got hardness; water particle has got humidity; fire has got heat and air particle has got motion. It is said that these four types remain in each constituted object in relative proportion. All these four primary elements are characterized with colour (*varṇa*) and shape (*saṁsthāna*).

Although Buddhism does not ignore the concept of space (*ākāśa*), but enters it in a list of six *dhātus* with *vijñāna*. In many respects it differs from the other four: it is a non-corporeal (*amūrta*) substance devoid of tactility (*sparśa*) and characterized by ubiquity (*vibhū*), absolute continuity and infinite magnitude. As such, unlike the other four substances, it is not, in the ultimate analysis, composed of atoms. Thus, although *ākāśa* is introduced as a *bhūta* (element), in view of its peculiar characteristics, it has to be distinguished from the other four and is, in a way, on a par with such intangible substances as *kāla*, time.

The four principle characteristics of matter are referred to and enumerated in many canonical texts.[9] This has also been elucidated in the commentarial works, viz. *Aṭṭhasālinī* and *Visuddhimagga*. They are called *mahābhūtas* or great primary elements, because of manifestation of greatness. It means they manifest with immense vastness with respect to phenomena 'grasped at' *(upādinna-santati)* and those of ungrasped at *(ana-upādinna-santati)*. In case of *upādinna-santati*, they appear as the material forms, as the bodies of various kinds of beings, like human beings, animals, birds, etc. But in case of *ana-upādinna-santati*, they appear into a world system, tremendously vast, traditionally calculated as 1203450 *yojanas* in circumference containing big waters, mountains, as well as the great famous trees like Jambu tree, Kappa tree, etc.[10]

These four primary elements are being elaborated as under:

Paṭhavī-dhātu (earth element):

The word *pṛthivī (paṭhavī)* is derived from the root *prath- (puttha-)*, meaning to expand or extend and directly refers to the vastness of the earth. It is the feminine form of the noun *pṛthu* which means vast, broad, expansive, etc. *Dhātu* means that which bears its own characteristic marks *(attano sabhavaṁ dhāretiti dhātu)*. So, the literal as well as nearer meaning of the term is 'the element of extension'. It does not stand only for geometrical extensions of length, width and height, but also for solidity and hardness. Whatever is hard and solid is the element of earth.

यं अज्झत्तं कक्खळं खरिगतं उपादिन्नं, सेय्यथीदं - केसा लोमा नखा दन्ता तचो मं सं ... यं वा पनञ्ञं पि किञ्चि अज्झतं पच्चत्तं कक्खळं खरिगतं उपादिन्नं। अयं वुच्यतावुसो, अज्झत्तिका पठवी धातु ॥[11]

So, the earth element is that which is hard (*kakkhaḷam*), rough (*khara-gatam*), hardness (*kakkhaḷattam*), rigidity (*kakkhaḷ abhavo*) both internal and external.

For the Abhidharma, too, *kakkhaḷa* and *khara* which mean hard and rigid respectively bring out the essential nature of earth element.[12] The first is said to represent its characteristic (*lakkhaṇa*) and the second, its mode (*ākāra*).[13] Similar definitions are met with in other schools of Buddhist thought. The *Mahāvastu* says that when the living beings who lived at a new evolution of the world began to eat whole mouthfuls of the essence of this earth as food, their bodies came to possess the characteristics of *gurutva* (heaviness), *kharatva* (roughness), *kakkhatatva* (hardness).[14] The *Abhidharma-kośa* and its commentary, too, use the latter two terms in defining the *paṭhavī-dhātu*. In the *Abhidharma Samuccaya* it is defined as '*kaṭhinatā*', a term which could be interpreted as meaning 'solidity'. As such this interpretation is almost the same as that explained by the Theravādins. Thus, there is a common outlook among the Buddhist scholars in maintaining that what is called primary element of earth stands for the phenomenon of hardness, solidity or compactness in matter. It is a repellent energy which gives to matter the characteristics of dimension, expansion, weight and pressure.

Āpo-dhātu (water element):

The term *ap* is derived from the root *āp-*, which means 'to pervade' or 'to obtain' (*āpnoti*). *Āpo-dhātu* represents the fact of viscidity (*sineha*) and cohesion or binding together in matter-'*rūpassa bandhanattam*'.[15] It is the binding quality of matter, as it acts as a binding force of the material elements. In the Sanskrit Buddhism, i.e. in the *Abhidharmakośa*, *āpo-dhātu* is defined in a similar manner. It stands for *dravatva* (liquidity) and *snehatva* (viscidity) in material things[16]. The Vaiśeṣika school also accepts '*ap*' substance with the same two characteristics as: '*rūpa-rasa-sparśa-vatya āpo dravāḥ snigdhaḥ*'[17]. But according to the Vaiśeṣikas liquidity and viscidity are qualities inherent in the '*ap*' substance. No such dichotomy is recognized by the Buddhists.

However, cohesion is that which diffuses itself throughout its co-existent qualities or that which increases the bulk of them.[18] Thus, although fluidity (*paggharaṇa*) is its distinctive characteristic, yet cohesion is its particular function. It is interesting to note that this quality of cohesion is not perceptible to the sense of touch or sense contact, for it is an entirely 'internal' quality which does not exert its energy in a way which can be apprehended by the sense organs.

Tejo-dhātu (fire element):

The word *tejas* (*tejo*) is derived from the root *tija-niśāne-* 'to be sharp' (cf. Greek *stigma*, Latin *in-stig-are*, English sting, German *stechen*, etc.). In Sanskrit, starting from Vedic times, *tejas* first expressed the meaning of a sharp ray of light, point of a flame and then fire and light. In Buddhism also *tejo-dhātu* signifies the phenomenon of heat, the term being used is *usmā* or *usumā*.[19] *Tejo* (*tejas*) is the essential material quality of thermal energy or temperature in its various aspects and degrees of cold (*sita-tejo*) and heat (*usma-tejo*). This, too, is a primary quality inherent in all matter. Both *paṭhavī* and *āpo* are essentially affected by changes in temperature; for heat can expand and even melt solids, while liquids are congealed by cold; evaporation and condensation are produced by changes in temperature and variations of caloricity.

It was only in the Nineteenth Century that Science found it possible to agree with Buddhism, when it was discovered that temperature was due to motion: the kinetic theory. *Tejas*, then, is that essential material quality which gives 'life' to matter, without which the other primary qualities could not function. It stands for the maturation of diseased matter, for digestion and assimilation of food (*paripācana*)[20], for evolution as well as involution. For this is the element which heats, matures, sharpens and imparts heat to all other material elements.

Vāyo-dhātu (air element):

The word *vāyu* (*vāyo*) is derived from the root *vā-* 'to blow', 'to move', etc.

The meaning of this word is also known as motion, vibration, oscillation and pressure. It is a material energy to keep the things in a particular position by generating pressure all around. It is defined as the air (*vāyu*), that which belongs to air (*vāyogatam*), fluctuation; and the inflation of form (*thambhitattaṁ rūpassa*[21]). The standard term used in the Pāli commentarial works to describe the *vāyo-dhātu* is '*samudīraṇa*', which means mobility or motion.[22] There is general agreement among the scholiasts that *vāyo-dhātu* is representative of mobility or motion (*īraṇa, samudīraṇa*).

This (air-element) is not to be understood merely as the movement of air, or of an object in space, but far more as the continuous adjustment between the two opposite forces of extension (earth), which repels and cohesion (*ap*) which attracts. This oscillation between attraction and repulsion causes a natural friction which is the generator of heat. Thus *vāyu* is as much a condition for the arising of *tejas*, as *tejas* is a condition for the origination of movement. It is through vibration that extension is felt as pressure; through vibration also cohesion becomes magnetic and centripetal. In a way, vibration is the most important of the four great elements as it is mainly through this essential quality that matter is known to us.

The general position assigned to the elements may now be examined If some one will examine how the elements are interpreted in other systems of Indian Philosophy one would notice that in Buddhist thought they are assigned a comparatively primary position. What the Sāṁkhya considers as elements are not the ultimate irreducible constituents of matter, for they are evolved immediately from the *tanmātras* and ultimately from the Prakṛti. According to the Vedāntins the elements are produced from the *sūkṣma-bhūtas*. For the Jains the ultimate constituents of *puggala* (matter) are not four elements (*dhātu-catukka)* but the homogeneous atoms. The latter are recognized as the essential causes of the former.[23] The Nyāya-Vaiśeṣikas postulate four kinds of atoms corresponding to the four elemental substances, viz. *pṛthivī, ap, tejas* and *vāyu*. This may be described as an attempt to reconcile the older theory of the elements with the later atomic theory.

In Buddhism, unlike in many other systems of Indian thought, the elements (*mahābhūtas*) are assigned a primary position in the sense that they are recognized as the ultimate irreducible data of matter. It is of course true that a given instance of matter consists of not only the four elements but also a set of *upadā-rūpas*, such as colour, smell, etc. But these so called *upadā-rūpas*, as conceived by the Buddhists, are always depended on, therefore secondary to the elements.

The Buddhist concept of *bhūtas* (atoms) may be compared with the atoms of ancient system of Greek Philosophy, Leibnitz's Philosophy of spiritual atomism and logical atomism of Vaiśeṣika Philosophy with the physical properties of modern science. The Buddhist conception of the atoms lying always in group seems to remove an ancient difficulty of Nyāya-Vaiśeṣika idea about a combination of two atoms (*dvyaṇuka*) and perceptible manifestation of the combination of three atoms (*trasareṇu*). Thus, these thinkers take recourse to *ārambhavāda* (theory of new origin) and *īśvara kāraṇatā-vāda* (theory of causal agency of God) in order to explain that combination. These two ideas on the other hand are criticized by the Buddhist thinkers. Buddhists view seems to be more rational when they hold that the atoms always are found together. Unlike the Monads of Leibnitz, the atoms, according to Buddhists, are not spiritual but physical. These atoms again are momentary and dynamic. This idea, however, is not generally found in Greek school of atomism; evidently, a scientific approach is seen here and the approach is very close to that of in modern Physics. These atoms in their composite state are subject to change from moment to moment.

Thus, although the modern conception of Physics, like field of forces, seat of energy, or dynamism or space time units are not clearly found in Buddhist thought, it is evident that these ancient Buddhist thinkers grasped the correct nature of the universe as multiversity, evanescent and changing at every moment. Though appearing as a continuous and a single one, the universe is a composition of momentary units just flowing on. These, abstract and hypothetical units whether they are thought as *dharmas* or atoms are only comparable with the views of modern scientists like John Eddington or Sir James Jeans.

From the foregoing description of the four primary elements it would appear that *pṛthivī* stands for solidity, heaviness and extension, *ap* for viscidity and cohesion, *tejas* for the temperature of cold and heat and *vāyu* for motion. These four elements are coordinate and represent four distinct forces or phenomena in the realm of matter. Besides, another fundamental feature of these elements is that they always remain together (*sahajāta*). No element can exist independently of the other three.[24]

Modern Scientific concept of material elements was latent, since the very out set of creation. Hence, in Buddhism the basic four material elements are discussed from the scientific outlook. In the Science three forms of matter exist-solid, liquid and gas. Solid is compared with earth element as it has mass (weight or heaviness), which also occupies space. Water element is a liquid form of matter, whereas heat (*tejas*) and air (*vāyu*) are considered as gaseous form of matter. This way, the basic material elements are analyzed in Buddhist thought bearing the idea of Modern Science.

REFERENCES

1. *Dhammasaṅgaṇi*, pp. 124-179.
2. *Saṁyutta Nikāya*, III.86.
3. *Abhidharmakośa Bhāṣya*, I.13.
4. *ibid.*, II.22.
5. *ibid.*, I.13.
6. *The Central Conception of Buddhism*, Ch. IV, p 14.
7. तत्थ भूतरूपं चतुब्बिधं - पथवीधातु, आपोधातु, तेजोधातु, वायोधातू ति। विसुद्धिमग्ग, निद्येस 14.35;

(cf. *bhūtāni pṛthivīdhāturaptejovāyudhātavaḥ—Abhidharmakośa*, I.12).

8. *saṁcitā daśarūpiṇaḥ—Abhidharmakośa*, I.35 (comm.) and *na vai paramāṇurūpamekaṁ pṛthagbhūtamasti*, *ibid.*, I.13.
9. Sāmaññaphala Sutta of the *Dīgha Nikāya*, I.76 (*cātumahābhūtiko*); Ānanda Vagga's fifth sutta of the *Aṅguttara Nikāya*, I.222; Upādāna parivaṭṭa Sutta of the *Saṁyutta Nikāya*, III.56, Saṅkha Sutta of the *Majjhima Nikāya*, I.185, etc. (*cattāro mahābhūta - paṭhavī-dhātu, āpo-dhātu, tejo-dhātu, vāyo-dhātu*).
10. *pātali-simbali-jambu, devānaṁ pāricchattako /*
 kadambo kapparukkhoca, sirisena bhavati sattamo// *Aṭṭhasālinī*, 242.
11. *Majjhima Nikāya,* Mahāhatthipadopama Sutta (I.185).
12. *Dhammasaṅgaṇi*, p. 177; cf. *Vibhaṅga Pāli*, p. 82 (P.T.S.).
13. *tattha paṭhamaṁ lakkhaṇa-vacanaṁ dutiyam ākāra-vacanam—Visuddhimagga*, p. 286 (P.T.S.).
14. *yato ca bhikṣavaste satvā taṁ pṛthivīrasamālopakāra - kamāhāram - ihārensuḥ atha teṣāṁ kāye gurutvaṁ ca kharatvaṁ ca kakkhaṭatvaṁ ca upanīpate—Mahāvastu,* I.339 (P.T.S.).
15. *Dhammasaṅgaṇi*, p. 226; *Vibhaṅga Pāli*, p. 83 (P.T.S.).
16. *Abhidharmakośa,* (comm.) I.
17. *Vaiśeṣika Sūtra*, II.1.2.
18. *āpeti sahajātarūpāṇi pattharati; appāyati vā brūheti vaḍḍhetīti āpo— Abhidhammāttha-vibhāvani*, p. 167.
19. *Dhammasaṅgaṇi*, p. 177; *Vibhaṅga Pāli*, p. 83 (*usmā usmārtataṁ usumaṁ usumāgatam ṛajjhattika tejodhātu*).
20. *Aṭṭhasālinī*, p.332.
21. *Vibhaṅga Pāli*, p. 84 (3.1.5).
22. *Aṭṭhasālinī*, p. 332; cf. *samudīraṇā vāyudhātu—Abhidharmakośa Bhāṣya* (Sphuṭārthā), II.22.
23. Cf. *adeśamattamutto dhātucatukkassa kāraṇaṁ jo du—so neo paramāṇo pariṇāmaguṇo sayamasaddo—Pañcāstikāyasāra*, p. 28.
24. *Abhidharmakośa*, Ch. II, p. 248.

Concept of *Indriya* in Buddhism

'Indriya' is one of the most comprehensive and significant categories of Buddhist (Pāli) psychological philosophy and ethics. The term *'indriya'* (neuter) is derived from the root *idi-* or *ind-*, meaning to be powerful (*idi paramaiśvarye*[1]), with the suffixes *rak* and *ghac (iya)*[2]. It is also derived from the root *indh-inddhe, indhāṁ-cakre* or *īdhe indhiṣyate, aindhiṣṭa, indhitum*[3], meaning to kindle, light and set on fire.[4]

In the *Aṣṭādhyāyī* the word *'indriya'* is defined as : "*indriyamindriyaliṅgam-indradṛṣṭam-indradṛṣṭam-indrajuṣṭam-indradattam iti vā.*"[5] It means the expression *indriya* is introduced to denote the following senses : (a) means (*liṅgam*) by which the Self is inferred (*indra*); (b) perceived by the Self (*indradṛṣṭam*); (c) created by the Self (*sṛṣṭam*); (d) nourished by Self (*juṣṭam*); or (e) given by the Self (*dattam*).

In the *Amarakośa*[6] there are three synonyms of the term *indriya*—"*hṛṣīkaṁ viṣayindriyam.*"[7]

The word *'indriya'* is noted several times in the Saṁhitās. The Vedic *'indriya'* (adj.) only in meaning 'belonging to Indra'—strength, might, but in specific Pāli sense "belonging to the ruler', i.e. governing, ruling or controlling principle.

In the *Abhidharma Kośa*, "*kaḥ punarindriyārthaḥ, idi paramaiśvarye tasya indantīti indriyāṇi, ataḥ ādhipatyārtha indriyārthaḥ*"[8]—means the root *idi-* signifies *'paramaiśvarya'* or supreme authority. Whatever exercises, the supreme power or authority is called *indriya*. Hence, in (Pāli) Buddhism, *indriya* which is translated as 'faculty'[9], meaning: (i) controlling principle, directive force, elan, in the perceptibility "faculty function", often wrongly interpreted, as 'organ'; (ii) with reference to objective aspects of form and matter "kind, characteristic, determinating principle, sign, mark" (cf. woman-hood; hood=gothic, *haidus* 'kind', form; (iii) with reference to moods of sensation and; (iv) to moral powers or motives controlling action, 'principle, controlling force'; (v) with reference to cognition and insight 'catergory'.[10]

So, the meaning of the term *indriya* is faculty or a special control over a special field. Each faculty, e.g. indicates an entry into a speical field constituted by various forces. Thus, each *indriya* is a faculty or a special power by which a particular field of conditions may be mastered

Classifications and Groups of Faculties:

There are twenty-two[11] *indriyas* or the faculties. These 22 controlling faculties[12] are:

(1) the faculty of eye, (2) the faculty of ear, (3) the faculty of nose, (4) the faculty of tongue, (5) the faculty of body, (6) the faculty of mind, (7) the faculty of famininity (womanhood), (8) the faculty of masculinity (manhood), (9) the faculty of life (vitality or vital/principle), (10) the faculty of pleasure (physical or bodily), (11) the faculty of pain (physical), (12) the faculty of joy (mental pleasure or mental gladness), (13) the faculty of grief (mental pain), (14) the faculty of equanimity (neutral feeling or indifference), (15) the faculty of faith (confidence), (16) the faculty of energy, (17) the faculty of mindfulness, (18) the faculty of concentration, (19) the faculty of wisdom (insight), (20) the faculty of initial enligtenment (come to know the unknown), (21) the faculty of intermediate enlightenment (gnosis), (22) the faculty of final enlightenment (final knower faculty). These are called the twenty-two controlling faculties (*indriyas*).

Out of these twenty-two *indriyas* listed above, may be detached into the several groups. 1-5 *indriyas* are the sense organs. The Nos. 7-8 *indriyas* are collectively called *bhāvindriya. Jīvindriya* (9) is both physical and mental. Nos. 10, 11, 12, 13 and 14 (*indriyas*) represent five kinds of feelings. 15, 16, 17, 18 and 19 (*indriyas*) are treated both *indriya* and *bala* (power), as they influence their co-adjuncts and as they overcome their opposing forces. The last three faculties (Nos. 20, 21 and 22) are very important and they pertain supramundane.

A DETAIL DISCUSSION ON THE FACULTIES:

1. *Cakkhuindriyam* (Faculty of Eye)

Eye is one of the twenty-two divisions of *indriya* and also one of the six sense-organs. The eye's characteristic is sensitivity of primary elements that is ready for the impact of visible data; or its characteristic is sensitivity of primary elements originated by *kamma (karma)* sourcing from desire to see. Its function is to pick up an object from visible data. It is manifested as the footing of eye consciousness. Its proximate cause is primary elements born of *karma* sourcing from desire to see.[13] This is called the controlling faculty of eye.

2. *Sotindriyam* (Faculty of Ear)

Ear is the second sensitive organ. Its characteristic is sensitivity of primary elements that is ready for the impact of sounds; or its characteristic is sensitivity of primary elements. Originated by *karma* sourcing from desire to hear, its function is to pick up (an object) among sounds. It is manifested as the footing of ear-consciousness. Its proximate cause is primary elements born of *karma* sourcing from desire to hear. This is called the controlling faculty of ear.[14]

3. *Ghānindriyam* (Faculty of Nose)

The nose's characteristic is sensitivity of primary elements that is ready for the impact of odours; or its characteristic is sensitivity of primary elements originated by *karma* sourcing from desire to smell. Its function is to pick up (an object) among odours. It is manifested as the footing of nose-consciousness. Its proximate cause is primary elements born of *karma* sourcing from desire to smell. This is called the controlling faculty of nose.[15]

4. *Jihvindriyam* (Faculty of Tongue)

Tongue is the third sensitive organ. Its characteristic is sensitivity of primary elements that is ready for the impact of flavours; or its characteristic is sensitivity of primary elements originated by *karma* sourcing from desire to taste. Its function is to pick up (an object) among flavours. It is manifested as the footing of tongue-consciousness. Its proximate cause is primary elements born of *karma* sourcing from desire to taste. This is called the controlling faculty of tongue.[16]

5. *Kāyindriyam* (Faculty of Body)

Body is one of the twenty-two divisions of faculty. It is also one of the 28 kinds of *rūpa*. The body's characteristic is sensitivity of primary elements that is ready for the impact of tangible data; or its characteristic is sensitivity of primary elements originated by *karma* sourcing from desire to touch. Its function is to pick up (an object) among tangible data. It is manifested as the footing of body-consciousness. Its proximate cause is primary elements born of *karma* sourcing from desire to touch. This is called the controlling faculty of body.[17]

6. *Manidriyam* (Faculty of Mind)

The aggregate of feeling, aggregate of perception, aggregate of mental concomitants, are called mind or the function of mind. The controlling faculty of mind is associated with contact. It is by the way of ten-fold division : eye consciousness ; body consciousness which is accompanied by pleasure, and pain, etc. Thus is controlling faculty of mind by way of tenfold division, and it may be of manifold division. This is called the controlling faculty of mind.[18]

7. *Itthindriyam* (Faculty of Femininity)

The femininity faculty has the female sex due to its characteristic. Its function is to show that 'this is a female'. It is manifested as the reason for the mark, sign, work and ways of the female.[19] If a man deports himself like a woman, it is said of him that; he goes like a woman.[20]

8. *Purisindriyam* (Faculty of Masculinity)

The masculinity faculty has the male sex due to its characteristic. Its function is to show that this is a 'male'. It is manifested as the reason for the mark, sign, work, and the ways of the male.[21]

If a woman has male characteristics, she is said to 'go like a man'.[22]

Vasubandhu explains[23] why these two, viz. *strīndriya* and *puruṣendriya* are separately categorised He says there are two separate sexual organs within the *kāyendriya,* or the organ of touch. These two organs are not distinct from the *kāyendriya :* they too congnize tangible things. But there is a part of the *kāyendriya* that receives the name of the male organ or female organ, because this part exercises predominance over masculinity or femininity is the physical form, the voice, the hearing, and the dispositions proper to women. The same for masculinity. Since the differences of these natures are due to these parts of the body, these two parts are predominant through their two natures. Hence, they constitute *indriyas.*

9. *Jīvitindriyam* (Faculty of Life)

The life faculty has the characteristic of maintaining conascent kinds of matter. Its function is to make them occur. It is manifested in the establishing of their presence. Its proximate cause is primary elements that are to be sustained And although it has the capacity, consisting in the characteristics of maintaining etc., yet it only maintains conascent kinds of matter at the moment of presence, as water does lotuses and so on.

Controlling faculty of life is of twofold division: (a) controlling faculty of material vital principle, (b) controlling faculty of non-material vital principle.[24]

10. *Sukhindriyam* (Faculty of Pleasure[25])

The controlling faculty of 'physical pleasure' is that which is bodily ease; bodily pleasure; pleasant experience born of bodily contact; easeful pleasant feeling born of bodily contact. This is called controlling faculty of pleasure.

11. *Dukkhindriyam* (Faculty of Pain[26])

The controlling faculty of 'physical pain' is that which is bodily uneasiness, bodily pain; uneasy painful experience born of bodily contact, uneasy painful feeling born of bodily contact. This is called controlling faculty of pain.

12. *Somanassindriyam* (Faculty of Mental Pleasure)

The controlling faculty of 'mental pleasure' is that which is mental ease, mental pleasure, easeful pleasant experience born of mental contact, easeful pleasant feeling born of mental contact. This is called controlling faculty of mental pleasure.

13. *Domanassindriyam* (Faculty of Mental Pain)

The controlling faculty of 'mental pain' or agony is that which is mental uneasiness, mental pain, uneasy painful experience born of mental contact, uneasy painful feeling born of mental contact. This is called controlling faculty of mental pain or grief.

14. *Upekkhindriyam* (Faculty of Equanimity)

The faculty of equanimity or indifference[27] is that which is neither mental ease nor uneasiness, neither painful nor pleasant experience born of mental contact, neither painful nor pleasant feeling born of mental contact. This is called controlling faculty of indifference or equanimity or neutral feeling.

15. *Saddhindriyam* (Faculty of Faith or Confidence)[28]

The controlling faculty of faith or confidence is that which is confidence, being confident, trust, implicit faith, controlling faculty of confidence is the power of confidence. This is called controlling faculty of faith or confidence.

16. *Viriyindriyam* (Faculty of Energy)[29]

The controlling faculty of energy is that which is the arousing of mental energy or mental *śakti*, toiling, endeavour, aspiring, effort, zeal, perseverence, vigour, stability, unfaltering endeavour, not relinquishing wish, not relinquishing the task, firm hold of the task, controlling faculty of energy, power of energy. This is called controlling faculty of energy.

17. *Satindriyam* (Faculty of Mindfulness)[30]

The controlling faculty of mindfulness is that which is constant mindfulness, recollection, attentiveness, act of remembering, bearing in mind, non-superficiality, non-forgetfulness power of mindfulness or heedfulness. This is called controlling faculty of mindfulness.

18. *Samādhindriyam* (Faculty of Concentration)[31]

The faculty of concentration is that which has stability, steadfastness, firmness of consciousness, non-distraction, non-wavering; mental imperturbability, calmness, controlling faculty of concentration, power of concentration and right concentration. This is called the faculty of concentration.

19. *Paññindriyam* (Faculty of Wisdom)[32]

The controlling faculty of wisdom (*jñānendriya*) is that which is (based on) understanding, investigation, research, truth investigation, discernment, discrimination, erudition, proficiency, subtlety, analysis, guidance, insight, awareness, right view and absence of dullness. This is called the faculty of wisdom.

20. *Anaññātaññassamītindriyam* (Faculty of Initial Enlightenment)[33]

The faculty of initial enlightenment or will-to-know what is unknown is that which for the realization of these states that are not known, not comprehended, not attained, not discerned, not realized, real identification of the thing through knowledge, understanding, and absence of dullness, truth investigation, right view, path constituent, included in the path. This is called the controlling faculty of initial enlightenment of the truth.

21. *Aññindriyam* (Faculty of Intermediate Enlightenment)[34]

The faculty of intermediate enlightenment is that which for the realization of those states that are known, comprehended, attained, discerned, realized, is wisdom, understanding, and absence of dullness, truth investigation, right view, path constituent, included in the path. This is called controlling faculty of intermediate enlightenment, i.e. one step before the final realization.

22. *Aññātāvindriyam* (Faculty of Final Enlightenment)[35]

The faculty of final enlightenment is that which for the realization of those states that are known fully, comprehended, attained, discerned, realized, is wisdom, understanding. It is the stage of attainment of the final realization of the truth, i.e. *Nirvāṇa*.

The last three faculties (Nos 20, 21 and 22) are very important and they pertain to the state of supramundane.

How these controlling faculties are rulers? By actions ; sense action, bodily action, mental action; the individual *kamma* (action or performance) is produced at every stage, constantly and with cessation. Sometimes, the *kamma* is weak, sometimes strong, according to the nature of craving (*taṇhā*). The controlling faculties which are in a sense show these infinite *kammas* as sorted out into particular groupings, exercise their direct control on the senses and on purely mental states by virtue of the relative strengths and interactions between the originated actions (*kammas*). Thus, if at a certain instant the controlling faculty of eye is weak, then the eye is not quick to see, it shows no keenness. If the controlling faculty at a given instant is strong, the eye is keen and quick to see the objects. So also with the other controlling faculties. If the resultant condition of a particular state is weak, then this *kamma* shows itself in the tendency of weakness in future activity of a related pattern; if the resultant is strong the tendency is to strengthen the appropriate controlling faculty.

Conclusion

Now, in short we will go through the various divisions of *indriyas* (faculties) and its impact in life. The first six faculties represent the six sense organs, which are predominant in their respective spheres. They refer to what is known as internal 'self-hood'. Famininity and masculinity indicate the two faculties with reference to which the distinction between the two sexes is made. The two faculties are also dependent on the life-faculty which comes next. The five faculties—bodily pleasure, bodily pain, joy, grief and equanimity represent the feelings that a living being experiences in course of his journey through the universe (*saṁsāra*). These experiences, in the widest sense, can be interpreted as suffering *(duḥkha)*. The next five ethical faculties—faith, energy, mindfulness, concentration and wisdom—lead to the cessation of suffering. The following are the last three faculties; the faculty that 'I shall realize what is not yet realized' (*anaññātaññassāmītindriyam'*) the faculty of partial realization (*aññindriyam*), and the faculty of final realization (*aññātāvindriyam*). Among them the first faculty is related to the first path stage, the second is related to the next path and fruition stages, and the third is related to the last fruition stage. Thus, the last three faculties belong to the supramundane state. It is clear from the short account given above that out of 22 faculties some give rise to the process of *saṁsāra* and others bring about cessation of the same, i.e. lead towards the emancipation.

However, (Buddhist) *indriyas* (faculties) play a very important role in the way of human life.

REFERENCES

1. *Pāṇinīya-Dhātupāṭha,* I.64.
   Cf. *indatervaiśvaryakarmaṇaḥ, Nirukta,* X.8. Also cf. *Mādhavīyā-Dhātuvṛtti,* (53), p. 74.
2. *Aṣṭādhyāyī,* VI.1.2.
3. (i) *Ṛgveda*, V.3.1.
   (ii) *Atharvaveda,* XIX.55.3-4.
4. *Pāṇinīya-Dhātupāṭha,* VIII.11; *Nirukta,* X.8.
5. V.2.93.
6. *trīṇi indriyāṇām—Amarakośa,* I.5.8.
7. *viṣayī viṣayāsakte....,—Medinī-kośa,* XX.108.
8. *Abhidharma-kośa,* II.1.
   Cf. *indanti paramissariyaṁ karontīti indriyāṇi—Aṭṭhasālinī,* p. 99.
   Cf. *adhipatyāṭṭhena indriyam, paggahanalakkhaṇe vā kāretīti indriyam—Aṭṭhasālinī,* 3.217.
   Also cf. *aiśvaryārtho vipaścidbhirindriyārtho' abhidhīyate, Abhidharmadīpakārikā,* 76ab, cf. *Visuddhimagga,* 16.6, etc.
9. (a) *Dhammasaṅgaṇipāli,* Introduction, p. xxxi (Bihar Govt. Pali Pub. Board, 1960 edition).
   (b) *Pāli-English Dictionary,* Rhys Davids, p. 121.
   (c) *Visuddhimagga,* English translation by Bhikkhu Ñyāṇamoli, P.T.S., vol II, Ch. 16, p. 559.
10. *Pāli-English Dictionary,* Rhys Davids, p. 121.
11. *indriyāṇi ti bāvīsati indriyāṇi, Visuddhimagga*, 16.1
    Cf. *dvāviṁsatimindriyāṇyadhikṛtyādhipativyavasthānaṃ veditavyam: Abhidharmasamuccaya Bhāṣyam,* p. 42, cf. *bāvīsati indriyāṇi? Vibhaṅga Pāli,* p. 122. Also cf. *Pāli English Dictionary,* Rhys Davids, pp. 121-122.
12. 1. *Cakkhunidriyam,* 2. *sotindriyam,* 3. *ghānindriyam,* 4. *jivhindriyam,* 5. *kāyindriyam,* 6. *manindriyam,* 7. *itthindriyam,* 8. *purisindriyam,* 9. *jīvitindriyam,* 10. *sukhindriyam,* 11. *dukhindriyam,* 12. *somanassindriyam,* 13. *domanassindriyam,* 14. *upekkhindriyam,* 15. *saddhindriyam,* 16. *viriyindriyam,* 17. *satindriyam,* 18. *samādhindriyam,* 19. *paññindriyam,* 20. *anaññātaññassamītindriyam,* 21. *aññindriyam* and, 22. *aññātāvindriyam.*
13. *Visuddhimagga,* 14.37, cf. *Vibhaṅga Pāli*, 1.5, p. 156; Also cf. *Abhidharma Kośa,* pp. 135-40.

14. *Visuddhimagga,* 14.38; cf. *Vibnaṅga Pāli,* 1.5, p. 156, also cf. *Abhidharmasamuccaya-Bhāṣyam, Samuccaya,* 1, p. 42; also cf. *Abhidharma-Kośa*, pp. 135-40.
15. *Visuddhimagga,* 14.39; cf. *Abhidharma-Kośa,* pp. 135-40, cf. *Abhidharma-samuccaya-Bhāṣyam, Samuccaya,* 1, p. 42, also cf. *Vibhaṅga Pāli,* 1.5, p. 156.
16. *Visuddhimagga,* 14.40, cf. *Vibhaṅga Pāli,* 1.5, p. 156, cf. *Abhidharma-Kośa,* p. 135-40, also cf. *Abhidharmasamuccaya, Samuccaya,* 1, p. 42.
17. *Visuddhimagga,* 14.41; cf. *Abhidharma-Kośa,* pp. 135-40, also cf. *Vibhaṅga Pāli,* 1.5, p.156.
18. *Vibhaṅga Pāli,* 1.5.4, pp. 156-57.
19. *Vibhaṅga Pāli,* I.5.5, p. 157, cf. *Visuddhimagga,* 14.58. Also cf. *Abhidharma-samuccaya-Bhāṣya, Samuccaya,* 1, p. 43.
20. *Dhammasaṅgaṇi,* p. 173.
21. *Vibhaṅga Pāli,* 1.5.6, p. 157; cf. *Visuddhimagga,* 14.58, cf. *Aṭṭhasālinī,* 4.61-65. Also cf. *Abhidharma-Kośa,* II.2.
22. *Dhammasaṅgaṇi,* p. 173.
23. *"Kāyendriyādeva strīpuruṣendriye pṛthak vyavasthāpyete... puṁsaḥ puṁstvam"— Abhidharmakośa-Bhāṣya*, II. 2cd.
24. *Vibhaṅga Pāli,* 1.5.7, pp. 157-58.
25. *(śātā sukham)/sukhendriyaṁ kāyikī śātā vedanā ; sātetyanugrāhikā sukhetyarthaḥ —Abhidharmakośa-Bhāṣya,* II.7bc.
26. *duḥkhendriyamaśātā yā kāyikī vedanā, Abhidharma-Kośa,* II. 7ab.
27. Vide, *Pāli English Dictionary,* Rhys Davids, p. 121.
28. *Vibhaṅga Pāli,* 1.5.13, p. 158.
29. *ibid.,* 1.5.14, p. 158.
30. *ibid.,* 1.5.15, p. 159.
31. *ibid.,* 1.5.16, p. 159.
32. *ibid.,* 1.5.17, p. 159.
33. *ibid.,* 1.5.18, p. 159.
34. *ibid.,* 1.5.19, p. 159.
35. *ibid.,* 1.5.20, p. 159.

Concept of *Bhūmi* in the Buddhist Literature with special reference to the *Daśabhūmika Sūtra*

The term '*bhūmi*' is derived from the root *bhū-* '*to be*', with the *uṇādi* suffix *mi* (by the *uṇādi* rule (IV.45) *bhūvaḥ kit*). Cf. Greek *phuśis*, Sanskrit *bhavati*. Rāyamukuṭa, a commentator of the *Amara Kośa* (II.12) has given the derivation of the same as: *bhuvaḥ kmin (bhū-+kmin)*. According to Hemacandra, *bhūmi* is explained as: *bhūmiḥ kṣītau sthānamātre.*[1] It is used to denote soil, earth, place (in general), ground, level, stage and state of consciousness, in Vedic and Sanskrit literature.

In the Buddhist literature *bhūmi* has also several meanings, including ground, plane, stage, level and state of consciousness.[2] In a metaphorical sense, it is employed in a general way to denote 'range', 'state', 'sphere', 'condition', 'function', etc.

In the *Abhidharma Kośa Bhāṣya*, the term *bhūmi* is used to denote 'the place of origin' (i.e., the place of origin of a *dharma* is the *bhūmi* of this *dharma*).[3] The author Vasubandhu has mentioned both the terms *mahābhūmi* and *mahābhūmika*. The *mahābhūmi* (great sphere) is so called because it is the sphere, the place of origin, of great *dharmas* (i.e., of *dharmas* of great extension, that are found everywhere). The *dharmas*, inherent in the *mahābhūmi* are called *mahābhūmika*, i.e. the *dharmas* which are always found in all minds.[4] Buddhaghosa in his commentary on the *Dīgha Nikāya* (I.54), explains the term *bhūmi* as: 'eight stations of people' (*aṭṭha puriso-bhūmiyo*), viz., *manda-bhūmi, khiḍḍā-bhūmi vīmaṅsana-bhūmi, ujugata-bhūmi, sekha-bhūmi, jina-bhūmi* and *pañña-bhūmi*. These are the stages of a person's life, from birth till the perfect stage of renunciation and mental equilibrium. In the *Dhammasaṅgaṇi, bhūmi* is synonymous with *magga* (path).[5] The *Visuddhimagga* (IV.9.3) uses *bhūmi* in word like *kāmāvacarabhūmi*, in the sense of plane.

The *Mahāvastu* (I, p.77), defines *bhūmi* by saying that every existence of the Bodhisattvas is shortly defined as an earth, whence has arisen the name *bhūmi*. As a matter of fact these *bhūmis* are the various stages of development of the attributes of a Bodhisattva towards which he progressively advances. He gradually ascends from one stage to the next, up to the last or the tenth stage. But the *Mahāyānasūtrālaṅkāra* states that the *bhūmis* are so called because beings enter into higher and higher immeasurable stages repeatedly. They are also known as *bhūmis*, as they deliver infinite beings from fear.[6] The *bhūmis* are also termed 'states (*vihāra*)' due to their manifold right aspirations.[7]

Though *bhūmis* are mentioned in the Buddhist Tantras[8] places of pilgrimage (*pīṭha*, etc.), they are identified with the stages of spiritual progress. Hence, a Bodhisattva is called 'Lord of the ten stages', *daśabhūmiśvara*.

In the *Yoga Sūtra* (II.27), *bhūmi* means stages of meditation: **तस्य सप्तधा प्रान्तभूमिः प्रज्ञा.** It means, his (*yogi's*) intellective vision possessed of 'final ground'[9] is seven-fold. Besides, it mentions[10] *dṛḍha-bhūmi, prānta-bhūmi,* etc.

Hence, *bhūmi* has become a philosophical term, meaning 'stage' or career, i.e. stages of spiritual progress for the attainment of perfect knowledge.

The concept of *bhūmi* goes back to a very early period in the history of Buddhist thought. Because the idea of establishing, 'stages' on the spiritual pilgrim's long journey occurred early to the Buddhist thinkers. The Hīnayānists developed the doctrine of the four stages, i.e., Hīnayāna recognises four states of spiritual progress, viz., (a) *sotāpanna* (entering upon the stream), (b) *sakadāgāmi* (returning once), (c) *anāgāmī* (a never returner), and (d) *arhat* (the state of an *arhat*).

In Mahāyāna, there is also the important factor of *bhūmi* or stage in the spiritual progress of a Bodhisattva. In the Mahāyāna works the number of *bhūmi* varies from text to text. But most of the available Buddhist Sanskrit works mention ten *bhūmis*. There are at least four different schemes of divisions in the principal Buddhist Sanskrit texts. The earliest treatment of the subject is in the *Mahāvastu,* which refers ten *bhūmis*.[11] The *Śatasāhasrikā-Prajñāpāramitā*,[12] and the *Daśabhūmika Sūtra*[13] also describe ten *bhūmis* each in different ways. The *Bodhisattva Bhūmi* mentions seven *bhūmis*[14] and thirteen *vihāras*[15]. The *Laṅkāvatāra Sūtra*, the *Pañcaviṁsati-sāhasrikā-Prajñāpāramitā*, the *Mahāyānasūtrālaṅkāra* and the like are also discussed a bit on the *bhūmis*.

The standard *bhūmis* accepted by the Mahāyānists are those referred to in the *Daśabhūmika Sūtra*, which is the most systematic and authoritative work on the subject. It also goes under the name of *Daśabhūmika Śāstra, Daśabhūmīśvara* and the like. Ācārya Asaṅga in his *Daśabhūmi* has referred to it by the name of *Daśabhūmika*. It is remarkable evidence of its supreme authority and immense popularity that it has been translated into the Tibetan, Chinese, Japanese, Mangolian and other languages. The author of the *Daśabhūmika Sūtra* manages to place almost all the important concepts and categories of Buddhist Philosophy in his scheme of ten *bhūmis*. Thus, for example, he puts the four *saṅgraha-vastus* in the first four *bhūmis*, the four Noble Truths in the fifth *bhūmi,* and so on. But his system exhibits a certain unity of plan on account of the parallelism between the ten *pāramitās* and the ten *bhūmis*. A Bodhisattva especially cultivates one of the *pāramitās* in each *bhūmi*.

Although the *Mahāvastu* speaks of ten *bhūmis,* but its account is scanty and incoherent. It does not give details according to any plan, but *Daśabhūmika Sūtra* allots a *pāramitā* to each *bhūmi*. The *Mahāvastu* declares that a Bodhisattva may fall back into a lower *bhūmi* on account of certain faults, but the *Daśabhūmika Sūtra* never speaks of the possibility of retrogation and always discusses virtues instead of sins. The names of *bhūmis* found in the *Mahāvastu* are different, except for one[16], from those found in the *Daśabhūmika Sūtra*.

The *Śatasāhasrikā Prajñāpāramitā* too mentions ten *bhūmis* to which it does not assign any names and mentions the same virtues and sins again and again. Its description on the *bhūmis* is not quite systematic. Hence, it also fails to evolve an intelligible system. The *Mahāyānasūtrālaṅkāra* too mentions ten Bodhisattva *bhūmis,* but explains these within nine verses.[17] The names of *bhūmis* and *vihāras* mentioned in the *Bodhisattva Bhūmi* are too different from those in the *Daśabhūmika Sūtra*. According to Har Dayal, an eminent scholar, "the author of the *Daśabhūmika Sūtra* has constructed the framework of his system on the basis of ten *pāramitās*, but the *Bodhisattva Bhūmi* divides a Bodhisattva's career up to a certain point according to the ancient triple formula of *śīla, samādhi (citta)* and *prajñā*. The two writers have not the same point of view. It is true that the author of the *Bodhisattva Bhūmi* makes an unsuccessful attempt to identify some of his *vihāras* with the *bhūmis* of the *Daśabhūmika Sūtra* and cites some passages from that treatise. But the principles underlying the two systems remain divergent in all essential respects."[18]

In the conception of the *bhūmis* the *Mahāvastu* seems to be the earliest, the *Prajñāpāramitā* texts the middle, the *Daśabhūmika Sūtra* and the like, the latest.[19] As already said that the *Daśabhūmika Sūtra* is the most systematic and authentic work on the subject, elaborates ten *bhūmis* (stages), through which a Bodhisattva must pass before he attains perfection. Here is given a brief account of each *bhūmi* of the *Daśabhūmika Sūtra*.[20]

1. *Pramuditā Bhūmi* :

The first stage is named *pramuditā*[21], which means 'perfectly delightful.' A Bodhisattva enters this stage just after the production of the thought of enlightenment which annihilates all his previous sins. This *bhūmi* is called *pramuditā,* because supreme delight permeates this stage. As said in the *Daśabhūmika Sūtra* (I, p. 8), "प्रमुदितायां बोधिसत्त्वभूमौ स्थितो बोधिसत्त्वः प्रमुदितो भवति।" It means, when a Bodhisattva is steadily established in the stage called *pramuditā,* he becomes highly delighted

The Bodhisattva realizes that he is now above an ordinary being and is liberated from rebirth in purgatory or any other inferior form of existence. He becomes exempt from five fears, viz., the fear of loss of livelihood, of reproachful language, of death, of evil destiny, and of diffidence in assemblies.[22] A Bodhisattva who abides in this stage makes the following great *praṇidhānas*: to pay homage to all the Buddhas, to preserve the teachings of the good doctrine of all Buddhas, to approach the great

Nirvāṇa after accomplishing all the deeds to a Buddha, to render all the stages immaculate in order to produce thought, to bring spiritual maturity of all creatures, to make knowable the diversity of the world-system, to bring about the purification of all the lands of the Buddha, to cause to enter into the great vehicle, to practice all the courses of conduct of the Bodhisattvas and to achieve irresistibility of the state of all efforts, to accomplish perfect enlightenment, great knowledge and intuition.[23]

The Bodhisattva now manifests many distinctive qualities and attitudes, selflessness, compassion, patience, humility, the study of all sciences, courage, bearing with others and patience, equanimity and truth are also listed in this connection. He gives away wealth, wife and children and his own limbs and life. He takes the ten great vows by means of ten *niṣṭhāpadas*[24] (inexhaustible vows), viz., *sattvadhātu-niṣṭhāpada, lokadhātu-niṣṭhāpada, ākāśadhātu-niṣṭhāpada, dharmadhātu-niṣṭhāpada, nirvāṇadhātu-niṣṭhāpada, buddhotpādadhātu-niṣṭhāpada, tathāgatajñānadhātu-niṣṭhāpada, cittālambanadhātu-niṣṭhāpada, buddhaviṣayajñānapraveśadhātu-niṣṭhāpada, lokavartanī dharmavartanī jñānavartanīdhātu-niṣṭhāpada.*

In this *bhūmi* he practises the perfection of giving (*dāna-pāramitā*) with zeal and also cultivates the other perfections according to his capacity. He earnestly desires to become the first, formost and best of all beings. He sets his energy in motion in conformity with his aspirations. He keeps company with the virtuous and longs for knowledge. As a result of it, he renounces his worldly belongings and adopts the religious instruction of the Buddha as a wandering monk, experiences hundreds of *samādhis,* live for a hundred aeons, and performs innumerable miracles. The *Mahāyāna-sūtrālaṅkāra*[25] states that this *bhūmi* is so called because a Bodhisattva rejoices exceedingly as he perceives that he will soon attain enlightenment and promote the good of all beings. According to the *Mahāvastu* (I, p.71), a Bodhisattva in the first *bhūmi* is enjoyed to practice liberality (*tyāga*), compassion (*karuṇā*), indefatigability (*aparikkheda*), humility (*amāna*), study of all the scriptures, heroism (*vikrama*), asking for permission or approval of people (*lokānujñā*) and fortitute (*dhṛti*). The Bodhisattva, in this stage, conceives the idea of attainment of perfect wisdom by means of accumulation of merits, the roots of goodness.

2. *Vimalā Bhūmi:*

The second level of consciousness is named *Vimalā* (the state of purity). Those who are the sons of the knower should know that Bodhisattva who performed well in the first level of consciousness desires to ascend the next level of consciousness of Bodhisattva, where after reaching there his mental dispositions (*āśayas*) is of ten kinds, viz., *ṛju, mṛdu, karmaṇya, dama, śama, kalyāṇa, asaṁsṛṣṭa, anapekṣa, udāra* and *māhātmya.*In this stage, a Bodhisattva takes the vow to get rid of all impurities. He always avoids the unwholesome course of actions of body, speech and mind, viz., killing, stealing, unlawful intercourse, lying, slandering, harsh speech, covetousness, ill-will and wrong views; and persuades other to do so. He knows that these unwholesome actions lead to rebirth in purgatory, or in the world of brutes, ghosts or men, undergoing manifold miseries. He therefore, observes the wholesome course of actions in life and commands its observance to all others. He becomes their friend, guide, protector, teacher, and leads them to the path of righteousness. He pays his best attention to kindly speech, one of the ground of popularity (*saṁgrahavastu*). Moreover, the Bodhisattva attains the primacy of the quality of speaking in a loving manner (*priyavadyatā*) and moral perfection (*śīlapāramitā*) in this realm.[26]

The *Mahāyānasūtrālaṅkāra*[27] states that this *bhūmi* is so called because a Bodhisattva is free from the dirt of the immoral conduct as also of the other *yāna,* i.e., Hīnayāna. The *Mahāvastu* (I, p. 85.) explains—a Bodhisattva in the second state (*bhūmi*) develops an aversion to all forms of existence and that herein their dispositions are good, amiable, sweet, keen, bountiful, charming, profound, not losing control, imperturbable, extraordinary, lofty, noble, resolute, sincere, pure, steadfast, independent, contented, intent on the person and infinite. Their lapses in this stage are too related in this treatise and on account of these lapses the Bodhisattvas fail to reach the third stage.

3. *Prabhākarī Bhūmi:*

The next stage of a Bodhisattva is called *prabhākarī,* which means 'luminous'.[28] A Bodhisattva's thoughts now are pure, constant, unworldly, dispassionate, firm, ardent, noble and maganimous. He realizes that all compounded things are impermanent, transient and momentary. They are the sources of manifold sufferings. He again thinks of misery, sins and folly of the living beings, and again resolves to help, teach and liberate them. He devotes himself day and night to the study of the Scriptures and the teachings of the Buddha in order to gain perfect knowledge. He practises the four meditations (*dhyānas*), the four attainments (*samāpattis*), the four sublime states (*brahmavihāras*) and five kinds of higher knowledge (*abhijñās*). He is freed from the four *āsravas*. He also overcomes lust, malice and delusion. In this stage, he cultivates the perfection of patience (*kṣāntipāramitā*) to the greatest possible extent without neglecting the other perfections.

The *Mahāyānasūtrālaṅkāra*[29] explains that this *bhūmi* is so called because Bodhisattva diffuses the great light of the noble doctrine among the all beings. In the *Mahāvastu*[30] it is stated that a Bodhisattva in the third *bhūmi* pays special attention to *tyāga* (renunciation) and is prepared even to buy one verse containing a wise saying with the sacrifice of wives and children. He wants to make all beings happy and he does this not for his own well-being, not even for the sake of his own attainment of enlightenment.

4. *Arciṣmatī Bhūmi:*

The fourth *bhūmi* is called *arciṣmatī*. A Bodhisattva who is enkindled with the loftiest ambition of attaining Bodhisattvahood moves ahead and lands on the fourth stage that bears the designation of *arciṣamatī,* means 'radiant', 'brilliant' or 'effulgent'.[31]

A Bodhisattva practises here the ten virtues[32] with the mature knowledge. He also practises thirty-seven virtues[33] that pave the way for the attainment of enlightenment. They are liable to be set forth in the following order: i. the four applications of mindfulness (*smṛtyupasthāna*), ii. the four righteous exertions, iii. four constitutive elements of supernatural power (*ṛddhipādas*), iv. the five moral faculties (*indriyas*), v. the five corresponding powers (*bala*) bearing identical names, vi. the seven constitutive members of true enlightenment (*saṁbodhiaṅga*), vii. and the noble eight-fold path (*āryāṣṭāṅgikamārga*). With the attainment of these qualities his mind becomes very soft and compassionate. His doubts are all removed and his mental dispositions become pure. He renounces the world in the doctrine of the Tathāgata. He practises the perfection of vigour (*vīryapāramitā*) to the greatest possible extent without neglecting the other perfections. As the fourth *saṁgrahavastu* he specially cultivates the state of equality (*samānārthatā*).

According to the *Mahāyānasūtrālaṅkāra*[34], this *bhūmi* is so called because the rays of the *bodhipakṣadharmas* consume both the obstruction of suffering (*kleśāvaraṇa*) and the obstruction of knowledge (*jñeyāvaraṇa*). The *Mahāvastu* (I, pp.101-102) explains, in order to qualify themselves for attaining the fourth *bhūmi* the Bodhisattvas do not create schisms in the *saṅgha,* nor do they raise *stūpas* to the ground, nor harbour any evil thoughts against a Tathāgata.

5. *Sudurjayā Bhūmi:*

The fifth *bhumi* is named *sudurjayā,* which means invincible, i.e. difficult to conquer. A Bodhisattva regards all the principles of Buddhahood, past, present and future, with pure thought and equanimity. He thinks in the same way of conduct, meditation, doubt, speculation, knowledge of right way and the perfection of all beings. He comprehends the four noble truths. He becomes conversant and enlightened with different types of truth, viz., 1. *saṁvṛtti satya* (relative truth), 2. *paramārtha satya* (absolute truth), 3. *lakṣaṇa satya* (the truth of characteristics), 4. *vibhāga satya* (truth of division), 5. *nistīrṇa satya* (truth of origination), 6. *vastu satya* (truth of things and phenomena), 7. *prabhava satya* (truth of decay), 8. *kṣayānutpāda satya* (truth of non-production), 9. *mārgajñānāvatāra satya* (truth of initiation into the knowledge of the way), 10. *tathāgatajñāna satya* (truth of the appearance of Buddha knowledge) and the like.[35] He acquires a knowledge of *skandha, dhātu, āyatana,* etc., and knows different divisions of *dharma.* He feels great compassion for all the beings who undergo manifold suffering and resolves to save and liberate them. In this stage he sincerely acquires the qualities of mindfulness, fortitude, discretion, and skilfulness in the choice of the means for attaining his ends. He achieves mastery of the different branches of popular science and literature, like mathematics, medicine, art, drama, astrology, etc., which reveal the infallible ways that lead to the material welfare and happiness of all creatures. He specially practises the perfection of meditation (*dhyāna*) and cultivates all the elements of popularity (*saṁgrahavastus*) in this *bhūmi*.

According to the *Mahāyānasūtrālaṅkāra*[36], this *bhūmi* is so called because a Bodhisattva performs the arduous task of ripening beings as also guarding his own mind. In the *Mahāvastu* (I, pp. 130-141) it is stated that a Bodhisattva now realizes that all existence is consumed with the fire of lust, hatred and delusion, and that it is devoid of protection and happiness.

6. *Abhimukhī Bhūmi:*

A Bodhisattva enters into the next stage which is named *abhimukhī,* means 'face to face', 'being in front', or 'showing the face'. He specially cultivates the perfection of *prajñā* (wisdom) without lacking in respect for the other *pāramitās*. He treads on this realm by reflecting upon the ten varieties[37] of equality and sameness of nature of all things and phenomena. When a Bodhisattva looks upon all things in this way, he acquires the *kṣānti* called *ānulomakī*. But he is not spiritually prepared to reach the threshold of the receptivity that concerns itself with the fact that they (states of being) are bereft of production (*anutpattika-dharma-kṣānti*)[38]. When he realizes them in their true light, he reflects on the origination and destruction of beings with increased concentration. His mind becomes saturated with love and compassion for them. He understands the profound truth that all worldly activities and behaviours owe their existence to adherence to the heretical notion of the self as a real existent. And he finds access into the truth that the cessation of the latter entails the cessation of the former.[39] He comprehends the formula of dependent origination (*pratītya-samutpāda*)[40], which from the absolute standpoint, means non-origination at all times. He realizes that all sins and errors depend upon the mind. He is also freed from the conceptions of 'I' and 'other', 'doer' and 'feeler', 'existence' and 'non-existence'. He reverse all connections with the compounded elements and experiences many *samādhis,* which are related to the principle of emptiness. He is now perfectly pure and steady. His mind truns to knowledge of the Buddha resolutely.

According to the *Mahāyānasūtrālaṅkāra*[41], this *bhūmi* is so called because the Bodhisattva practising the perfection of wisdom (*prajñāpāramitā*), now stands face to face with both *saṁsāra* and *Nirvāṇa*. The *Mahāvastu* (I,pp. 142-150) states that a Bodhisattva now feels and knows that this 'whirlpool' of the world is very terrible and yields little joy and satisfaction. He cannot rise to the seventh *bhūmi* and abide in it, if he desires to attain the trance of the cessation-of-perception and feeling, or listens complacently to his own praises as a great man and a self-restrained saint.

7. *Dūraṅgamā Bhūmi:*

The seventh stage of a Bodhisattva is called *dūraṅgamā,* means which 'goes far' or 'far-reaching'. In this stage he is provided with intelligence, knowledge, and skill in devices conducive to the effectuation of ten beginnings of a new way.[42] And it is intended for spiritual emancipation of the mass of creatures. His mind reaches an ideal state of rarefication due to the ceaseless practice of three mystic contemplations, viz., *śūnyatā, ānimitta* and *apraṇihīta*. He acquires and aguments the quantum of merit and enlarges the frontiers of his knowledge as equipments for attaining the ultimate end of his life. He comprehends that all states of existence and the so-called things are devoid of ego and essence. He never forshakes the four *brahmavihāras,* viz., *maitrī, karuṇā, muditā* and *upekṣā*. The Bodhisattva ardently practises the ten *pāramitās*.[43] Besides, he practises the four elements of popularity (*saṁgrahavastas*) and resolution (*adhiṣṭhānas*), viz., *satya, tyāga, upaśama,* and *prajñā*; thirty-seven constituents of enlightenment; and three thresholds of spiritual liberation. He understands the thoughts of others and is pure in his thoughts, words and deeds. He transcends the lower wisdom of the Hīnayāna. He attains liberation, but does not realize personal *Nirvāṇa.* But under no circumstances he goes astray from the path of righteousness. In this stage he specially cultivates the perfection of *upāyakauśala* without neglecting the others.[44]

The *Mahāyānasūtrālaṅkāra*[45] states that this *bhūmi* is so called because it leads to the end of the only path, i.e. to the discipline. According to the *Mahāvastu* (I, pp. 161-164), a Bodhisattva practises self-control and through the thought of great compassion he advances from the seventh *bhūmi* to the eighth.

8. *Acalā Bhūmi:*

The Bodhisattva is approaching closer and closer to the ultimate goal of his life, i.e. liberation. He pursues his spiritual career and ascends the eighth stage. This stage is named *acalā,* 'immovable' or 'steadfast'. The Bodhisattva, because of the attainment of this eighth stage of steadiness becomes free from the taste of delight of enjoyment there, attains the state of non-relishment and becomes free from longing towards body, speech and mind. He becomes the knower of all shorts of inner motion, even then he remains unperturbed and free from thought constructs and therefore, remains well-established in the ripening state of absorption.[46]

So it signifies that in the career of a Bodhisattva, this stage is progressive spiritual realization is immovable and as such precludes the possibility of retrogression.[47] A candidate for Bodhisattvahood who succeeds to enter into it by discarding false discriminations becomes endowed with an exalted state of realization.[48] After the attainment of this stage, he realizes the futility of all his efforts and all his previous spiritual preparations become deprived of their significance. He reached the preceding seven-stages by relentless endeavour, but in this stage he had nothing to strive for and every act of his is spontaneous.

Even after the attainment of this *bhūmi*, called the immovable, the Bodhisattva is not entitled to enter *Nirvāṇa.* Since this would brings about a termination of all activities directed towards redemption of all creatures. It is owing to this reason that the Bodhisattva refrains from entering into the state of *Nirvāṇa* and elects to continue his worldly existence. But the activities of his body, voice and mind come to a complete cessation. The functioning of his previous vows takes place without encountering any hitch and his spiritual progress reaches the pattern of perfection.

In this stage, a Bodhisattva pays special attention to the perfection of aspiration (*praṇidhāna*), without lacking in respect of other *pāramitās*. He also achieves ten controls (*vaśitā*) and ten *balas* (DBhūSū, p. 46). He now possesses everything which makes him a Buddha. He belongs to the member of Tathāgata family and is served by all the gods.

According to the *Mahāyānasūtrālaṅkāra*[49] this stage is so called because a Bodhisattva can not be disturbed by the two ideas of course and absence of cause. The *Mahāvastu* (I, pp. 161-164) states that a Bodhisattva is now perfectly pure and may be described as *avaivartaka* (not capable of turning back). He should be honoured in the same way as Buddha.

9. *Sādhumatī Bhūmi:*

The Bodhisattva reaches in the ninth stage called *sādhumatī,* means 'stage of the good beings' or 'good thoughts'. He now knows all phenomena and principles truly and certainly whether they are mundane or supra-mundane, conceivable or inconceivable, compounded or uncompounded He understands the minds and actions of all beings. He acquires a knowledge of the numerous obligations of the *Śrāvakas, Pratyeka-Buddhas* and *Bodhisattvas*. He becomes a great preacher and acquires the four-kinds of special knowledge, i.e., direct inner intuition (*pratisṁvids*)[50]. His desire transcends all limitations. What he desires is brought into actual realization.

The Bodhisattva pays special attention to the perfection of '*bala*' (strength), without disregarding other *pāramitās*. He also experiences thousands of meditations and is in possession of magical spells (*dhāraṇī*). He never goes out of the sight of Buddhas and is not lacking in any way in respect of his spiritual practices. According to the *Mahāyānasūtrālaṅkāra*[51], this *bhūmi* is so called because a Bodhisattva has good mind or thoughts on account of the intuitive knowledge (*pratisaṁvids*) that he acquires. But the *Mahāvastu* gives no details of this stage. It enumerates hundreds of names of the precious, powerful, renowned Āryān Buddhas under whom Śākyamuni Buddha acquired the root knowledge, while he advanced from the first to the seventh stage. Then the text (*Mahāvastu*, I. pp.164-167) again mentions hundreds of the host of Āryān Buddhas in the ninth stage.

10. *Dharmameghā Bhūmi:*

The Bodhisattva now reaches the end of his quest. His tenth and the final stage of progressive spiritual realization receives the significant designation of *dharmameghā,* means 'cloud of Virtue' or 'cloud of the Doctrine'. He becomes entitled to realize innumerable varieties of contemplations including the ten unique types of them.[52]

And at the end the contemplation (*samādhi*), called '*sarvajñajñānaviśeṣābhiṣeka*'[53] also becomes manifest to him. As soon this realization takes place, he is beheld to be seated upon a luminous seat that bears the significant name '*mahāratnarājapadma*' and including other ten varieties of seat. It emits a myriad of radiant rays which illuminate all the ten quarters and work-out innumerable miracles. The Buddhas appear before him. Rays also come forth from the foreheads of the assembled Buddhas and touch his head. He is thus consecrated (*abhiṣikta*) as a fully enlightened Buddha (*samyaksambuddha*). Thus, this *bhūmi* is also known as *abhiṣekabhūmi*[54], i.e. stage of holy consecration. Through his proficiency in mindfulness he bears in mind all the clouds of '*dharmas*' showered on him by the Buddhas, and hence received the designation of '*dharmameghā*'.

Dharmamegha is also the name of a *samādhi* in the *Yoga Sūtra*. Patañjali has elucidated the essential nature of the spiritual contemplation called *dharmamegha* in the way indicated below:

प्रसङ्ख्यानेऽप्यकुसीदस्य सर्वथा विवेकख्यातेर्धर्ममेघः समाधिः। (IV.29)

It means, the spiritual absorption known as the cloud of virtue comes to him who, being possessed of the intellective revelation in all respects, is not professional even on the full payment.

Vidyāraṇya the author of *Pañcadaśī* (I.60) has also made the following significant observation:

धर्ममेघमिमं प्राहुः समाधिं योगवित्तमाः।
वर्षत्येष यतो धर्मामृतधाराः सहस्रशः।।

This means, the experts in *yoga* call this *samādhi* a rain cloud of *dharma*, because it pours forth countless showers of the bliss of *dharma*.

The *Mahāvastu* (I, pp. 167-186) states nothing particular about the tenth *bhūmi*. It mentions the birth of the Bodhisattvas in the *tuṣita* heaven and their longing for human existence. According to the *Mahāyānasūtrālaṅkāra*[55] this *bhūmi* is so called because it is pervaded by the modes of concentration and magical spells, just like the sky covered with clouds. Hence, a Bodhisattva in this *bhūmi* is a personification of love and sympathy, which freely issue from the fount of his inner will. He pays special attention to the perfection of knowledge (*jñāna*) without neglecting other *pāramitās*.

While concluding the discussion on *bhūmi* as referred in the *Daśabhūmika Sūtra*, it can be summarized as follows:

Pramuditā is so called because seeing *bodhi* and the salvation of beings nearby a great joy arises. *Vimalā* is so called because all tendency towards evil conduct is removed to confer purity. *Prabhākarī* is named from the fact that it illumines the great truth. *Arciṣmatī* derives its name by burning out duality and brigtening the factors conducive to enlightenment. *Sudurjayā* is so described because it matures sentient beings and protects ones own mind and is hence difficult to conquer. *Abhimukhī* relies on *prajñāpāramitā* and confronts both *Saṁsāra* amd *Nirvāṇa*. *Duraṅgamā* cleaves to the one path, the *Acalā* is unmoved by duality. *Sādhumatī* has the attainment of inward intuition. *Dharmameghā* has the sky of truth (*dharma*) pervaded with the cloud of non-duality.

In this way, a brief survey of the ten stages (*bhūmis*) with their special emphasis on their salient features have been presented The account of the stages given above presents an idea of the gradation in the spiritual life of a Bodhisattva. It further gives an idea of the ideal life to be pursued in Mahāyāna. The transition from one state to the other takes place according to the progress made by the Bodhisattva in respect of certain virtues. However, after going through these stages, a Bodhisattva who is enkindled with the loftiest ambition of attaining Bodhisattvahood, finally succeeds to attain Enlightenment or *Nirvāṇa*. This is the main aim of the author to elaborate systematically the ten spiritual stages (*bhūmis*) of the Bodhisattva for the quest of perfection or realization of the true knowledge.

REFERENCES

1. *Haima Kośa*, II.335; also cf. *Medinī Kośa*, XXV.22.
2. *Pāli-English Dictionary*, R.W. Rhys Davids and W. Stede, (Reprint edn., 1989), p. 508.
3. Vide, English tr. by L.M. Pruden, Vol. I, Ch. II.23cd, p.189.
4. भूमिर्नाम गतिविषयः। यो हि यस्य गतिविषयः स तस्य भूमिरित्युच्यते। तत्र महती भूमिरेषामिति महाभूमिकाः, ये सर्वत्र चेतसि भवन्ति। *Abhidharma Kośa Bhāṣya*, II.23cd.
5. 277, see also English translation by C.A.F. Rhys Davids, P.T.S. Publication (1974), pp.74-75.
6. भूयो भूयोऽमितास्वासु ऊर्ध्वगमनयोगतः।
   भूतामिताभयार्थाय त एवेष्टा हि भूमयः।। MSūAI XX-XXI.40, p.519.
7. विविधे शुभनिर्हारे रत्या विहारणात्सदा।
   सर्वत्र बोधिसत्त्वानां विहारभूमयो मताः।। *ibid.*, V. 39.
8. *Amṛtakaṇikā* on *Āryamañjuśrīnāmasaṅgīti,* (Sarnath edn., 1994), p. 29. Cf. *Hevajra Tantra*, I.7.10-18.
9. 'Final ground' denotes that this Intellective Vision has its cessation; so this happiness should be avoided by the highest Non-attachment.
10. *Yoga Sūtra,* I.14, II.27, II.31, etc.
11. *Durārohā, Baddhamānā, Puṣpa-maṇḍitā, Rucirā, Cittavistāra, Rūpavatī, Durjayā*, *Janmanideṣa,* and *Abhiṣeka.*
12. This treatise mentions ten *bhūmis*, to which it does not assign any names. Vide, Har Dayal, *The Bodhisattva Doctrine,* Ch. VI, p.275.
13. *Pramuditā, Vimalā, Prabhākarī, Arciṣmatī, Sudurjayā, Abhimukhī, Dūraṅgamā, Acalā*, *Sādhumatī,* and *Dharmameghā.*

14. *Gotra, Adhimukti-caryā, Śuddhā-śaya, Caryā-pratipatti, Niyata, Niyata-caryā,* and *Niṣṭhāgamana.*
15. *Gotra, Adhimukti-caryā, Pramudita, Adhiśīla, Adhicitta, Adhiprajñā, Adhiprajñā No.1, Adhiprajñā-vihāra No.2, Sābhoga-nirnimitta, Anābhoga-nirnimitta, Pratisaṁvid, Parama,* and *Tathāgata.*
16. It is *Durjayā-bhūmi* (difficult to conquer) in the *Mahāvastu*, but *Sudurjayā-bhūmi* (invincible) in the *Daśabhūmika Sūtra.*
17. *Bhūminiruktivibhāge nava ślokāḥ,* vide, MSūAI, XX-XXI, p. 514.
18. *The Bodhisattva Doctrine,* Ch. VI, p.272.
19. Dutt, N., *Aspects of Mahāyāna Buddhism and its Relation to Hīnayāna,* p. 327.
20. The *Daśabhūmika Sūtra* consists of two sections, viz. (i) prose section, (ii) poetry (*gāthā*) section. The *gāthās* are not available in its oldest manuscripts. Besides, the *gāthās* occuring in the last chapter of the Johannes Rahder's edition are conspicuous by their absence in its earlier Manuscripts. Hence, most of the scholars of Mahāyāna Buddhism agree to accept the *gāthās* 'as later edition'. P.L. Vaidya in his Editorial remarks states: " ....I am inclined to believe that the *gāthā* portion of *Daśabhūmika Sūtra* is a positively late edition (*gāthāvibhāga,* p.69). The present study is based on the prose section of the *Daśabhūmika Sūtra.*
21. The form *'muditā'* is also found in the *Laṅkāvatāra Sūtra* and in the *Mahāyānasūtrālaṅkāra.*
22. यदिदमाजीविकाभयं वा अश्लोकभयं वा मरणभयं वा दुर्गतिभयं वा पर्षच्छारद्यभयं वा, तानि सर्वाणि व्यपगतानि भवन्ति। ...DBhūSū, p. 9.
23. For details, see DBhūSū, p. 10.
24. तानि च महाप्रणिधानानि दशभिर्निष्ठापदैरभिनिर्हरति। *ibid.*, p. 11.
    Also cf., *Laṅkāvatāra Sūtra*, XII.37.
25. पश्यतां बोधिमासन्नां सत्त्वार्थस्य च साधनम्।
    तीव्र उत्पद्यते मोदो मुदिता तेन कथ्यते।। XX-XXI.32, p. 514.
26. तस्य च चतुर्भ्यः संग्रहवस्तुभ्यः प्रियवद्यता अतिरिक्ततमा भवति। दशभ्यः पारमिताभ्यः शीलपारमिताऽतिरिक्ततमा भवति। DBhūSū, *Vimalā Bhūmi,* p. 18.
27. दौः शील्याभोगवैमल्याद्विमला भूमिरुच्यते।
    दौः शील्यमलस्यान्ययानमनसिकारमलस्य चातिक्रमाद्विमलेत्युच्यते। (Comm.) XX-XXI.33ab, p.515.
28. DBhūSū, *Prabhākarī Bhūmi*, p.19.
29. महाधर्मावभासस्य करणाच्च प्रभाकरी। XX-XXI. 33cd, p.515.
30. त्यागे प्रवर्तते चित्तं बोधिसत्त्वानमावुसो। X.(91.2ab), p. 106; cf. त्यागेन त्यागसंपन्ना बोधिसत्त्वा.... चन्द्रभानुरिवांशुभाम्। X. (79.1), p. 91.
31. *Arciṣmatī Bhūmi*, p. 24.
32. अप्रत्युदावर्त्याशय, त्रिरत्नाभेद्यप्रसादनिष्ठागमन, संस्कारोदयव्ययविभावन, स्वभावानुपत्याशयता, लोकप्रवृत्तिनिवृत्याशयता, कर्मभवोपपत्त्याशयता, संसारनिर्वाणाशयता, सत्त्वक्षेत्रकर्माशयता, पूर्वान्तापरान्तकर्माशयता, एवम् अभावक्षय। DBhūSū, p. 24.

33. (For details see) *ibid.*
34. अर्चिर्भूता यतो धर्मा बोधिपक्षाः प्रदाहकाः।
अर्चिष्मतीति तद्योगात्सा भूमिर्द्वयदाहतः।। XX-XXI.34, p. 515.
35. A detail explanation of these terms has been furnished in the DBhūSū, p. 27.
36. सत्त्वानां परिपाकश्च स्वचित्तस्य च रक्षणा।
धीमद्भिर्जीयते दुःखं दुर्जया तेन कथ्यते।। XX-XXI.35, p. 516.
37. यदुत सर्वधर्मानिमित्त... अलक्षण... अनुत्पाद... अजात... विविक्त... आदिविशुद्ध... निष्प्रपञ्च... अनाव्यूहानिर्व्यूह. ..मायास्वप्नप्रतिभास- प्रतिश्रुत्कोदकचन्द्रप्रति- बिम्बनिर्माण... भावाभावाद्वय समतया च। आभिर्दशभिर्धर्म-समताभिरवतरति। DBhūSū, p. 31.
38. *ibid.*
39. ...यावत्यो लोकसमुदाचारोपपत्तयः सर्वाः ताः अत्माभिनिवेशतो भवन्ति। आत्माभिनिवेशविगमतो न भवन्ति लोकसमुदाचारोपपत्तयः...। DBhūSū, p. 31.
40. ...एवं बोधिसत्त्वोऽनुलोमाकारं प्रतीत्यसमुत्पादं प्रत्यवेक्षते...। *ibid.*
41. आभिमुख्याद् द्वयस्येह संसारस्यापि निर्वृतेः।
उक्ता ह्यभिमुखी भूमिः प्रज्ञापारमिताश्रयात्।। XX-XXI.36, p. 516.
42. स दशभिरुपायप्रज्ञाज्ञानाभिनिर्हृतैर्मार्गान्तरारम्भविशेषैराक्रमति। कतमैर्दशभिः? यदुत शून्यतानिमित्ताप्रणिहितसमाधि सुपरिभावितमानसश्च भवति। DBhūSū, p. 36.
43. *Dāna, śīla, kṣānti, vīrya, dhyāna, prajñā, upāyakauśala, praṇidhāna, bala* and *jñāna*.
44. तस्य दशभ्यः पारमिताभ्यः उपायकौशल्यपारमिता अतिरिक्ततमा भवति, न च परिशेषा न समुदागच्छति... । DBhūSū, p. 41.
45. एकायनपथश्लेषाद्भूमिर्दूरंगमा मता। XX-XXI.37ab, p. 517.
46. अचला नाम अष्टमी भूमिः। बोधिसत्त्वोऽस्या अष्टम्या अचलाया बोधिसत्त्वभूमेः सहप्रतिलम्भात्सर्वाभोग विगतोऽनाभोगधर्मताप्राप्तः कायवाक्चित्तौत्सुक्यापगतः सर्वञ्जितमन्यनास्पन्दितविकल्पापगतो विपाकधर्मतावस्थितो भवति। ..., DBhūSū, *Acalā Bhūmi*, p. 42.
47. The DBhūSū has stated that the eighth *bhūmi* receives the following designations, viz., *anivartya, durāsava, kumāra, janma, pariniṣpanna, pariniṣṭhita, nirmāṇa (nirvāṇa), adhiṣṭhāna,* and *anābhoga,* for details see pp. 46-47.
48. ... अवतीर्णोऽनुत्पत्तिकधर्मक्षान्तिप्राप्त इत्युच्यते। DBhūSū, p. 42.
49. द्वयसंज्ञाविचलनादचला च निरुच्यते। XX-XXI. 37cd, p. 517.
50. स धर्मप्रतिसंविदा स्वलक्षणं धर्माणां प्रजानाति। अर्थप्रतिसंविदा विभक्तिं धर्माणां प्रजानाति। निरुक्तिप्रतिसंविदा असंभेददेश धर्माणां प्रजानाति। प्रतिभानप्रतिसंविदा अनुप्रबन्धानुपच्छेदतां धर्माणां प्रजानाति। DBhūSū, p. 51.
51. प्रतिसंविन्मतिसाधुत्वाद्भूमिः साधुमति मता। XX-XXI.38ab, p. 517.
52. The ten *samādhis* are: *vimala, dharmadhātu vibhakti-praveśa, bodhimaṇḍ-ālaṅkāravyūha, sarvākarar-aśmikusuma, sāgaragarbha, sāgarasamṛddhi, ākāśa-*

dhātuvipula, sarvadharmasvabhāvavicaya, sarvasa-ttvacittaparitānugata and *pratyutpannasarva-buddhasaṁmukhāvasthita*. DBhūSū, p. 55.

53. स तस्य सर्वज्ञज्ञानविशेषाभिषेकवतः समाधेः सह प्रतिलम्भात्तस्मिन् महारत्नजपद्मे निषण्णः संदृश्यते। *ibid.*

54. सर्वाकार सर्वज्ञ ज्ञानाभिषेकभूमिप्राप्त इत्युच्यते।
DBhūSū, p. 55.

55. धर्ममेघा द्वयव्याप्तेर्धर्माकाशस्य मेघवत्।।
XXI.38cd, p. 517.

Māra in the Buddhist Literature

Māra is a multi-layered concept in the Buddhist literature. The term '*māra*' is derived from the root *mṛ-* with the suffix *ghañ*, meaning 'to kill, to slay', etc. In the *Amarakośa*, Māra is stated as an epithet of Madana, the gods of Kāma *(madano manmatho māraḥ)*.[1]

In the *Atharvaveda*, the word Māra is used in the sense of Yama, Death, the destroyer and evil killer:

"यमो मृत्युरघमारो निर्ऋथो बभ्रुःशर्वोऽस्ता नीलशिखण्डः।"[2]

The above *mantra* is a prayer for protection from the enemy or danger. The gods like Yama, 'Death', killer of the evil and others are being prayed to protect our heroes.

At another place in the Atharvaveda, Māra is known as 'Pāpman', i.e. evil one.

अव मा पाप्मन्त्सृज वशी सन् मृडयासि नः।
आ मा भद्रस्य लोके पाप्मन् धेह्यविह्रुतम्।।[3]

In the *Śatapatha Brāhmaṇa*, 'Death' *(mṛtyu)* is explained as Pāpmā.[4] Māra is called Namuci in the Buddhist Literature. In the Pāli text like *Sutta Nipāta*[5] *(Namuci karuṇaṁ vācam)* and Bhddhist Sanskrit texts like *Mahāvastu*[6] and *Lalitavistara*[7], Māra is called Namuci. In the *Ṛgveda* also Namuci is described as a demon *(asura)*.[8] The words like: Māra, Namuci and Pāpman *(pāpimā)* are found in the pre-Buddhist Literature in the sense of non-liberator, i.e. an opponent of liberation or *Nirvāṇa*.

In the Pāli Buddhist texts, *Māra* is known as Kaṇha. The *Sutta Nipāta*, however, describes it as :

कण्हस्स सोतं दीघरत्तानुसयितं । अतारि जातिमरणं असेसं।[9]

The Buddha has passed beyond all birth and death, the stream of Kaṇha, which has long been latent (in him). The *Dīgha Nikāya*[10] also describes Māra as Kaṇha *(pisāce pi kaṇhā ti sañjānanti)*.

In the Buddhist Mythology Māra possesses a very prominent figure. It always follows Buddha's religious and true austerity life. Due to Māra's bad intension for providing different materialistic happiness to the Buddha, his austerity life became prejudiced But the great Buddha's *sādhanā* was free from Māra's bad influence and inert effort. The Māra was a dominant figure in Gautama Buddha's period as he has an assembly. In the Mahāparinibbāna Sutta of *Dīgha Nikāya*, Buddha tells Ānanda, one of his great disciples, that (out of eight *pariṣadas*)[11] the wicked Māra has a regular assembly (*Māra-parisā*), through which he was controlling over religious and saintly minded persons as well as Bodhisattvas. In Māratajjaniya Sutta of the *Majjhima Nikāya,* Mahā Moggalāna says that he was formerly a Māra, named Dūsī (in the sense of *duṣṭa* or *pāpi* or wicked in nature), and committed a number of sins in that life. As said in the text:

"भूतपुब्बाहं, पापिम, दूसी नाम मारो अहो सिं।"

It is known that Māra's nature and intention was not proper and favourable for the Buddha's austerity life. The Mārasaṁyutta chapter of *Saṁyutta Nikāya* contains twenty-five suttas (sub-chapters), which elaborately describes Māra's true nature and his real intension through various interesting and practical experiences of the Buddha's *sāttvika* life. These Suttas (Sūtras) which deal with Māra's bad influence to disturb Buddha's true effort to obtain *Nirvāṇa* (enlightenment) as under:

(1) Tapaḥkarma Sutta, (2) Hastirājavarṇa Sutta, (3) Śubha Sutta, (4) Prathama Mārapāśa Sutta, (5) Dvitīya Mārapāśa Sutta, (6) Sarpa Sutta, (7) Svapiti Sutta, (8) Nandati Sutta, (9) Prathama Āyuḥ Sutta, (10) Dvitīya Āyuḥ Sutta, (11) Pāṣāṇa Sutta, (12) Kinsusiṁha Sutta, (13) Śakalika Sutta, (14) Pratirūpa Sutta, (15) Mānasa Sutta, (16) Pātra Sutta, (17) Ṣatsparśāyatana Sutta, (18) Piṇḍa Sutta, (19) Kṛṣaka Sutta, (20) Rājya Sutta, (21) Sambahula Sutta, (22) Samṛddhi Sutta, (23) Godhika Sutta, (24) Saptavarṣānubandha Sutta, and (25) Māradhītā Sutta.

In these above Suttas, Māra tries either to threaten Buddha through various furious and wicked ways or to attract him through different worldly enjoyments for disturbing or not allowing him to move towards Bodhisattvahood. As is known that a number of hurdles come in the religious path of the Buddha's through *māyā* or Māra or any other ill motivated characters. The same happened in the case of Buddha when Māra appears in two different forms, viz. an elephant and a snake, in order to frighten him.[12] In addition to this, Māra assumes the form of a peasant and disturbs Buddha's ideal preaching.[13] He even tries to distract the audience by making a terrific noise.

It is found in the suttas of Mārasaṁyutta, that Māra and his associates have advised Buddha to enjoy all the worldly enjoyments or pleasures to dwell in his father's place as long as he possessed youth and health, to rule his prosperous kingdom and make himself fit and active for immortal godhood by offering the various sacrifices. This way, Māra has tried his best to offer all shorts of worldly amenities to Buddha for diverting his mind from the way of *sādhanā* or meditation.

Lord Buddha, however, replied Māra that he had no use for the tiniest of merits, but he wanted to attain the state where there was no return (cf. *yad gatvā na nivartante tat dhāma paramaṁ mama*).[14] No body, he said to Māra, has power to stop his bright efforts in that direction. He has strongly desired to offer fight to Māra's hosts which consisted of desire, discontent, hunger, thirst, craving, sloth and torpor, fear, doubt and pride, etc. Only a cowardly person cannot overcome this host of Māra—so replied the Bodhisattva, but he was sure that inspite of Māra he would be able to reach the place where all ills cease. After this the wicked Māra along with his cruel associates vanished from sight. Even Māra's three daughters (Tṛṣṇā, Arati and Raga) have left the place, being defeated by the Lord. But in spite of their defeat, Māra has praised the virtuous eternal spiritual qualities of the Lord and said his daughters as:

सेलं व सिरसूहच्च, पाताले गाधमेसथ ।
स्थाणुं व उरमासज्ज, निब्बिज्जापेथ गोतमा 'ति॥
दद्दल्लमाना आगच्छुं, तण्हा, च अरती रगा।
ता तत्थ पनुदी सत्था, तूलं भट्ठं व मालुतो 'ति॥

—संयुत्तनिकाय, मारसंयुत्तं, I.127 (P.T.S.)

In Mahāvagga of· the *Vinaya Piṭaka*, Māra appears twice and tries to assert his evil power over Buddha, who sternly repels and repudiates him.[15] In Nidānakathā of the *Jātaka*, he attacks Buddha with nine different storms of rain, wind, rocks, weapons, charcoal ashes, sand, mud and darkness; and his mighty elephant is 150 leagues in height.[16] However, in different Pāli texts Māra is described as: *adhipati* (chief), *antegu* (destroyer), *pamatabandhu* (friend of the passionate), *maccu* (death), *kaṇha* (black), *namuci* (non-liberator entity of *Nirvāṇa*), active, mischievous imp and a celestial being. This is his personal aspect that he is considered as a mythlogical Puruṣa (being), with a distinct individuality, like Sakka and other *devas*. But there is also an impersonal aspect of Māra. In various texts he is regarded merely as the symbol of evil, sin, wicked, desire and temptation. Māra is even addressed as '*pāpi*' by the Divine Lord in the *Majjhima Nikāya*.[17] Various sensuous pleasure, i.e. worldly enjoyments and the sixfold 'sphere of sense', viz. *śabda, sparśa (kāya), rūpa, rasa, gandha* and *manas* are said to be Māra's domin (*pāpima, cakkhu, tava rūpā tava cakkhusamphassaviññāṇāyatanam*).[18] He cannot obtain entrance (*otāra*), if a monk practises virtue and self-control *(labhati tassa māro otāraṁ labhati tassa māro ārammaṇam)*.[19] In Padhāna Sutta of the *Sutta Nipāta*, Māra's mythical personality is not prominent, he serves only as a symbol of temptation. When Buddha was meditating near the Nirañjanā River, Māra tried in vain to obstruct his effort for attaining enlightenment. He said that the way of meditation or *sādhanā* or *tapasyā* is very difficult and it is not even easy to obtain *Nirvāṇa* (*duggo maggo padhānāya, dukkaro durabhisambhavo*).[20] In spite of several obstructions by Māra, the Buddha was not disappointed. He addressed Māra as '*pamattabandhu*', '*pāpi*' and said: 'why you have come here? I do not seek your advice to perform Agnihotra sacrifices and to step down from this tedious path of meditation. Because you are not a pious and faithful adviser, as sensual pleasures are your first *senā* (army), discontent is called your second; your third is hunger and thirst; the fourth is called craving. Sloth and torpor are your fifth; the sixth is called fear; the seventh is doubt; hypocrisy and obstinacy are your eighth *senā*':

कामा ते पठमा सेना, दुतिया अरति वुच्चति।
ततिया खुप्पिपासा ते, चतुत्थी तण्हा पवुच्चति।।
पञ्चमं थीनमिद्धं ते, छट्ठा भीरु पवुच्चति।
सत्तमी विचकिच्छा ते, मक्खो थम्मो ते अट्ठमो।।[21]

The Māra's eight armies are always creating problems for the *brāhmaṇas*, *śramaṇas* and other *sādhakas*. One who is not a *asura* cannot conquer it, but having conquered it one obtains happiness—"न तं असूरो जिनाति, जेत्वा च लभते सुखं"[22]. But the Buddha having positive approach in mind has defeated Māra's great army through his Divine wisdom and power. Thus, Māra had followed the Buddha for seven years, looking for any weakness in him, but finally failed to get an opportunity against the fully enlightened one, who possesses mindfulness. In the words of Māra:

सत्त वस्सानि भगवन्तं, अनुबन्धिं पदा पदं।
ओतारं नाधिगच्छिस्सं, सम्बुद्धस्स सतीमतो।।[23]

The Māra has also a personal and an impersonal aspect as found in the Buddhist Sanskrit literature. In his personal aspect, he is the chief of the *devatās*, who are collectively called 'the *mārakāyikas*.'[24] There are good numbers of these gods.[25] In the *Buddhacarita* of Asvaghosa, Māra is known as the Lord of Kāma or Kāmadeva and also designated as the enemy of the eternal law and liberation (**कामप्रचाराधिपतिं तमेव मोक्षद्विषं मारमुदाहरन्ति**).[26] He is the supreme ruler of the world where passions have their free play, and beings are all subject to disease, decay and death. When Siddhārtha was sitting at the foot of the Bodhi tree to obtain omniscience, Māra with his three sons, Vibhrama (caprice), Harṣa (gaiety) and Darpa (wantonness) and with his three daughters Arati (discontent), Prīti (delight) and Tṛṣṇā (thirst) and himself armed with the flowery arrow (*puṣpa-śara*), came to the Aśvattha tree to disturb him.[27] His army consists of his followers who appear in many ghastly forms and carry various weapons. Some have the faces of boars, fishes, horses, asses, and camels, or the countenances of tigers, lions, and elephants; some are one-eyed, many-mouthed, three headed, with pendulous bellies and speckled bellies.[28] All conceivable ugly, horrible and terrific shapes, forms and countenances are given to them. All grimaces, frowning, frightening, hurling, brandishing, wild orgies are described as their characteristic actions. Māra is a stubborn fighter and artful at the same time. All means he tries from the hurling of rocks and mountains down to coaxing and cajoling, enticing and softening to keep all under his sway. His daughters are the bewitchers of hearts of men, his sons are generators of violent passions in them, while his forces are suckers of the vital essence and of the mind. However, in a different manner Māra tries to allure Siddhārtha (Buddha), the mighty *kṣatriya* and advised him to follow his own *dharma*, i.e. *kṣātradharma* (to rule over the country as a king) and give up the *dharma* or path of liberation. Subdue the world both with arrows and with sacrifices and obtain the world of Vāsava, i.e. get the *loka* of Indra or Indrapada through the duty of a true *kṣatriya*. As the poet says in his words:

उत्तिष्ठ भोः क्षत्रिय मृत्युभीत चर स्वधर्मं त्यज मोक्षधर्मम्।
बाणैश्च यज्ञैश्च विनीय लोकं लोकात्पदं प्राप्नुहि वासवस्य।।[29]

Māra tried to tempt Buddha in various ways, but in vain and finally, he left the Lord in despair.

In the *Saundarananda Kāvya*, Asvaghosa also describes Buddha's victory over Māra and his army, through his deep meditation and firm patience. By defeating Māra he has achieved the great eternal abode or graceful *Nirvāṇa* (मारबलमजयदुग्रमथो बुबुधे पदं शिवमहार्यमव्ययम्।)[30]. The gods are delighted on Buddha's victory over Māra and his army. But on the contrary the associates of Māra are totally disappointed and returned

Fetters of Māra (*Māra Bandhana*):

Māra, the greatest opponent of enlightenment, is depicted in different Pāli texts in the appearance of a thoroughly personified supernatural and bitterest enemy of the Buddha, rather than in the form of an abstract (*nirākāra*) idea of metaphysical character; the idea of the evil and ignorance in opposition to the good and insight. The fetter of Māra was really an obstacle for Buddha in the way of his religious journey.

One is entangled in the snares (*pāśa*) of Māra, if he has any attachment towards any beautiful form, tasty food, attractive things, etc. Hence, it is recorded in the *Saṁyutta Nikāya*[31] :

सन्ति, भिक्खवे, चक्खुविञ्ञेय्या रूपा इट्ठा कन्ता मनापा प्रियरूपा कामूपसंहिता रजनीया। तं चे, भिक्खु, अभिनन्दति अभिवदति अज्झोसाय तिट्ठति-अयं वुच्चति, भिक्खवे, भिक्खु आवासगतो मारस्य, मारस्य वसं गतो, पटिमुक्कस्स मारपासो। बद्धो सो मारबन्धनेन यथाकामकरणीयो पापिमतो ...... पे.।

Especially, a Bhikkhu who is practising meditation for obtaining *Nirvāṇa* should remain separate from the worldly alluring things. Hence, it is observed that a Bhikkhu, who has some worldly attachment, is entangled by the snares of Māra.[32]

The *Dhammapada* is one of the most popular books of the Tripiṭaka. It is a collection of the moral teachings of Lord Buddha. The pious discourses of Buddha advise to the Bhikkhus for controlling over their sense organs in order to stay disentangled from the fetters or snares of Māra. The *kilesamāra* or the defilements hindering the realization of *Nirvāṇa*, is as follows:

शुभमनुपश्यन्तं विहरन्तं इन्द्रियेषु असंवृतम्।
भोजने चामात्राज्ञं कुसीदं हीनवीर्यम्।
तं वै प्रसहते मारो वातो वृक्षमिव दुर्ब्बलम्।।[33]

The verse clearly states that a Bhikkhu who keeps his mind on enjoyable objects, who is uncontrolled in his senses, immoderate in eating, and in lazy and lacking in energy, is overpowered by wicked Māra, just like a weak tree, uprooted in the stormy wind.

Those who can restrain their mind and check his propensities can escape from the snares of Māra.

अशुभमनुपश्यन्तं विहरन्तं इन्द्रियेषु सुसंवृत्तम्।
भोजने च मात्राज्ञं श्रद्धं आरब्धवीर्यम्।
तं वै न प्रसहते मारो वातः शैलमिव पर्वतम्।।[34]

The Bodhisattva or the Bhikkhu who keeps his mind on the impurities of the body, who is well-controlled in his senses, moderate in his food, confident and energetic, cannot be overthrown by Māra, just as stormy winds cannot shake a mountain of rock.

Hence, it is clear that the Māra will certainly overthrow a Bhikkhu or a Bodhisattva who is unrestrained in his senses, immoderate in his food, idle and weak.

One should fight with Māra with the weapon of Divine knowledge or Spiritual wisdom.

दूरङ्गमं एकचरम् अशरीरं गुहाशयम्।
ये चित्तं संयस्यन्ति मुच्यन्ते मारबन्धनात्।।[35]

Going far, wandering alone, formless and lying or sleeping in a cave is the nature or function of mind. Those who control over their mind from the worldly objects and enjoyments are freed from the fetters of Māra.

Lord Buddha always advised to his disciples to keep distance from *vāsanā*, *taṇhā, kāma,* etc. for obtaining Bodhisattvahood or *Nirvāṇa*. He says: dig up the root of craving, just as one who wishes to have the fragrant root, digs up the *bīraṇa* grass. Do not let Māra to destroy you again and again, like the flood which destroys the reeds on the river bank. In the words of Buddha:

तण्हाय मूलं खणथ, उसीरत्थो व बीरणं।
मा वो नलं व सोतो व, मारोभञ्जि पुनप्पुनं।।[36]

The Lord further states: 'O Bhikkhus! Give up the past, future and present. Having reached the end of existences, with a mind freed from all conditioned things, you will not again undergo birth and decay (*jarā*).' He who delights in quieting his thoughts, who meditates on what, is unpleasant, and who is ever mindful in every aspect, will definitely get rid of craving. Finally, he cut the fetters of Māra. As rightly said:

वितर्कोपशमे च यो रतोऽशुभं भावयते सदा स्मृतः।
एष खलु व्यन्ती करिष्यति एष छेत्स्यति मारबन्धनम्।।[37]

Hence, a desireless (without *vāsanā*) person can be freed from the bond of Māra.

According to Buddhism, the best of paths is the Eightfold Path (*aṣṭāṅgika-mārga*). This is the path pointed out by Buddha for liberation from the round of existences. According to the *Dhammapada* one can make oneself free from Māra, if one has attained the noble Eightfold Path.

एष वो मार्गो नाऽस्त्यन्तो दर्शनस्थ विशुद्धये।
एतं हि यूयं प्रतिपद्यध्वं मारस्यैष प्रमोहनः।।[38]

This is the only Path, and there is none other that leads to the completely pure vision, i.e. understanding. Follow this Great Path and finally it will bewilder Māra.

The text further records that true meditation is the only way through which one can be freed from the fetters of Māra.[39] Because, those who practise the tranquility and insight meditation are freed from the snares of Māra.

Besides *Dhammapada*, some other Pāli texts also record the discussion on the fetters of Māra and the means to release from it. The Buddha had a strong belief that Māra cannot destroy the *Dhammacakka*, i.e. Wheel of Law.[40] According to the *Udāna*, a Bhikkhu whose mind is not protected, who has false belief and who is idle, comes under the control of Māra.

अरक्खितेन कायेन मिच्छादिट्ठिगतेन च।
थीनमिद्धाभिभूतेन, वसं मारस्स गच्छति।।[41]

It means, as a result of body being unguarded, and as a result of being slain by wrong view, as a result of being overcome by sloth and torpor, a Bhikkhu comes under the direct control of Māra.

The *Visuddhimagga* exclusively states that who has freed himself from the ties of the world, is fit to overcome Māra with his strong associate army.[42] A *yogī* or *sādhaka*, who remains fixed in his seat spending his whole time in meditation, can easily subdue over Māra.[43] It is very interesting to note that Bhikkhus living within the Buddha's state are not overcome by the fetters of Māra. The Buddha assumed to the Bhikkhus by saying that if you regularly live within the state of your father or *guru* or Lord (i.e. Buddha), you will not be subdued by Māra.[44] According to the *Itivuttaka*, Māra is conquered by a Bhikkhu who is totally free from worldly attachment, and who has exalted triumphant over all pains and sufferings and will not born again in this world.[45] Those who are under the domain of passion, delusion, anger and illusion, are really ignorant of the *āryadharmas* and they cannot liberate themselves from the snares of Māra.[46] The *Aṅguttara Nikāya* asserts that a Bhikkhu who follows true *dharma* can conquer over Māra. The text refers as:

धर्माधिपो च अनुधम्मचारी, न हीयति सच्चपरक्कमो मुनि। पसय्ह मारं अभिभुय्य अन्तकं, यो च फुसी जातिक्खयं पधानवा। सो तादिसो लोकविदू सुमेधो, सब्बेसु धम्मेसु अतम्मयो मुनी "ति"।।[47]

On the basis of *dharma*, if the *muni* meditates God he never sees behind on the way of his religious journey. True devotion and sincere effort in practising austerity must help him to vanquish over Māra. At another place in the *Aṅguttara Nikāya* it is clarified that a Bhikkhu who puts forth the right effort in performing *yoga* and transcendental meditation in a proper direction, and who has conquered the kingdom of Māra, is not subject to rebirth and death.

सम्मप्पधाना मारधेय्याभिभूता,
ते असिता जातिमरणभयस्स पारगू।
ते तुसिता जेत्वा मारं सवाहिनिं ते अनेजा,
सब्बं नमुचिबलं उपातिवत्ता ते सुखिता "ति"।।[48]

Finally, after destroying the evil power of Namuci (i.e. Māra), the *muni* lives in the *Tuṣita* world with full Bliss.

Māra went to that place where Buddha was staying and having approached him he addressed the Blessed One by the following verse:

बद्धो सि सब्बपासेहि ये दिब्बा ये च मानुसा।
महाबन्धनबद्धोसि न मे समण मोक्खसी 'ति'।।[49]

You are bound by Māra's fetters, human being and Divine. Thou art bound by strong fetters of mine and hence you will not be delivered from me, O Śramaṇa (Buddha).

Buddha, having pious thought in mind strongly replied Māra in the following words:

मुत्ताहं सब्बपासेहि ये दिब्बा ये च मानुसा।
महाबन्धनमुत्तोम्हि निहतो त्वमसि अन्तका ति।।[50]

Being a Man or Divine, I am totally free from the strong fetters of Māra. You know this fact. Then the Māra understood that the Blessed One recognized me and my evil intension and vanished away.

It is properly advised that those monks who know the great suffering provided by Māra are really unbearable in the way of their meditation. Hence, to be freed from the snares of Māra they must go for the shelter of Lord Buddha. This is the only way to get success in their spiritual life. The *Majjhima Nikāya* rightly says:

यो एतमभिजानाति, भिक्खु बुद्धस्स सावको।
तादिसं भिक्खुमासज्ज, कण्ह दुःखं निगच्छसि।।[51]

The Supernatural Powers of Buddha always protect Bhikkhus from the evil influence of Māra, because without proper guidance and kind Blessings of Lord Buddha it was difficult for the monks to attain the Highest Bliss.

Māra was confusing and ill-motivating to the Bhikkhus through his wicked sons, daughters and army personals. Although the sons of Māra are innumerable as the sands of the Ganges, but according to the *Lalitavistara* their number can find to thousand (मारस्य पापीयसः पुत्रसहस्रम्).[52] Some of the prominent sons of Māra as mentioned in the text[53] are: Sārthavāha, Durmati, Madhuranirghoṣa, Śatavāhu, Subuddhi, Ugratejā, Sunetra, Dīrgavāhu, Prasādapratilabdha, Bhayaṅkara, Ekāgramatirāha, Avatārapreksī, Puṇyālaṅkāra, Anivartī, Dharmakāma, Anupaśānta, Siddhārtha, Ratilola, Dharmamati,

Vātajava, Acalapati, Brahmamati, or Mandamati,Siṁhamati, Sarvacaṇḍāla, Siṁhanādī, Duścintitācintī and Sucintitārtha.

Bhadrasena, the chief commander of Māra's army said to the Māra that "all the *devatās, gandharvas, kinnaras* are sincerely extending their regards and devotions to the Buddha. Besides, your wise and mighty sons are even liking and greatly respecting him".[54] The *Mahāvastu* simply states that Māra's son Sārthavāha and Janīsuta tried to dissuade him from attacking the Bodhisattva.[55]

According to the *Lalitavistara* (chapter XXI; 377-378, P.T.S.), Māra dreams a dream with thirty-two ominous signs that seem to foretell his doom. Some of his dreams are described as: (1) Māra's place has been overshadowed by darkness; (2) he runs away through fear; (3) he sees that he is leaving his crown; (4) he sees that the feathers of goose, crane, peacock, etc. are falling; (5) he sees that musical instruments, e.g. drums, kettle drums, conches, etc. break into pieces and fall down on the ground. For this Māra advised his followers to be careful and addressed them by saying, "One who is endowed with all the good signs and who has undergone many difficulties, comes of the Śākya family, and will subdue the members of the devil's power and strength." I have heard from the heaven that the Buddha, the Blessed One, has obtained the Highest Bliss, i.e. *Nirvāṇa.* So it is not bearable for us, because, after *bodhiprāpti*, Buddha will definitely seek the release of his disciples. Henceforth, you, all my followers, go there, i.e. near *Bodhivṛkṣa*, to puzzle the Blessed One, so that his mind will be diverted from the high spiritual path.[56] Durmati, one of the Māra's devil son, has assumed to his father for destabilizing the Buddha. He said, "my eye-sight can render twain hearts of beings whom it will touch, and can divide the essence of the oldest tree in the world. No being, who shall fall my sight, can survive. Hence, I fix my cruel eyes on the Buddha, he will have no power to breathe again or survive."[57] Another devil son of Māra was also in a terrific mood. He also threatened Buddha to throw him into the deep sea. He further adds:

सबोधिवृक्षमुत्पाट्य क्षेप्स्ये पाण्या दिशो दश॥[58]

(I will throw the Bodhivṛkṣa in ten different directions after cut into pieces.)

On the contrary, even some sons of Māra are worshipping and respecting Buddha as a 'symbol of peace'. These honest and spiritual minded sons of Māra are: Sārthavāha, Madhuranirghoṣa, Subuddhi, Sunetra, Prasāda-pratilabdha, Ekāgramati, Puṇyālaṅkāra, Dharmakāma, Siddhārtha, Dharmarati, Siṁhanādī, Sucintitārtha, Acalapati, etc. They said to Māra and their wicked brothers: Buddha is a saintly minded man. He is pure in body, mind and speech (*vāc*). He has seen your frightful and terrible army but does not get frightened Surely he will conquer you all as a great hero. It is impossible, you must not think of harming him, but be humble and have faith in Buddha, the Blessed One. Hence, it is better to go back without fighting with him.[59] Māra's religious minded sons this way tried to dissuade him from attacking the Buddha. But the wicked Māra being ignored the advice of his spiritual minded sons ordered his army to attack the Buddha for the last time with such a violent force as would not spare his life. Māra's strong army charged the Buddha with all sorts of weapons and implements and with various satanic means but their hopes and cruel attempts was frustrated His evil followers were utterly defeated by the Divine Power of Buddha. The *Lalitavistara* has elaborately discussed the victory of Buddha over the enemy Māra in a most commanding way:

देवासुरा गरुड राक्षस किन्नरेन्द्रा
ब्रह्माथ शक्र परनिर्मित साकनिष्ठाः।
भाषन्ति तस्य विजयं जय लोकवीर
यत्रेदृशी नमुचिसेन त्वया निरस्ता॥[60]

At the end, the Devendra (Indra), Asurendra, Garuḍendra, Rākṣasendra, Kinnarendra, Brahmā and other gods including the gods of *Bodhivṛkṣas*[61] had congratulated Lord Buddha for his great victory over the evil power Māra and his army. Then, while Buddha was being worshipped and honored by the *devatās* and Lord Brahmā with flowers, etc., Māra's religious minded (pious) sons brought an umbrella and a big canopy for the Buddha and with folded hands they eulogized the Great Lord in these words: "Oh Blessed One, we bow to you with sincere devotion and great respects, because you have defeated us. You are only Divine Being who exerts for the welfare of the beings in this universe. The devils and other harmful powers could not oppose your religious activity, nor could they shake you from your place of meditation under the pious Bodhi tree. Finally, Māra came to the Buddha and told him that it was the time for his attainment of *Nirvāṇa* and after obtaining this he should leave this universe. But Buddha was not pleased with the advice of Māra, rather he said, "My disciples are devoted and quite firm in their faith; until I see them free from sufferings and constantly establish in the world the name of Buddha, Dharma and Saṅgha, I shall not leave this world." It is known that Lord Buddha has defeated Māra and obtained *Nirvāṇa,* while he was sitting in *Bhūmisparśa-mudrā*. The earth even has witnessed this great victory.

It can be safely concluded that the fight of the Buddhas or Bodhisattvas with Māra is a struggle against the fetters and hindrances that stand in the way to achieve the emancipation, i.e. *Nirvāṇa*. It is just a war between good and bad ideology and between *daivī-pravṛtti* and *āsurī-pravṛtti*, just like the war of Indra and Vṛtra, as described in the *Ṛgveda*.[62] However, this may be a war among the *indriyas* of human beings as happening in our day to day life. Sometimes, it is also seen, when we intend to perform any religious ceremony, many obstacles come before us to complete it. As said: '*śreyāṅsi bahu vighnāni*'. So, Māra may be known as some weak state of mind through which the right decision or any auspicious work cannot be taken or performed properly. However, by controlling over one's own mind and sense organs one can control over Māra, and finally he will reach at the destination of his life, i.e. emancipation or *Nirvāṇa*.

REFERENCES

1. *Amarakośa*, I.1.25.
2. *Atharvaveda*, VI.93.1.
3. *ibid.*, VI.26.1.
4. तानि अस्य गर्भ एव सन्ति पाप्मा मृत्युरगृह्णात् । ..... सर्वाणि भूतानि पाप्मनो मृत्योः स्पृणोति .... ॥ शतपथब्राह्मण, VIII.4.2.1-2; cf. कृष्णबन्धु पापीमं .... । महावस्तु अवदान, II.238(7).
5. Padhāna Sutta, Verse 2 (P.T.S. 426).
6. नमुचि करुणां वाचं भाषमाण इहागमत्। महावस्तु अवदान, II.238 (II.26.2).
7. XXI.173.
8. युवं सुरामनाश्विना नमुचावासुरे सचा। ऋग्वेद, X.131.4.
9. सुत्तनिपात, verse 355; (II.12.13), cf. कण्हस्स पक्खेति, *ibid.*, 967.
10. I.93.10.
11. (अट्ठ खो) (इमा, आनन्द, परिसा। कतमा अट्ठ?) The eight *pariṣadas* are: (1) खत्तियपरिसा, (2) ब्राह्मणपरिसा, (3) ग्रहपतिपरिसा, (4) समणपरिसा, (5) धातुमहाराजिकपरिसा, (6) तावतिंसपरिसा, (7) मारपरिसा, and (8) ब्रह्मपरिसा। दीघनिकाय, II.109 (P.T.S.).
12. महन्तं हत्थिराज वण्णं अभिनिमिनित्वा.... - संयुक्तनिकाय, I.103 ff. (and महन्तं सप्पराज वण्णं ....).
13. *Saṁyutta Nikāya*, I, p. 114 (P.T.S.).
14. *Bhagavad Gītā*, XV.6.
15. *Vinaya Piṭaka*, I, pp. 21-22 *(baddho'si sabba pāsehi, etc.)*.
16. *Jātaka*, I. 72-73 (P.T.S.).
17. 'मारो अयं पापिमा' - इति विदित्वा.... संयुत्तनिकायपालि, मारसंयुत्तं 1 (P.T.S. I.103); cf. .... मारं पापिमन्तं एतदवोच - मज्झिमनिकाय, मारतज्जनीयसुत्तं, Sutta 50.1.
18. *Saṁyutta Nikāya*, I.115 (IV.19).
19. *Majjhima Nikāya*, III.94.
20. *Sutta Nipāta*, 429 (III.2.5).
21. *ibid.*, 436-37 (III.2.12-13); cf. *Mahāvastu Avadāna*, II.240 (verse 19-21).
22. *ibid.*, 439 (III.2.15).
23. *ibid.*, 446 (III.2.22).
24. सर्वमारमारकायिक देवता निर्जेतुकामेन निर्जेतुकामेन सर्वावरणीयानि....। शिक्षासमुच्चय, XIV.20 (244, P.T.S.).
25. *Lalitavistara*, 283.20.
26. *Buddha Carita*, XIII.2cd.
27. ततो धनुः पुष्पमयं गृहीत्वा शरान् जगन्मोहकरांश्च पञ्च ।
    सोऽश्वत्थमूलं ससुतोऽभ्यगच्छदस्वास्थ्यकारी मनसः प्रजानाम्॥ *ibid*; XIII.7.
28. *ibid.*, XIII.19.
29. *ibid.*, XIII.9.
30. *Saundarananda*, III.7cd.
31. सळायतनसंयुत्तं, लोककामगुणवग्गो दुतियो, पठममारपाससंयुत्तं (Vol. IV, p. 91, P.T.S.).
32. संयुत्तनिकाय, खन्ध संयुत्तं, अरहन्त वग्गो, उपादियमानसुत्तं (Vol. III, p. 73, P.T.S.).
33. *Dhammapada*, Yamakavagga, verse 7.

34. *ibid.*, verse 8.
35. *ibid.*, Cittavagga, verse 5.
36. *ibid.*, Taṇhāvagga, verse 4.
37. *ibid*, Taṇhāvagga, verse 17.
38. *ibid.*, Maggavagga, verse 2.
39. प्रतिपन्नाः प्रमोक्ष्यन्ते धयायिनो मारबन्धाना; *ibid.*, verse 4.
40. *Nettiprakaraṇa*, pp. 8-9 (P.T.S.).
41. *Udāna* (मेघियवग्ग) IV.2 (P.T.S. 38).
    Cf. अरक्खितेन चित्तेन ....वसं मारस्य गच्छतीति। नेत्तिप्रकरण, III.13.1 (p. 85, P.T.S.).
42. *Visuddhimagga*, Vol. I, p. 73 (P.T.S.).
43. *ibid.*, Vol. I, p. 79 (P.T.S.).
44. *Niddesa*, Vol. I, p. 475 (P.T.S.).
45. *Itivuttaka*, p. 58 (P.T.S.).
46. *ibid.*, p. 92 (P.T.S.).
47. अंगुत्तरनिकाय, तिक्कनिपातो, देवदूतवग्गो, अधिपतेय्यसुत्तं (I.150, P.T.S.).
48. *ibid.*, चतुक्कनिपातो, चरवग्गो, पधानसुत्तं (II.15, P.T.S.).
49. विनयपिटक, महावग्ग, I.12.
50. *ibid.*
51. मज्झिमनिकाय, मारतज्जनीय सुत्त (337, P.T.S.).
52. *Lalitavistara*, 387 (Ch. XXI.24).
53. Chapter XXI (P.T.S. 387-397).
54. ये च तवेमे पुत्रः प्रज्ञा मेधाविनश्च बलिनश्च।
    ते बोधिसत्त्वहृदयं अनुप्रविष्टा नमस्यन्ति।। ललितविस्तर, XXI.68 (398, P.T.S.).
55. *Mahāvastu,* II.408.10ff.
56. *Lalitavistara*, XXI.163 (P.T.S. 426).
57. का शक्तिरस्ति मम दृष्टिहतस्य तस्य।
    संजीवितुं, जगति मृत्युहतस्य वाऽस्तु ।। *ibid.*, XXI.26 (P.T.S. 388).
58. *ibid.*, XXI.39cd (P.T.S. 391).
59. तस्मान्निवर्तामहे तात सर्वे । *ibid.*, XXI.52 (393, P.T.S.).
    Cf. निवर्तितव्यं क्षमं प्राज्ञैः । *ibid.*, XXI.74 (398, P.T.S.).
    Also cf. श्रेयो भवे प्रतिनिवर्तितुमद्य तात।। *ibid.*, XXI.137 (421, P.T.S.).
60. *ibid.*, XXI.199 (438, P.T.S.).
61. The gods of (eight) *Bodhivṛkṣas* are: Śrī, Vṛddhi, Tapā, Śreyasī, Vidu, Ojobalā, Satyavādinī and Samaṅginī.
    अथ खलु भिक्षवस्तस्मिन् समयेऽष्टौ बोधिवृक्षदेवताः। तद्यथा–श्रीः, वृद्धि, तपा, श्रेयसी, विदुः, ओजोबला, सत्यवादिनी समङ्गनी च। *ibid.*, 139, Prose text (421-422, P.T.S.).
62. *Ṛgveda* I.32 (cf. Griswold, H.D., *The Religion of the Ṛgveda*, pp. 178-86, Oxford, 1923).

Nature of the Absolute in Kashmir Śaivism

Kashmir Śaivism is a well developed monistic system which deserves a significant place amongst the great philosophies of the world. It is called Kashmir Śaivism because the writers who enriched its literature belonged to and flourished in this area.[1]

This Śaiva system is purely a monistic system of philosophy which represents the absolutistic development of Śaiva tradtion, and may be described as theistic absolutism, "*Īśvarādvayavāda*". Since ancient times Advaitism appears to be a very favourite concept of the Indians. Elements of Advaitism can certainly be traced in Saṁhitās. It was popular both in the Upaniṣads as well as in the Epics. Different forms of absolutism prevailed during early days. The elements which gave rise to the growth of integral Śaiva Absolutism were present in the ancient Śaiva theology.[2] But before the emergence of absolutistic Śaivism, the Buddhist thought was predominent in Kashmir. Though Śaivism has its own ancient tradition and seems to be the native faith of Kashmir, there has been a tremendous influence of Buddhism upon its development. Prior to the advent of Buddhim in Kashmir, Śaivism was confined to a simple form of worship.[3] It is the Buddhist concept of *Śūnyatā* which provided the metaphysical foundation for the growth of integral Advaitism within the Śaiva tradition. The influence of *Śūnyavāda* upon Tantricism has been widely recognised

It has also been said that Śaṅkara had close affinity with Tantricism. There are some indications of Śaṅkara's affinity to Pratyabhijñā thought. Śaṅkara himself was a great devotee of Śrīvidyā which has many similarities with the Pratyabhijñā. The authorship of *Prapañcasāra* also has been attributed to Śaṅkara. There prevailed the popular view that Śaṅkara wrote the commentary on the *Brahma Sūtras* after repeatedly reflecting upon *Sūta-Saṁhitā*[4] which contains teachings similar to Śaiva Absolutism. If *Dakṣiṇāmūrti Stotra* could be regarded as a work of Śaṅkara, then his relationship with Tantricism can easily be established[5] The fact that many adherents of Śaivism and Śāktism, like Bhaskara Ray and others, referring to Śaṅkara as an authority after his death also points out the relationship.[6] Moreover, Śaṅkara's influence of Kashmir Śaivism can very well be judged from the fact that this system could develop only after Śaṅkara had visited Kashmir. The visit of Śaṅkara proved to be of great help to the local Śaivites in their struggle against Buddhism which had been a serious challange to them. It appears as if the great master of Vedānta cleared the way for the rise and advancement of Śaiva Absolutism.

The term 'absolute' is quite vague and elusive in its metaphysical usage. The absolute is a term used by philosophers to signify the ultimate reality regarded as one and yet as the source of variety, as complete and perfect, and as not divorced from the finite, imperfect world.[7] Every absolutism is infact an advaitism or *advayavāda*, a nondualism. The absolute is the sole and supreme reality in the Mādhyamika, the Yogācāra, the Vedānta, and the Kashmir Śaivism.

Kashmir Śaivism believes in the existence of one reality which has been variously called as the Supreme Śiva (Parama Śiva), Supreme Lord (Parameśvara), Supreme Saṁvid (*Para Saṁvid*) and supreme experiencing principle. The essential characteristic of Śaiva Absolute is the free act of consciousness. The Śaivite interpretation of the Supreme Self is unique in itself and is not found anywhere else. The act of Consciousness, or the characteristic feature of the agent in the act of consciousness, is spoken of as the self. Unlike the Vedāntin who conceives consciousness as pure consciousness, the Śaivite regards it essentially as free consciousness. It can not be described as *Śūnya* which is wholly negative in character. Freedom alone is the distinguishing feature of the absolute. It is the cause of real, not illusory manifestation of the world. So, the Śaiva absolute might be described as essentially free being. The term "*svātantrya*" indicates that the essence of consciousness consists in great Lordship (*Māheśvarya*). It represents the chief characteristic of the absolute according to Śaivite. In this respect, Paramaśiva differs from Brahman.[8] *Svātantrya Śakti,* being essentially the power of consciousness, is also known as *cit śakti*. Sometimes it also stands for self consciousness. The term "*svātantrya*" has also frequently been used in the Śaiva literature. So the Śaiva Absolutism has often been described as "*Svātantryavāda*".

Although the terms like *svātantrya*, *śakti*, *ahaṁtā*, *sphūrattā*, *vimarśa*, etc. represent the dynamic aspect of the absolute, all of them do not equally emphasize the same form of dynamism. While *ahaṁtā* emphasizes the dynamism of integration, *sphūrattā* indicated the manifestation of the unmanifest. Similarly, *vimarśa* expresses the determination of the indeterminate and *svātantrya* stands for the capacity to perform the impossible.

In its essential nature, the absolute has been conceived as being, consciousness and bliss (*sat, cit, ānanda*), in both Śaiva and Vedānta Absolutisms. But, unlike the Vedānta Absolutism, there is no clear cut distinction between the accidental characteristics of the Absolute in the Śaiva Absolutism. Accordingly, we shall be confined mainly to considering the distinction between the concepts of "*saccidānanda*" in the two systems. It has rightly been said that although each of these three terms denotes one and the same entity, each does so differently. These terms are not concepts or predicates, each is *'Sui generis'* the self. Being, Consciousness and Bliss are employed only to differentiate them from their opposites, signifying that self is not non-being, etc. But this does not amount to Buddhist *apohavāda,* which means exclusion from all other, e.g. the concept 'blue' means merely that is not yellow, not red, etc.[9] Both the Śaivite and Vedāntin reject the view that existence is momentary. They commonly hold that the eternal existence is the ground and support of all variable and finite existence. But whereas the Vedāntin regards the finite and momentary existence as limitation of the absolute pure existence, the Śaivite holds it to be a real manifestation of the infinite existence. The Vedāntin holds that the 'red' is such that its nature remains constant and unreal.

In the Śaiva system, the absolute is taken to be the fullest and richest existence. It is the all, the transcedent and integral reality of all finite existence. It is one, or same, which is the perfect harmony of opposites. There is no negation of finitude, but merely a rejection of discord in it. It is being, such as does not include not being; it is consciousness which manifests even the absence of consciousness.[10] The Vedāntin puts '*sat*' before the beginning of everything and regards it to be the ultimate principle. According to them existence would cease to be eternal, if it is also varied with the variable. So it can not be denoted by words which, like 'being', in the usual sense signify a category of things. Being or existence has to be regarded as coeval with consciousness, without consciousness, existence would be nothing in itself. That is why the Śaivite and the Vedāntin both agree that existence and consciousness can not be related to each other as substance and attribute.

In the Śaiva Absolutism, '*cit*' or consciousness, like existence, is illimitable and infinite. In the absolute existence consciousness, there is an inherent freedom or power which is infinite in itself. Consciousness in its very essence is conscious power (*cit śakti*). Unlike the Vedāntin, who conceives consciousness, the Śaivite regards it essentially as free consciousness. As there is no conception of '*cit śakti*' in the Vedānta, there can be no place for the doctrine of absolute self consciousness in it. In Śaiva Absolutism, the Absolute is *ānanda*, because, besides being the *bhūma*, it is also freedom or *vimarśa*, or self consciousness. This brings out the main difference of the Śaiva conception of *ānanda* from that of the Vedānta. Parama Śiva is itself described as *ānanda* and there is also the experience of *ānanda* in it. If there were no conscionsness of *ānanda*, there could be no sense in describing the absolute in terms of Bilss. We have to accept that in the absolute there is an experience of *ānanda*. But in Vedānta, on the other hand, the absolute does not have any conciousness of *ānanda*; it is *ānanda* itself. *Ānanda* can not be regarded as an object of experience, as there is no subject-object relationship within Brahman. An admission of such distinction would amount to a division of the indivisible non-dual Reality. So obviously, the description of the Absolute as '*saccidānanda*' has different implictions in the two systems. According to Śiva Absolutist, Parama Śiva is ever a personal-impersonal God. Will (*Icchā*), Knowledge (*Jñāna*), and Action (*Kriyā*) constitute the essential nature of '*saccidānanda*' and the world is a real manifestation of it. The two highest power, viz., Cit Śakti, and Ānanda Śakti, are fully manifest both at the transcedent and empirical levels. The other three Śaktis : Icchā, Jñāna and Kriyā, become manifest only during Creation. So He is all pervading and at the same time He is also all transcending. That is to say His nature has a 'two fold'[11] aspect. The first one is an immanent aspect (*viśvātmaka*) in which form He pervades and permeates the entire universe and is one and all. In the later form he transcends all and is beyond all universal manifestations in which aspect (*viśvottīrṇa*). He has been called *Anuttara*[12] and *Tattvātīta* or *Paratattva*.[13] The word *anuttara* implies that it is a reality beyond which there is nothing. It is not to be spoken of as 'this' or 'that' nor as 'not this' or 'not that'. This concept of *anuttara* is very much similar to that of pure Brahman of Vedāntin. The Śaivite also agrees with Vedāntin in accepting the world as non-different from Brahman, but rejects the Vedāntic view that the world is illusery. For them (Śaivites) the world is a real manifestation of the Absolute. The universe is essentially identical with the Absolute.[14]

The Śaiva absolutist describes Parama-Śiva as '*caitanya*'.[15] The Vedāntins also conceive Brahman, the Supreme Reality as of the nature of *caitanya* which is self-effulgence light. But according to Trika school, *caitanya* is not merely the nature of *Śuddha Prakāśa* which does not always shine and illumine but also possesses power of self-illumination or self-manifestation. The *caitanya* in the Trika system, is therefore, described as *prakāśa-vimarśamaya*. *Prakāśa* stands for the pure changeless witness aspect of the universal consciousness. *Vimarśa*, on the other hand, stands for the power which gives rise to self-consciousness, self-knowledge and action successively. *Prakāśa* and *Vimarśa* are inseparable. *Prakāśa* is regarded as the 'Śiva' and *Vimarsa* is regarded as '*śakti*' and the *nityasāmarasya* of Śiva and Śakti is Paramaśiva. But Vedāntins do not admit the above view of Śaivites. Neither do they admit to *Māyā* as a *Śakti* of Brahman, nor they admit that there is an inherent relation between Brahman and *Māyā*. Hence, in this respect Śaivites are clearly opposed to Vedāntins.

The Śaiva absolutist also describes the Parama Śiva as the Absolute subject (*Para-pramātā*). The Absolute is the supreme "I" the all-inclusive Reality. The conception of the Absolute as the supreme ego enables the Śaivite to avoid the two extremes of the danger of drifting towards the abstract of pure monism of the Vedānta type and drowning into the great void of the Mādhyamika. But it is not necessary to reject either the subject or the object, the knower or the known, in order to arrive at the notion of the Absolute. For, it is the very nature of the self to manifest itself simultaneously as the knower and the known, as it ever performs the transcendental functions of *nigraha* and *anugraha*, self concealment and self revelation. The 'I' is the integral and all-comprehensive reality and indicates the all-inclusive and the all-pervading nature of Absolute. The use of the pronoun of the first person (*I* or *aham*) shows that Śiva is the essential ego or the subject of thought in all forms of consciousness. The '*ah*' in '*aham*' represents all the letters of the Devanāgarī alphabetic system from '*A* to *H*' and as such, signifies all the basic ideas manifested by the absolute consciousness. '*AM*' stands for '*bindu*' and signifies that the Absolute, the Anuttara, though manifesting itself in the various forms of thought does not lose its essential nature but ever remains in its own unbroken light of consciousness.[16] All the ideas, which are represented by the letters form '*A* to *H*' arise from the rest in the Absolute in so far as they are the manifestation of its power of freedom.[17]

As we have seen, the Śaiva Absolutist insists that the Absolute being the integral reality in all, it is both *Nirguṇa* as well as *Saguṇa* and is always endowed with the power of free consciousness. What the Vedāntin describes as the Highest reality, the *Nirguṇa* Brahman, is in Reality a lower form of reality. Beyond the *Nirguṇa*, there are higher forms of manifestation of the Absolute which can not be limited to this or that form. The main concern of the Śaivite is to establish the absoluteness of God. According to them, the God of religion is itself the Absolute and Ultimate Reality. We have also seen that in the Śaiva Absolutism, the Absolute is regarded not merely as being consciousness but also as the being which is at the same time self-consciousness. However, unlike the Mādhyamika Absolute which does not even have a nature (*svarūpa*) of its own, the Vedānta Absolute is being itself. But according to Śaiva Absolutists, the Vedānta absolute lacks consciousness. Possession of both being and consciousness constitutes the essential nature of the Śaiva Absolute.

In the final analysis, we have to admit that every Absolutism, in spite of its similarities with others, has its peculiar characteristics owing to its unique tradition and approach which provide it an individuality. Like wise, the nature of Absolute (Supreme Reality) in Kashmir Śaivism, which has been explained, is completely different from other *āstika darśanas* in Indian Philosophy. In this Kashmir-Śaiva-system, the Absolute is said not to be limited or conditioned by *Kāla*, i.e. *trikālabādhita*, *deśa* and form. Also his real *svarūpa* has been characterised as *viśvātmaka* and *viśvottīrṇa* in this system. In this respect His (Parama Śiva) nature appears to be more clear than any other *āstika darśanas* and as a result, it deserves a unique place amongst other philosophies of the world.

REFERENCES

1. *The Cultural Heritage of India,* Vol. IV, Part-I, p. 79, 2nd Edition, 1956, Kolkatta.
2. Zimmer, M.: *Myths and Symbols in Indian Art and Civilization.* Ed. by Joseph Campbell, Washington, Panthen Books,1946, Part-III, Ch. V.
3. Panday, K.C.: Abhinavagupta, *An Historical and Philosophical Study.* Varanasi, Chowkhamba, 1929, Also cf. Kaviraj, G., *Philosophy of Eastern and Western,* Vol. 1, page 192.
4. *tamastandaśadhālocya śaṅkara śūtasaṁhitāṁ cakre śārīrakaṁ bhāṣyaṁ sarva-vedāntanirṇayam.*
5. In this point Prof. S.S. Sūryanārāyaṇa Śāstrī holds that it is possible that more than one Pratyabhijñā work has derived from Advaita sources, where in a work like the *Dakṣiṇāmūrtistotra*, there are many points common to *Advaita* and

Pratyabhijñā, it will rest without further evidence to conclude the derivation of either of the two.....Collected Papers, University of Madras, 1961, pp. 223-24.

6. Kaviraj, G.: *Bhāratīya Saṁskṛti aur Sādhanā,* Patna, 1957 (Ist Hindi Edition), p. 292.
7. *The Encyclopaedia of Philosophy,* Vol. I, The Macmillan Co., and the Free Press, New York, 1967.
8. *"Śvātantrya" śabdo brahmavādavailakṣaṇam ācakṣaṇaḥ cito māheśvarysāratāṁ brūte—Pratyabhijñāhṛdayam,* I, Comm. (K.S.T.S.).
9. Chaudhury, A.K.: *Self and Falsity in Advaita Vedānta,* p. 111.
10. *Paryanta Pañcāśikā,* 2-3 (K.S.T.S.).
11. *Viśvātmaka and Viśvattīrṇa, Śrīmat paramaśivasya punaḥ viśvottīrṇaviśvātmaka paramānandamaya prakāśaikaghanasya—Pratyabhijñā Hṛdaya,* p. 8 (K.S.T.S.).
12. *"na vidyate uttaraṁ praśnaprativatorūpam"—Parātrīṁśikā Vivaraṇa,* p. 19 (K.S.T.S.).
13. *"yat paratattvam"—Paramārthasāra*, Kā-11, edited by J.C. Chatterji, Srinagar, 1916.
14. *Pratyabhijñā Hṛdaya* of Kṣemarāja, Vol. III (K.S.T.S.).
15. *"Caitanyamātmā" –Śiva Sūtra,* 1, Comm. p.3 : *"Caitanya rūpopi svayam..... Paramārthasāra,"* Kā—1, Comm., p.3.
16. *Tantrāloka*, (Abhinavagupta) Edited with Comm. of Jayaratha, Srinagar (K.S.T.S.), 1918, pp. 193-194.
17. Pāṇini's *Aṣṭādhyāyī*, II. 2.72; see also *Tantrāloka*, 11, p.196.

Abhinavagupta on Mystical Experience

Mystical experience is, as old as humanity, undoubtedly one of the original grounds of personal religion, and does not stand or fall with the truth or falsity of the metaphysically formulated doctrine of mysticism. It is marked by the emergence of a type of consciousness which is not sharply focalized or clearly differentiated into a subject-object state. Whatever is seen, heard or felt in these moments is flooded within rush from the abysses (spiritual profundity) of the inner life. Deep-lying powers, not ordinarily put into play, seem suddenly liberated The usual insulations which keeps apart our inner life into something like compartments, seem shot through. The whole being is an integral and undivided experience finds itself. Not only so, but transcendent energies from beyond the margin appear to invade the individual self, a larger, environing consciousness, an enfolding presence, makes itself felt. Lofty appreciation of beauty or sublimity, absorbed enjoyment of music, serene companionship with nature, sudden insight into the meaning of a truth, the awakening of love, moral exaltation of life in the pursuit of duty, illustrate some types of experience which immensely transcend 'knowledge'—experiences in which subject and object are fused into an undifferentiated one, in which self is identified with object.

'Mysticism' on the other hand, in its narrow and exact historical significance is a doctrine of union with the Absolute. In this context, it implies a certain metaphysical conception of God and of the soul, and it implies further, 'a mystic way' of attaining union with the Absolute.

Abhinavagupta was the leading exponent and staunch adherent of the Trika philosophy of Kashmir. He was a mystic, a profoundly religious man, a scholar of great intellectual powers, a philosopher and a literary critic of great repute. He revolutionised Indian aesthetics by providing a strong and philosophical foundation. He succeeded largely in confirming the aesthetic experience of all art forms—poetry, music, dance, drama, etc. with mystic and religious status of ecstasy. He visualised and established intimate associations between on philosophy and aesthetics. Besides, his philosophical works contain a detailed discussion on mystical experience. Being a chief exponent of this monistic system of Śiva thought he has written a large number of books and commentaries. The important works are: *Tantrāloka, Tantrasāra, Tantravaṭa-dhānikā, Mālinī-Vijaya-Vārttika, Paramārthasāra, Īśvara Pratyabhijñā Vimarśinī* and *Īśvara Pratyabhijñā Vṛtti Vimarśinī*. These works definitely contain the central ideas of mystical experience.

The distinguishing features of Abhinavagupta's conception of the Supreme Reality is that He (Supreme Being) is of immanent Reality who pervades and permeats the entire creation and therefore is called the *Ātman*[1] or *Caitanya,* at the same time He transcends the entire creation and as transcendental Reality. He is named as *Anuttara* and *Tattvātīta* (Absolute). The two aspects of His nature symbolise His integral character. This is because Abinavagupta holds the Supreme Reality to be endowed with Divine *Śakti,* which ceaselessly functions, thereby manifests Divine Glory sometimes as the cosmos and at after times as Supreme Being or Supreme Lord. Śaivites consider the whole world to be real as if Parama Śiva Himself who becomes fettered being (*śiva eva gṛhīta paśubhāvaḥ*).[2] Abhinavagupta deals this as a Kashmir Śaivite point of view like as Śiva, He is perfectly free from all the impurities, i.e., three *malas*. But when He is associated with *māyā,* His own volition or free will manifests Himself as limited being (*cidaṇu*). At the same time, He is known as *paśu* or *jīva*, the bound one. Really there is no essential difference between the Supreme Reality and the man (*jīva*). Because, it is His real nature or *svabhāva* to manifest, i.e., manifest as the beings or *paśus*. Abhinavagupta says the universe is a real manifestation of the Absolute.[3] The universe comprising thirty-six *tattvas* shines the Supreme element, which is radiant, mightily, blissful from its being merged in the Self, fully stored with will and without origination and dissolution. During the state of creation the Self is called *sakala,* as it is subject to all the impurities. These experiencers being associated with organs are related with the objects or actions are covered with body.[4] The *sakalas* are only embodied *paśu pramātās* and as such they are said to be covered by all the three *malas,* viz. *āṇava*, *kārma,* and *māyīya*. The *sakalas* which includes the entire range of being, beginning with planets and creepers up to various duties, are also classified under three heads, viz. human, superhuman and sub-human *sakalas*. The human being constitute only a part of the vast range of creation, but owing to their procession of *kārmadeha* (a type of body) which enable them to enjoy fruits of their deeds. The super human *sakalas* are called *deva,* the human *sakalas* are called *manuṣyas* and the sub-human *sakalas* are called the *tiryak sakalas*.

Each human being has normally an experience of three states of consciousness—waking, dreaming and deep-sleep. The fourth state is known as *turya*[5] and the fifth is called *turyātīta*. These states corresponds to the different stages of manifestation. The waking state is called *viśva,* or the *virāj* form of Brahman because of differentiation. The dreaming state is called *tejas,* i.e., the *tejas* form of Brahman, because of the greatness of the light. The deep sleep is called *prajñā* or understanding, i.e., the *prajñā* form of Brahman. The fourth state is *turya*. Every man's consciousness functions only in three states, viz. *jāgrat, svapana* and *suṣupti*. When *udāna śakti* becomes active in the *suṣumnā,* one developes the consciousness of *turya* or the fourth state in which one has unity-consciousness and the sense of difference disappear. This consciousness is full of Bliss. In the first of waking condition, the body, *prāṇa, manas* and senses are active. In the second or dreaming condition, the *prāṇa* and *manas* alone are active. In the third or the state of deep sleep, even the *manas* stops functioning, and *ātman* or pure consciousness is in association with mere void. In the *turya* state *ātman* is detached from these limitations, and remains pure consciousness and Bliss. Micro-cosmically, it is the fourth state holding together the three functions (*kṛtyas*) of *sṛṣṭi, sthiti* and *saṁhāra.*

Turyātīta is fifth and final state. This state is beyond the *turya* state. It is called *turyātīta,* in which the *turya* state transcended It is that state which is full of uninterrupted divine rapture of I-consciousness. There is no question of phases of this state. It is the state of fullest realization. There is no need of any *yogic* practice now. In it even the distinction between the transcendent and the immanent disappears. Everything appears to the individual as Śiva.

In order to attain the divinity or liberation the Divine Grace is direly needed for the human being. Divine Grace or *śaktipāta* leads the individual to the path of spiritual realisation. It is the last act of the Supreme Power, which leads to the attainment of final release. Abhinavagupta arrives at the conclusion that Divine Grace is absolutely undetermined and unconditioned The postulation of conditions or qualifications would be against the doctrine of free will of the absolute which carries on the sport of self bondage and release.[6] It has been stated in the *Tantrāloka* that *śaktipāta* is in essence the descent of the highest light on the limited soul. It is free from all limitations and is of the characteristic of pure consciousness.[7] It should be remembered in this context that *śaktipāta* is really of the nature of *icchā* or *arugraha* of the Lord. Divine Grace has been classified into various types as slow, fast, faster, etc. depending upon the nature of its intensity. Throughout all these forms, it is the Lord who illumines His own nature. In reality, there is no other cause of these manifestations excepts His freedom, which alone gives rise to *mokṣa*. Depending upon the degree in which the Divine Grace has fallen upon him, the initiate adopts a particular means for self-realisation. While describing the nature of *mokṣa,* Abhinavagupta says in the *Paramārthasāra* that there is no separate reason of it, nor one is to proceed towards it, but it is to be realised by piercing the knots of ignorance by virtue of full development of one's own power of freedom.[8] *Mokṣa* should not be considered as the effect of *jñāna* and the later the cause of it, but it is the manifestation of the real nature of *ātman.*[9] Four successive means (*upāyas*) of attaining release have been prescribed in Śaivism. They are called *Āṇavopāya, Śāktopāya, Śāmbhavopāya* and *Anupāya.*[10] All of these means do not directly lead to self realisation. The preceding one among them leads to the succeeding one and, accordingly, only the last, viz. *Anupāya,* can be regarded as the direct means of release. These *upāyas* are recommended to get rid of the *malas* so that one may fit for receiving grace.

In the state of release, the *yogin* realises his identity with the whole universe, and attains perfect and Supreme Egoity. The invidividual who has the cognition of identity and regards the universe to be a sport and is always united with it, is undoubtedly liberated in life. To him the entire objective world appears merely as a reflection in the self. The released soul looks upon the universe as his own self. To him this entire universe appears as Bliss and identical with *Vimarśa.* The released soul realises that the universe consists in the unfolding of his own nature, so says the sacred tradition concerning them. At the final stage the *yogin* realises that all activity of the mind evolves from the Supreme Power and that the universe is really absolute being identical with the Absolute. This true conception figures in his consciousness by the activity of the mind. He sees that the universe revealed to him in modes of imagination as an operation of the mind is real and identical with the light, for conscious is present in it through and through.[11] The difference between the bound and released souls is that while the bound understands and experiences the objects as different from himself, the released looks upon them as one with himself. The *yogin* regards himself to be identical with the Absolute Ego, which is the prompter of all subjects from Sadāśiva to a worm. Accordingly he thinks, 'all that can be object of a congnition in the universe is also mine, similarly, what is my object of cognition, the same is the object of cognition of all beings in the universe'. That object is a part of myself and so are others also. Thus, all figure in his consciousness as ultimately merged in the pure unity of the self.[12] It is like the embrace of the dearest beloved for the first time, wherein one has no consciousness of sleep. It is sheer awareness, pure consciousness and objectlessness.

The Indian theory of *Pratyabhijñā* or recognition is based similarly on the essential unity of subject and object. All kinds of knowledge are of the nature of recognition, for its subject and object are essentially identical and united at a primary timeless stage, all perceptions are bound to be recognitions. According to Abhinavagupta the language of divine or pure self consciousness is so united with itself that it may be truely called its self. He further clarified the unity of word with meaning. In the most primary state, word is so united with its meaning that it may be said that word is meaning and meaning is word; intuition is expression and *vice-versa*. In the primary state thus, word is consciousness and meaning is self or existence. Both are completely united It is not possible to distinguish existence from consciousness then. In the second stage, word is an intuitive expression felt distinct but not separate from intuition. Here word is Divine will or percept. In the third stage, word is Divine knowledge or concept.

These three states of word as consciousness, will and knowledge are all divine and are known as *parā, paśyantī* and *madhyamā* respectively. In these states word is a kind of divine intuitive light. Such a unity of word and meaning is the highest manifestation of truth and being, language and thought, subject and object, existence and consciousness. Regarding the divine *mantras* Abhinavagupta says:

हृदयं च नाम प्रतिष्ठास्थानमुच्यते.....सर्वस्य हि मन्त्र एव हृदयम्, मन्त्रश्च विमर्शनात्मा, विमर्शनं च परा वाक्शक्तिमयम्।[13]

Hṛdaya means main stay or resting place. For, the heart, the resting place (*hṛdaya*) of all is *mantra,* which, in its essence, is nothing but free consciousness, which also is simply the power of the transcendental speech (*parā vāk*).

The following statements have been made in the Āgamas just because of this:

न तैर्विना भवेच्छब्दो नार्थो नापि चितेर्गतिः।[14]

This means without the *mantras* there will be no sound nor meaning nor the grasp of light of consciousness. The same has been asserated by Bhartṛhari also and thus Abhinavagupta quotes the verses of the *Vākyapadīya.*

न सोऽस्ति प्रत्ययो लोके यः शब्दानुगमादृते।
अनुविद्धमिव ज्ञानं सर्वं शब्देन गम्यते।।

वाग्रूपता चेदुत्क्रामेद् अवबोधस्य शाश्वती।
न प्रकाशः प्रकाशेत सा हि प्रत्यवमर्शिनी।।[15]

There is no congnition in the world (*loka*) in which the word does not figure. All knowledge and experiences at the time we have them, are as it were presented by word.

If the internal identity of thought (knowledge) and the word were to disappear, cognition would not be cognition, because it is this *vāgrūpatā* which brings about the identification and the mutual determination of the word meanings.

It is from this unity that all the letters of the alphabet and all the objects of the universe as well as our consciousness of them derived Thus the relation between subject and object is spoken of in the Trika Philosophy as a relation between the word and its meaning. In this context it will be discussed about of nature of *mātṛkā, bindu* and *varṇa*.

A threefold form of limited knowledge is in the form of threefold *mala*. Of this threefold limited knowledge that which makes oneself consider himself as incomplete and imperfect is the *āṇava mala;* that which brings a sense of difference in everything is *māyīya mala;* that which makes one perform good or bad deeds is *kārma mala*. Of this threefold limited knowledge, *mātṛkā* (or alphabet form '*a*' to '*kṣa*'), the mother of the entire universe is the presiding deity. So, ultimately it is *mātṛkā* which is responsible for the limited knowledge, i.e., three *malas*. She is called *mātṛkā,* because she is unknown and unintelligible. It is through *mātṛkā*, therefore, that all human activities are carried on. So long as the mystery of *mātṛkā* is not understood, we are only involved in the 'fret and fever'of life. If a person wants to understand the mystery of life, if he wants to turn to the source of his being, he will have to understand the mystery of *mātṛkā*. When unknown, the *mātṛkā* impels people towards all kinds of worldly activities and feelings. When the *mātṛkā* is known, i.e., when her saving power is realized, she leads one to liberation (*mokṣa*).

Mātṛkā is the subtle form of gross speech. The *parā vāk* or the I-consciousness of the Supreme is the reason for existence of the *mantras*. So, *mantras* are consisting of letters or words. These letters are not meaningless jargon. They are symbols of the creative *śaktis* of the Divine. These *śaktis* inherent in the letters are collectively known as *mātṛkā*.[16] This *mātṛkā* is the secret of all the *mantras*. The word for 'I' in Sanskrit is '*ahaṁ*'. This '*a*' of '*aham*' symbolizes *anuttara* (the Highest Reality) and the '*ha*' of this '*aham*' symbolizes *visargaśakti*. Thus, '*aham*' of the Supreme, contains all the letter of Sanskrit alphabet which contains 50 letters. All the vowels (*a, i, u, ṛ, ḷ*) represent the inner life of Śiva. Of all the vowels '*a*' the representative of *anuttara-śakti* is the most important. As Jayaratha puts it in his commentary on the *Tantrāloka:*

"अकारः सर्ववर्णानामन्तर्यामितया स्थितः"[17]

This means '*a*' (*akāra*) resides in the letter as their inner controller. Hence, these vowels give rise to the various consonants which symbolize different *tattvas* from Pṛthivī to Sadāśiva. It is Śiva, therefore, who dwells in the heart of all the letters and all the creatures, and expresses all manifestation as identical with Himself. As '*a*' represents Śiva, likewise '*ha*' in its subtle form is constantly being sounded inside each creature without any effort on its part. In the *Tantrāloka* Sri Abhinavagupta says:

"विसर्गोऽयमव्यक्तहकलात्मकः।"[18]

The *bindu* (or *anusvāra*) in '*aham*' indicated by a dot on the letter '*ha*', suggesting the fact that Śiva in spite of the manifestation of the universe is undivided In the definite calm of *anuttara* or Highest Reality, there arises a metaphysical point of stress. This is known as *bindu*. Abhinavagupta interprets *bindu* to mean heart (*hṛdaya*) and awareness (*vedana*) in the *Parātrīṁśikā Vivaraṇa*.[19] While interpreting all the phonemes, he takes *bindu* as the fifteenth vowel *am* which denotes awareness of the very nature of the Reality that is pure consciousness and get immersed in the *anuttara* state.[20] In the *Tantrāloka*, Abhinvagupta states that which is undivided light, that which in spite of all differentiation does not change, remains uneffected and does not deviate from its inherent oneness is known as *bindu*.[21] In the *Abhinava Bhāratī* (comm. on *Nāṭya Śāstra*) Abhinavagupta explains *bindu* as *anusandhāna*, i.e. the process of unification.[22]

Hence, it is clear now that *śakti* as such should be known as *mātṛkā* and *mātṛkā* should be known as the nature of Śiva. Abhinavagupta in his *Tantrāloka*[23] clearly states *mātṛkā* as:

"स आत्मा मातृका देवी शिवो देहव्यवस्थितः।"

Jayaratha, the commentator explains it thus:

इत्याद्युक्त्या मातृका देवी पारमेश्वरी शक्तिः शिवश्च नरशक्तिशिवात्मतया स एव परिस्फुरेदित्यर्थः।

The Śaiva Philosophy of Kashmir is generally called '*Trika Śāstra*', because it is the philosophy of the triad, i.e., *Śiva, Śakti* and *Nara*. Here *nara* is *ātmā, śakti* is *mātṛkā* and Śiva is Supreme Lord, the cause of everything. The *ātmā* is also Śiva *rūpa*. This limited *ātmā* shines as *haṁsa* and it is nothing but (*Pārameśvarī*) *Śakti* and this *Pārameśvarī-Śakti* is known as *mātṛkā*, which is non-different from Śiva and dwells in every *nara* or *jīva*. The collective *śaktis (cakras)* of *mātṛkā* pertain to *icchā, jñāna* and *kriyā śaktis* of Śiva which evolve the world of words and objects.

The words or the *varṇas* though basically are considered as sound, yet for conveying thought to the others this sound assumes the form of syllables which in the Āgama is known as *mātṛkās*. These *varṇas* are not only permeating the entire literature of the world, but it is abiding in every living and non-living object as *prāṇa*. According to Abhinavagupta, the unmanifest, inarticulate sound or *nāda* is known as *varṇa*.[24] Regarding *nāda,* he writes in the *Tantrāloka*[25] as:

एको नादात्मको वर्णः सर्ववर्णविभागवान्।
सोऽनस्तमितरूपत्वादनाहत इहोदितः॥

This means, there is one *varṇa* in the form of *nāda*, in which all the *varṇas* lie latently in an undivided form. As it is ceaseless, it is called *anāhatanāda*. All the *varṇas* originate from this *nāda,* so it is called *varṇa* prolifically. *Anāhata-nāda*[26] literally means unstruck sound. It is a sound that goes on vibrating within spontaneously without any impact. The subtlest *nāda* vibrates in *prāṇa-śakti* present in *suṣumnā*. *Prāṇaśakti* is, in the universe, representative of *parāśakti,* the *śakti* of Parama Śiva. It is the essential energy of consciousness, the spiritual *spanda*. When the *yogī* concentrates on this *nāda,* he forgets everything of the external world, is gradually lost in the internal sound and is finally absorbed in *cidākāśa,* i.e., in the vast expanse of consciousness. So he attains to Brahman or Parama Śiva. This kind of *yoga* is known as *varṇa* in *Āṇava upāya* of *śaiva yoga,* as *nādānusandhāna* is some of the older Upaniṣads. Abhinavagupta interprets *nādātmaka varṇa* in the following verse:

अव्यक्तानुकृतिप्रायो ध्वनिर्वर्णः स कथ्यते।
सृष्टिसंहारबीजं च तस्य मुख्यं वपुर्विदुः॥[27]

The commentator Jayaratha explains the above verse of *Tantrāloka* as:

तस्य च सृष्टिबीजं संहारबीजं चेति बीजद्वयं 'मुख्यं वपुः' प्रधानमभिव्यक्तिस्थानमित्यर्थः।

It can be certified as: the sound that slightly imitates the unmanifest sound is called *varṇa*. Its chief form is known to be consisted of two seed letters, viz. the seed of creation (*sṛṣṭi bīja*) and the seed of dissolution (*saṁhāra bīja*). Here one form is *sṛṣṭi bīja* (*sa*) or the mystic letter denoting expiration and another form is *saṁhāra bīja* (*ha*) or the mystic letter denoting inspiration.[28]

Hence, *anāhata-nāda* is referred to here as *varṇa* (syllable). It is named as *varṇa* for two reasons: (a) it remains associated with all the syllables, and (b) it is the cause of them, though it remains unassociated with them.

After having the knowledge of *mātṛkā, varṇa* and its true relations, a few most critical and secrets subject in the Tāntric *sādhanā,* like *dīkṣā, guru, dhyāna, japa* and *śarīra* will be discussed here from the viewpoint of Abhinavagupta.

It is quite obvious and most difficult for a *sādhaka* to get *anugraha* or Divine Grace without the blessings and guidance of *guru* and *dīkṣā*. The word *dīkṣā* (initiation) means that which imparts *divya-jñāna* and causes *kṣaya* (destruction) of evil. The initiation ceremony pertaining to a disciple by which spiritual knowledge is imparted and the residual traces of his evil deeds are purified Abhinavagupta says:

एवं यो वेत्ति तत्त्वेन तस्य निर्वाणगामिनी।
दीक्षा भवेदिति प्रोक्तं तच्छ्रीत्रिंशकशासने॥[29]

This means in the *Parātriṁśikā* text it has been mentioned that he who knows the Supreme Reality perfectly attains initiation (*dīkṣā*) leading to liberation (*mokṣa*).

It is also noted that the highest kind of spiritual knowledge is obtained from holy texts. One who is uninitiated is not considered to be the right person to receive *śāstra*.[30] Hence, *dīkṣā* is essential. Then, who is known as *guru* or a teacher? A *guru* is one who imparts the essential Truth and Knowledge. He may be said to be the power of divine grace. As it is said in the *Mālinīvijaya*:

"शक्तिचक्रं तदेवोक्तं गुरुवक्त्रं तदुच्यते।"

That the power of divine grace has been said to be the collective whole of *śaktis,* which has been said to be the mouth of the *guru,* i.e., the *guru's* power of grace. So, *guru* who has attained self-realization can only help the aspirant in acquiring it.[31] According to Abhinavagupta, an aspirant who is unable to attain the level of pure consciousness of *śuddhavidyā* should go to the *guru* in order to receive spiritual knowledge (lessons) of the holy texts from him and follow the order as directed by him.[32] In the *Tantrāloka,* Abhinavagupta has mentioned two types of spiritual guides (*guru*). One is *akalpita,* and another is *akalpita kalpaka*. The *guru* who has attained the highest perfection without any help from any other source (*ācārya*) is known as *akalpita*, i.e., he has attained the reality by himself. The second category of *guru* is also *akalpita kalpaka* because he has also attained perfection spontaneously but he has to delve deep into the *śāstra* first and only then has attained the real import of it. As the *śāstra* has shaped his inner being, he is known as *akalpitakalpaka*. So, *guru* has the immense power of grace and that power of grace, affording a favourable opportunity to the aspirant, is the means to unravel the secret of the *mantra,* which leads to liberation.[33]

The disciple on initiation is instructed to meditate on the oneness of the *mantra,* the *devatā* and *guru*. Abhinavagupta has also given importance on the meditation (*dhyāna*), *japa* and worship (*pūjā*). By this process the *yogī* or *sādhaka* is able to concentrate and purify his mind (*citta*). The purpose of *dhyāna* is to acquire supreme powers. Abhinavagupta explained *dhyāna* in the following way:

ध्यायते परमं ध्येयं गमागमपदे स्थितम्॥
परं शिवं तु व्रजति भैरवाख्यं जपादपि।[34]

While commenting on the above verse the commentator Jayaratha says:

परमं ध्येयं शिवलक्षणं परमकारणं ध्यायते स्वात्माभेदेन परामृश्यते।

The object of meditation is the Parama Śiva, who is the chief source (*yoni*) of all the creation and who is to be meditated on as non-different from one's own self. So in a pure mind if someone meditates on Śiva he attains that *parama pada,* i.e., he becomes identified with the consciousness of Śiva. So by the way of meditiation the mind of the aspirant (*yogī*) acquires *samāveśa* or absorption into the divine consciousness. As Abhinavagupta clarifies this in the *Tantrāloka:*

आवेशश्चास्वतन्त्रस्य स्वतद्रूपनिमज्जनात्।
परतद्रूपता शम्भोराद्याच्छक्त्यविभागिनः॥[35]

Here *āveśa* (*samāveśa*) means the subordination or disappearance of the personal ego of the aspirant and his identification with the divine nature of Śiva. *Samāveśa* with the Highest Lord means identification of the individual self with the Universal Self. The individual, in this state, feels that he is nothing else than Śiva. *Samāveśa,* also means taking possession of the individual by the Dvine. *Samāveśa* is directly obtained from the Parama Śiva but not from the *Śakti* etc. although he never detached from *Śakti*.

As it is already mentioned that in the Tāntric *sādhanā, japa* has a very significant place. The *sādhaka* should concentrate his mind in one object (Parama Śiva) by recitation of a *mantra*. Besides, *japa* in its real sense is the *bhāvanā* or contemplation on one's essential self. According to Abhinavagupta, *japa* freed of all ideas of *ens*, and non-*ens* is the constant contemplation of Śiva's nature.

तत्स्वरूपं जपः प्रोक्तो भावाभावपदच्युतः॥[36]

The commentator Jayaratha explains the same as follows:

तस्य शिवस्य, स्वरूप परावाक्स्वभावम् आत्मरूपम् अर्थात् भूयो भूयः परामृश्यमानं जपः।

This means the constant mindfulness of the real nature of Parama Śiva, which is *Parāvāk* or self is *japa*.

Regarding the *mantras* of the *japa* it is said the *sādhaka* always recites *mantra 'haṁsa'.* This *haṁsaḥ* (I am He, i.e., *'so aham'* —I am Śiva or the Divine) is the *ādi prāṇa*, i.e., the initial *prāṇa* which is the first evolute or transformation of consciousness. This *mantra 'haṁsa'* is repeated by every *sādhaka* automatically in every round of expiration-inspiration. This automatic *japa* is technically known as *ajapā japa.* The alphabet *ha* (in *haṁsa*) denotes Śakti and *saḥ* denotes Śiva. *'Am'* (*bindu*) in *haṁsa* denotes the *jīva* (*paśu*-individual). This is known as *trika mantra* also, as it includes in itself the three realities of Śiva, Śakti and *nara*. So the *sādhaka* has to concentrate on *'am'*, which is the *sandhi* point of *'ha'* and *'saḥ'*. Abhinavagupta has clearly explained this in the *Tantrāloka* and *Parātrīṁśikā Vivaraṇa*. The aim of *japa* is to recognize one's own self identical with Parama Śiva. Hence, finally it can be said: "the *sādhaka* or the aspirant should practise the meditation over and over again with the *japa* of his senses both in an extroverted way in which he regards objective manifestation (*sṛṣṭi*) as Śiva and in an introverted way in which he regards the withdrawal of manifestation (*saṁhāra*) also as Śiva" (*sa eva eṣa satatodito hṛdaya japaḥ*).[37]

Perhaps in no other system of Indian spiritual thought has the body (*śarīra*) received greater symbolical and spiritual meaning as in *tāntric* and *yogic* system. In Tāntric *sādhanā,* body is not considered as an obstacle on the spiritual and cultural path, but as an instrument which is described and used in all its subtle dimensions. It also has been accepted to a major means for fulfilling the purpose of *sṛṣṭi* and *līlā* at the macro level and *bhoga* at the micro level. Hence, the body is an important means in meditation and worship, which finally leads to liberation. According to Abhinavagupta the body is the excellent place of worship. In the *Tantrāloka* he says:

देह एव परं लिङ्गं सर्वतत्त्वात्मकं शिवम्।
देवताचक्रसंजुष्टं पूजाधाम तदुत्तमम्॥

तदेव मण्डलं मुख्यं त्रित्रिशूलाब्जचक्रखम्।
तत्रैव देवताचक्रं बहिरन्तः सदा यजेत्॥[38]

The body is the highest abode of all the *tattvas.* All the *devatās, vidyās, cakras, triśulas, maṇḍalas*, etc. are normally existing in the body. Beyond this there is no other best *dhāma* (place) which could be found suitable for perfect worship. So, Abhinavagupta further adds that it is the house of the divine, where He enjoys with his consort. Being a great *sādhaka* he has expressed his internal feelings and experiences of worship by the following words:

त्वां देव्या सह देहदेवसदने देवार्चयेऽहर्निशम्॥[39]

शिवानन्दरसापूर्णं षट्त्रिंशत्तत्त्वनिर्भरम्॥
देहं दिवानिशं पश्यन्नर्चयन्स्याच्छिवात्मकः।[40]

In a mystic way he explains when the body filled with divine that shines in the core of the universe, it is to be meditated upon, to be worshipped, to be propitiated and the one who becomes fully possessed of it, gets liberated

When we proceed further to know about his mystical experiences we find *advaita bhāva* in his real feelings. According to him whatever we are experienced in our life like pleasure, pain, consciousness, unconsciousness, bondage, liberation, etc. all these are synonymous terms like *ghaṭa* and *kumbha*. There should be no feelings or existence of '*dvaita bhāva*', which occurs due to *śābda bheda,* because in reality all words are one and identical with Brahman or Śiva. *Bheda* or difference occurs due to *māyā* and in the final stage when the *yogī* or *sādhaka* attains *'tattva jñāna'* then *māyā* disappears and he feels that he is nothing else than Śiva and everything is also Śiva. In the words of Abhinavagupta:

अस्यां भूमौ सुखं दुःखं बन्धो मोक्षश्चितिर्जडः।
घटकुम्भवदेकार्थाः शब्दास्तेऽप्येकमेव च॥[41]
सम्यग् ज्ञानं च मुक्त्येककारणं स्वपरस्थितम्।[42]

Regarding the *mantra* and *vidyā* Abhinavagupta says there are more secret and mystical knowledge, beyond of one's mind to express and explain in a practical and complete way, by which the disciple or the *yogī* can receive and understand. The sacred *mantras,* mystic *tattvas* and other *rahasyamaya-vidyās* can be achieved only by intuitive knowledge and one's own keen interest in this subject. This *Śāstra* is open to all, and by sincerely going through it one can get the *amṛta rasa svāda*—the reạl taste of human life. In his words:

न पठ्यते रहस्यत्वात्स्पष्टैः शब्दैर्मया पुनः।
कुतूहली तूक्तशास्त्रसंपाठादेव लक्षयेत्॥[43]

This way, to my mind, I describe regarding the mystical experience of the great Ācārya Abhinavagupta. In a short article it is very difficult to elaborate the mystical meanings and explanation of the secret subjects like *tattvas, varṇas, mātṛkā, dhyāna, japa, śarīra, mokṣa* and other related subjects. However, it is Śiva Himself, of unimpeded will and pellucid consciousness, who is ever sparkling in my heart. Finally, I conclude this with the glorious words of Abhinavagupta:

इदमभिनवगुप्तोदितसंक्षेपं ध्यायतः परं ब्रह्म।
अचिरादेव शिवत्वं निजहृदयावेशमभ्येति॥[44]

REFERENCES

1. आत्मैव धर्म इत्युक्तः शिवामृतपरिप्लुतः।
   प्रकाशावस्थितं ज्ञानं भावाभावादिमध्यतः॥ *Tantrāloka,* I.84.
   cf. सकृद्विभातोऽयमात्मा। *Tantrāloka,* under verse XXIX.80; Also cf. चैतन्यमात्मा। *Śivasūtra,* I.1.
2. *Paramārthasāra,* verse 5; cf. *Tantrāloka,* I.223.
3. *Paramārthasāra,* verse 11.
4 *ibid.,* verse 23 and the comm. of Yogarāja.
5. *ibid.,* verse 34-35; cf. *Māṇḍukya Upaniṣad,* I. 3-6; also cf. *Śivasūtra,* I.7.
6. *Mālinīvijaya Vārttika,* verse 611-690.
7. *Tantrāloka,* XIII. 254-255.
8. मोक्षस्य नैव किंचिद् धामास्ति न चापि गमनमन्यत्र।

अज्ञानग्रन्थिभिदा स्वशक्त्यभिव्यक्तता मोक्षः।।
Paramārthasāra, verse, 60.

9. मोक्षस्य हि नाम नैवान्यः स्वरूपप्रथनं हि सः। *Tantrāloka*, I.56.
10. *Tantrāloka*, I.230..
11. *Paramārthasāra,* verse 77.
12. *Īśvara Pratyabhijñā Vimarśinī,* IV. I. 13.
13. *ibid.*, I. 5.14.
14. *ibid.*, quoted by Abhinavagupta here.
15. *Vākyapadīya,* I. 123-124.
16. सर्वे वर्णात्मका मन्त्रा स च शक्त्यात्मकाः प्रिये।
शक्तिस्तु मातृका ज्ञेया सा च ज्ञेया शिवात्मिका।।
Tantrasadbhāva—a lost text (now); cf. *Yoginīhṛdaya,* II.20.
17. Jayaratha quotes in his comm. on *Tantrāloka,* III.113cd-114ab.
18. *Tantrāloka,* III.146, see also the comm. of Jayaratha.
19. भैरवात्मवेदनरूपतया बिन्द्वात्मकं हृदयम्। comm. under verses 16-18, p. 82.
20. परित्यज्य तथाविधोपाधि.....पुरुषतत्त्ववेदनारूपबिन्दुमात्रावशेषेण वपुषा तथानुत्तरपदलीने अमिति। *Parātīṁśikā-Vivaraṇa* comm. under verses 5-8, p. 61.
21. अविभागः प्रकाशो यः स बिन्दुः परमो हि नः।
Tantrāloka, III. 111cd. Cf. *Vijñānabhairava,* verse 90.
22. *Abhinavabhāratī* on *Nāṭyaśāstra,* XIX.23.
23. XXIX.90; cf. *ibid.*, XV. 402, XXVII. 35;
Also cf. *Svacchanda Tantra,* I.31.
24. *Tantrāloka,* V.131.
25. *ibid.*, VI.217.
26. *Vijñānabhairava,* verse 38.
27. *Tantrāloka,* V.132.
28. सकारेण बहिर्याति हकारेण विशेत्पुनः।
हंस-हंसेत्यमुं मन्त्रं जीवो जपति नित्यशः।।
Kṣemarāja quotes this verse while interpreting III.27 Sūtra of *Śivasūtra.*
29. *Tantrāloka,* IV.50.
30. Vide comm. of *Tantrāloka,* under verse XV.12; cf. *Svacchanda Tantra,* IV.79.
31. *Mālinīvijaya Vārttika,* II.10; cf. *Spanda Kārikā,* IV.1; cf. *Śivasūtra,* II.6.
32. *Tantrāloka,* IV.69cd-70ab.
33. *ibid.*, IV. 59; XIII.158; XVI. 269cd-270; XXVIII.193; cf. *Yoginī Hṛdaya,* II.50-51ab; *Kulārṇava Tantra,* XVII.7-8, etc.
34. *Tantrāloka*, I.89cd-90ab; cf. *Vijñānabhairava,* verse 146.
35. *Tantrāloka,* I.173.
36. *ibid.*, I.90; cf. *Yogasūtra,* I.28 (*tat japaḥ tadartha-bhāvanam*).
37. Explained by J. Singh in *Parātrīṁśikā Vivaraṇa,* verse 35,p.266 (Delhi Edition, 1988).
38. *Tantrāloka,* XXIX. 171-172.

39. *ibid.*, XXIX. 176cd.
40. *ibid.*, XV. 285cd-286ab.
41. *ibid.*, II.19.
42. *ibid.*, I.233.
43. *ibid.*, XXIX.169.
44. *Paramārthasāra,* verse, 104.

Symbols and Śakti Worship

[Symbols represent a number of deities: male and female. At the time of Śakti worship (*devīpūjā*), some symbols are directly and indirectly used or worshipped for Śakti. Śakti is symbolized as women or the mother. In the *Mahānirvāṇa Tantra,* Śakti has been addressed as Kālī, Tāriṇī, Durgā, Ṣoḍaśī, Bhuvaneśvarī, Dhūmāvatī, Bagalā, Bhairavī, Vāgdevī and Śivā. Śakti is worshipped through various symbols, like: (i) *yantras,* (ii) *maṇi,* (iii) plants, and (iv) *pīṭha/maṇḍapa*, etc. As it is known that *yantras* are symbolic representation of the goddess in her different manifestations. *Yantras* are innumerable. *Śrīyantra* is the most celebrated of all Tāntric *yantras.* There are ten *Mahāvidyās*, viz. Kālī, Tārā, Ṣoḍaśī, Bhuvaneśvarī, Chinnamastā, Bhairavī, Dhūmāvatī, Bagalāmukhī, Mātaṅgī and Kamalā. These *Mahāvidyās* or Divine Śaktis are worshipped in their respective *yantras.* Nine plants (Nava-patrikās) are symbolically treated as the *nava Śaktis* or *nava Durgās* during *Durgā-pūjā. Pīṭha* of the goddess Kālī/Durgā signifies the wholeness of Divine Śakti.]

Symbols have great significance for understanding early Indian religion, beliefs, traditions, art and culture. Symbols are not confined to any particular period, place or people. They are found among the most uncivilized as well as the most civilized and sophisticated people. They have been traced right from the beginning of human experience down to our present times. They are found in all countries of the world. Of these symbols, some are widely current and continued to be in use for several centruries and are found delineated in sculpture, architecture, poetry, paintings, (*pūjā*) rituals, etc.

It is widely known that symbols represent a number of deities—male and female. For example, *Śālagrāma* is the symbolical representation of Lord Viṣṇu. When we worship *Śālagrāma śilā,* it indicates that we are worshipping Nārāyaṇa-Viṣṇu. Similarly, a *liṅga* symbolically represents to Lord Śiva. This way, at the time of Śakti worship (*devī-pūjā*), some symbols are directly and indirectly used or worshipped for the female deities. Before dealing various symbols used in the Śakti worship, first of all the meaning and concept of Śakti would be clarified Śiva is commonly said to be the male principle and Śakti is the female principle. As a matter of fact they are neither male nor female, nor they are neuter. The man who worships the wisdom (*jñāna*) aspect of Reality, commonly called the male principle, is a Śaiva; and he who worships the power aspects, or the female principle, is called a Śākta. When Lord Śiva is worshipped, his consort is also worshipped, as these two are inseparable. For the same reason when Śakti is worshipped, Śiva is also worshipped Śakti is an immanent principle of Śiva.[1] Without Śakti, Śiva is inactive. Devoid of Śakti, Śiva would be insentient (*jaḍa*) and consequently, as good as 'dead' (*śava*). Śiva knows Himself only through His Śakti. But Śakti also depends upon Śiva for its functioning. Both are essentially dependent upon each other.[2] Śakti is symbolically represented as the spouse of Śiva and hence She is the immanent principle of Śiva.

Śakti is symbolized as a woman or the mother. In the *Mahānirvāṇa Tantra*[3], Śakti has been addressed as Kālī, Tāriṇī, Durgā, Ṣoḍaśī, Bhuvaneśvarī, Dhūmāvatī, Bagalā, Bhairavī, Chinnamastakā, Annapūrṇā, Vāgdevī, Kamalālayā, and Śivā. In the *Saundarya Laharī*[4], Śakti has been called Aruṇā, Aparṇā, Pārvatī, Caṇḍī, Umā, Bhavānī, Satī, Samayā, besides Jananī, Mātṛ, *Devī* and Ambā. In the *Lalitāsahasranāma,* Śakti has been named Kālī, Karālī, Kalyāṇī, Kalāvatī, Kamalā and Kalidarpaghnī. So Śakti is known by different names. Her different names have occurred due to her various functions, qualities, and forms. The *pūjaka* worships the *Devī* directly through *mūrti* or *pratimās* and indirectly through various symbols, i.e. *yantra, kalaśa,* etc.

In the Indian tradition *Śakti* or *Devī* is also worshipped symbolically or through various symbols. An attempt has been made in this paper to highlight the various traditional symbols related to Śakti worship. The *Durgā-pūjā-paddhati* may differ from place to place in India, but since Bengal is rich in Durgā/Kālī worship, hence the traditional *pūjā paddhati* of Bengal is mostly followed in other parts of India. .Those symbols which are used in Śakti worship can be classified as under:

(i) ***Yantras* and Śakti worship,**

(ii) ***Maṇi* and Śakti worship,**

(iii) **Plants/trees and Śaktı worship,**

(iv) ***Pīṭha/maṇḍapa* and Śakti worship.**

Yantras and Śakti worship:

The *yantras* are symbolic representation of the goddess in her different manifestations. In a Tāntric *pūjā*, the *yantra* of the main deity/*devī* is always worshipped as a symbol of the goddess. *Yantra* worship is the essential part of Śaiva *sādhanā* and it is also a mystic process of awakening the divine power. *Yantra* is a mystic diagram and it is an apparatus by which anything is accomplished Every *yantra* is a sacred enclosure, a dwelling or receptacle of *iṣṭa-devatā*. It is a substitute for an anthropomorphic image of the deity; like Kālī *yantra* is meant for goddess Kālī. At the time of Kālī worship one should worship the Kālī *yantra* for the better prosperity. The *yantra* thus, restrains the restless movements of the mind and helps it to concentrate on the diagram representing the deity worshipped

It is said that *yantra* removes all pains arising from love and anger. It further held that if the worship is made with *yantra,* the deity is pleased Because *yantra* is ensouled by *mantra* and the deity is in the form of *mantra.* So the deity is immediately satisfied if he is worshipped in the *yantra.* As said in the *Kulārṇava Tantra:*

यन्त्रं मन्त्रमयं प्रोक्तं देवता मन्त्ररूपिणी।
यन्त्रे सा पूजिता देवी सहसैव प्रसीदति।।[5]

Yantra worship is employed for fourfold of human desires, viz. *dharma, artha, kāma* and *mokṣa.* Every desire can be fulfilled if some one sincerely and devotedly worships *yantra devatā* or *devī*. The *Śāradātilaka* discusses in detail the formation and esoteric significance of different *yantras.* According to it, *yantras* are innumerable. Different *yantras* are employed for different objectives. According to it, *yantra* is that which fulfills all desires of the *sādhaka/pūjaka.*[6] *Śrīyantra* is the most celebrated of all Tāntric *yantras*. In the *Mahānirvāṇa Tantra*[7], this *yantra* is known as *yantrarāja* and *sarvatobhadra* in the *Gautamīya Tantra.*[8] *Śrīyantra* is also known as *Śrīcakra. Śrīyantra* is geometric representation of goddess Lalitā or Tripurā (*Śrī*). It is a diagram of nine *cakras* intermingled to form a concentric figure, in which the central point is conceived as the seat of Tripurā. The goddess Tripurā or Lalitā is worshipped in this *yantra,* as the source and essence of all the universe represented by the diagram. This *yantra* of the goddess Lalitā is most popularly worshipped all over India. In the following verse, the parts of this *yanta* have been described:

बिन्दुत्रिकोणवसुकोणदशारयुग्म–
मन्वस्त्रनागदलसंयुतषोडशारम्।
वृत्तत्रयं च धरणीसदनत्रयं च
श्रीचक्रराजमुदितं परदेवतायाः।।[9]

The *Śrīcakra* consists of a *bindu, trikoṇa* (triangle), *aṣṭakoṇa* (eight triangles), *antardaśāra* and *bahirdaśāra* (the pair of ten triangles), *caturdaśāra* (fourteen triangles), *aṣṭadala* (eight petals), *ṣoḍaśadala,* (sixteen petals), and *bhūpuras* (three circles). So, *Śrīcakra* consists of nine *yonis* and forty three triangles. In the nine *yonis,* five Śakti *cakras* and four Śiva *cakras* are present. The five Śakti *cakras* are: (1) *trikoṇa,* (2) *aṣṭakoṇa,* (3) *antardaśāra,* (4) *bahirdaśāra,* and (5) *caturdaśāra.* The four Śiva *cakras* are: (1) *bindu,* (2) *aṣṭadala,* (3) *ṣoḍaśadala,* and (4) *bhūpura.*

The *Śrīcakra* is one of the chief instruments of instruction of the *Śrī vidyā* form of worship which consists essentially in the use of an esoteric fifteen syllable *mantra* representing the Supreme Divine power manifested as a form of the universe. In the *Lalitā Sahasranāma,* Devī Lalitā advises to the devotee to worship her in the *Śrīcakra.* She says:

श्रीचक्रे मां समभ्यर्च्य जप्त्वा पञ्चदशाक्षरीम्।।[10]

So *Śrīvidyā* was the chief form of worship of a number of renowned sages[11] and has survived among all sects of Tantrism.

Regarding the object of *Śrīyantra* Sir John Woodroffe says: "the object of worship of the *yantra* is to attain unity with the Mother of the Universe in her forms as Mind, Life and Matter and their *devatās*, as preparatory to *yoga*-union with Her as She is in Herself as pure consciousness. The world is divinized in the consciousness of the worshipper or *sādhaka*. The *yantra* is thus transformed in his consciousness from a material object of lines and curves into a mental state of union with the Universe, its Divinities and Supreme Deity. This leads to auto-realization as mindless consciousness. The *Śrīyantra* is thus the Universe and its one causal power of various aspects. The worshipper, too, is a *Śrīyantra,* and realizes himself as such."[12]

So, in the *pūjā* of *Śrīcakra* or *Śrīyantra* the personal and impersonal aspects of Brahman are harmonized Ritual and meditation lead to the knowledge of oneness, having gained which one attains to Supreme Peace and Highest Bliss.

Śakti worship and Ten *Mahāvidyās:*

The forms of Śakti are numerous. A number of them are classed as the *Mahāvidyās* or *Vidyās* and the *Nityās*. The *Tantrasāra* quotes two lists of *Mahāvidyās* from the *Mālinīvijaya* and the *Muṇḍamālā Tantra,* of which the following list consists of ten names, are very popular in Eastern India: (1) Mahākālī, (2) Tārā, (3) Ṣoḍaśī, (4) Bhuvaneśvarī, (5) Chinnamastakā, (6) Bhairavī, (7) Dhūmāvatī, (8) Bagalāmukhī, (9) Mātaṅgī, (10) Kamalā.[13]

These above *Mahāvidyās* or Divine Śaktis are being worshipped in their respective *yantras*. The *yantras* of these ten *Mahāvidyās* are also very famous in the Tāntric rituals. While worshipping these Śaktis, the *sādhaka* or *pūjaka* has to worship the goddesses in their respective *yantras*. Without *yantra pūjana,* Śakti (or Devī) worship has no value, says the Tantra Śāstra.

Regarding the symbolic worship of *yantras* as well as the importance of ten *Mahāvidyās* Prof. Madhu Khanna, a Tāntric scholar, says: "There are specific *yantras* devoted to each of the ten *Mahāvidyās* each named after a goddess and explaining her nature, *yantra*, mode of ritual, and the benefits that are gained from her ritual. Two main centers of the *daśa-mahāvidyā* worship are Bengal and Mithila in Bihar state, eastern India. In Mithila, when a child is born the local priest assigns one of the ten *Mahāvidyās,* as his chosen deity (*iṣṭa-devatā*) and the individual generally adheres throughout his life to the worship of the deity in either a *yantra* or image form."[14]

(1) Kālī & Śakti worship:

Kālī is considered to be the most important and popular of the Śakti deities in Eastern India. She is worshipped on different occasions under different names and forms, all fearful and ferocious, manifesting the spirit of destruction which she represents. The Kālī *yantra* bestows the *sādhaka* for the fulfilment of all his desires, wealth, comforts of life. The *japa mantra* of Kālī is: "*Oṁ krīṁ kālikāyai namaḥ*; *Oṁ kapālinyai namaḥ*". The worshipper should meditate on Kālī with the following *mantra:*

शवारूढां महाभीमां घोरदंष्ट्रां हसन्मुखीम्।
चतुर्भुजां खड्गमुण्डवराभयकरां शिवाम्॥
मुण्डमालाधरां देवीं ललज्जिह्वां दिगम्बराम्।
एवं सञ्चिन्तयेत् कालीं श्मशानालयवासिनीम्॥

—शाक्तप्रमोद—कालीतन्त्र

Kālī pūjana yantra: Minor differences are also noticed in the *Kālī yantra* in different Tantra works. In the Mahidhara's *Mantramahodadhi*, the *Kālī yantra* is described as:

आदौ षट्कोणमारच्य त्रिकोणत्रितयं ततः।
पद्ममष्टदलं बाह्ये भूपुरं तत्र पूजयेत्॥[15]

It means, first of all, writing a six triangled hexagon and then enclosing it, make three triangles each over the other. Around the traingles draw an eight petalled lotus and finally, outside the petals, draw a *bhūpura* (mystic square shapped outline). The *sādhaka/pūjaka* should worship goddess Kālī on the (above mentioned) *Kālī yantra* with the *bīja mantra 'krim'*.

(2) Tārā (*yantra*):

Goddess Tārā is regarded as the *devī* of knowledge. She is called *parāvāk.* Tārā *devī* should be worshipped on a *yantra* consisting of a hexagonal pericarp, eight petals and surrounded by a square pedestal.[16] Tārā is also considered as a goddess of Buddhist pantheon. In order to destroy the enemies and achieve every success in life it is essential to worship and meditate upon *devī* Tārā by the following *mantra* (*aim auṁ hriṁ kriṁ hūṁ phaṭ*):

प्रत्यालीढपदार्पिताङ्घ्रिशवहृद्घोराट्टहासापरा।
खड्गेन्दीवरकर्त्रिखर्प्परभुजा हुंकारबीजोद्भवा॥
खर्व्वा नीलविशालपिङ्गलजटाजूटैकनागैर्य्युता।
जाड्यन्यस्य कपालकर्तृ जगतां हन्त्युग्रतारा स्वयम्॥

(3) Ṣoḍaśī (*yantra*):

Devī Ṣoḍaśī is the third *Mahāvidyā.* She represents the power of perfection and sustenance. In the Tantra she is known as *Tripurasundarī* and *Śrīvidyā. Kāma* is the main aspect in worshipping *Tripurasundarī.* She is the main *devī* of *Śrīvidyā* form of worship and is invoked either in the *Śrīyantra* or in her own *yantra.*[17]

For getting every success and prosperity in life *devī Ṣoḍaśī* should be meditated by the following *mantra* :

(*hrīṁ ka e ī la hrīṁ ha sa ka ha la hrīṁ sa ka la hrīm)*

बालार्कमण्डलाभासां चतुर्बाहान्त्रिलोचनाम्।
पाशाङ्कुशशरांश्चापन्धारयन्तीं शिवाम्भजे॥

—शाक्तप्रमोद-षोडशीतन्त्र

(4) Bhuvaneśvarī (*yantra*):

Bhuvaneśvarī is the fourth of the ten *Mahāvidyās*. She appears in her *yantra* seated on a star hexagon, which is associated with the transcendent immensity of both the male and female principles as one. With the colour of the rising sun and moon as her diadem, her anthropomorphic image placed in the center of the *yantra* is surrounded by two rings of eight and sixteen petalled lotuses.[18] In the *Bhuvaneśvarī Tantra* She is described as:

बालरविद्युतिमिन्दुकिरीटां तुङ्गकुचां नयनत्रययुक्ताम्।
स्मेरमुखीं वरदाङ्कुशपाशाभीतिकरां प्रभजे भुवनेशीम्।।

—शाक्तप्रमोद—भुवनेश्वरीतन्त्र

(5) Chinnamastā (*yantra*):

Chinnamastā is also called *pracaṇḍa-caṇḍikā*. *Chinna-mastā Tantra* and *Śakti-saṅgama Tantra,* etc. describe her real form, *yantra, mantra* and the procedure of worship. In the *Mantramahodadhi,* the *yantra*, *mantra* and the procedure of worship of goddess Chinnamastā are described as under:

त्रिकोणमध्यषटकोणपद्मभूपुरमध्यतः।
बाह्यावरणमारभ्य पूजयेत्प्रतिलोमतः।
भूपुराद्बाह्यभागेषु वज्रादीनि प्रपूजयेत्।।[19]

It means, on a *yantra* consisting of a triangle, hexagon, eight petals and a square, the *pūjaka,* beginning from the outer covering and proceeding in an inverse order, perform the worship. In the external side of the square the *vajra,* etc. weapons should be worshipped

(6) Tripurā Bhairavī (*yantra*):

Tripurā Bhairavī is the sixth *Mahāvidyā*. There are many forms of Bhairavī known by different names such as *Siddhi-Bhairavī*, *Caitanya-Bhairavī, Kamaleśvarī-Bhairavī,* etc. Her *yantra* is a hexagon placed within a circle of lotuses. The *Śāradātilaka* describes Tripurā Bhairavī as:

उद्यद्भानुसहस्त्रकान्तिमरुणक्षौमां शिरोमालिनीं
रक्तालिप्तपयोधरां जपवटीं विद्यामभीतिं वराम्।
हस्ताब्जैर्दधतीं त्रिनेत्रविलसद्वक्त्रारविन्दश्रियं
देवीं बद्धहिमांशुरत्नमुकुटां वन्दे समन्दस्मिताम्।।[20]

(7) Dhūmāvatī (*yantra*):

Devī Dhūmāvatī is known as the goddess of *uttarāmnāya,* who moves in a chariot having the flag marked by a crow. Dhūmāvatī is to be worshipped in her own *yantra* for the prosperity and destruction of enemies. In the *Mantramahodadhi*[21] the nature and importance of the *devī* are described Her *bīja-mantra* is *'dhūm'*. Dhūmāvatī's *yantra* is a hexagon within an eight-petalled lotus. Goddess Dhūmāvatī should be worshipped by the following *mantra*:

धनहृष्टा धनपुष्टा दानाध्ययनकारिणी।
धनरक्षा धनप्राणा धनानन्दकरी सदा।।
शत्रुग्रीवाच्छिदाच्छाया शत्रुपद्धतिखण्डिनी।
शत्रुप्राणहराहार्य्या शत्रून्मूलनकारिणी।
मदिरामोदयुक्तो वै देवीध्यानपरायणः।
तस्य शत्रुः क्षयं याति यदि शक्रसमोऽपि वै।।

(8) Bagalāmukhī (*yantra*):

Goddess Bagalāmukhī is the eighth *Mahāvidyā*. Bagalāmukhī is meditated upon as holding the tongue of the enemy with one hand, and thrashing him with a club. By the grace of the *devī* the adept becomes powerful enough to enchant the world.[22] The *yantra* of Bagalāmukhī consisting of triangle, six triangles (hexagon), eight petals, sixteen petals and a *bhūpura*. As said in the *Mantramahodadhi*:

चन्दनागुरुचन्द्राद्यैः पूजार्थं यन्त्रमालिखेत्।
त्रिकोणं षड्दलाष्टास्त्रषोडशारधरापुरम्।।[23]

This means, the *devī* should be worshipped in the center of the *yantra* with sandal-paste, *agara* and camphor. Her *bīja-mantra* "*hlrīm*" should also be meditated upon.

(9) Mātaṅgī (*yantra*):

The ninth *Mahāvidyā* is Mātaṅgī. She is known by various names, such as : Sumukhī, Ucchiṣṭacāṇḍālinī and Mahāpiśācinī. Mātaṅgī is also appears in various forms and names, such as : Rāja-mātaṅgī, Vaśya-mātaṅgī, Karaṇa-mātaṅgī, etc. *Devī* Mātaṅgī represents the power of domination, dispels evil and dispenses justice to all. The *Mantramahodadhi* states regarding her *yantra* and the *pūjana vidhi* as:

त्रिकोणाष्टदलद्वन्द्वं कलास्त्रचतुरस्त्रकम्।
पीठं कृत्वा यजेत्तस्मिन्पीठशक्तीर्नवेष्टदाः।।[24]

This means, making a *yantra* (of Mātaṅgī) consisting of triangle, two set of eight petals, then sixteen petals and above it a square *bhūpura,* following nine Śaktis, who are fulfillers of desires, should be worshipped on that pedestal.

(10) Kamalā (*yantra*):

Devī Kamalā is the tenth of the *Mahāvidyās*. From the name and the description it appears that Lakṣmī, the goddess of wealth and fortune of the Purāṇas is identical with the goddess Kamalā. The *yantra* of Kamalā is a hexagon placed within a circle of lotuses. The *Śāradātilaka* describes goddess Kamalā as:

कान्त्या काञ्चनसन्निभां हिमगिरिप्रख्यैश्चतुर्भिर्गजै-
र्हस्तोत्क्षिप्तहिरण्मयामृतघटैरासिच्यमानां श्रियम्।

विभ्राणां वरमब्जयुग्ममभयं हस्तैः किरीटोज्ज्वलां
क्षौमाबद्धनितम्बबिम्बलसितां वन्देऽरविन्दस्थिताम्॥[25]

This way, the above ten *Mahāvidyās* should be worshipped symbolically on their respective *yantras,* for attaining *dharma, artha, kāma* and *mokṣa.*

Maṇi and Śakti worship:

Maṇi (metallic stone) is also used as a symbol for Śakti worship. According to P.V. Kane "five kinds of stones were used in worship, viz. Bāṇa liṅga from Narmadā in Śiva worship, Śālagrāma in Viṣṇu worship, metallic stone in Durgā worship, crystal for sun worship and red stone in Ganesh worship."[26] Detail references are not available on the symbolical worship of *maṇi.*

Trees/Plants and Śakti worship:

On the seventh day of the *Durgā pūjā,* with all its subsidiary rituals, starts with the bathing of the *navapatrikās* or the nine trees and plants (nine sprouts), bound together with an *aparājitā* creeper and covered with a *sārī* in the manner of a newly married girl. It is called *kalā-bau* in Bengalī. *Kalā-bau* or *kalā-badhu* (plantain-wife) consisting of nine plants and trees symbolically represent nine female deities, which are called nine Śaktis or *nava-Durgās.* At the time of worship each *patrikā* stands for a particular form of the goddess, which can be mentioned as under:

	Patrikās	**Presidding deities**	***Bīja mantras***
1.	Rambhā (*Kadalī*)	Brahmāṇi	*oṁ rambhādhiṣṭhātryai brahmāṇyai namaḥ*
2.	Kacvī	Kālī (Kālikā)	*oṁ kacvyadhiṣṭhātryai kālīkāyai namaḥ*
3.	Haridrā	Durgā	*oṁ haridrādhīṣṭhātryai durgāyai namaḥ*
4.	Jayantī	Kārtikī	*oṁ jayantyādhiṣṭātryai kārttikyai namaḥ*
5.	Bilva	Śiva	*oṁ bilvādhiṣṭhātryai śivāyai namaḥ*
6.	Dāḍima	Raktadantikā	*oṁ dāḍimvyādhiṭhātryai raktadantikāyai namaḥ*
7.	Aśoka	Śokarahitā	*oṁ aśokādhiṣṭhātryai śokarahitāyai namaḥ*
8.	Māna	Cāmuṇḍā	*oṁ mānādhiṣṭhātryai Cāmuṇḍāyai namaḥ*
9.	Dhānya	Lakṣmī	*oṁ dhānyādhiṣṭātryai lakṣmyai namaḥ*

These are the nine plants and trees (*nava-patrikās*), which are symbolically treated as the *nava-śaktis* or *nava-Durgās* during *Durgā pūjā.* In no way, these *patrikās* are considered as mere plants/trees, but on the other hand they are worshipped as the Divine Mothers through this symbolic (*kalā-badhū*) tree.

Tulasī plant and Śakti worship:

Besides these *nava patrikās,* Tulasī plant is also symbolically represents Tulasī *devī,* whom we worship as one of the most sacred plants. This plant reserves a special position in the heart of every religious Indian women. One who worships Tulasī plant ultimately *devī* Tulasī bestows on him peace, happiness and prosperity. In the *Tulasīmāhātmya,* it is truely said:

ध्यायेच्च तुलसीं देवीं श्यामां कमललोचनाम्।
प्रसन्नां पद्मकह्लारवराभयचतुर्भुजाम्।।
किरीटहारकेयूरकुण्डलादिविभूषिताम्।
धवलांशुकसंयुक्तां पद्मासननिषेदुषीम्।।[27]

Pīṭha and Śakti worship:

After *visarjana* of the goddess Durgā/Kālī, the skeleton of that goddess placed on the plank or *pīṭha* is worshipped symbolically. This is due to the all pervadingness of the *devī*, whose creation and destruction is not possible practically. So it is clear that the *pīṭha* of the goddess Kālī/Durgā signifies the wholeness of the Divine Śakti.

Conclusion:

It may safely be concluded that various symbols like: *yantra, maṇi,* plants and trees, etc. are used as the inherent essence of the Śakti worship, which are most essential to get every success, prosperity and final liberation (*mokṣa*). Though some minor differences are noticed in the various *yantras* or diagrams of the *daśa-mahāvidyās*, still there is an attempt for the unification of the symbolic *yantras* and the Divine Goddess or Divine Śakti.

REFERENCES

1. *Śaktiḥ sā śivasya śaktiḥ—Ānanda Sūtra*, verse-2.2.
2. न शिव: शक्तिरहितो न शक्तिर्व्यतिरेकिणी।। शिवदृष्टि, III.2cd.
   Cf. शिव: शक्त्या युक्तो यदि भवति शक्त: प्रभवितुम्।
   न चेदेवं देव: न खलु कुशल: स्पन्दितुमपि।। आनन्दलहरी, 1.
   Also cf. शक्तिश्च शक्तिमद्रूपाद् व्यतिरेकं न वाञ्छति।। बोधपञ्चाशिका, 3.
3. त्वं काली तारिणी दुर्गा षोडशी भुवनेश्वरी।
   धूमावती त्वं वगला भैरवी छिन्नमस्तका।।
   त्वमन्नपूर्णा वाग्देवी त्वं देवी कमलालया।
   सर्वशक्तिस्वरूपा त्वं सर्वदेवमयी तनु:।। महानिर्वाणतन्त्र, IV.13-14.
4. Vide versess 17 to 55.
5. *Kulārṇava Tantra*, VI.85-86.
6. अथ वक्ष्यामि यन्त्राणां भेदांस्तन्त्रेषु गोपितान्।
   यै: साधयन्ति सततं मन्त्रिणो निजवाञ्छितम्।। शारदातिलकतन्त्र, XXIV.1.
7. V.171-173.

8. 30.102-109.
9. *Rudrayāmala Tantra*, quoted in *Kāmakalāvilāsa*, under verse 31.
   Also cf. *Kāmakalāvilāsa*, verses 29-31.
10. *Lalitāsahasranāma*, I.44, p. 17 (Nag Publishers, Delhi, 1985).
11. मनुश्चन्द्रः कुबेरश्च लोपामुद्रा च मन्मथः।
    अगस्तिरग्निः सूर्यश्च इन्द्रः स्कन्दः शिवस्तथा।
    क्रोधभट्टारको देव्या द्वादशामी उपासकाः।।
    Twelve *upāsakas* of *Śrīvidyā* from twelve sects.
12. Woodroffe, Sir John: *Śakti* and *Śākta,* ch. XX, p. 274-275 (Ganesh & Company, Madras, 1998, reprint).
13. काली तारा महाविद्या षोडशी भुवनेश्वरी।
    भैरवी छिन्नमस्ता च विद्या धूमावती तथा।
    वगला सिद्धविद्या च मातङ्गी कमलात्मिका।
    एता दश महाविद्याः सिद्धविद्याः प्रकीर्तिताः।।
    –मुण्डमालातन्त्र। cf. *Prāṇatoṣinī Tantra*, V.6.
    Quoted in : *Tantras*: *Studies on their Religion and Literature,* by C. Chakravarti, Ch. X, p. 86 (Kolkatta edition, 1972).
14. Khanna, Madhu; *Yantra,* Ch. IV, p. 58 (Thomas and Hudson Ltd., London, 1979).
15. *Mantramahodadhi*, III.11.
16. For more details, Vide, *Mantramahodadhi*, ch. IV. 83-88.
17. *ibid.,* Ch. XI. 3-10.
18. Khanna, Madhu: *Yantra,* Ch. IV, p. 58.
19. *Mantramahodadhi*, VI. 12cd-13, cf. vide, VI.6.
20. *Śāradātilaka*, XII.31.
21. अत्युच्चामलिनाम्बराखिलजनोद्वेगावहा दुर्मना
    रूक्षाक्षित्रितया विशालदशना सूर्योदरी चञ्चला।
    प्रस्वेदाम्बुचिता क्षुधाकुलतनुः कृष्णातिरूक्षप्रभा
    ध्येया मुक्तकचा सदाप्रियकलिर्धूमावती मन्त्रिणा।। मन्त्रमहोदधि, VII.43.
22. बगलामुखीं त्रिजगतां संस्तम्भिनीं चिन्तयेत्।। *ibid.,* X.5cd.
23. *ibid.,* X.7, also cf. X.1.
24. *ibid.,* VII.72.
25. *Śāradātilaka*, VIII.4.
26. Kāṇe, P.V.: *History of Dharmaśāstra,* Vol. II, part II, Ch. XIX, p. 716.
27. Quoted in the *Elements of Hindu Iconography,* by T.A., Gopinath Rao, Vol. I, Part II, Appendix, p. 131 (MLBD, Delhi, 2nd edn., 1993).

Fig. 15.1. *Yantras* of Mahāvidyās

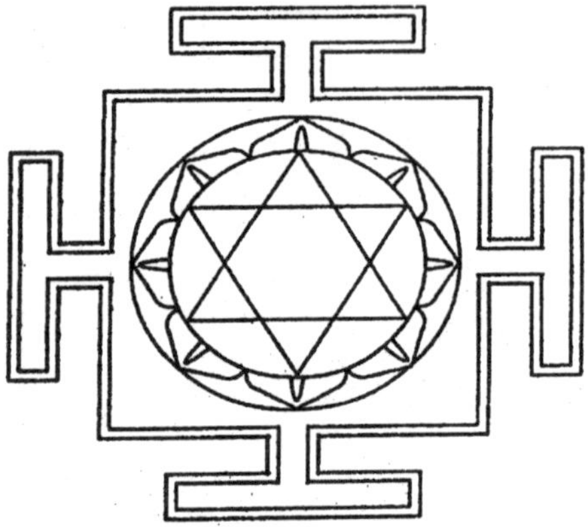

Dhūmāvatī Yantra

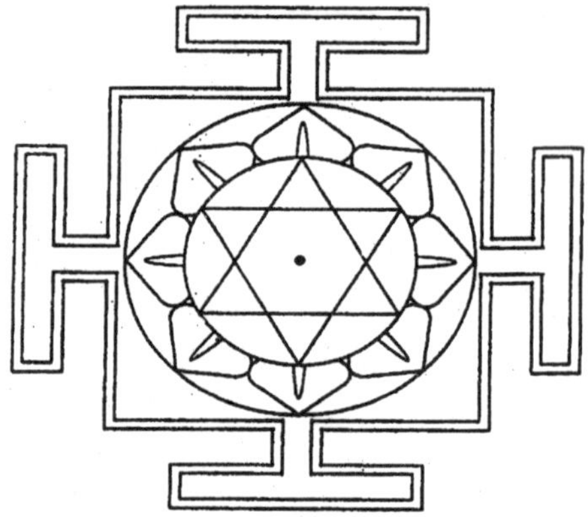

Kamalā Yantra

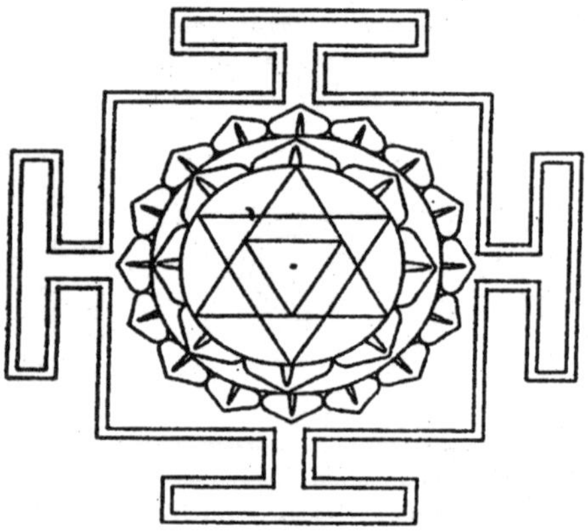

Bagalāmukhī Yantra

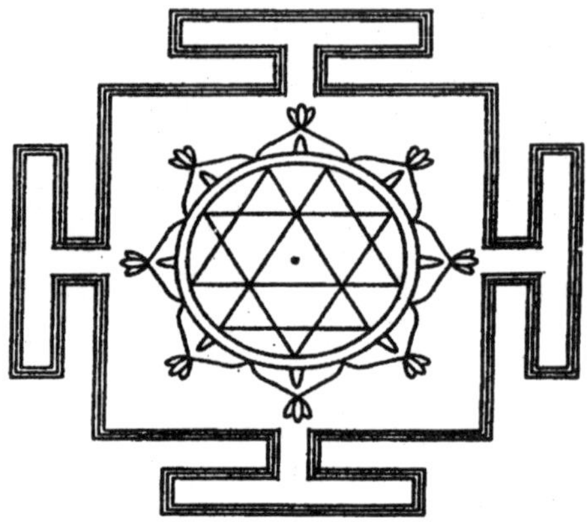

Durgā Yantra

Mātaṅgī Yantra

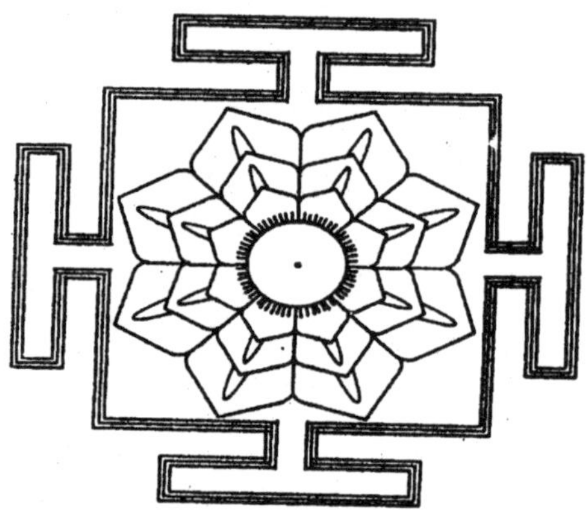

Śiva Yantra

Fig. 15.2. *Yantras* of Mahāvidyās along with Śiva and Durgā Yantra

Geographical Data in the *Meghadūta*

Kālidāsa occupies a unique place in the literature of the world. He is unquestionably the most popular poet in the Sanskrit literature. His highly creative powers, massive intellect, his immense imagination, marvellous poetical fluency, and his supreme culture, place him in the very front rank of the great poets of all ages.[1] He is the great representative of India's spirit, grace and genius. The Indian national consciousness is the base from which his works grow. The great qualities make his works belong to the literature of the world.

It seems that Kālidāsa possessed considerable knowledge of the contemporary topography of India, as his works bear a lot of evidence to his accurate and detailed geographical knowledge of this country. He knows the climatic conditions, physical features, and natural products of most parts of India, the names and exact location of rivers, mountains, lakes, forests and cities situated therein. The *Meghadūta,* especially Pūrvamegha which describes step by step the cloud messenger's northward course from Rāmagiri to Alakā will no doubt the truth of our assertion. Generally, during June-July the direction of monsoon wind is from east to west and finally towards north direction, i.e., to the Himālayas, as the route of clouds depicted in the *Meghadūta*. This also indicates the meteorological knowledge of Kālidāsa.

The Yakṣa who sends the cloud with the message to his wife was according to Kālidāsa at Rāmagiri,[2] which is identified by H.H. Wilson with Rāmaṭek or Rāmaṭekaḍī, which in Marāṭhi language means the same import Rāmagiri, 'Rāma's hill'. Both Vallabhadeva[3] and Mallinātha[4] say that it is Citrakūṭa, a mountain in Bundelakhaṇḍa. M.M. Haraprasada Shastri identifies Rāmagiri with Mount Rāmagarh of the former Sirgujā state in Madhya Pradesh. But there is a traditional belief still prevalent there that Rāma, Sītā and Lakṣmaṇa in their southward course during exile had bathed there. Foot-prints are still discernible on the rocky surface of this mount, somewhere in the middle, which the residents of this place in devotional fervour point out to the visitors as Rāma's. Mount Rāmagiri is spoken in the *Meghadūta* as bearing such sacred prints. In the words of Kālidāsa:

आपृच्छस्व प्रियसखममुं तुङ्गमालिङ्ग्य शैलं
वन्द्यैः पुंसां रघुपतिपदैरङ्कितं मेखलासु ।[5]

While explaning *'amuṁ śalim'* of the above verse G.R. Nandargikar says "this mountain must be Rāmagiri that stands a short distance (around 28 miles) north of Nagpur, and not Citrakūṭa given by Mallinātha in his commentary."[6] Besides these, Prof. V.V. Mirashi is of the opinion that we are inclined to take Rāmagiri to be the same as Rāmaṭek. He adds : "two copper-plate grants of the Vākāṭaka Queen Prabhāvatīguptā, one discovered in distant Poona and the other at Riddhapur in Berar, lend support to our view that Rāmagiri is Rāmaṭek today. Both the grants were made by the Dowager queen near the feet of the Bhagavat (i.e., Rāma) at the time of *pāraṇā* after observing a fast on Kārttika *śukla ekādaśī* (cf. 'शापान्तो मे भुजगशयनादुत्थिते शार्ङ्गपाणौ—*Uttaramegha,* 50). The Riddhapur plates actually describe the god Rāmachandra as 'the lord of Rāmagiri[7]'? He further adds, "the Riddhapur plates show that Prabhāvatīguptā, mother of Pravarasena II and daughter of Chandragupta II Vikramāditya, often visited Rāmagiri, which was close to her capital Nandivardhana, in order to worship the sacred shrine of Śrī Rāma situated on the top of it."[8] So, considering the matter from all points of view, it is now clear that Rāmagiri is modern Rāmaṭek.

In the verse "मार्गं तावच्छृणु कथयतस्त्वत्प्रयाणानुरूपम्"[9] Kālidāsa begins to instruct the cloud about the route to be followed by him. While commenting on this verse H.H. Wilson writes "we will now begin the geographical part of the poem; which, as far as it can be made out through the difference of ancient and modern appellations, seems to be very accurately conceived The two extreme points of the cloud's progress are the vicinity of Nagpur and the mountain Kailāsa or rather, the Himālaya range. During this course, the poet notices some of the most celebrated places, with the greater number of which we are still acquainted In the first instance, we have here his direction due north from the mountain of Rāmagiri and we shall notice the other points as they occur."[10] Then the cloud is to start towards north and he is first of all to get up Mālakṣetra[11], the high plateau containing the black cotton soil. Mallinātha[12] takes *māla* to be the name of an elevated hilly spot. But other commentators[13] interpret it as: *mālākhyaṁ deśam,* the district of that name. Mallinātha's sense is better, as the cloud would like to ascend an elevated spot rather than a district. H.H. Wilson, however, takes *māla* to be the name of a town called Māldā, a little to the north of Ratanpur, the chief town of the northern province of Chattisgarh.

Next the poet takes the cloud to the hill of Āmrakūṭa.[14] This must be the mountain now known as Amarakaṇṭaka,[15] from which the river Narmadā and other rivers spring and which form the eastern part of the Vindhya mountain. Kālidāsa describes the Narmadā or Revā, a thin stream flowing by the foot of the Vindhya, after it comes down from the top of Amarakaṇṭaka.[16] Then the cloud is to pass from hill to hill and then to reach the country of the Daśārṇas, which is dark with the ripe berries of the *jambu* tree and which is frequented by the Swans only for a few days. The word *daśārṇa* means 'the country of ten citadels'. It is the name of a country laying south-east of

Madhyadeśa.[17] Daśārṇa is the name of a river rising in the Vindhya mountain, the ancient Dasarene. This country is the eastern part of Mālvā. According to Prof. H.H. Wilson, Daśārṇa may be identified with modern Chattisgarh. It is watered by many rivers, Vetravatī being the foremost of them. The modern name of Vetravatī is Betavā. It rises on the north side of the Vindhya chain and pursuing a north-easterly course of 340 miles, traverses the province of Mālvā and the south west corner of Allahabad and falls into the Yamunā. The early part of its course, it passes through Bhilsā or Vidiśā. Vidiśā is known as the capital of Daśārṇa and situated on the bank of river Betavā in the province of Mālvā. The Purāṇas associate the people of Daśārṇa country with the Mālavas, Kārūṣas, Mekalas, Utkalas and Naiṣadhas. In the *Rāmāyaṇa*[18] their country is connected with those of the Mekalas and Utkalas, where Sugriva sent his monkey-army in the quest of Sītā. But Prof. B.C. Law says: "it should be noted that the Daśārṇa country of the *Rāmāyaṇa* and Purāṇas seems to be different from the Daśārṇa country of the *Meghadūta*."[19]

After visiting the capital Vidiśā[20] and after tasting the rippling water of Vetravatī, the cloud should rest on the Nicaiḥ,[21] a hillock of little importance 'most likely the Sāñcī of modern maps'. There are so many Buddhist monuments remains even now round about this place. Then the poet leads the cloud by the gardens on the banks of the *Vananadī*. The commentator Mallinatha explains this in the sense of 'forest rivers'. According to H.H. Wilson[22] it may have been the name of a small river west of the Betavā named Pārvatī, which rising in the Vindhya chain runs north-west, till it joins another called the Śiprā; and the two together fall into the Chambal.

Now the poet Kālidāsa makes the Yakṣa apologize to the cloud and request him to turn a little from his straight path towards the west, to make a detour so as to include the famous city of Ujjayinī, which must have been very dear to the heart of the poet. In the words of Kālidāsa:

वक्रः पन्था यदपि भवतः प्रस्थितस्योत्तराशां
सौधोत्सङ्गप्रणयविमुखो मा स्म भूरुज्जयिन्याः।[23]

Ujjayinī, situated on the bank of Śiprā river, was the capital of the country called Avantī. It has many other names, viz. Viśālā, Avantī, Avantikā, Puṣpakaraṇḍinī.[24] It has been the place of great importance from the earliest period of Hindu tradition down to the present day. The famous Mahākāla temple of Śiva is also situated in this city. So, it is one of the seven sacred cities in India.[25] The most important thing is to be noted here that the Hindu geographers calculate their longitude from this city, taking it as their meridian. The modern Ujjayinī or Ujjain is about a mile south of the acncient city. Hiuen Tsang describes the capital of *U-she-yen-na*, or Ujjayinī as 80 *li,* or 5 miles, in circuit, which is only a little less than its size at present day. The kingdom was 16000 *li,* or 1000 miles in circuit.[26] Between Vidiśā and Ujjayinī, i.e., between the Vetravatī and the Śiprā, Kālidāsa mentions two other streams. There are many water courses in the regions and the Nirvindhyā and the Sindhu belong to them. These two have been identified with Pārvatī and the Kāli Sindh respectively. Reaching Ujjayinī the poet speaks of the Śiprā[27] upon which stands the temple of Chandesvara and the river Gandhavatī and famous Mahākāla temple of Śiva. The river Gandhavatī which was fine stream at the time of Kālidāsa, has now shrunk to a mere drain, as M.M. Haraprasada Shastri, who has carefully gone over these parts of the country with the express object of identifying the geographical names given by Kālidāsa observes.[28] He says about Gandhavatī that this river does not exist at the present time. In Kālidāsa's time it formed the boundary of the temple gardens of Mahākāla.[29] The cloud is asked to wait at the temple till sunset to witness the evening worship of Śiva there and then to resume its journey after sunrise on the following day.

Leaving Ujjayinī, thereafter, the cloud is asked to cross the Gambhirā, a small river in Mālvā province. Along the side of river Gambhirā the poet would lead the cloud to a certain distance and then take him to Devagiri hill on which Lord Kārttikeya dwells. H.H. Willson has identified it with Devagaḍa, situated south of the Chambal, in the centre of the province of Mālvā, and precisely in the line of the cloud's progress.[30] Then the poet makes the cloud cross the Carmaṇvatī river (modern Chambal) and again makes him deviate from the direct route in order to reach Daśapura or Mandasora. This river known as the Carmaṇvatī, because it was formed of the blood of many cows slaughtered by Rantideva, when he performed cow-sacrifices in ancient times.[31] According to the plan of the journey the cloud uses the rivers as his watering stations. The long stream of the river with its sparkling water would look like a pearl-necklace with the cloud hung in the middle as a pendant of sapphire.

Daśapura is identified with the modern mandasor in Western Mālvā division of central India. The ancient Daśapura stood on the north or left bank of Siwana river. From Daśapura the cloud is asked to go straight towards the north and stops at the Kurukshetra in old Brahmāvarta land. The modern Kurukshetra, one of the sacred places of the Hindus, lies a little to the south-east of Thāneśvara. It is mentioned by the sage Manu as situated between the divine rivers Sarasvatī and Dṛṣadvatī.[32] The modern city Thāneśvara is a correct form of Sthāṇvīśvara or God of Śiva. The Sarasvatī, one of the holy rivers of (ancient) India, falls from the southern portion of the Himālayas and runs into the great desert where it is lost in the sands. Kālidāsa has some definite knowledge about this holy river as well as the city of Sthāṇvīśvara. So he makes the cloud to drink the water of Sarasvatī.[33] From the Sarasvatī, ignoring the Yamunā, which, however is mentioned by name in verse I. 54 (as 'स्यादस्थानोपगतयमुनासंगमेवाभिरामा'), the cloud is to go to Kanakhala, which is a holy place near Haridwara, where the Ganges descends into the low ground of Hindustan. In the words of Kālidāsa:

तस्माद् गच्छेरनुकनखलं शैलराजावतीर्णां,
जह्नोः कन्यां सगरतनयस्वर्गसोपानपङ्क्तिम्।[34]

Here, Kālidāsa mentions the place Kanakhala, but omits Haridwara another sacred spot of the Hindus. H.H. Wilson observes, "it is rather extraodinary that Kālidāsa should have omitted the name of Haridwara and preferred Kanakhala,[35] especially as the former occurs in the Purāṇas..."[36] Besides, Kanakhala may be more famous place than Haridwara in the time of Kālidāsa. The poet also mentions a word *caraṇanyāsa* in verse I. 58. The spot here alluded may have some connection with a neighbouring hill at Haridwara called Harkāpāyaṛī *(pauḍī)*, the foot of Hara (Śiva). It is called *Śrīcaraṇa-nyāsa* in the *Śambhurahasya.*[37] So, *Śrīcaraṇanyāsa* is a sacred spot on the Himālayas, where there is supposed to be a foot-print of Śiva, a sight of which was supposed to qualify the pilgrim for rebirth, a sight of which was supposed to qualify the pilgrim for rebirth as *gaṇa* of Śiva.

After Kanakhala the cloud is asked to go to Himālaya mountain; arriving at the snow-clad peaks of the Himālayas, the cloud is invited to rest on some breezy height. Viewing the several wonders of this great mountain, the cloud should pass to the north through Krauñcarandhra,[38] and come upon mount Kailāsa, at the foot of which lies limpid lake Mānasarovara[39] abounding in golden lotuses. The Mānasa lake is situated on Mount Kailāsa, which runs parallel with it on the north of that chain. It is the favourite haunt of flamingoes which migrate to it at the commencement of the rainy season. Kailāsa is the name of a mountain in the Himalāyas, north of the Mānasa lake. It is the abode of Lord Śiva and also of god Kubera. H.H. Wilson observes, "Kailāsa, as it here appears, a part of the Himālaya range, is, in fable, a mountain of costly gems or of crystal, the site of Kubera's capital, and the favourite haunt of Śiva."[40] On the top of this mountain stands the city of Alakā, the city of perfect glory and bliss. It is the capital of Kubera, the god of wealth and the regent of the north, so called because of its grandeur. This is the destination of the cloud, as said by Kālidāsa in the following verse:

गन्तव्या ते वसतिरलका नाम यक्षेश्वराणां,
बाह्योद्यानस्थितहरशिरश्चन्द्रिकाधौतहर्म्या।[41]

So, Alakā, the mythical abode of Kubera, supposed to be situated on the Himālayas.

Conclusion

From the above description of cloud route, we can surmise a physical map of ancient India, especially northern part which is almost the same as we find in the modern geography, only with some changes in the names of places (cities, etc.), hills and rivers. These types of changes are quite natural even today (e.g. from Madras to Chennai). No doubt, Kālidāsa has some sharp witted knowledge on geography of India, on the basis of which he has accurately sketched the exact position of the towns, rivers, hills and lakes of ancient northern India. Hence, *Meghadūta* may be treated as a geograhical *kāvya* of Kālidāsa.

However, from this study some questions may arise in the minds of modern researchers/thinkers : firstly, why Kālidāsa, being a devotee of Lord Śiva has not shown the shortest cloud route through Vārāṇasī (Kāśī), place of Lord Viśvanātha? Secondly, was there any physical map of ancient India before Kālidāsa?

NOTES AND REFERENCES

1. *Meghadūta* (tr. into English) by M.R. Kale, Introduction, p. XV.
2. कश्चित्कान्ताविरहगुरुणा स्वाधिकारात्प्रमत्तः ... रामगिर्याश्रमेषु। —*Meghadūta*, I.1.
3. रामगिर्याश्रमेषु चित्रकूटाचलतपोवनेषु वसतिं चक्रे। Vallabhadeva's Comm. on *Meghadūta*, I.1.
4. रामगिरेश्चित्रकूटस्याश्रमेषु वसतिम्। Mallinātha's Comm. on *Meghadūta* I.1.
5. *ibid.,* I.12.
6. Note on Verse I.11 of *Meghadūta*, p. 17 (1998 edn.); cf. *Meghadūta* by M.R. Kale, notes on Verse I. 12.
7. *Kālidāsa* by V.V. Mirashi & N.R. Navlekar, p. 153 (1969 edn.).
8. *ibid.,* cf. V.V. Mirashi's *Studies in Indology,* Vol. I (Second edn. 1968), p. 12 f.
9. *Meghadūta,* I. 13.
10. Note on verse I. 13 of *Meghadūta* by H.H. Wilson.
11. सद्यः सीरोत्कषणसुरभि क्षेत्रमारुह्य मालम्...। *Meghadūta,* I.16.
12. मालं मालाख्यं क्षेत्रं शैलप्रायमुन्नतस्थलम्। मालमुन्नतभूतलम् इत्युत्पलमालायाम्। I. 16 of *Meghadūta.*
13. मालं-मालाख्यं देशम्। मालं देशे वनेऽप्युक्तं मालं ग्रामान्तराटवी। मालं मालवदेशे च वसतेर्भूमिरुर्ध्वका इति सुमतिविजयभाष्यम्। मालं क्षेत्रसमूहम्। मालाख्यं देशं वा। वनभूमिं वा इति सारोद्धारिणीभाष्यम्। मालं-मालमुदारक्षेत्रम् इति वल्लभाचार्यभाष्यम्। मालं-ग्रामान्तराटवी। मालाभिधानं देशमारुह्य इति मेघलताभाष्यम्। मालं-मालवदेशमारुह्य इति अवचूरिभाष्यम्।
14. सानुमानाम्रकूटः। *Meghadūta,* I.17.
15. H.H. Wilson rightly identifies Āmrakūṭa with mountain Amarakaṇṭaka.
16. रेवां द्रक्ष्यस्युपलविषमे विन्ध्यपादे विशीर्णाम्...।। *Meghadūta,* I.19.
17. In *Manusmṛti* (II.21), the position of Madhyadeśa is described as:

    हिमवद्विन्ध्ययोर्मध्यं यत्प्राग्विनशनादपि।
    प्रत्यगेव प्रयागाच्च मध्यदेशः प्रकीर्तितः।।
18. *Kiṣkindhākāṇḍa,* 41.8-10 (Gītā Press Edition).
19. Law, B.C.: *Geographical Aspects of Kālidāsa's Works,* p. 27 (Kolkatta 1954 edn.).
20. The ancient city of Vidiśā identified with Bhilsā in the Gwalior state was situated at a distance of 26 miles north-east of Bhopal. In the *Mārkaṇḍeya Purāṇa,* it is mentioned that Vidiśā was one of the western neighbours of Avantī. Since the time of Aśoka it became an important centre of Buddhism and later on of Vaiṣṇavism. Its importance was due to its central position on the lines of communication between the sea-ports of the western coast and Pāṭaliputra and between Pratiṣṭhāna Śrāvastī.
21. *Nicaiḥ* is a small hill near Vidiśā town; vide, *Meghadūta : Ek purānī kahāni* by Acharya Hazari Prasad Dvivedi, pp. 42-43.
22. Commentary on *Meghadūta,* verse I.27.

23. *Meghadūta,* I. 28.
24. उज्जयिनी स्याद्विशालावन्ती पुष्पकरण्डिनी। *Haima Kośa,* IV.42.
25. अयोध्या मथुरा माया काशी काञ्ची अवन्तिका।
    पुरी द्वारावती चैव सप्तैता मोक्षदायिकाः।।
26. Law, B.C., *Geographical Aspects of Kālidāsa's Works,* p. 26.
27. Vallabha says : "सिप्राख्योज्जयिन्यां नदी"। *Meghadūta,* I. 32 ;cf.
    सिप्रातरङ्गानिलकम्पितासु विहर्तुमुद्यानपरम्परासु। *Raghuvaṁśa,* VI.35.
28. *JBORS,* Vol. I. Part 2, p. 202.
29. It is one of the twelve *Jyotirliṅgas*, viz. सौराष्ट्रे सोमनाथं च श्रीशैले मल्लिकार्जुनम्। उज्जयिन्यां महाकालमोंकारे परमेश्वरम्।। केदारं हिमवत्पृष्ठे डाकिन्यां भीमशङ्करम्। वाराणस्यां च विश्वेशं त्र्यम्बकं गौतमीतटे।। वैद्यनाथं चिताभूमौ नागेशं दारुकावने। सेतुबन्धे च रामेशं घुश्मेशं च शिवालये।। (एतेषां दर्शनादेव पातकं नैव तिष्ठति)।। *Śivapurāṇa, Koṭirudrasaṁhitā* (4), I. 21-23.
30. *Meghadūta,* tr. into English by H.H. Wilson, I.45.
31. *Meghadūta*, I. 48; cf. "यतो हि रन्तिदेवेन राज्ञा गोमेधयज्ञेषु शतशो धेनव आहूतास्तद्रक्तनदीप्रवाहेण चर्मण्वती नदी जातेति प्रसिद्धः।" Sumativijaya Bhāṣya of *Meghadūta,* I.48.
32. कुरुक्षेत्रं च मत्स्याश्च पञ्चालाः शूरसेनकाः।
    एष ब्रह्मर्षिदेशो वै ब्रह्मावर्तादनन्तरः।। *Manusmṛti*, II 19; cf, II.21-22.
33. *Meghadūta*, I. 51-52.
34. *ibid.,* I. 53.
35. तीर्थं कनखलं नाम गङ्गाद्वारेऽस्ति पावनम्। यत्र काञ्चनपातेन जाह्नवी देवदन्तिना। *Kathāsaritsāgara,* III.4.

    Cf. गङ्गा कनखले पुण्या कुरुक्षेत्रे सरस्वती।
    ग्रामे वा यदि वारण्ये पुण्या सर्वत्र नर्मदा।।
    Also cf. गङ्गाद्वारं कनखलं सोमो वै तत्र संस्थितः।
    स्नात्वा कनखले तीर्थे पुनर्जन्म न विद्यते।। *Harivaṁśa,* quoted in G.R. Nandargikar's edition of *Meghadūta*, I.54.
36. *Meghadūta*, edited by H.H. Wilson, 3rd edition, London, 1843, p. 50.
37. Mallinātha's Comm. on *Meghadūta*, I.58.
38. The *Krauñcarandhra* was apparently a part of the mountain Krauñca. This 'pass' is situated somewhere in the Himālayas, and is said to have been opened by Paraśurāma with his arrows to make a passage from Kailāsa to the southwards. The *Vāyu Purāṇa* attributed the splitting of the mountain to Kārttikeya.
39. The Mānasa lake is called *Brahman saraḥ* (*Raguvaṁśa,* XIII. 60) having been created by Brahman from his mind. According to the *Rāmāyaṇa* the river Sarayū issues from it:

    कैलासपर्वते राम मनसा निर्मितं परम्।। ब्रह्मणा नरशार्दूल तेनेदं मानसं सरः।
    तस्मात्सुस्राव सरसः साऽयोध्यामुपगूहते। सरःप्रवृत्ता सरयूः पुण्या ब्रह्मसरश्च्युता।।
    Rāmāyaṇa, Bālakāṇḍa, XXIV.8-10.
40. Vide, notes on the *Meghadūta*, edited by H.H. Wilson.
41. *Meghadūta*, I.7.

Socio-economic Thoughts in the *Śukranītisāra*

Economic thought in any age only reflects its life and economic opinion moves with the variations of economic condition. Our Ancient Indian thinkers like Kāmandaka, Kauṭilya, Śukrācārya, etc. have focused a lot on the socio-economic life of the people in different times. The economic theories and ideas suggested by these great thinkers definitely enabled the king and their subjects to enliven their life in a general way in the society. The understanding of the Ancient Indian attitude towards economic study and towards economic questions may also lead to a better appreciation than we now have of Indian attitude towards life and knowledge.

As regards to the Ancient Indian conception of economics is concerned there is no single expression in our languages which have attempted to coin equivalents for the term 'economics' in such expressions as : *Arthanīti, Arthavijñnāna, Artha-mīmāṁsā, Arthaśāstra* and *Vārtāśāstra.* The last two however have specialized meanings of their traditional sense. There are two expressions in Sanskrit, which relate to subjects having a large economic content. These are *Arthaśāstra* and *Vārtā*. The literature of Dharmaśāstras and Nītiśāstras also deal largely with the economic matter. Anyway, to appreciate the position of *Arthaśāstra* and *Vārtā* in the circle of Ancient Indian science, it is necessary to understand first the traditional Indian attitude towards knowledge as a whole and its different branches. Every division of knowledge, which is systematized, was conceived as *vidyā* or a *śāstra*. The *vidyās* are four in number as stated by Kauṭilya in his *Arthaśāstra*:

आन्वीक्षिकी त्रयी वार्ता दण्डनीतिश्चेति–चतस्र एव विद्या॥[1]

This means *vidyās* are four in number, viz., (1) *Ānvīkṣikī,* (2) *Trayī,* (3) *Vārtā*, and (4) *Daṇḍanīti*. Each of these divisions comprises a number of subjects or sciences. The name *Ānvīkṣikī* stands for the sciences derived from subjective or metaphysical speculations involving keen introspection. Three such different subjects or systems of thought and philosophy are known to Kauṭilya, viz., Sāṁkhya, Yoga, and Lokāyata.[2] But Śukrācārya, the author of the *Śukranītisāra* regards Nyāya and Vedānta as the primary sub-divisions of *Ānvīkṣikī*.[3] '*Trayī*' means the Veda and is made to comprehend all branches of revealed knowledge and their auxiliaries, such as the four Vedas, six

Vedāṅgas, Itihāsas, Purāṇas, Nyāya, Mīmāṁsā *śāstras,* etc.[4] The word '*vārtā*' generally means *vṛtti,* i.e., profession. It is defined as the subject, which treats of agriculture, cattle rearing, trade and commerce.

In the *Śukranītisāra* it is said that money-lending, agriculture, commerce and cattle-protection are comprised in *Vārtā.*[5] "A good man who is blessed by *Vārtā* never has a fear on account of his occupation," says Śukrācārya.[6] *Daṇḍanīti,* the fourth of the branches of *vidyā* (knowledge) is virtually the same as *Nītiśāstra,* the Science of polity,[7] i.e., the Science and art of government.

The *Arthaśāstra* is called Arthaveda and classed as an Upaveda. As a term, *Arthaśāstra* was of wider import than either *Vārtā* or *Daṇḍanīti*. It appears to have had a vogue of popularity after the days of Kauṭilya. But the *Arthaśāstra* was obiviously wider in scope than economics. The Indian doctrine of *puruṣārtha* indicates a fourfold division of the aims of human existence. These *puruṣārthas* are: *dharma, artha, kāma* and *mokṣa*. There are two spheres of human activity indicated in the *śāstras*. One is *vyavahārika* and another is *pāramārthika*. Of the four aims of human existence, the first three, viz., *dharma, artha* and *kāma,* representing the moral and religious, the economic and aesthetic values are ending in this worldly life—the life of *vyavahāra*, of *pravṛtti*—action, the cause of bondage, the *karmamārga*, the path of action taught in the *śāstra*. But the latter *mokṣa* takes a man to *pāramārthika* stage, where a certain negation of earthly good as well as a certain transvaluation of earthly values takes place, i.e., *nivṛtti mārga*. *Nivṛti* is inaction. It is the cause of liberation, the path of *sāmānya* (cf. *Gītā*, XVIII. 30).

The old Indian attitude towards 'scicence' and 'art' reflects the beliefs in the interdependence of all branches of knowledge and all stages of life, and in the ultimate sanction for all secular sciences being found in religion and philosophy. Thus, it came to pass that in Ancient India economic laws had to find their ultimate justification in metaphysics and religion, and their immediate sanction in politics and law as much as in their own rationality and practicability. This is rightly indicated in Śukrācārya's definition of *Arthaśāstram*, which he defines as:

श्रुतिस्मृत्यविरोधेन राजवृत्तादिशासनम्।
सुयुक्त्याऽर्थार्जनं यत्र ह्यर्थशास्त्रं तदुच्यते॥[8]

It means, *Arthaśāstra* is that science which describes the actions and administration of kings in accordance with the dictates of revelation and of law as well as the means of appropriate livelihood.

In the *Nirukta*[9], Yāska gives two possible etymologies of the word *artha* : (a) *artho' rteḥ,* (b) *araṇastho vā,* which means that the word is to be derived either from the root *ṛ-+than (Uṇādi*—I. 61) 'to go' or from *araṇa*+root *sthā*-'to remain in a distant or forcign place'. The commentator Durga tries to explain these etymologies as applicable to *artha* in the sense of 'wealth'. *Artha* from the root √*ṛ*-'to go', because wealth is sought (lit. gone to) by those desirous of it; (2) *artha* from *araṇa* +√*sthā*-, because when the owner of the wealth goes from this world to another world (*araṇa=gamana*), it does not go with him to the next world, but stays behind (root√*sthā-*) in this world.[10] Durgācārya then adds that *artha* 'meaning (of a word)' has arisen secondarily from *artha* 'wealth' owing to similarity with it (*tat sāmānyād itaro' pi śabdārtho' rtha ucyate*).[11]

The commentary ascribed to Skanda-Maheśvara, on the other hand, explains the etymologies first with reference to *artha* 'meaning', and secondarily with reference to *artha* 'wealth'. *Artha* 'meaning' is derived from the root √*ṛ-* 'to go', because it is understood (lit. gone to) from the word. *Artha* is derived from the same root, because in business it 'goes' from person to person since time immemorial.[12]

The *Amarakośa* explains the world *artha* as:

अर्थोऽभिधेयरैवस्तुप्रयोजननिवृत्तिषु।[13]

Artha means 'meaning', 'thing', 'purpose', and prohibition. According to the *Medinīkośa*[14], *artha* denotes *viṣaya* (subject), *dhana* (wealth, money), and *vastu* (material), etc. The *Arthaśāstra* clarifies the term *artha* as : *manuṣyāṇāṁ vṛttirarthaḥ, manuṣyavatī bhūmirityarthaḥ*[15]—the source of the livelihood by men following various occupations constitutes *artha*..... Likewise the *Viṣṇusahasranāma Bhāṣya* explains *artha* as :

सुखस्वरूपत्वात्सर्वैरर्थ्यत इति अर्थः।[16]

However, *artha* as a subject of *Arthaśāstra* has two other meanings, besides wealth. As a synonym for wealth,[17] it is less commonly used than *dhana* being specialized in two other senses. In the first of these senses, it refers to the aims of life (*puruṣārtha*). In the second, it refers one of the *puruṣārtha,* viz. that which satisfies human desire. Hence, *artha* or wealth is highly essential for every human being as it is a means of welfare and happiness irrespective of cast and creed Even for a Brahmin, according to Maharshi Manu,[18] the earning of wealth (*arthārjana*) is a duty, though he is enjoined to eke out this means of subsistence in such a manner as to cause little or no pain to others. Even the grains and moments should make accumulation of wealth and learning. The man who is desirous of acquiring both, shall neglect neither the grains nor the moments because they are trifling says Śukrācārya in the following verse:

क्षणशः कणशश्चैव विद्यामर्थं च साधयेत्।
न त्याज्यौ तु क्षणकणौ नित्यं विद्याधनार्थिना।।[19]

In the same spirit, prodigality and extravagance are sternly reprobated Social and civil penalties are prescribed for extravagance, over and above the penalty of natural consequences. Among those whom Śukrācārya would banish from the country or imprison, the prodigal has a prominent place.

Expenditure, for mere ostentation, on trifling matters is condemned,[20] and a warning is sounded that even good impulses (as through indiscriminate charity) might lead, if not properly restrained, to poverty and ruin. On the other hand, the accumulation of big hoards, which would withdraw capital from production of enjoyment, is also disapproved A name for wealth '*bhogya*' is suggested that wealth exists to be enjoyed The ideal is held that the aim of accumulation and of earning is to provide for oneself and for one's dependents. Thus Śukrācārya elaborates as :

सुभार्यापुत्रमित्रार्थं हितं नित्यं धनार्जनम्।।
दानार्थं च विना त्वेतैः किं धनैश्च जनैश्च किम्।[21]

This means, the daily acquisition of wealth is proper for the man and wife, children and friends. It is also necessary for charity. Without these, what is the good existence to man?

In the society any difficult task can be done through wealth or money. A wealthy person gets every success and happiness in the society. Money is the best means of every worldly pleasure. Hence, Ācārya Bhartṛhari rightly says :

यस्यास्ति वित्तं स नरः कुलीनः स पण्डितः स श्रुतवान् गुणज्ञः।
स एव वक्ता स च दर्शनीयः सर्वे गुणाः काञ्चनमाश्रयन्ति।।[22]

Śukrācārya has also stressed for proper accumulation of wealth in order to maintain a healthy and prosperous life. He adds:

अस्ति यावत्तु सधनस्तावत् सर्वैस्तु सेव्यते।।
निर्धनस्त्यज्यते भार्यापुत्राद्यैः सगुणोऽयतः।

संसृतौ व्यवहाराय सारभूतं धनं स्मृतम्।।
अतो यतेत तत्प्राप्त्यै नरः सूपायसाहसैः।[23]

It means, one should carefully preserve wealth, which can maintain him in the future. So long as there is wealth, one is respected by all. But even a qualified man without wealth deserts by his wife and sons. In this world, wealth is the means to all pursuits. He further states :

सुविद्यया सुसेवाभिः शौर्येण कृषिभिस्तथा।।
कौसीदवृद्ध्या पण्येन कलाभिश्च प्रतिग्रहैः।

यया कया चापि वृत्त्या धनवान्स्यात्तथा चरेत्।।
तिष्ठन्ति सधनद्वारे गुणिनः किङ्करा इव।[24]

Let men therefore try to acquire wealth in legitimate ways, as by learning, service, valour, agriculture, commerce, the practice of crafts, and even by mendicancy. Owing to insufficiency of wealth, people occasionally become slaves of others.

To control the day-to-day family expenditure Śukrācārya recognizes the importance of maintaining 'accounts'. He recognizes that for the transaction of business as much for family solvency, the absence of a written record of the incomings and outgoings is fatal. He accordingly rules that for businessman there is nothing more important than the maintenance of written accounts, and that the wise businessman never transacts business without documents and accounts.

नैवास्ति लिखितादन्यत् स्मारकं व्यवहारिणाम्।।
न लेख्येन विना कुर्याद् व्यवहारं सदा बुधः।[25]

The rigorous enforcement of such precepts in our sacred Dharmaśāstras and Nītiśāstras might lead one to conclude that the standard of living must have been comparatively low in Ancient India. That this was not so in actual practice, is borne testimony to not merely by foreign visitors, but by such light as our secular literature and our old epigraphic records throw upon the conditions of consumption in those epochs. Saving, rather than stinting, is what our old economists praise. For instance, in language, which sounds startlingly modern, Śukrācārya condemns the stinting of necessaries as wasteful. In a picturesque phrase Śukrācārya lays down that, in feasts and in law-suits, the wise person should abandon timidity and not hold himself back till fully satisfied[26]

In Ancient India, the agents of production appear to have been counted as four, viz., land, labour, capital and organization. This is remarkable, since organization as a factor of production, obtained recognition in the West only in recent times. On the other hand, the modern attempt to reduce all primary factors of production to two, viz., land and labour, has also its parallel in our Ancient economic theory. Without going to the length to which the Physiocrats carried the doctrine, as it is found in the *Śukranītisāra* the dictum "land is the source of all type of wealth"—'*khaniḥ sarva-dhanasyeyam*'[27] ...."For it, the kings have laid down even their lives. Men for enjoyment, desire wealth and life. What has else the man, who has wealth and life, but has not cherished land?" says Śukrācārya in the following verse:

उपभोगाय च धनं जीवितं येन रक्षितम्।
न रक्षिता तु भूर्येन किं तस्य धनजीवितैः।।[28]

Besides the importance of wealth, labour is also recognized with equal status in the *Śukranītisāra*. So, it is with capital, as is evident from the exhortations on thrift, addressed to both individuals and kings.[29] Land is mainly used for agricultural purpose. Hence, it can easily be understood that the pre-eminence given to rural economics in India, ancient and modern; since in both ages, agriculture has been marked as the best occupation of the people. Two of the most important sections of *vātrā* were agriculture and cattle-rearing, including dairy farming under the latter (modern). The importance attached to agricultural pursuits by our economists is shown by the injunctions to kings to study *vārtā,* and by the precept that a considerable part of king's own revenue should be derived, both directly and indirectly, from the proceeds of agriculture and the rearing of cattle. As an occupation, agriculture was prescribed for *vaiśyas*, and for *śūdras* only in a less degree. It was also permitted to the other two castes, i.e. *brāhmaṇa* and *kṣatriya*. Even a Brahmin could take to agriculture, provided he did not himself hold the plough. Regarding different professions (*vṛttis*) Śukrācārya clearly states as under :

कृषिस्तु चोत्तमा वृत्तिर्या सरिन्मातृका मता।।
मध्यमा वैश्यवृत्तिश्च शूद्रवृत्तिस्तु चाधमा।
याच्ञाऽधमतरा वृत्तिर्ह्युत्तमा सा तपस्विषु।।
क्वचित् सेवोत्तमा वृत्तिर्धर्मशीलनृपस्य च।[30]

Apart from the *Śukranītisāra*, *Arthaśāstra*, *Manusmṛti* and other Smṛti texts show the high degree of perfection to which agriculture had attained as an art and of the thoroughness with which our old economists understood the details of agricultural pursuits.

Śukrācārya has discussed a lot on wages and the conditions of labour. It is, in regard to wages that we find the most elaborate treatment in our old economic literature. The dignity of labour is affirmed A clear distinction is made between 'pure' and 'impure' types of labour, and between one's own land and labour for hire.[31] According to our old literature the position of the domestic slave was distinctly better than that of a hired labourer. The life of a labourer was not secured in ancient times, so Śukrācārya has prescribed some rules and regulations on labour laws for the economical benefit of the labourer. He has even stressed for the upliftment of the social and economical status of the servants. Therefore, in his *Śukranītisāra*, he suggests that a labourer should be remunerated according to his productivity and qualification and that the wages should be such as would maintain the labourer and his family intolerable comfort. In a maxim pointing to the bad economy of low wages, Śukrācārya opines, "servants who get low wages are enemies by nature and are plunderers."

ये भृत्या हीनभृतिकाः शत्रवस्ते स्वयंकृताः।
परस्य साधकास्ते तु छिद्रकोशप्रजाहराः।।[32]

For domestic servants, Śukrācārya provides for leave of absence for recreation and on the occasion of festivities. He provides leisure for three hours in the day and nine hours in the night. His scales of sickness, accident and pension benefits are very reasonable. A bonus of three months'pay is due to a servant who has served five years, and of six months'wages to one who has been long ill. A fortnight's leave with allowance is due to one who has been employed for a year, a life pension of one-half the pay to a public servant who has served for forty years, and half the amount to his widow or minor children in case he dies in service, a bonus of one eighth of the salary for an efficient servant for every year of his service, with compensation to the family, in case of a worker who dies in harness. Śukrācārya realizes fully the value of kind treatment as one of the alleviations of labour, and has many great words of advice on the subject.[33] No provisions of equal liberality are to be found in other parts of our old economic literature. Whether the precepts of Śukrācārya reflects only his own ideals or the attempts to cope with a historical situation, we have now no means of knowing, nor whether his humane and sane precepts merely reflect the wisdom and experience of an economist of vision, or whether they are deductions from the actual treatment of a difficult labour situation of his age. However, it can be said that Śukrācārya has a positive and favourable attitude towards the better and prosperous life of the labourers and servants in the Ancient Indian society.

After prescribing labour laws and due recommendations for financial benefits to the labourers and servants, Śukrācārya then defines the price (*mūlya*) of the commodity as that by spending which one gets the possession of the commodity, he thereby strikes the modern definition of price as the exchange-value of a commodity and comes very close to present-day economic theory. So he lays down first that price (*mūlya*) is what is paid (in money) for acquiring an article and secondly, that prices are high or law, according to articels are obtainable with or without any difficulty, and according to they posses or do not possess utility.[34] There is no *mūlya* for things which cannot be put to use. Every article which has utility, need not be valuable. Scarcity is a necessary cause of value. Those articles priced high in the world, are rare.[35] Articles without utility have no value.[36] The influence of time as a factor of value is also understood. In laying down the maxims for the guidance of governments and traders, who have to fix prices, *Śukranītisāra* says :

यथादेशं यथाकालं मूल्यं सर्वस्य कल्पयेत्॥[37]

This means, one should fix the price of an article according to time and place, i.e., according to the availability of things or articles, the prices should be fixed Besides, variations in the demand for commodities in accordance with variations in prices, leading to a rise in demand with a fall in prices, and a fall in demand with a rise in prices, are implied in Śukrācārya's warning not to forget that in sales as considerations of high, low and middle prices are of importance. The doctrines of Śukrācārya, when analyzed, show that the two points to be considered in determining the price are : (a) cost of production as determing the supply (referred to as : *sulabhāsulabhatvāt*—the easy or difficult attainment of a commodity), and (b) the demand for the article as determined by its utility or power of satisfying wants (*aguṇatvaguṇasaṁśraya*). Similarly, these are also implied in the rules of the *Arthaśāstra* for the fixing of prices of commodities. So being followed the traditional economic guidelines of Achārya Śukra and Bṛhaspati, Kauṭilya clearly states that the head of trade and commerce shall be conversant with the condition of high and low prices, and the quick and slow saleability of various kinds of goods, whether brought into the country by land routes or by water routes. He should also know the appropriate time for buying in and selling out, and also for expanding or contracting his stock.[38]

A number of references are recorded regarding the medium of exchange in our ancient Indian Nītiśāstras, Smṛtiśāstras, Dharmaśāstras and Arthaśāstras. In our ancient exchange system, the uses of coins as currency, and of credit are both in evidence. The bulk of retail transactions, however, were by barter, i.e. a trade by exchange. The reason for this is to be sought, not merely in the scarcity of currency, but in such circumstances as the comparatively low prices of the articles to be sold, and the prohibition of the use of gold and silver to many classes of the population in the society. In urban areas financial economy or monetary unit is more common. This is shown by the elaborate rules for maintaining a proper currency, which we find in the *Śukranītisāra* and *Arthaśāstra*. Gold was the metal accepted for the standard coin (currency). It is not clear whether silver coins were also part of the standard currency. Token coins were either in copper or in cowry-shells (*varātika*). If gold and silver circulated side by side, the ratio of exchange was settled by the interaction of supply and demand, and there was no State ratio as in the Persian Empire. In the *Śukranītisāra,* Śukrācārya gives a practical ratio, viz., that gold is sixteen times as valuable as silver and silver is also eighty times valuable than copper.

रजतं षोडशगुणं भवेत् स्वर्णस्य मूल्यकम्।
ताम्रं रजतमूल्यं स्यात् प्रायोऽशीतिगुणं तथा।।[39]

But it is not possible to say whether the above ratio was actually current or was only a recommendation. Silver though known and prized in Ancient India was comparatively scarcer than gold, since silver had to be imported It came in usually in exchange (along with gold) for the export of silk, spices and gems.

The revenue and taxation system suggested by Śukrācārya was much favourable to the kings for the upliftment of socio-economical status of their subjects. In true sense, sound finances are the backbone of a stable, strong and prosperous state. Good collection of revenue is meant for the maintenance of the armed forces and the subjects and for the performance of sacrificial works.[40] The armed forces save the country from the outsider's attack as well as protect the life and property of the people. Likewise, sacrifice too boost the life span of the people and finally it helps the people to get the liberation.[41] Hence, it is legal and moral duty of the king to collect revenue from his subjects. Accordingly, the king should not give up even *aṅgula* of land in such a way as to part with rights to it[42]. In a difficult time like war, drought and flood, the king, according to Śukrācārya, has to use harsh means to collect taxes, but in ordinary circumstances, the revenue is to be realized-without causing hardship to the subjects. Śukrācārya also condemns the raising of the revenue for the personal benefit of the king and his family. The collection of revenue, according to him, when for wife and children as for self-enjoyment leads to hell and does not give pleasure hereafter. That which is earned unlawfully or illegally is the cause of sin. The kingdom where wealth is amassed by forsaking morality and by oppressing the people is destroyed As said in the *Śukranītisāra :*

त्यक्त्वा नीतिबलं स्वीयप्रजापीडनतो धनम्।
सञ्चितं येन तत्तस्य सराज्यं शत्रुसाद् भवेत्।।[43]

On taxation policy a good number of references are noted in Kośanirūpaṇa Prakaraṇa of the *Śukranītisāra*. The modern criterion of tax is that it is a compulsory levy by the state. The old Indian ideas of taxation are implied in the very conception of a tax. As Śukrācārya states :

स्वभागभृत्या दास्यत्वे प्रजानां च नृपः कृतः।
ब्रह्मणा स्वामिरूपस्तु पालनार्थं हि सर्वदा।।[44]

It is due to the king, because its payment is divinely ordained, because it flows from an original contract, and also because it is the price for the security afforded to the subject by the existence of a settled government. The state may not only levy its share from the owner's own property, but it can compel even the property-less person to contribute by his labour.[45] Śukrācārya suggests the principle of taxation of the art of a gardener who deprives the trees of their products but not of their life. Though taxation is a painful necessity but must not be heavy enough to kill the people. The collector of taxes is to be like a gardener who collects flowers and fruits after having duly nourshed the trees with care.[46] Further, he explains this point by adding that the tax is to be realized in the fashion of the weaver of the garland and not of the coal merchant. As the coal-merchant sets fire to the woods to make charcoal and thus destroys the entire property, like-wise the king should not extract tax by destroying the productive capacity of the subjects.[47] But, as the weaver of garlands plucks from the tree only those flowers which are fully bloomed and preserves the rest as well as the trees for future use, similarly, the king should collect tax from his subjects by well-preserving and sustaining their life and livelihood.

According to Śukrācārya, in normal times the king should not intend to increase his treasure by augmenting land revenues and duties and by taking dues from holy places and properites consecrated to divine purposes. But on the other hand, the king is allowed to receive from his subjects special grants of fines, duties, etc., when he has to maintain and raise defense forces to destroy the enemy of his kingdom.[48] In critical and danger period Śukrācārya allows the king to receive treasure of the wealthy persons. But when he is free from danger, he should return the amount to them together with due interest[49] and if he refuses to do so, the people, the state and the king, all are destroyed In the *Śukranītisāra,* Śukrācārya makes three categories of kings on the basis of realization of revenue. Therefore, he opines :

मालाकारस्य वृत्त्यैव स्वप्रजारक्षणेन च।
शत्रुं हि करदीकृत्य तद्धनैः कोशवर्धनम्।।

करोति स नृपः श्रेष्ठो मध्यमो वैश्यवृत्तितः।
अधमः सेवया दण्डतीर्थदेवकरग्रहैः।।[50]

It means, the best king is he, who following the practice of the weaver of garlands protects his subjects, makes the enemies tributaries and increases the treasure by their wealth. The second category (*madhyama*) king is one who does this by following the practice of Vaiśya, i.e., he collects money through business (*vaiśyavṛttis*). And the third category (*adhama*) king is he who extracts money from services, fines and also by imposing tax on holy places, temples and other sacred institutions.

Śukra, the great ancient economist divides the source of revenue of the king into *śulka* and *bhāga*. *Śulka* or 'duty' is the kings's share received from the buyer and seller.

विक्रेतृक्रेतृतो राजभागः शुल्कमुदाहृतम्।।[51]

The regions of duty (*bhāga*) are the market places, special tax collection counter and roads of the market. The duties (*śulka*) are to be levied on goods only once. Because double taxation is viewed as unfair by Śukrācārya in his *Śukranītisāra:*

वस्तुजातस्यैकवारं शुल्कं ग्राह्यं प्रयत्नतः।।
क्वचिन्नैवासकृत् शुल्कं राष्ट्रे ग्राह्यं नृपैश्छलात्।[52]

According to the *Śukranītisāra,* the king should receive the thirty-secondth (1/32) portion from the seller or buyer and the twentieth or sixteenth part, as the duty, is not drawback upon the price. The king should not realize duty from the seller when he receives what is less than just equal to the cost. He should receive it from the buyer after seeing that he is a gainer. Besides, the revenue from the land whether great, middling or small is to be taken when the amount of the produce has been ascertained This means, it is repeatedly urged that what a person should pay as a tax should depend upon his capacity. The land tax is not to be collected if the harvest does not leave a margin out of which the tax can be paid.[53] The schedule of taxes on commodities and sales is to be prepared only after calculating cost of production, normal profits of the trader and other middle-men, length of time for which the article will remain unsold, possibility of clearing the entire stock and the functions of the market.

Śukrācārya suggests that the king should collect tax as one-third, one-fourth or one-half, from places which are irrigated by tanks, canals and wells, by rains and by rivers, respectively.[54] He should have one-sixth tax from the barren and rocky lands. If people undertake new industries or cultivate new lands and dig tanks, canals, wells, etc., for their welfare, the king should not demand any tax from them until they realize profit twice of the real expenditure.[55] The aim is always that, after the payment of the tax, a surplus should remain in the pocket of the cultivator or the investor, i.e., the net return to the cultivator should be double his outlay. However, it is also suggested by Śukrācārya that the king should give to each cultivator the deed of rent (written document or original receipt) having his own mark-seal. He should receive rents from houses and abodes as from cultivated lands, also have land tax from shopkeepers. For the maintenance and repair of the roads, he should collect tax from those who use the roads. This is known as road tax paid by the subjects to the king. This way, the king, by collecting tax from the subjects should protect their life and livelihood like a servant of the people.[56]

Finally, Śukrācārya's view on the ratio of public expenditure (to state income) will be discussed here. It must be, however admitted, in fairness to Śukrācārya, which he has made an attempt to give what he regards as the ideal proportions, in relation to the income, of the various items of public expenditure. He recommends that the heads of the villages are to receive one-twelfth of the income from the village, that the army is to be maintained by three such part, charity is to be met to the extent of half such part, and people be entertained with half of such a part, officers are to be paid half such part, the king's personal expenditure is to be met out of half such a part, and the treasury is to have the balance. It is rightly said in the *Śukranītisāra* as:

ग्रामस्य द्वादशांशेन ग्रामपान् संनियोजयेत्।
त्रिभिरंशैर्बलं धार्यं दानमर्धांशकेन च।।
अर्धांशेन प्रकृतयो ह्यर्धांशेनाधिकारिणः।
अर्धांशेनात्मभोगश्च कोशोंऽशेन च रक्ष्यते।।
आयस्यैवं षड्विभागैर्व्ययं कुर्यात् तु वत्सरे।[57]

The king, thus, collecting revenue from his subjects, should spend it for the welfare of state. However, Śukrācārya's views and suggestions on tax collection and its proper expenditure are appropriate and are relevant even to modern times.

This way, the *Śukanītisāra* records a number of financial aspects (theories) for the upliftment of the status of people of different times. Before conclude, it may be noted some of the major recommendations of economic policy of Śukrācārya, found in the *Śukranītisāra*, which are more relevant in today's economic concept. Śukrācārya is very realistic in his approach when he observes that workers getting low wages become enemies by nature, auxiliaries to others and always look for opportunities for trouble and are plunderers of treasure and people. He, therefore, as in modern times, recommends provisions, which give real benefits to servants and daily labourers. Like modern bonus system, a servant is to receive one-eighth of his salary by way of reward every year. He advises the king to pay interest on property in his custody, which also reflects modernity, for the present day government also pays interest to the capital, which it borrows from public. When Śukrācārya defines the price (*mūlya*) of the commodity as that by spending which one gets the possession of the commodity, he thereby strikes the modern definition of price as the exchange-value of a commodity and comes very close to present day economic concept. These are the formulations, which confirm the then existing concept of the welfare of the state. Thus, on the basis of observation of the above facts, the economic order reflected in the *Śukranītisāra* resembles the trend found in the capitalistic society of modern times.

REFERENCES

1. *Arthaśāstra,* I. 2.1 ; 8 (Vidyāsamuddeśa).
   Cf. आन्वीक्षिकी त्रयी वार्ता दण्डनीतिश्च शाश्वती।
   विद्याश्चतस्र एवैता अभ्यसेन्नृपतिः सदा।।
   Śukranītisāra, I. 152, p. 24 (Edited and translated into Hindi by Brahmashankar Mishra, Chowkhambha Sanskrit Sansthan, Varanasi, second edition, 1987).
   Cf. आन्वीक्षिकी त्रयी वार्ता दण्डनीतिश्च शाश्वती।
   विद्याश्चतस्र एवैताः लोक-संस्थिति-हेतवः।।
   Kāmandakīyanītisāra, II.2.
   Also cf. चातुर्विद्यं च कीर्तितम्। *Mahābhārata* (Gita Press edition) XII. 59. 140d.

2. साख्यं योगो लोकायतं चेति आन्वीक्षिकी।
Arthaśāstra, I. 2. 10.
3. आन्वीक्षिक्यां तर्कशास्त्रं वेदान्ताद्यं प्रतिष्ठितम्।
Śukranītisāra, I. 153ab, p. 24.
4. त्रय्यां धर्मो ह्यधर्मश्च कामोऽकाम: प्रतिष्ठितम्।
अङ्गानि वेदाश्चत्वारो मीमांसा न्यायविस्तर:।
धर्मशास्त्रपुराणानि त्रयीदं सर्वमुच्यते।।
ibid., I. 153ab, 155, p. 24.
5. अर्थानर्थौ तु वार्तायां... ... ...।
कुसीदकृषिवाणिज्यं गोरक्षा वार्तयोच्यते।
सम्पन्नो वार्तया साधुर्न वृत्तेर्भयमृच्छति।।
ibid., I. 154ab, 156, p. 24.
Cf. कृषिपाशुपाल्ये वाणिज्या च वार्ता।
Arthaśāstra, I. 4.1.
Cf. कृषिवाणिज्यगोरक्षा कुसीदं तुर्यमुच्यते। वार्ता ... ...।।
Bhāgavata Purāṇa, X. 24. 21.
Also cf. *Kāmandakīyanītisāra,* XIV. 27.
6. *Śukranītisāra,* I. 156, p. 24.
7. दम्भो दण्ड इति ख्यातस्तस्माद्दण्डो महीपति:।
तस्य नीतिर्दण्डनीतिर्नयनान्नीतिरुच्यते। *ibid.,* I. 157, p. 24.
8. *ibid.,* IV. 3, 55-56, p. 230.
9. *Nir* I.18.
10. अर्थोऽर्ते: गतिकर्मण:। अर्यते ह्यसावर्थिभि:। अरणस्थो वा। यदा ह्यस्य स्वामी अरति गच्छतीतो लोकादमुं लोकं तदायमिहैव तिष्ठति, न अनेनैव सहामुं लोकं गच्छति दीनारादिरर्थ:। Commentary of Durgācārya on *Nirukta*, I. 18.
11. *ibid.*
12. अर्थोऽर्ते: गत्यर्थस्य। यस्तावच्छब्दस्यार्थ: स तस्माद् गम्यते, यो हिरण्यादि: सोऽप्यनादिना व्यवहारेणान्यस्मात् पुरुषाद् अन्यं गच्छति।
Commentary of Skanda-Maheśvara on *Nirukta,* I. 18.
13. *Amarakośa*, III.3.86.
14. अर्थो विषयार्थनयोर्धनकारणवस्तुषु।
अभिधेये च शब्दानां निवृतौ च प्रयोजने।।
Medinīkośa, XVII.2.
15. *Arthaśāstra,* XV. 1.1.
16. *Viṣṇusahasranāma Bhāṣya*, 59.
Cf. *arthāḥ viṣayāḥ, arthyante jñāyanta ityarthaḥ– Abhidharmakośa Bhāṣya*, I.9 (vide, Sphuṭārthā, p. 30).
17. द्रव्यं वित्तं स्वापतेयं रिक्थमृक्थं धनं वसु।
हिरण्यं द्रविणं द्युम्नमर्थरैविभवा अपि।।
Amarakośa, II.9.90.

18. *Manusmṛti*, I. 88 and X.75.
19. *Śukranītisāra*, III. 176cd-177ab, pp. 154-155.
20. न च व्ययाधिकं कार्यं कर्तुमीहेत पण्डितः।।
    लाभाधिक्यं यत्क्रियते स सेवेद् व्यवसायिभिः।
    ibid., III. 265cd-266ab, p. 170.
21. *ibid.*, III. 177cd-178ab, p. 155.
22. *Nītiśataka* (of Bhartṛhari) 41.
23. *Śukranītisāra*, III. 181cd-183ab, p. 155.
24. *ibid.*, III. 183cd-185ab, p. 156.
25. *ibid.*, III. 189cd-190ab, p. 157; also cf. III. 188, 192, 193, etc.
26. आहारे व्यवहारे च त्यक्तलज्जः सुखी भवेत्।
    ibid., III. 194, p. 157.
27. *ibid.*, I. 179, p. 28.
28. *ibid.*, I. 180, p. 28.
29. न यथेष्टव्ययायालं सञ्चिते न धनं भवेत्।
    सदागमाद्विना कस्य कुवेरस्यापि नाञ्जसा।।
    ibid., I. 181, p. 28.
30. *ibid.*, III. 276cd-288ab, p. 172; also cf. III.278-279, etc.
31. कर्मापि द्विविधं ज्ञेयमशुभं शुभमेव च।
    अशुभं दासकर्मोक्तं शेषं कर्मकृतः स्मृतम्।।
    Nārada Smṛti, V. 5, Vol. I, p. 282.
32. *Śukranītisāra*, II. 403cd-404ab, p. 118; also cf. II. 404cd-407ab, etc.
33. *ibid.*, II. 407-419, pp. 119-121.
34. येन व्ययेन संसिद्धस्तद्व्यस्तस्य मूल्यकम्।।
    सुलभासुलभत्वाच्चागुणत्वगुणसंश्रयैः।
    यथाकामात्पदार्थानामर्घं हीनाधिकं भवेत्।।
    Śukranītisāra, II. 358cd-359ab, pp. 111-112.
35. रत्नभूतं तु तत्तत्स्याद्यद्यदप्रतिमं भुवि।
    ibid., IV. 102ab, p. 217.
36. *ibid.*, IV. 2. 103, p. 217.
37. *ibid.*, IV. 2. 102cd, p. 217.
38. पण्याध्यक्षः स्थलजलजानां नानाविधानां पण्यानां स्थलपथवारिपथोपयातानां सारफल्ग्वर्धान्तरं प्रेयाप्रियतां च विद्यात्। तथा विक्षेपसंक्षेपक्रयविक्रय प्रयोगकालान्।
    Arthaśāstra, II. 16. 1.
39. *Śukranītisāra*, IV. 2. 90, p. 215.
40. येन केन प्रकारेण धनं सञ्चिनुयान्नृपः।
    तेन संरक्षयेद्राष्ट्रं बलं यज्ञादिकाः क्रियाः।।
    ibid., IV. 2. 2, p. 201.
41. बलमूलो भवेत् कोशः कोशमूलं बलं स्मृतम्।
    ...कोश राष्ट्रवृद्धिररिक्षयः...प्रजासंरक्षणेन वै।।

यज्ञार्थं द्रव्यमुत्पन्नं यज्ञः स्वर्गसुखायुषे।
अर्थभावो बलं कोशो राष्ट्रवृद्ध्यै त्रयं त्विदम्।।
ibid., IV. 2. 14cd-16, pp. 203-234.

42. न दद्याद् द्व्यङ्गुलमपि भूमेः स्वत्वनिवर्तकम्।
वृत्त्यर्थं कल्पयेद्वापि यावद्ग्राहस्तु जीवति।।
ibid., I. 211, p. 32.

43. *ibid.*, IV. 2. 8, p. 202.

44. *ibid.*, I. 188, p. 29.

45. धर्म्यं शुल्कमवहारयेत्।। *Āpastamba Dharmasūtra,* II. 10. 26. 9, p. 360, (Chowkhamba, third edition, 1892).
Cf. कारुकान् शिल्पिनश्चैव शूद्रांश्चात्मोपजीविनः।
एकैकं कारयेत् कर्म मासि मासि महीपतिः।।
Manusmṛti, VII. 138.

46. वृक्षान् सम्पुष्य यत्नेन फलं पुष्पं विचिन्वति।
मालाकार इवात्यन्तं भागहारस्तथाविधः।।
Śukranītisāra, II. 173, p. 82.

47. *ibid.*, IV. 2. 110, p. 218.

48. यदा शत्रुविनाशार्थं बलसंरक्षणोद्यतः।
विशिष्टदण्डशुल्कादि धनं लोकात्तदा हरेत्।।
ibid., IV. 2. 10, p. 202.

49. *ibid.*, IV. 2. 11, p. 203.

50. *ibid.*, IV. 2. 18-19, p. 204.

51. *ibid.*, IV. 2. 104cd, p. 217.

52. *ibid.*, IV. 2. 105cd-106ab, p. 217.

53. *ibid.*, IV. 2. 108cd-109, p. 218.

54. *ibid.*, IV. 2. 112-113, p. 218.

55. तस्य वृद्ध्यै तडागं वा वापिकां कृत्रिमां नदीम्।।
कुर्वन्त्यन्यत् तद्विधं वा कर्षन्त्यभिनवां भुवम्।
यद्व्ययद्विगुणं यावन्न तेभ्यो भागमाहरेत्।।
ibid., IV. 2. 119cd-120, p. 219.

56. तथा चापणिकेभ्यस्तु पण्यभूशुल्कमाहरेत्।
मार्गसंस्काररक्षार्थं मार्गगेभ्यो हरेत् फलम्।।
सर्वतः फलभुग् भूत्वा दासवत् स्यात्तु रक्षणे।
ibid., IV. 2. 127-128ab, p. 221.

57. *ibid.*, I. 315cd-317, p. 46.

Bibliography

ORIGINAL TEXTS

Abhidharmakośa Bhāṣya: Ed. P. Pradhan, second revised edition, ed by Aruna Haldar, Patna: K.P. Jayaswal Research Institute, 1975.

______ tr. into English by L.M. Pruden, Berkeley: Asian Humanities Press, 4 Vols, 1988.

Agni Purāṇa: tr. into Hindi by Tarinisha Jha & G. Tripathi, Allahabad: Hindi Sahitya Sammelan, 1998.

____ tr. into English by J.L. Shastri, Delhi: Motilal Banarsidass, 4 Vols, reprint, 1998.

Aitareya Āraṇyaka: with the comm. of Sāyaṇa, ed by K. Shastri, Ananda Ashram Sanskrit Granthavali-32, Poona: Ananda Ashram, 2 Vols, 1979.

____ ed & tr. into English by A.B. Keith, Oxford: Oxford University, 1909.

Aitareya Brāhmaṇa: ed with comm. of Sāyaṇācārya, by Sudhakar Malaviya, Pracyabharatiya Granthmala, 14 Vols I-II, Varanasi: Tara Printing Works, 1986.

____ tr. A.B. Keith, Ṛgveda Brāhmaṇas, ed by C.R. Lanman, Harvard Oriental Series, Vol. 25, 1920, reprint, Delhi: Motilal Banarsidass, 2nd edn., 1981.

Āpastamba Dharma Sūtra: ed with Ujjvalā comm. of Haradatta, by U.C. Pandey, Kashi Sanskrit Series No. 93, Varanasi: Chowkhamba Sanskrit Samsthan, 3rd edn., 1992.

Āpastamba Gṛhya Sūtra: ed with Anākūlā comm. of Haradatta, ed U.C. Pandey, Kashi Sanskrit Series No. 59, Varanasi: Chowkhamba Sanskrit Series Office, 1971.

Arthaśāstra: ed with comm. by T. Ganapati Shāstri, Delhi: Bharatiya Vidya Prakashan, reprint, 1990.

Aṣṭādhyāyī of Pāṇini: tr. into English by S.C. Basu, Delhi: Motilal Banarsidass, 1988.

Āśvalāyana Gṛhya Sūtra: ed with Vṛtti of Nārāyaṇa, Kārikā of Bhaṭṭakumārila by V.S.R.R.G.S. Gokhale, Ānandāśrama Sanskrit Series No. 105, Poona: Ānandāśrama, 1978.

Atharvaveda Saṁhitā: ed by S. Damodar Satvalekar, Paradi: Svadhyaya Maṇḍala, 1985, 4 Vols

____ tr. M. Bloomfield: Hymns of the Atharvaveda, ed by F. Max Mýlar, S.B.E., Vol. 42, 1897, reprint, Delhi: Motilal Banarsidass, 1979.

____ tr. R.T.H. Griffith: Hymns of the Atharvaveda, Vol. I-II, 1895-96, reprint, Delhi: Munshiram Manoharlal Publishers Pvt. Ltd., 1985.

____ tr. W.D. Whitney: Atharvaveda Saṁhitā, ed by C.R. Lanman, Harvard Orien-tal Series No. 7-8, Vol. I-II, 1905, reprint, Delhi: Motilal Banarsidass, 1984.

Aṭṭhasālinī (Comm.on Dhammasaṅgaṇi): ed by P.V. Bapat & R.D. Vedekar, Poona: B.O.R.I.,1942.

Baudhāyana Dharma Sūtra: ed with Vivaraṇa comm. of Sri Govinda Swami by U.C. Pandey, Kashi Sanskrit Series No. 104, Varanasi: Chowkhambha Sanskrit Sansthan, 4th edn., 1994.

Baudhāyana Śrauta Sūtra: ed by W. Caland, Vol. I-II, 1903-04, Delhi: Munshiram Manoharlal Publishers Pvt. Ltd., 2nd edn., 1982.

Bhagavad Gītā: with the comm. of Śaṅkara, tr. into English by A. Mahādeva Sastry, Madras: Samatā Books, reprint, 1995.

_____ with Śāṅkara Bhāṣya, Gorakhpur: Gita Press edn., 1967.

____ tr. into English by R.C. Zaehner, London: Oxford University Press, 1981.

Bhāgavata Purāṇa: with English translation, Gorakhpur: Gita Press edn., 3 Vols, 4th edition, 1995.

Bodhapañcadaśikā & Paramārtha Carcā: with Vivaraṇa by H.B. Shastri, ed by Pt. J.Z. Shastri, Srinagar: The Research and Publication Dept.. J.K. Govt., 1947.

Brahma Sūtra (Śāṅkara Bhāṣya): ed with comm. of Bhāṣyaratnaprabhā of Govinda-nanda, Bhāmatī of Vācaspati Miśra & Nyāyanirṇaya of Ānandagiri, J.L. Shastri, reprint, Delhi: Motilal Banarsidass, 1996.

____ tr. G. Thibaut: S.B.E. Series 34, 38, Delhi: Motilal Banarsidass, 1890, 1896, 2 Vols

Bṛhadāraṇyaka Upaniṣad: ed with Śāṅkara Bhāṣya, Gorakhpur: Gita Press, 8th edn., 2055 V.S.

____ tr. with comm. of Śaṅkarācārya, by Swami Madhavananda, Calcutta: Advaita Ashram, 5th Imp., 1993.

Buddhacarita of Aśvaghoṣa: ed & tr. into English by E.H. Johnston, Delhi: Motilal Banarsidass, 1992.

Caraka Saṁhitā: tr. into English by P.V. Sharma, Varanasi: Chowkhamba Orientalia,3 Vols, 1981, 1983, 1985.

Chāndogya Upaniṣad: ed with the comm. of Śaṅkarācārya, Gorakhpur: Gitā Press, 8th edn., 2052 V.S.

_____ tr. with the comm. of Śaṅkarācārya, by Swami Mādhavānanda, Calcutta: Advaita Ashram, 8th Imp., 1993.

Daśabhūmika Sūtra: ed by P.L. Vaidya, Darbhaṅgā, Bihar: Mithila Research Institute, 1967.

Devī Bhāgavatam: ed by M. Abhimanyu, Varanasi: Sanskrit Pustakalaya, 1995.

_____ tr. into English by Swami Vijñānānanda, New Delhi: Munshiram Manoharlal Pvt. Ltd., 1921, 4th edn., 1992.

Dhammapada: Pāli & Sanskrit texts, English tr. & notes by D.M. Tin, Sarnath: Central Institute of Higher Tibetan Studies, 1990.

____ ed & tr. into English by C.R. Lama, Sarnath, Varanasi: Central Institute of Higher Tibetan Studies, 1982.

Dhammasaṅgaṇi: ed by P.V. Bapat and R.D. Vedekar, Poona: B.O.R.I., 1st edn., 1940.

______ English tr. by C.A.F. Rhys Davids, P.T.S. Translation Series, No. 41, London: The Pali Text Society, 3rd edn., 1974.

Dīgha Nikāya Pāli: ed & tr. into Hindi by Swami Dwarikadas Shastri, Varanasi: Bauddha Bharati, 3 Vols, 1996.

Garuḍa Purāṇa: ed by Khemaraja Sri Krishna Dass, Delhi: Nag Publishers, 1984.

Gopatha Brāhmaṇam: ed by Vijayapala Vidyavaridhi, Calcutta: Savitri Devi Bagadia Trust, 1980.

Harivaṁśa Purāṇa: ed by Khemaraja Srikrishna Dass, Delhi: Nag Publishers, 1985.

Īśānaśivagurudevapaddhati: ed by T. Ganapati Shastri, Delhi: Bharatiya Vidya Prakashan, 4 Vols, 1988.

Īśvarapratyabhijñā Kārikā of Utpaladeva: with Vimarśinī by Abhinavagupta, ed by M.S. Kaul, K.S.T.S., Srinagar: Research Dept., Jammu & Kashmir, 2 Vols, 1918, 1921.

Īśvarapratyabhijñā Vimarśinī of Abhinavagupta: with the comm. of Bhāskarī, ed by K.A. Subramaniya Iyer & K.C. Pandey & tr. into English by K.C. Pandey, Delhi: Motilal Banarsidass, 3 Vols, 1986.

Jātaka: ed by V. Fausboll, P.T.S., London: Messrs Luzac & Company Ltd., 7 Vols, reprint, 1962-1964.

Jātakamālā: ed & tr. into Hindi by S.N. Chaudhari, Delhi: Motilal Banarsidass, reprint, 1991.

_____ tr. into English by J.S. Speyer, Delhi: Motilal Banarsidass, reprint, 1991.

Kāmakalāvilāsa: ed & comm. by Syamakanta Dvivedi, Varanasi: Chowkhamba Surabhārati Prakashan, 1st edn., 1997.

Kāmandakīya Nītisāra: ed by R.R.L. Mitra and tr. into English by S.K. Mitra, Calcutta: The Asiatic Society, reprint, 1984.

Kāṭhaka Saṁhitā (Yajurvedīya): ed by Sripad Damodar Satvalekar, Pardi: Svādhyāya Maṇḍala, 1985.

Kauṣītaki Brāhmaṇa Upaniṣad: ed by E.R.S. Sarma, Gen. Editor K. Kunjuni Raja, tr. into English by A.G.K. Warrier, Madras: The Adyar Library & Research Centre, 1st edn., 1990.

Kulārṇava Tantra: ed Taranatha Vidyaratna with Introduction of Arthur Avalon and readings of M.P. Pandit, Delhi: Motilal Banarsidass, reprint, 1984.

____ tr. into Hindi by Paramahamsa Mishra, Varanasi: Chowkhamba Surabhārati Prakashan, 1st edn., 2002.

Kumārasaṁbhava: ed & tr. into English by M.R. Kale, Delhi: Motilal Banarsidass, 1986.

Kūrma Purāṇa: ed by Nāga Śaraṇa Singh, Delhi: Nag Publishers, 1983.

_____ critically ed by Anand Swarup Gupta, Ramnagar, Varanasi: All India Kashiraj Trust, 1971.

_____ tr. into English by G.V. Tagare, Delhi: Motilal Banarsidass, 2 Vols, reprint, 1997-98.

Lalitasahasranāma: ed by W.L. Shastri Pansikar, Delhi: Nag Publishers, reprint, 1985.

Lalitavistara: ed by P.L. Vaidya, Buddhist Sanskrit Texts No. 1, Darbhanga: The Mithila Institute, 1958.

_____ tr. into English (Chs 1-15) by R.L. Mitra, Delhi: Sri Satguru Publications, 1998.

_____ tr. into Hindi by Santibhikshu Sastri, Lucknow: Uttar Pradesh Hindi Sansthan, 1st edn., 1984.

Laṅkāvatāra Sūtra: ed by P.L. Vaidya, Darbhanga: Mithila Research Institute, n.d.

_____ tr. into English by D.T. Suzuki, London: Routledge & Kegan Paul Ltd., reprint, 1956.

Mādhyamaka Śāstra of Nāgārjuna: with the comm. of Prasannapadā by Candrakirti, ed by P.L. Vaidya, Darbhanga: Mithila Institute, 1960.

Mahābhārata: Gorakhpur, Gita Press edition, 2053 V.S.

____ tr. into English by M.N. Dutt, Delhi: Parimal Publications, 7 Vols, 1988.

Mahāyānasūtrālaṅkāra, tr. into English by S.V. Limaye, Delhi: Sri Satguru Publications, 1st edn., 1992.

Maitrāyaṇī Saṁhitā: ed S.D. Satavalekar, Pardi: Svādhyāya Maṇḍala, 1942.

Majjhima Nikāya: ed & tr. into Hindi by Dwarika Das Shastri, Varanasi: Bauddha Bharati, 5 Vols, 1989-1993.

Mālinivijayottara Tantra: ed by Madhusudan Kaul, K.S.T.S. No. 37, Bombay: Research Department, Jammu & Kashmir, 1922.

Māṇḍukya Upaniṣad: with Śaṅkara Bhāṣya, Gorakhpur: Gita Press edition, 17th edition, 2055 V.S.

Mantra Mahodadhi: with Sanskrit comm., Mumbai: Sri Venkateswar Press, 1999.

_____ tr. into English by Ram Kumar Rai, Varanasi: Prachya Prakashan, Vol. I-II, 1st edn., 1992.

Manusmṛti: ed with the comm. of Kullūka Bhaṭṭa, by J.L. Shastri, Delhi: Motilal Banarsidass, reprint, 1990.

_____ The Laws of Manu: tr. into English by G. Buhler, S.B.E. Series-25, Delhi: Motilal Banarsidass, reprint, 1993.

Matsya Purāṇa: Bombay: Laksmi Venkatesvara Press, 1980.

___ ed by Nag Sharan Singh, Delhi: Nag Publishers, 2 Vols, 1983.

Meghadūta: with the comm. of Mallinatha, ed & tr. into English by M.R. Kale, Delhi: Motilal Banarsidass, reprint, 1987.

Milindapañha Pāli: ed and tr. into Hindi by Dwarikadas Shastri, Varanasi: Bauddha Bharati, 1990.

Mīmāṁsā Sūtra: ed with Śābara Bhāṣya by Ratna Gopal Bhatta, Varanasi: Chowkhamba Publications, 1910.

____ ed by Ganesh Shastri Joshi, Poona: Ananda Ashram Sanskrit Granthavali No. 97, Ananda Ashram, 6 Vols, 1981.

Nārada Smṛti: ed with extracts from the comm. of Asahāya and others by J. Jolly, Bib. Ind., Calcutta, 1885.

Nāṭyaśāstra with Abhinavabhārati: ed by M. Ramakrishna Kavi and J.S. Pade, Gaekward's Oriental Series 36, 68, 104-105, Baroda: Baroda Oriental Institute, 4 Vols (Vol. I, chapters 1-7, 1956; II- chapters 8-18, 1934; III- chapters 19-27, 1954; IV-chapters 28-37, 1964).

Nighaṇṭu and the Nirukta: ed and tr. into English by Lakshman Sarup, Delhi: Moti-lal Banarsidass, reprint, 1984.

Nīti and Vairāgya Śatakas of Bhartṛhari: ed & tr. into English by M.R. Kale, Delhi: Motilal Banarsidass, 1971.

Nyāya Sūtra: with the comm. of Vātsyāyana, ed & tr. into Hindi by Dwarikadas Shastri, Varanasi: Bauddha Bharati, fourth edn., 1989.

Padma Mahā Purāṇa: ed by Khemaraja Sri Krishnadasa, Delhi: Nag Publishers, 4 Vols, 1984.

Pañcadaśī: tr. into English by Swami Svahananda, Madras: Sri Rama Krishna Matha, 4th Imp., 1967.

Paramārthasāra of Abhinavagupta: tr. into English by B.N. Pandit, Delhi: Munshiram Manoharlal Publishers Pvt. Ltd., 1st edn., 1991.

Parātrīśikā Vivaraṇa of Abhinavagupta: ed by B. Baumer, and tr. into English by Jaideva Singh, Delhi: Motilal Banarsidass, 1988.

Paryanta Prakāśikā: ed in a book entitled 'Abhinavagupta and his Works' by V. Raghavan, Varanasi: Chaukhambha Orientalia, 1981.

Prapañcasāra Tantra: revised by A. Avalon, ed by Atalananda Sarasvatī, Tantric Text Series 19, Delhi: Motilal Banarsidass, 2 parts in one Vol., reprint, 1989.

Pratyabhijñā Hṛdaya: tr. into English by Jaideva Singh, Delhi: Motilal Banarsidass, Reprint, 1991.

Raghuvaṁśa: tr. into English by G.R. Nandargikar, Delhi: Motilal Banarsidass, 1982.

Rāmāyaṇa of Vālmīki: text with English translation, 3 Vols, Gorakhpur: Gita Press edition, 4th edition, 1995.

Ṛgveda Saṁhitā: ed by S. Damodar Satavalekara, Pardi: Svadhyaya Maṇḍala, 4 Vols, 1985.

___ The Hymns of Ṛgveda: tr. into English by R.T.H. Griffith, Varanasi: Chaukhamba Sanskrit Series Office, 2 Vols, 1971.

Sāmaveda Saṁhitā: ed & tr. into English by Devi Chand, Delhi: Munshiram Manoharlal, 1980.

___ ed by S.D. Satvalekar, Pardi: Svādhyāya Maṇḍala, 4th edn., 1956.

___ tr. into English by R.T.H. Griffith, Varanasi: Chowkhamba Prakashan, 1976.

Sāṁkhya Kārikā: with Yuktidīpikā comm., ed by Ram Chandra Pandey, Delhi: Motilal Banarsidass, 1967.

Śāradātilaka: ed Arthur Avalon, Delhi: Motilal Banarsidass, 1933.

Śatapatha Brāhmaṇa: with the Vedārthaprakāśa Bhāṣya of Sāyaṇācārya & comm. of Harisvami, Delhi: Gian Publishing House, 5 Vols, 1987.

___ tr. into English by J. Eggeling, S.B.E. Series-12, 26, 41, 43, 44, Delhi: Motilal Banarsidass, reprint, 1986.

Ṣaṭrimsattattva-sandoha: ed & tr. into English b D.B. Sen Sharma, Kurukshetra: B.N. Chakraborty University (now Kurukshetra University), 1977.

Saundarananda: ed & tr. into English by E.N. Johnston, Delhi: Motilal Banarsidass, 1975.

Śivadṛṣṭi: with Vṛtti by Utpaladeva, ed by M.S. Kaul Shastri, K.S.T.S. and Studies-54, Srinagar: Research Department, Jammu & Kashmir, 1934.

___ with Vyāsa Bhāṣya: tr. into English by Bangali Baba, Delhi: Motilal Banarsidass, reprint, 1982.

___ tr. into English by J.H. Woods, Delhi: Motilal Banarsidass, reprint, 1988.

Yoginī Hṛdaya: with Dīpikā comm. of Amṛtānanda and Setubandha of Bhāskarācārya, ed by M.M. Gopinath Kaviraj, Banaras: Govt. Sanskrit Library, Saraswati Bhavan, 1923.

____ ed by Vrajavallabha Dwivedi, Varanasi: Motilal Banarsidass, 1988.

Yajurveda Saṁhitā: ed by S. Damodar Satavalekara, Pardi: Svadhyaya Mandala, 1957.

____ tr. into English by R.T.H. Griffith, Banaras: E.J. Lazarus & Co., 1957.

MODERN WORKS

Agrawala, V.S.: India as Known to Pāṇini, Varanasi: Prithivi Prakashan, 1963, 2nd revised edn.

____ The Thousand Syllabled Speech, Vol. I, Varanasi: Vedāraṇyaka Ashram, 1963.

____ Vāmana Purāṇa—A Study, Varanasi: Prithivi Prakahan, 2nd edn., 1983.

____ Vedic Lectures, Varanasi: Prithivi Prakashan, 2nd edn., 1981.

Aurobindo: Bankim, Tilak and Dayananda, Pondicherry: Aurobindo Ashram, 1955.

____ Dayananda: Man and His Work, Allahabad: Star Press, 1917.

Bhattacharya, Haridas (Ed.): The Cultural Heritage of India, Vol. IV, Calcutta: The Ramakrishna Mission Institute of Culture, reprint, 1993.

Bulke, Kamik: Rāmakathā (Hindi), Prayag, Allahabad: Hindi Parishad, 2nd edn., 1964.

Bunce, Fredrick, W.: The Yantras of Deities & Their Numerological Foundations (an Iconographic Consideration), New Delhi: D.K. Printworld (P) Ltd., 2nd impression, 2006.

Chaubey, B.B.: Śukla Yajurveda Saṁhitā (Ch. 1-3), Hoshiarpur: Katyayana Vaidika Sāhitya Prakashan, 2005.

C. Chakravarti: Tantras—Studies on their Religion and Literature, Calcutta: Punthi Pustak, 1963.

Chatterji, J.C.: Kashmir Śaivism, Jammu & Kashmir: Govt. Publication, 1962.

Coomaraswami, A.K.: History of Indian and Indonesian Art, London, 1927.

Das, A.C.: Ṛgvedic Culture, Calcutta: R. Cambray & Co., 1925.

____ Ṛgvedic India, Calcutta, 1922.

Dasgupta, S.N.: A History of Indian Philosophy, Delhi: Motilal Banarsidass, Part II-IV, reprint, 1991, Part I, reprint 1997.

Dharmadhikari, T.N. (Ed.): Yajñāyudhāni, Pune: Vaidika Saṁśodhana Maṇḍala, 1989.

Gällmo, Gunnar: A Few Facts About Buddhism, New Delhi: D.K. Printworld (P) Ltd., 1988.

Guy, John (Ed.): Indian Art & Connoisseurship, New Delhi: Indira Gandhi National Centre for the Arts, Ahmedabad: Mapin Publishing Pvt. Ltd., 1995.

Har Dayal: The Bodhisattva Doctrine in Buddhist Sanskrit Literature, Delhi: Motilal Banarsidass Publishers, reprint, 2004.

Kane, P.V.: History of Dharmaśāstra, Vol. V, Part II, Part I-II, Poona: B.O.R.I., 2nd edn., 1974.

Kaviraj, Gopinath: Bhāratīya Saṁskṛti aur Sādhanā, 2 Vols, Patna: Bihar Rashtrabhasa Parisad, 1st Vol., 1963, 2nd Vol. 1964.

Khanna, Madhu: Yantra, London: Thomas & Hudson Ltd., 1979.

Law, B.C.: Geographical Aspects of Kālidāsa's Works, Calcutta, 1954.

____ India as Described in Early Texts of Buddhism and Jainism, London: 1941.

Macdonell, A.A.: A History of Sanskrit Literature, 1899, reprint, Delhi: Motilal Banarsidass, 1971.

Miller, Barbara Stoler, ed & tr. into English: The Gītagovinda of Jayadeva, Delhi: Motilal Banarsidass, 1984.

Mookerjee, Radha Kumud: Ancient Indian Education (Brahmanical and Buddhist), Delhi: Motilal Banarsidass, reprint, 1998.

Mukhopadhyaya, Govindagopal: Studies in the Upaniṣads, Delhi: Pilgrims Book Pvt. Ltd., 1st edn., 1999.

Narada: The Buddha & His Teachings, Malaysia: Buddhist Missionary Society, reprint, 1988.

Pandey, K.C.: Abhinavagupta, An Historical and Philosophical Study, Varanasi: Chowkhamba, 1929.

Pandey, Rajavali: Hindu Saṁskāras, Delhi: Motilal Banarsidass, reprint, 2002.

Pushpendra Kumar: Śakti Cult in Ancient India, Varanasi: Bharatiya Publishing House, 1974.

Rao, T.A.G.: Elements of Hindu Iconography, Vol. I, Part II, Delhi: Motilal Banarsidass, 2nd edn., 1993.

Sharma, L.N.: Kashmir Śaivism, Varanasi: Bharatiya Vidya Prakashan, 1st edn., 1972.

Sharma, R.C.: The Splendour of Mathura Art and Museum, New Delhi: D.K. Printworld (P) Ltd., 1994.

Sivaramamurti, C.: Śrī Lakshmī in Indian Art and Thought, New Delhi: Kanak Publications, 1st edn., 1982.

Upādhyaya, Baladeva: Purāṇa Vimarśa, Varanasi: Chowkhamba Vidyabhavan, 3rd edn., 1987.

V. Raghavan (ed): Abhinavagupta and his works, Varanasi: Chaukhambha Orienta-lia, 1981.

Woodroffe, Sir John: Śakti and Śākta, Madras: Ganesh & Company, reprint, 1998.

Zimmer, M.: Myths and Symbols in Indian Art and Civilization, ed by J. Cambell, Washington: Panthen Books, part III, chapter-V, 1946.

REFERENCE WORKS

Amarakośa, ed with the comm. of Ramāśramī, by Pt. Hargovinda Shastri, Varanasi: Chowkhambha Sanskrit Sansthān, 2nd edn., 1982.

Buddhist Dictionary (Manual of Buddhist Terms and Doctrines) by Nyanatiloka, ed by Nyanaponika, Ceylon (Colombo): Frewin & Co. Ltd., revised edn., 1972.

Buddhist Hybrid Sanskrit Grammar and Dictionary, ed by F. Edgerton, Vol. I & II, Delhi: Motilal Banarsidass, reprint, 1998.

Concordance to the Principal Upanishads & Bhagavadgītā, ed by G.A. Jacob, Delhi: Motilal Banarsidass, 1985.

A Dictionary of Buddhist Terms & Terminologies by K. Krishna Murthy, New Delhi: Sundeep Prakashan, 2nd revised edn., 1999.

Dictionary of the Vedic Rituals, C. Sen, Delhi: Concept Publishing Company, 1978.

Encyclopaedia of Buddhism, ed by G.P. Malalasekera, Ceylon: The Government of Ceylon, Sri Lanka, 1964.

Encyclopaedia of Religion and Ethics, ed by James Hastings, Edinburgh: T and T Clark, 12 Vols, 1979.

Encyclopaedic Dictionary of Sanskrit on Historial Principles, Gen. Editors: A.M. Ghatage & S.D. Joshi, Poona: Deccan College Postgraduate & Research Institute, 5 Vols, 1976-1995.

Glossary of Indian Religious Terms & Concepts, N.N. Bhattacharya, New Delhi: Manohar Publishers & Distributors, reprint, 1999.

Kalātattvakośa, Gen. Ed. Kapila Vatsyayan, New Delhi: Indira Gandhi National Centre for the Arts & Motilal Banarsidass, 4 Vols, 1988, 1992, 1996, 1999.

Medinī Kośa, ed by J.S. Hoshing, Varanasi: Chowkhambha Sanskrit Series, 3rd edn., 1968.

Nānārtha-Ratnamālā of Irugapa Daṇḍādhinātha, critically ed by B.R. Sharma, Poona:Deccan College P.G. & Research Institute, 1st edn., 1954.

Pali-English Dictionary, ed by T.W. Rhys Davids & William Stede, New Delhi: Munshiram Manoharlal Pub. Pvt. Ltd., reprint, 1989.

The Practical Sanskrit English Dictionary, V.S. Apte, Delhi: Motilal Banarsidass, reprint, 1992.

A Practical Vedic Dictionary, ed by Suryakanta, Delhi: Oxford University Press, 1981.

Purāṇic Encyclopaedia, ed by Vettam Mani, Harvard Oriental Series-10, Delhi: Motilal Banarsidass, reprint, 1964.

A Sanskrit English Dictionary, M. Monier-Williams (Oxford University Press, 1899), Delhi: Motilal Banarsidass, 9th reprint, 1986.

Sanskrit-Wörterbuch, O. Böhtlingk & R. Roth, Delhi: Motilal Banarsidass, 7 Vols, reprint, 1990.

Vaijayantī Kośa, ed by Pt. Haragovinda Sastri, Varanasi: Chowkhambha Sanskrit Series Office, 1971.

Vedic Bibliography, ed by R.N. Dandekar, Govt. Oriental Series, 5 Vols, Poona: B.O.R.I., 1946-93.

Vedic Index of Names & Subjects, ed by A.A. Macdonell & A.B. Keith, Delhi: Motilal Banarsidass, 2 Vols, 1982.

Glossary

Abhidharma **:** Philosophical exposition of the *dharma*. The Philosophy of *Abhidharma* was compiled in Sanskrit by Vasubandhu in a book of eight chapters, known as Abhidharmakośa. *Abhidharma* is one of the branches of Buddhist Tripiṭaka. It is the higher doctrine of the Buddha, expounds the quintessence of his profound teachings. The Abhidharma Piṭaka is composed of the following seven works: (1) Dhammasaṅgaṇi (classification of Dharma), (2) Vibhaṅga (divisions), (3) Dhātukathā (discourse on elements), (4) Puggala Paññati (the book on individuals), (5) Kathāvatthu (points of controversy), (6) Yamaka (the book of pairs), (7) Paṭṭhāna (the book of causal relations). To the wise truth-seekers, Abhidharma is an indispensable guide and an intellectual treat.

Agni & Soma **:** Literally it means fire and moon. Agni and Soma are symbolic terms. Agni symbolizes the *prāṇa śakti* and Soma symbolizes the *apāna śakti*. The *prāṇa* and *apāna śaktis* are associated with the *prāṇa* and *apāna* breaths. *Prāṇa* is the breath of expiration and *apāna* is the breath of inspiration.

Ahiṁsā **:** Lit. means non-vilolence, harmlessness, absence of cruelty. Both Buddhist and Jainas lay great stress on virtue of *ahiṁsā*. The thought of non-violence is one of the three constituents of Right Thought.

Ānanda **:** Bliss; the nature of śakti; the essential nature of Parama-śiva along with *cit*. It is the state of *mukti*, *mokṣa* or *nirvāṇa* in which the self becomes free from all fetters. In Indian philosophical conditions *ānanda* or Bliss is a characteristic of Brahman, others being *sat* and *cit*.

Aṇu **or *paramāṇu*** **:** Both the terms are synonymous and denote an atom, i.e. an indivisible particle of matter.

Araṇī **:** *Araṇīs* are prepared out of wood of Aśvattha tree grown in Śami tree or of Aśvattha even not grown in Śami tree. It helps to kindle the light. In the Ṛgveda (III.29.2) it is said that '*araṇyor nihito jātavedāḥ*—the fire is available in *araṇīs*.

***Arhat* :** A Buddhist monk or Bodhisattva, who has attained the forth and final path (*magga*) and for whom existences have come to an end, i.e. he is freed from further rebirth (*punarjanma*).

***Ariya* :** The noble one; one who has entered the path, i.e. one who has realized at least one of the four *maggas* (*mārgas*).

***Āstika darśana* :** The orthodox or Vedic systems of Indian Philosophy, viz. Nyāya, Vaiśeṣika, Sāṁkhya, Yoga, Mīmāṁsā, and Vedānta. These six system of Indian thought believe in the Supreme authority of the Veda.

***Asura* :** Lit. means an evil spirit, demon, a general name for the enemies of gods, known as *daityas* and *dānavas*.

This term also appears in the Pāli scriptures. Whenever there is a discussion about *devaputras* (sons of gods), there is a reference to the *asuras* in the same context. The gods are famous for their pious deeds and the *asuras* for their evil deeds (Saṁyutta Nikāya, Vol. I, 228). The *asuras* are considered and classed with inferior deities, such as *yakṣas, gandharvas,* etc. It is evident from the Asura Vagga that the *asuras* are generally considered to be wicked, who indulge impious deeds (Aṅguttara Nikāya, Vol. I, p. 96). According to the Mahāsamaya Sutta, the *asuras* lived in the Ocean (Dīgha Nikāya, Vol. II, p. 192). The *asuras* whose names are mentioned in the Buddhist scriptures are: Rāhu, Pahārada, Baicitrāsura, etc.

***Bhairava* :** Lit. means terrible, frightful, horrible, formidable, etc.. The letter '*bha*' of this word indicates *bharaṇa* or maintenance of the world, and '*va*' indicates *vamana* or projection of the world. Thus, Bhairava is one who brings about the *sṛṣṭi, sthiti* and *saṁhāra* of the universe. He is Lord Śiva who is known as Bhairava. A Tāntric *sādhaka* may consider himself as a Bhairava.

***Bhikṣu* or *Bhikkhu* (Pāli) :** A Buddhist monk, who follow the rules of Saṅgha.

***Bhūmisparśa-mudrā* :** The earth touching posture of Buddha images. The right hand (of Buddha) exhibits this *mudrā*; the palm turned inward and the fingers outstretched with the tips touching the earth. This *mudrā* indicates that Buddha has defeated Māra and obtained *Nirvāṇa*. It is a symbol of victory over Māra. The earth has witnessed this great victory.

***Bhūta* :** Lit. means being, existing, gross physical element, etc. *Bhūta* is primarily the concept of creature with both idea of being or originated and becoming or in process. It is an entity which 'was produced' a creature, living or insentient. The term refers to the whole process of evolution and to particular stages at the same time. There are five *bhūtas* (elements), viz. earth, water, fire, air and space. These are also known as *mahābhūtas*. Buddhism, generally accepts four elements, i.e. excluding space (*ākāśa*).

***Bimba* :** It means the disc of the sun or moon or any round or disc-like surface. In the commentary of Amarakośa, Kṣīrasvāmin explains the term as: '*bimbati bhāti bimbam ābhogaḥ.*' *Bimba* is derived from the root *bimba-*, 'to shine' and *ābhoga* here means circuit, circumference, etc. Hence, *bimba* denotes a solar or lonar orb, shape and any round surface (*maṇḍala*), face, mark, shadow or reflected form, etc. The Buddhacarita of Aśvaghoṣa mentions that Buddha sees the whole world reflected within himself just like a reflection in mirror.

***Bodhisattva* :** In the Buddhist thought it generally means all the previous existences of Gautama Buddha. The Pāli term Bodhisatta is composed of *bodhi* which means 'wisdom' or enlightenment and *satta* means 'devoted to' or 'intent-on'. A Bodhisatta, therefore, means one who is devoted to, or intent on, wisdom or enlightenment. The popular term is Bodhisattva which means 'wisdom being' or a being aspiring to become a Buddha. The methods of becoming a Bodhisattva and the stages or *bhūmis* of his mental, moral and intellectual attainments to the extent of realising *dharmaśūnyatā* were carefully outlined The Bodhisattvas take keen interest in all forms of homage. The image of Buddha is a great inspiration to them. It should be understood that Buddhists do not worship an image. They pay homage to what it represents and reflects on the virtues of the Buddha. A Bodhisattva always intends the good and welfare of the world. He loves all beings as a mother, who loves her only child. Therefore, it is known that he is like a mother, a father, a friend, a teacher, to all beings in this universe.

***Bodhivṛkṣa* or Bodhi tree** (*Fiscus religious*) **:** The most religious tree at Bodhgaya under which Lord Buddha meditated and finally got *Nirvāṇa*. This tree is also known as the symbol of the enlightened Buddha.

***Caitanya* :** Absolute Consciousness characterized by *svātantrya*, absolute autonomy and knowledge (*jñāna*) and activity (*kriyā*).

***Citi* :** It means the Absolute Consciousness, i.e. consciousness in its initial, unconditioned state. The consciousness-power of the Absolute that brings about the world process. It is also known as *cit*.

***Citta* :** 'The empirical mind'. The limited individual consciousness, the psychological status of the individual.

***Dakṣiṇā* :** It is known as sacrificial fee and also the fee for making a gift, consisting of cow or other animals and other things, like cloths, chariots, slaves, corns, etc. A sacrifice becomes singed (*prakṣāma*) if no fees are paid, and the sacrificer becomes short-lived Even a non-brahmin may get fees if he is learned

***Darbha* :** A kind of sacrificial grass (*kuśa*) required in various rituals or rites for strewing over the hearth and for purifying the *ājya*.

Darśa-purṇamāsa **:** One type of *yajña* or sacrifice. *Darśa* literally means *amāvāsyā,* i.e. new-moon and *purṇamāsa* means the moment when the moon is full, i.e. full-moon. The Āpastamba Śrauta Sūtra describes it as a sacrifice which is to be performed throughout a man's life. It is regarded as the archetype of all other *iṣṭis*.

Deva / devatā **:** Lit. means god, deity. The term *deva* is derived from the root *div-* 'to shine' with the suffix *ac*. In the Nirukta (VII.15), Yāska has given the etymology of *deva* as: *devo dānādvā, dipanādvā, dyotanād vā, dyusthāno bhavati iti vā, yo devaḥ sā devatā*. In the Ṛgveda (X.158.1) the three principal deities of three regions are priased for protection, i.e. Sūrya from heaven, Vāyu from atmosphere and Agni from earth. Further the number of gods is raised to thirty-three (Ṛgveda, III.6.9) and sometimes increased to 3339 (Ṛgveda, III.99). However, He is one but invoked by sages in various names.

Dharma **:** Lit. means religion, sect, law, usage, practice, custom, ordinance, etc. The term is derived from the root *dhṛ-* 'to hold' with the suffix *man*, denoting 'one that holds or sustains'. Various meanings of *dharma* like religious merit (*puṇya*), *yama*, fitness, nature, uses and drinker of a Soma, etc. are recorded in the Amarakośa (*dharmāḥ puṇyayamanyāyasvabhāvācārasomapāḥ*—III.3.138). According to the Gautama Dharmasūtra, *dharma* is that which is enjoined by the Vedas and Smṛtis. Etymologically the term *dharma* conveys the concept of eternal custom of disciplined people. According to Mīmāṁsakas *dharma* is identical with Vedic laws which enjoins the performance of a variety of actions in different walks of life. *Codanālakṣaṇo'rtho dharmaḥ*—Mīmāṁsā Sūtra, I.1.2). This interpretation was followed in the Brāhmaṇical tradition which equated *dharma* with law and behaviour. According to Buddhism, *dharma* is one of the three jewels (*triratna*) with Buddha and Saṁgha and one of the ten Recollections (*anussati*). The Buddha used the term *dharma* to denote the moral laws prescribed by him. Consequently, the term came to be used in the sense of nature, duty, and phenomenon or elements, truth, doctrine, justice, virtue, laws, quality, etc. in Buddhism. The *dhamma* or *dharma* as the liberating law discovered and proclaimed by the Buddha, is summed up in the four Noble Truths. *Dharma*, as an object of mind (*dhammāyatana*) may be anything past, present or future, corporeal or mental, conditioned or not, real or imaginary.

Dharmacakra **:** Wheel of the Law and also the symbol of Buddha's first sermon (*upadeśa*) at Sarnath (Varanasi), coupled with the symbol of *triratna*.

Dhātu **:** The word *dhātu* is derived from the root *dhā-*, 'to place, to put', with the suffix *tu*. In the Nirukta (I.20), Yāska defines *dhātu* as '*dhāturdadhāteḥ*'-

dhātu is so called, because it puts words in a proper form. The word can also be traced back to the root *dhṛ-* 'to hold or to bear'. The basic idea of supporting or holding has developed into different technical nuances in different systems which offer different etymologies of *dhātu*. Āyurvedācārya Suśruta gives the etymology of *dhātu* from the root *dhṛ-*, which holds true for all body elements as: '*ta ete śarīradhāraṇāddhātava etyucyante*' (Suśruta Saṁhitā, Sūtra-sthāna, XIV.20). In the Buddhist text Abhidharmakośa (III.3cd), *dhātu* is derived from the root *dhṛ-* with a different meaning like: '*svalakṣaṇadhāraṇād dhātuḥ*'—physical and material elements are called *dhātus*, because of holding their own characteristics. Here, *dhātu* is used in the sense of element (*bhūta*). The four physical elements (*dhātu* or *mahābhūta*), popularly called earth, water, fire and wind are to be understood as the primary qualities of matter. They are named in Pāli as: *paṭhavī dhātu, āpo dhātu, tejo dhātu* and *vāyo dhātu*. The Buddhists speak of eighteen *dhātus* which include the six sense organs, their objects, as well as their perceptions, like: *cakkhudhātu, rūpadhātu, cakkhuvijñāṇadhātu, sotadhātu, saddhadhātu*, etc. (Vibhaṅga Pāli, 401- 402, P.T.S.). The Pāli texts speak of three states of existence, viz. *kāmadhātu* 'element of desire', *rūpadhātu* 'element of form' and *ārūpyadhātu* 'element of formlessness'. However, in the Buddhist literature both in Pāli as well as in Sanskrit, the term *dhātu* conveys psychophysical states (*viññāṇa*) of human personality in respect of all elements. It also denotes mortal remains of Lord Buddha which are worshipped as the relics.

***Dīkṣā* :** Lit. means consecration for a religious ceremony, initiation in general. *Dīkṣā* is of two kinds, viz. Vedic and Tāntric. In order to lead a religious life as prescribed by the Vedas and texts of Vedic tradition, a formal initiation is required, but it is not as important as in the case of Tāntric *sādhanā*, in which it is an essential precondition. Abhinavagupta defines *dīkṣā* as a process of imparting real knowledge (*jñāna*) and a preceptorial instruction which removes the bondage of *pāśa*. Such kind of benediction and benevolent act is known as *dīkṣā* (*dīyate jñāna sadbhāvaḥ kṣīyate paśuvāsanā / dāna kṣapaṇasaṁyuktā dīkṣā teneha kīrtitā//* Tantrāloka). According to the Śāradā Tilaka, that which gives spiritual knowledge (*divyajñāna*) and brings the annihilation of baset propensities (*pāpa*) are verily the initiation (*dīkṣā*). The Kulārṇava Tantra presents a detailed analysis of different categories of initiation. It speaks about seven kinds of *dīkṣā*, viz. *kriyā, varṇa, kalā, sparśa, vāk, dṛk,* and *mānasa*. According to the Rudrayāmala, *dīkṣā* is of three types, viz. *āṇavī, śāktī, śāmbhavī* .

Hence, *dīkṣā* is a spiritual enrolment to carry on scientific research with the self. It is not a religious anointment but an esoteric discipline. It is not a faith but an inner conviction. It is not ritualistic ostentation but a mystic necessity. However, in Tāntric *sādhanā* the evil deeds are purified through *dīkṣā*.

Dukkha : Lit. means suffering, sorrow, misery, pain, etc. The first of the four Noble Truths preached by Lord Buddha. As a feeling *dukkha (duḥkha)* means that which is difficult to be endured As an abstract truth *dukkha* is used in the sense of contemptible ('*du*') and emptiness ('*kha*'). The world rests on suffering, hence it is contemptible. It is devoid of any reality, hence it is empty or void. Hence, *dukkha* is meant 'existence in the world with concomitant pain and pleasure' which are without any real substance (*anattā*) and are impermanent (*anicca*). The Visuddhimagga (498.99) refers to seven kinds of *dukkha*, viz. *dukkha, vipariṇāma, saṅkhārā, paticchanna, appaṭicchanna, pariyāya* and *nippriyāya*. There is a way leading to this cessation of suffering. There is an ethical and spiritual path (eight fold path) by following which misery may be removed and *Nirvāṇa* or liberation can be attained All the systems of Indian Philosophy basically deal with *dukkha* and the permanent means to remove it.

Durgā : She is called Durgā as she destroys or removes the difficulties of her devotees. Durgā is called *mūla prakṛti*, and the creation, destruction and nourishment of the world; these three activities are ascribed to her, and She is called Mahāsarasvatī, Mahālakṣmī, and Mahākālī (Devī Bhāgavata, IX.56.60). She is called '*durgatināśinī*', i.e. one who puts down calamities. Durgā is addressed as Ambikā in the Vājasaneyi Saṁhitā. The Taittirīya Āraṇyaka (X.18) mentions her as the consort of Śiva. Details about her nature and worship are found in the Purāṇas and the Tantras.

Guru : A teacher or a preceptor who teaches the essential truth is known as *guru*. Guru may be said to be the power of Divine Grace. That power of Grace affording a favourable opportunity to the aspirant is the means to unraveling of the secret of the *mantra*. The word *guru* is often used in the sense of any elderly person, male or female, who is entitled to get respect. The parents and *ācāryas* are often regarded as the three highest *gurus*. According to the Manusmṛti (II.141-42), *guru* is one who performs the *saṁskāras* and imparts Vedic education. *Guru* is the pivot of Tāntric *sādhanā,* the one who dispels darkness. The Śivasūtra (II.6) says: '*gururupāyaḥ*.' It means, the *guru* who has attained self-realization can alone help the aspirant in acquiring it. The Mālinīvijaya Tantra (II.10) also says: '*sa gururmatsamaḥ prokto mantravīryaprakāśakaḥ*.' Here, Lord Śiva is addressing Pārvatī as: "One who knows all the principles in their essentials, being able to throw light on the virility or efficiency of *mantras*, is a real *guru* like me." Hence, it is said '*gṛṇāti upadiśati tāttvikamarthamiti guruḥ*.'

Īśvara : Lit. *means god. The word* Īśvara *is derived from the root* Īś- 'to rule, be master of', with the suffix *varac* according to the Aṣṭādhyāyī (III.2.175). The Nirukta (III.12) says: *'īśvaraḥ-sarveṣāmindriyāṇāṁ gopāyitātmā'*, i.e. *Īśvara* is treated here as as the soul. The Vedas believe in Īśvara. The Cārvāka, Bauddha, Jaina, Sāṁkhya and Mīmāṁsā *darśanas* do not believe in God. But, on the other hand Nyāya, Vaiśeṣika, Yoga, Vedānta *darśanas* believe in Īśvara (God).

***Jīva* :** Lit. means a bonded being, *paśu, aṇu, puruṣa*, etc. The term is also used to denote 'individual self or soul'. The Buddhists reduce it to a stream of thought or a series of cognitions. The Nyāya-vaiśeṣikas hold it as a unique substance, to which all cognitions, feelings and conations belong as attributes. The Mīmāṁsaka says that it is a substance which has the capability of consciousness. *Jīva* remains under the control of *māyā* and seeks for liberation through the performance of various auspicious deeds, sacrifices, *vratas*, serious meditation and regular practice of *yogic sādhanās*.

***Kālī* :** Lit. means 'the Black one'. Goddess Kālī is one of the most popular deities, worshipped by Hindus. In the Devīmāhātmya section of Mārkaṇḍeya Purāṇa (VII.5ff.) it is stated that She merged from the forehead of the Divine Mother who became black with anger as the demons headed by Caṇḍa and Muṇḍa came to attack her. Kālī came out with a big hideous face and a dreadful appearance. More or less fearful forms of the deity with the name Mahākālī or Bhadrakālī are described in the works like the Kāraṇāgama, Bhaviṣya Purāṇa, Devī Purāṇa, etc. Kālī is generally considered in twelve aspects or forms. The twelve Kālīs as presented by Abhinavagupta, a great scholar of Kashmir Śaivism, are: (1) Sṛṣṭi Kālī, (2) Rakta Kālī, (3) Sthitināśa Kālī, (4) Yama Kālī, (5) Saṁhāra Kālī, (6) Mṛtyu Kālī, (7) Bhadra Kālī, (8) Mārtaṇḍa Kālī, (9) Paramārka Kālī, (10) Kālāgnirudra Kālī, (11) Mahākāla Kālī, (12) Mahābhairavaghora-Chaṇḍakālī.

Kālī or Parāśakti or Parāsaṁvid or the Universal consciousness manifests powers of *sṛṣṭi, sthiti* and *saṁhāra*.

***Kalpa-vṛkṣa* :** The wish fulfilling tree was churned as a jewel from the ocean at the time of '*sāgara-manthana*'. It is known as a tree of heaven, with gods seated on its branches and leaves. The main significance of this tree is that 'what one wishes under this 'Divine *vṛkṣa*' one obtains, i.e. one gets out of it as one desires.

***Kañcuka* :** The five limiting *tattvas* of a finite being, viz. *kalā, (aśuddha)vidyā, rāga, niyati,* and *kāla*. These five *kañcukas* are known as the coverings of *māyā*, throwing a pall over pure consciousness and thus converting Śiva into a *jīva*.

Karma **:** Lit. means work, action, deed, etc. In the early Vedic ideas *karma* denotes sacrifice, a religious rite. Our Vedas, *śāstras*, seers, teachers, etc. have advised us to perform good, auspicious, and religious acts for obtaining desirable things. Different systems of Indian philosophy, i.e. Bauddha, Jaina, Nyāya, Sāṁkhya, Yoga, Mīmāṁsā, Vedānta, etc. have explained the term according to their own principles.

Karuṇā **:** Lit. means compassion, pity, tenderness, etc. *Karuṇā*, a strong emotion of deep compassion, is a dynamic force, a source of human inspiration, which compels one to live and die for the suffering mankind.

In Buddhism, *karuṇā* is one of the four qualities of character significant of a human being who has attained enfranchisement of heart (*cetovimutti*) in the four sentiments.

Liṅga **:** Lit. means a mark, sign, token, an emblem, a badge, symbol, distinguishing mark, characteristic, etc. From etymological sense *liṅga* is that by which mark, one being or word is cognized whether one is male, female, eunuch or masculine, feminine, neuter. The commentator of Amarakośa, Rāmāśramī comments on the term as : '*liṅgayate anena, ligi gatau halaśca iti ghañ.*' The Ajitāgama (Kriyāpāda, III.17cd-18ab) defines *liṅga* as: '*layaṁ gacchanti bhūtāni saṁhāre nikhilāni ca nirgacchanti yataścāpiliṅgo-ktistena hetunā.*' The Tantrāloka (V.113-114) also says: '*atra viśvamidaṁ līnam atrāntaḥsthaṁ ca gamyate*'—it is from the *liṅga* the universe comes into being and dissolves in it. Generally, *liṅga* has been a popular object of worship in India from prehistoric to modern period. The Āgamic tradition uses the term *liṅga* mostly in the sense of arch-symbol and formal representative of Lord Śiva. The Kūrma Purāṇa describes the origin of *liṅga* and its worship. The Liṅga Purāṇa speaks about the Śivaliṅga and its symbolical components. It also praises the style of worshipping *liṅga* along with its pedestal. The Vāmana Purāṇa lauds several holy places where ancient *liṅgas* are established There are twelve (*dvādaśa*) *jyotir-liṅgas* of Lord Śiva being worshipped in India since ancient times.

Loka **:** The term *loka* is derived from the root *lok-* or *loc-* (*bhvādi*) 'to see, to behold, to perceive' or *lok-* or *loc-* (*curādi*) 'to recognize, to know', etc. The second deriving root of *loka* is *ruc-* (*bhvādi*), which means 'to shine, to bright or radiant or resplendant'. An important synonym of *loka* is *bhuvana*. The Amarakośa (III.3.2) defines *loka* as: '*lokastu bhuvane jane*'. Here *loka* means world and people. *Loka* is generally defined as : '*lokyate iti loka*' or '*lokyate asau loka*' (*loka* + *ghañ*). Generally speaking there are three *lokas*, viz. *svarga, pṛthivī* and *pātāla*. According to the Lakṣmī Tantra (XIV.50) *lokas* are fourteen (*lokāścaiva caturdaśa*), seven higher regions rising from the earth one above the other, viz. *bhūloka, bhuvarloka,* *svarloka, maharloka, janaloka, tapaloka,* and *satyaloka* (cf. Viṣṇu Purāṇa, I.22.80), and the seven successively lower regions, descending from the earth one below the other, viz. *atala, vitala, sutala, rasātala, talātàla, mahātala* and *pātāla*.

In the Brahmasūtra Bhāṣya (IV.3.4), *loka* is used to denote 'places of enjoyment of living beings.' In the Caraka Saṁhitā (Śārīrasthāna, V.4) *loka* is conceived as an aggregate of six *dhātus* (5 elements and Brahman). In the Sarasvatīkaṇṭhābharaṇa (I.146), *loka* is accepted as one of the *pramāṇas* and also described as the behaviour of the mobile and immobile beings. According to the Kāvyālaṅkāra Sūtra (I.3.1), *loka* is known as one of the three limbs of *kāvya*.

The Buddhist text Abhidharmakośa Bhāṣya (I.8cd) explains *loka* as: '*lujyata iti loka*'—*loka* is so called because it is in the process of dissolution and discomposition. It is also identified with the body or *yoni*, i.e. form of existence (station) fixed by birth (IV.1). In Jaina philosophy, *loka* is conceived as the conglomeration of five *astikāyas*, viz. *dharma, adharma, ākāśa*, *jīva* and *pudgala* (Tattvārthasūtra Bhāṣya, III.6).

***Mala* :** Lit. means dross, dirt, impurity, dust, any impure Matter, etc. According to Kashmir Śaivism *mala* is what covers and conceals the real nature of Divine Consciousness. It is a limiting condition. which hampers the free expression of the spirit. It is of three types, viz. *āṇava mala, māyīya mala* and *kārma mala*.

Āṇava mala is the primary limiting condition which reduces the universal consciousness to an *aṇu* or the empirical individual. *Māyīya mala* is the limiting condition brought about by *Māyā* that gives to the soul its gross and subtle body. *Kārma mala* is the limiting condition brought about by the *vāsanās* under the influence of desire. It is the force of those *vāsanās* that carries the *jīva* from one life to another.

***Maṇḍala* :** Lit. means round, circular. The Amarakośa defines the term *maṇḍala* as: '*cakravalaṁ tu maṇḍalam* (I.3.6), *bimbo'strī maṇḍalaṁ triṣu* (I.3.15) and *pariveṣastu paridhirūpasūryaka, maṇḍale* (I.3.32).' It means, a sensible horizon, a circle or ring, disc of the sun or moon and halo. In the Taittirīya Saṁhitā (V.3. 9.2) '*maṇḍaleṣṭakā*' is used to denote circular bricks. The Bṛhadāraṇyaka Upaniṣad (V.5.2) refers to the person in the orb (*maṇḍala*) of the sun (*etasmin maṇḍale puruṣa*). In the later Vedic and Sanskrit Literature *maṇḍala* is used to mean a circular diagram or figure drawn on any altar and *pūjā* ritual. In Śulbasūtras also it specifically refers the squaring of a circle (*caturaśraṁ maṇḍalam*—Āpastamba Śulbasūtra, III.2-3).

Maṇḍala worship is very popular and even important in Tāntric rituals. In

Śaivite tradition various *maṇḍalas* are worshipped in different months. Several *maṇḍalas* are described in the Śāradā Tilaka, Pauṣkara Saṁhitā and other Tāntric texts. The Buddhist Tantras also describe *maṇḍalas*, e.g. Sarvatobhadra etc. Now a days *maṇḍala* worship is a common feature in any *pūjā* rituals.

***Mantra* :** It is a sacred or mystic formula for recitation. The word *mantra* is composed of two letters '*man*' and '*tra*'. *Man* implies *mananāt* (by pondering), and '*tra*' implies '*trāyate* (protects). Hence, *mantra* means that which protect or save by pondering. Yāska says: *mantrā mananāt* (Nirukta, VII.12) which means Vedic verses are derived from the root *man*-, 'to think'. The Kulārṇava Tantra says '*mantra*' is so called since it saves from all dangers, as the aspirant thereby is led to ponder over God of immeasurable refulgence that is the only principle in the world. The Śāradā Tilaka (VI.3) devides *mantras* into three categories, viz. male *mantra*, female *mantra* and neuter *mantra*. The masculine *mantras* end in '*hum*' and '*phaṭ*', female with '*svāhā*' and neuter *mantras* with '*namaḥ*'. Purāṇas and some Smṛtis prescribe short *mantras* of five, six, eight, twelve, thirteen and more syllables as very efficacious for securing all objects. The best Vedic *mantra* is the Gāyatrī (Ṛgveda, III.62.10). The Atharvaveda (XIX.71.1) calls it Vedamātā. The Tāntric works (rituals) have their own sacred *mantras*, but they also employ Vedic *mantras*, e.g. '*tryambakaṁ yajāmahe sugandhiṁ*'.... (ṚV VII.59.12) is addressed to Rudra, but is known as *mahā-mṛtyuñjaya mantra* or *mṛtasañjīvanī mantra* in Tāntric works and is prescribed for purifying the mind in the Mahānirvāṇa Tantra (VIII.243). Similarly, the Gāyatrī *mantra* is employed by the Tāntrikas (vide Śāradā Tilaka, XXI.108 and Prapañcasāra Tantra, which devotes two chapters, i.e. 19 & 30 for explaining *praṇava mantra* or *oṁkāra*). The Mahānirvāṇa Tantra (III.14-37) recommends that '*om sac-cid-ekaṁ brahma*' is the best of *mantras*, that those who perform the *pūjā* & *upāsanā* of the Highest Brahma or Supreme Lord, are in need of no other *sādhanā* and that by the mere perfection of that sacred *mantra* the individual self merges in Brahma.

The Buddhist Tantras also claimed to show the way to the attainment of various worldly objects and even *Nirvāṇa* through the *mantras*.

***Māyā* :** Generally it means deceit, jugglery, witchcraft, fraud, trick, etc. The Amarakośa (II.10.11) records the term in the sense of magic (*indrajāla*) and Kṣīrasvāmin comments on this as: '*mātyasyāṁ viśvaṁ māyā*.' According to the Abhidharmakośa Bhāṣya (V.49), *māyā* is used in the sense of magic which deceives others (*parvañcanā māyā*). The term is very frequently used in the Ṛgveda in the sense of magic (*māyābhiraśvinā yuvam*—ṚV V.78.6; *indromāyābhiḥ pururūpa īyate*—ṚV VI.47.18). According to Śaṅkara the world is called *māyā*, because of its unreality. So, *māyā* is the root of every creation. But different philosophical schools develop different thoughts on this concept of *māyā*. According to Kāshmir Śaivism Parama Śiva has two forms of Śakti—Cit Śakti and Māyā Śakti. They may be called Vidyā-māyā and Avidyā-māyā. The nature of Vidyā-māyā is to help in the attainment of Parama Śiva with her power of *hlādinī* and *saṁvita*. It accelerates the process of evolution.Whereas Avidyā-māyā brings about the crudification of self. It creates the phenomenal world. With the power of her *āvaraṇa* and *vikṣepa* it obscures, limits and blinds the Self. But these two powers or functions of Śiva are not independent and separable. *Māyā* creates five principles or powers known as *kañcukas*, which limit the knowledge and power of the Universal Self. These five *kañcukas* are: *kalā*, *(aśuddha) vidyā*, *rāga, niyati & kāla*. It is with these sheaths that *māyā* enwraps *puruṣa*. The microcosm goes into deep slumber and forgets his Divine nature and origin.

Mokṣa : Lit. means salvation, liberation, emancipation, release, *nirvāṇa, mukti, apavarga*, etc. It is the last of the four goals of a human being (*puruṣ-ārtha*), the remaining three being righteousness (*dharma*), material well-being (*artha*), and sexual pleasure (*kāma*). The Amarakośa (I.5.6) records the term *mokṣa* as a synonym of *mukti* along with other terms like: *kaivalya, nirvāṇa, śreyas, niḥśreyas, amṛta* and *apavarga*. Kṣīrasvāmin comments on the same as: *mokṣaḥ pāśebhyaḥ ātmanaḥ pṛthakbhāvaḥ*—free from the bindings of one's self. The Laghu Yoga-Vāsiṣṭha (VI.1.9) defines the term as: *aśeṣeṇa parityāgo vāsanānāṁ ya uttamaḥ, mokṣa ityucyate*, i.e. abandonment of all sorts of desires (*vāsanās*) is the best means of liberation. Hence, to be freed from all sorts of sufferings is known as *mokṣa*. It is rightly defined by Śabdakalpadruma as: '*mokṣyate duḥkhamanena.*'

This is the main subject of discussion in all the Indian philosophical systems. The Vedānta, Sāṁkhya, Yoga, Nyāya-vaiśeṣika, Mīmāṁsā, Bauddha, Jaina, Kashmir Śaiva Darśana, etc. have treated it according to their own philosophical thought.

Mudrā : Lit. means a seal, an instrument for sealing or stamping; a stamp, print, mark, impression; an image, a sign; name of certain positions of fingers practised in devotion or religious worship. Generally it is known as posture of the body, especially of hands needed for *yogic* exercise and spiritual attainment. It is called *mudrā* (root *mud-* 'to rejoice', 'to please', with the suffix *rak* and *tāp*), because it gives the bliss of spiritual consciousness. The derivative meaning of the term *mudrā* is: '*mudaṁ harṣaṁ rāti dadāti iti mudrā*'—it gives delight in the heart. *Mudrās* like Abhaya, Varada, Dharmacakra, Bhūmisparśa, Namaskāra, etc. are commonly found in iconic representation symbolising the quality associated with the deity. The Haṭhayoga Pradīpikā devotes a complete chapter on *mudrās*. Some of which are: Mahāmudrā, Mahāvedha, Khecarī, Mahābandha, Uḍḍīyyāna-bandha, Mūlabandha, Jālandhara-bandha, etc. However, the scholars explain *mudrā* in different ways denoting 'mystic pose of the hand', 'manual signs indicative of various ideas', finger signs, hand poses adopted during meditation or exposition.

Nāstika-darśana : The heterodox schools of Indian Philosophy denying the authority of the Veda. As said '*nāstiko vedanindakaḥ*.' These *Nāstika-darśanas* are: Cārvāka, Jaina and Bauddha.

Nāda : Lit. means a loud roar, shout, cry and sounding in general. The Amarakośa (I.6.22) refers it as a synonym of *śabda*. The Nighaṇṭu (III.16.9) records it as a synonym of *stoṭa*, i.e. 'one who praises'. However, most of the related words of *nāda* bear the etymological sense of the verbal root *nad-* 'to sound' or 'to praise'.

In the Tāntric literature *nāda* is related with creation. When the Supreme Being or Parama Śiva begins to manifest itself in creation, its first vibration or the primordial sound is known as *nāda*, which is actually the manifestation of the consciousness of the Supreme Being revealed as sound. The Divine pleasure of this union, i.e. Śiva and Śakti is called *nāda*. As the supreme seed, the primeval sound *nāda* abides in all living beings.

Nirguṇa : The term *guṇa* means quality, virtue, cord, etc., while *nirguṇa* which is opposite to *saguṇa*, means having no cord or string or without good qualities or virtues, bad, worthless, vicious, etc. The term *nirguṇa* appears several times in the Upaniṣads in the sense of devoid of all qualities or properties. Basically the terms *saguṇa* and *nirguṇa* are associated with Brahman, viz. Saguṇa Brahma and *Nirguṇa* Brahma. *Nirguṇa* Brahman is unqualified Absolute. The best method of describing it, therefore, is by negative terms (*neti-neti*). The concept of *Nirguṇa* is found in the Upaniṣads, Epics, Purāṇas and other texts of Indian tradition. In the Śvetāsvatara Upaniṣad (VI.11), Brahman or God is described as omnipotent, omniscient, omnipresent, an observer and devoid of all qualities. Hence, *nirguṇa*, devoid of (*guṇas*) qualities is an attribute of Brahman, and without which Brahman cannot be defined in the traditional texts.

Nirodha : Lit. means confinemet, restraint, check, suppression, control, etc. In Buddhism, it denotes extinction of all sufferings and is regarded as one of the four noble truths, *dukkha-nirodha*.

Parama-Śiva : He is known as the Supreme or the Absolute of Tantra Philosophy. Parama-Śiva is the *purṇa-ahantā*, self-luminous and pure-consciousness. The *purṇa-ahantā* is the essence of Parama-Śiva. He is also known as the Supreme Reality. Besides, He is of the nature of Bliss and complete in himself. He holds in Himself the unmanifested universe as an idea. That reality out of which thirty-six *tattvas* evolve and into which all of them get absorbed At the same time, He transcends the Universe. He is the transcendental Reality, Pure Intelligence as well as the one all-including Supreme Experience. Hence, Parama-Śiva is both transcendent and immanent. He is Truth, Consciousness and Bliss.

Parā-vāk : Cosmic ideation holding within it all forms of knowledge, spiritual as well as mundane. It is the *svātantrya śakti*, the free, unfettered, absolute will-power, the main glorious supreme sovereignty of the Divine. It is called *parā*, because it is supreme and perfect. It is called *vāk,* because it sounds forth, utters forth, the universe by its 'I-consciousness'.

Pariṇāma-vāda : The Sāṁkhya theory of causation according to which an effect is not a new entity but only a changed phase of its cause. The theory is known as *satkārya-vāda*.

Paśu : The empirical individual bound by ignorance (*avidyā*) or spiritual nescience is known as *paśu*. Abhinavagupta explains it in his Paramārthasāra (verse 16) as: '*māyāparigrahavaśād bodho malinaḥ pumān paśurbhavati.*' *Puruṣa* is the finite subject who takes a finite individual I-consciousness, having limited powers to know and to do, as his self. Having lost his finiteness, he is known as '*aṇu*', a finite being. He sees everything and everyone as different from him. Such viewpoint of diversity and such finitude are the main impurities of such individual I-consciousness, which being fastened by the chains of ignorance and finitude, is known as *paśu*, a bonded being.

Perception : *Pratyakṣa* or *pratyakṣa-pramāṇa*. It is the first kind of means of knowledge based on sense.

Pīṭha : Lit. means a seat, a chair, stool or shrine of a deity (usually a goddess). In the Amarakośa (II.6.138) the term is recorded as a synonym of *āsana* to mean 'seat' or more specifically a chair or stool. At present the term is mostly focused on the senses of the seat of a deity, an altar, a pedestal, a religious seat, or throne of the *āśramas*.

Various holy *pīṭhas* of Goddess Śakti are famous in India. Tantracūḍāmaṇi records a list of 51 *pīṭhas*, widely known as holy resorts of Śakti, origin of which is associated with Dakṣayajña legend describing the falling of 51 pieces cut-off from the body of Satī. Each *pīṭha* is supposed to contain a limb of *devī* Satī, a presiding goddess and her Bhairava. Some of the famous Śakti *pīṭhas* are: Varanasi, Kañcī, Kāmākhyā, Kurukshetra, Ujjayinī, Hiṅgulā, Jvālāmukhī, etc. There are also some minor *pīṭhas*, known as *upapīṭhas*.

The Hevajra Tantra and Kālikāpurāṇa enumerate four *pīṭhas*, viz. Jālandhara, Uḍḍīyāna, Pūrṇagiri, and Kāmarūpa. The Devī Bhāgavata

Purāṇa records 108 *pīṭhas*. A complete list of 108 Śakti *pīṭhas* along with the 108 names of the goddess is formed for the first time in the Matsya Purāṇa (XIII.25-53). The Tāntric and Purāṇic texts have elaborately discussed various Śakti *pīṭhas* and its religious importance.

Prajñā : It stands for perfect knowledge, which liberates an individual mind from the miseries and torments of life and removes the veil of ignorance. In Buddhism, it (*paññā*) denotes transcendental wisdom, divine intuition and also counted as one of the six *pāramitās*.

Prāṇa : Lit. means breath. It is derived from the root *pṛ-* 'to fill, to nourish, to satiate. The term *prāṇa* is traditionally derived from the conjunction of *pra-an* + *ac* (cf. *ānīdavātaṁ svadhayā tadekam*—Ṛgveda X.129.2), which means 'breathing forth' and *prāṇiti jīvati*, means breathes properly and goes on living. The root *an-*, 'to breathe' with the suffix *kvip* means one who breaths. *Prāṇa* is defined in the Chāndogya Upaniṣad (I.3.3) as: '*yad vai prāṇiti sa prāṇaḥ*'—that which breaths, is truly breath. In the narrow sense *prāṇa* denotes one of the vital airs of which five are usually distinguished, viz. *prāṇa, apāna, vyāna, udāna,* and *samāna*. *Prāṇa* is *brahman*. It is an all-conditioning, yet inscrutable agent. This is said in the Kena Upaniṣad (I.9) as: '*yatprāṇena na prāṇiti yena prāṇaḥ pranīyate, tadeva brahma tvaṁ viddhi*.' In accordance with the Upaniṣads, Abhinavagupta in his Tantrāloka states that the vital energy is basically one, but it assumes the five specific modes, viz. *prāṇa, apāna*, etc.

Pratītya-samutpāda : The Buddhist causal theory is called Dependent Origination, i.e. there being one thing, the other follows. It explains how the three successive births, viz. past, present & future of a man is related to one another. It is based on a twelve-point law of causation. *Avidyā* (ignorance) in a past- life creates *saṁskāras* (impressions), which lead an individual to *vijñāna*, i.e. birth consciousness of the present life. From this originates the *nāma-rūpa* or mental and physical faculties developing *ṣaḍāyatana*, or internal organs of sense and mind leading to *sparśa* or contact with the corresponding objects. Contact further leads to *Vedanā* (sensation), which results in *taṇhā* or desire to reborn. From the latter arises *upādāna* (grasping) leading to *bhava*, i.e. becoming, the basis of *jāti* or birth in the next birth. Finally, when the birth takes place it is sure to lead to old age and death (*jarāmaraṇa*). This is the theory of causation in Buddhism.

Pratyabhijñā : A name of Kāshmir Śaivism. *Prati+abhi+jñā* = *Pratyabhijñā*. *Prati* means *pratipam*, i.e. contrary, in other words though known, now appearing as forgotten through delusion. *Abhi* means facing, i.e. close at hand. *Jñā* means illumination or knowledge. Hence, *pratyabhijñā* means recognition of the real self. Since the term means recognition it refers to the way of realising the soul's identity with Lord Śiva.

Rājasūya : Name of a sacrifice, especially the rite of royal consecration, performed by a *kṣatriya* king for achieving sovereignty. It lasts more than two years beginning with a *dīkṣā* on the first day of the bright half of *phālguna* (February-March).

Rakṣasa or ***Rākṣasa*** : Lit. means a demon, an evil spirit, an imp, a goblin, etc. In the Pāli texts the word *rākṣasa* is also occurred several times. It is often mentioned along with the words like: *yakṣa, gandharva, asura, nāga*, etc. (Jātaka, Vol. I, p. 127; Vol. VI, p. 464). Because of their association with inferior gods, *rākṣasas* are treated as minor supernatural beings. Due to their evilmindedness they are considered as demons in the *śāstras*.

The term *rākṣasa* is explained in the sense of a harmful non-human being. They are supposed to possess supernatural powers, excellent valour and energy. It is also said that they can assume any form (*ākāra*) they like. (Jātaka, Vol. I, pp. 556-57).

Ratha : Lit. means a wagon, carriage, chariot, car, vehicle, cart, etc., Especially a war chariot (cf. *yaṁ kumāra navaṁ rathamacakraṁ manasākṛṇoḥ*—ṚV X.135.3; *ratho vomābhyāṁ cakrābhyāṁ vartamānaḥ*—Chāndogya Upaniṣad, IV.16.5; *taṁ rathaṁ sūryasaṅkāśaṁ sītā hṛṣṭena cetasā*—Rāmāyaṇa II.40.13). In the Amarakośa several synonyms of *ratha* are recorded, e.g. *śatāṅga, syandana*, etc. Different types of *rathas* are mentioned in the Sanskrit literature. *Rathas* made of gold, silver, wood, etc. are found in the Vedic period. *Rathas* of different gods could be identified from their special structure and symbol. *Rathas* of different planets are described in the Purāṇas. The wheels of chariots are also different in number, e.g. one wheeled, two-wheeled, three-wheeled, four-wheeled, etc. which give the idea of different types of modern vehicles. In the Mahābhārata (VI.8.15-16) Lord Viṣṇu's golden eight-wheeled *ratha* is beautifully described

The most famous *rathayātrā* (car festival) of the Lord Jagannatha, Balabhadra and *devī* Subhadrā on the second lunar day of the bright fortnight in *āṣāḍha* (June-July) month held at Puri (Orissa) and other places in India.

Śakti : Lit. means energy, power, especially the creative energy that generates and continues to activate the universe. The term *śakti* is derived from the root *śak-* 'to be able', 'to be powerful', with the suffix *ktin*. Kṣīrasvāmin, the commentator of the Amarakośa comments on the term as: *śakyate anayā jetuṁ śakti*. The derivative sense of *śakti* is 'that through which it is possible to conquer or through which something can be conquered (*śakyate jetum ābhiḥ śaktyaḥ*). The Aṣṭādhyāyī of Pāṇinī (III.2.129) uses the term *śakti* in the sense of capability. The primordial female principle or the power of the Supreme Being is treated *śakti* through the manifestation of the universe is affected *Parāśakti* is conceived as female principle. It is the energy of Lord Śiva and regarded as the instrumental cause of creation. Besides, Śakti is symbolically represented as the spouse of Śiva and hence She is the immanent principle of Śiva. Devoid of Śakti, Śiva would be insentient (*jaḍa*) and consequently, as good as 'dead' (*śava*). Śiva knows Himself only through His Great Śakti. She is also the power of freedom of the Lord. Śakti has been addressed as *janani, mātri* and *ambā*. Generally, Śakti or Devī is identified with Vidyāmāyā. With the help of Vidyāmāyā, *jīva* proceeds towards spiritual sublimity. Śakti or Devī helps *jīva* in moving towards Paramaśiva. Without the help of Śakti it is not possible for the *jīva* to attain the Supreme Oneness with Paramaśiva.

Śaktipāta **:** It means the descent of Divine Śakti. *Śaktipāta* on an individual means the imparting of *anugraha* or Divine Grace to him, through which he realizes his essential Divine nature.

Samādhi **:** Collectness of mind in which there is cessation of the fluctuations of the mind; mental absorption. The experience of higher consciousness is known as *samādhi*. It is an advanced state of contemplation, and implies a thought-free mind. In the beginning the strain of the mind is felt in a subtle form, and is, therefore, called *savikalpa samādhi*. It is attained with effort in order to curb mental disturbances. Then there is the higher state known as *nirvikalpa samādhi*, in which the mind is totally quiescent and the experience effortless. The mind gets dissolved in the bliss of higher consciosness.

Samāpatti **:** Sustained deep mental absorption; sustained absorption in concentration.

Samāveśa **:** It means, *samādhi* in which there is unity of experience, i.e. in which the entire universe appears as Self, in which the consciousness of the empirical self is completely subordinated, and it becomes identified with the consciousness of Śiva. *Samāveśa, samādhi* and *samāpatti* are known as the superconscious experience of the Ultimate Reality.

Sambodhi **:** Enlightenment that came to Lord Buddha after heroic struggle. The seven qualities or attributes of *sambodhi* are: self-control, understanding of the *dharma*, zeal, tranquility of mind, joy, concentration and compassion.

Saṁhitā **:** Lit. 'collection', but usually referring to the gathering together of the lore known today as the four Vedas, viz. Ṛgveda, Yajurveda, Sāmaveda, and Atharvaveda.

Śaṁkara : This is another name of Śiva. '*Saṁ karoti iti Śaṁkaraḥ*', i.e. one who brings about happiness and welfare is known as Śaṁkara.

Saṁsāra **:** Lit. means passage, course, i.e. the course or circuit of worldly life, mundane existence, the world. '*Saṁsarati iti saṁsāraḥ*', i.e. that which is always on the move. Etymologically the word '*saṁsāra*' also means 'wandering through' (a succession of states) of the *jīva* or individual soul.

Saṅgha **:** The word *saṅgha* means 'a community' or group, collection, multitude; as *maharshi-saṅgha, manuṣya-saṅgha*, etc. In Buddhist context it means an assembly of Buddhist priests. The community or society of Buddhist monks or mendicants, both (male) *bhikṣu* and (female) *bhikṣuṇī*. The *saṅgha* in widest sense is meant, a community of all those who are walking the Buddhist path. As the third of the three gems (*triratna*) and three refuges (*trisaraṇa*), i.e. *Buddha, Dharma* and *Saṅgha*, it applies to the *ariya-saṅgha*, the real community of the saints. It is the oldest monastic order in the world.

Śānti **:** Lit. means peace, tranquility, etc. The term *śānti* (fem.) is a multi-dimensional concept in the Vedic, Purāṇic, Tāntric & Buddhist Literature. It is a word of current usage in the sense of peace or calmness of mind, absence of passion, averting of pain, quiet, etc. It is derived from the root *śam-* 'to be appeared', 'to kill', 'to stop', etc. Kṣīrasvāmī, the commentator of Amarakośa (III.2.3) says: '*kāmakrodhādyabhāva śānti*'—absence of lust, anger, etc. is known as *śānti*. The indeclinable particle *śam* means welfare, happiness, prosperity, and it is also used in the sense of peace, quiet, etc. Though the word *śānti* does not occur in the Ṛgveda, but '*śam*' occurs several times in this text. Similarly, in the Vājasaneyi Saṁhitā also '*śam*' occurs a number of times. The word *śānti'* is occurred many a times in the Taittirīya Saṁhitā (VI.1.7.7-8, VI.2.2, VI.3.5, etc.) as well as in the Atharvaveda (XIX.9.14). In the Upaniṣads, the word *śānti* is used in the sense of 'peace'. According to Atharvaveda Pariśiṣṭa (LXX.10.4), *śānti* does not occur / happen on account of the following reasons:

apūjanāttu pūjyasya tathāpūjyasya pūjanāt /
antaḥkaraṇadoṣācca hetoḥ śāntirnajāyate//

It means, persons those who are not honouring one who is honourable, honouring one who is not honourable, and blemishes in the mind. So, due to these reasons the peace desiring people never get peace in their life time.

The Gītā uses the words *śānti* and *nirvāṇa* to indicate the Bliss of the person who abides in God (*śāntiṁ nirvāṇa paramām.....*). According to the Viṣṇusahasranāma Bhāyṣa (75), Brahman is known as *śānti*, as those who have abandoned all attachments find peace in Him. The Agni Purāṇa (263.7-8) describes eighteen *śāntis*. The Kūrma Purāṇa (I.12.66) describes *śānti* as a goddess, whereas it is counted as *parva* in the Mahābhārata, i.e. *śānti parvan*. In Buddhism, *nirvāṇa* is known as the best *śānti* (peace). The Dhammapada rightly says: '*natthi śānti paramaṁ sukham*'—there is no Bliss, which surpasses the perfect peace. The Nārada Bhakti Sūtra (VI.1.60) records that love is the nature of peace and it is of the nature of Supreme Bliss.

Sarvāstivāda **:** one of the oldest schools of Hīnayāna sect of Buddhism.

Śāstra **:** *Śaṁsanāt śāsanāt śāstraṁ śāstramitrabhidhīyate. Śiṣyate anena śāstram* (root *śās* + *stran*). The word *śāstra* has several meanings, viz., (1) an order, a command, rule, precept; (2) a sacred precept or rule, scriptural injunction (cf. *tasmāt śāstraṁ pramāṇam te kāryākāryavyavasthitau*—Bhāgavata Purāṇa, XVI. 24; (3) a religious or sacred book, scripture, (4) any department of knowledge, science (cf. *iti guhyatamaṁ śāstram*—Bhāgavata Purāṇa, XV.20; *śāstreṣu kuṇṭhitā buddhiḥ*—Raghuvaṁśa, 1.19); often at the end of the compound after the word denoting the the subject, or applied collectively to the whole body of teaching on that subject, like Vedānta-śāstra, Nyāya-śāstra, Alaṅkāra-śāstra, etc.; (5) what is learnt, knowledge; (6) a work, treatise; (7) theory (opposite of *prayoga* or practice); (8) the mate-rial and spiritual science together

(cf. *tattvābhedena yacchāstraṁ tat kāryaṁ nānyathāvidham /*
asamīkṣyaiva karmāṇi nītiśāstraṁ yathāvidhi // Mahābhārata, XII.267.9)

Śāstrakāra **:** (1) an author of a *śāstra* or sacred book; (2) an author In general; (3) a sage, saint.

Śāstrajña **or** ***śāstravid*** **:** A person who is well-versed in the *śāstras* or scriptures are known as *śāstrajña*. It also means a mere theorist, i.e. one who is expert in the theoretical side of a subject (*siddhānta-śāstrī* or *siddhāntācārya*, etc.)

Śāstra-yoni **:** The source of the *śāstras*.

Siddhis**:** Super-natural powers attained through the practice of *yoga*. These *siddhis* are eight in number, viz. *aṇimā, laghimā, mahimā, garimā, prāpti, prākāmya, vaśitva*, and *īśitva*.

Śilpa**:** Lit. means an art, a fine or mechanical art, craft, etc. The term *śilpa* is a multi-dimensional concept of Indian tradition. Generally, it implies art or action or skill in action. The Nighaṇṭu (*śilayati śīlatīti vā*—Devarāja Yajvan's comm. II.1) regards it as one of the synonyms of *karman*, which indicates its association with activity. The Śatapatha Brāhmaṇa (III.2.1.5) defines it as; '*yad vai pratirūpaṁ tacchilpam*'. A proper imitation of any act is a real art. However, in Vedic texts *śilpa* occurs both in the sense of a *śāstra*, which is 'recited' (*śilpāni saṁsanti*—Aitareya Brāhmaṇa, VI.27) as well as an act which is performed (*śilpāni kriyanta*—Kauṣītaki Brāhmaṇa, XXV.2) during Agniṣṭoma sacrifice. In the Vedic Saṁhitās and Brāhmaṇas *śilpa* denotes 'devine acts' or skill (Tāṇḍya Brāhmaṇa, III.32.1), as it supports the cosmic elements or brings them into being (Kauṣītaki Brāhmaṇa, XXIX.5).

Art is synonymous with *śilpa* and *kalā* or more precisely with *śilpa-kalā*, which is the subject matter of Śilpa Śāstra. So, Śilpa Śāstra means the technical treatises on Arts & Crafts. It consists of a number of Śilpa texts, which deal with the major technical subjects like: Art & Architecture, crafts, painting, image making, construction of temples, buildings, royal palaces, *vimānas*, chariots of the deities, planning and construction of towns, villages, *maṇḍapas, caityas, stūpas*, etc. Though a number of Purāṇic & Āgamic texts deal with the above subjects, but there are two schools of Indian Śilpa tradition, viz. the Southern or Dravidian School (School of Maya) and Northern or Aryan or Nāgara School (School of Viśvakarmā). The major Southern Śilpa treatises are: Mānasāra, Mayamata, Aṁśumad-bheda, Agastya-sakalādhikāra, Śilparatna, etc. Similarly, the major Northern Śilpa treatises are: Viśvakarmā Prakāśa, Samarāṅgaṇa Sūtradhāra, Aparājita Pṛcchā, Rūpa-Maṇḍana, etc.

These Śilpa texts exhaustively deal with the various subjects on Indian *vāstu-vidyā,* Art, architecture & iconography.

Śrī **:** Goddess Lakṣmī, the deity and consort of Lord Viṣṇu, who embodies the qualities of prosperity and beauty. She is worshipped especially by the Vaiṣṇavas as inseparable from Viṣṇu.

Sruc **:** It means laddle and it is made of wood. In the Ṛgveda (VI.II.5) the *sruc* is described as '*suvṛkti*', i.e. well fashioned Generally, Juhū, Upabhṛt and Dhruvā are denoted by the term *sruc*. Even Paracaraṇī and Agnihotra *havaṇīs* are termed as *sruc*. Juhū is used to offer oblation and Agnihotra-*havaṇī* is also used for offering Agnihotra oblations. The *sruc* should have the length of a *bāhu*.

Sruva **:** It means a dipping spoon. It is generally made of Khādira or Parṇa wood. It is made of gold, silver, copper, bronze, at the Śānti, Pauṣṭika and Abhicāra rites. *Sruva* is utilized for scooping liquid oblations in different sacrifices.

Śuddha tattva **:** It means Parama Śiva or the Highest Śiva, the Absolute Principle.

Śuddhavidyā **:** Kashmir Śaivism recognises thirty-six *tattvas*. *Śuddhavidyā* is the fifth *tattva*, counting from Śiva. In this *tattva* the consciousness of both 'I' and 'This' is equally prominent.

Śūnya **:** Lit. means empty, void. According to Buddhism it is a state in which there is no distinct consciousness of knower, knowledge and known; an indefinable state of Reality. But according to Kashmir Śaivism it is a state in which no object is experienced

Śūnya-pramātā **:** The experiment who is identified with the void, *pralayākala* (Kashmir Śaivism).

Sūtra **:** Lit. thread. It means that which like a thread runs through or holds together certain ideas, a rule, a formula, a direction. A *sūtra* must contain the fewest possible words, must be free from ambiguity, must be meaningful and comprehensive, must not contain useless words and pauses and must be faultless.

Svastika **:** It is an auspicious symbol accepted by Bauddhas, Jainas and Hindus.

Svātantrya **:** Absolute freedom of will. It literally means self-dependence. It is a technical term in Kashmir Śaiva philosophy. It includes three important ideas: (1) absolute freedom to create, complete autonomy of Will, not depending on any external material or means for its activity, absolute sovereignty or lordship (*aiśvarya*), (2) Vimarśa or ever present self-consciousness, a self which is all inclusive (knower, known and means of knowing), (3) *jñāna* or *kriyā*. The absolute freedom to create, includes *jñāna* and *kriyā,* i.e. knowledge and activity. Lord Śiva in this system is not like the inactive Brahman of Śaṅkara Vedānta. He has *svātantrya*, unimpeded Will, absolute knowledge, absolute power of creativity, and absolute Self-consciousness.

Taṇhā **:** Lit. thirst. 'Craving' is the chief root of suffering, and of the ever continuing cycle of rebirths. According to the Dependent Origination, craving is conditioned by feeling. The most frequent synonyms of *taṇhā* are *rāga* and *lobha*.

Tathāgata **:** A title of Buddha, used by his followers, and also by himself when speaking of himself. It is now usually derived from *tathā-āgata* (thus come) and *tathāgata* (thus gone) and has given the meaning as: he who has come and gone as former Buddhas. The Mahāyāna school says that one who has attained full realization of thatness (*tathātā*), i.e. become one with the Absolute.

Tattva **:** Thatness, the very being of a thing; constitutive principle; category of Reality; Ultimate Reality. According to Kashmir Śaivism *tattvas* are thirty six in number.

Tripiṭaka **:** Lit. means 'the three baskets'. It is the name for the three main divisions of the Pāli canon, viz. Vinaya Piṭaka (the basket of Discipline), Sutta Piṭaka (the basket of Discourses), and Abhidhamma Piṭaka (the basket of Philosophy).

Triratna **:** Lit. means 'three Jewels or three Gems, which by all Buddhists are revered as the most venerable things, are the Buddha, the Dhamma and the Holy Saṅgha.

Trisaraṇa **:** 'Threefold refuge', in which every faithful adherent of the Buddha puts his whole trust, consists in the Buddha, the Dhamma and the Saṅgha. Lord Buddha, the Enlightened One, is the teacher who by himself has discovered, realized and proclaimed to thc world of deliverance. The Dhamma is the law of deliverance. The Saṅgha is the community of the holy monks, who have truly realized or are striving to realize the law of deliverance. In Pāli this is known as: *Buddhaṁ śaraṇaṁ gacchāmi, Dhammaṁ śaraṇaṁ gacchāmi* and *Saṅghaṁ śaraṇaṁ gacchāmi.*

***Tuṣita Heaven* :** The heaven of the thirty three gods, the last of the paradises in the sky from where Lord Buddha descended to this earth.

***Upāsanā* :** It literally means to 'come near' a thing. Śaṅkara defines *upāsanā* as the steady maintenance of one-pointed devotion of thought towards a particular object, in the way sanctioned by the scriptures, uninterrupted by any other thought.

***Vaibhāṣika* :** One of the four schools of the Buddhist Philosophy.

***Vedi* :** Sacrificial altar, an elevated or excavated plot of ground, strewn with *darva* grass, where sacrificial materials, utensils and implements are placed The term *Vedi* (from root *vid-*, 'to know') is explained in the Amarakośa (II.7.18) as cleansed quadrangular ground for sacrifice (*vediḥ pariṣkṛtā bhūmiḥ*). The commentator Kṣīrasvāmin explains it as: *vidantyenāṁ vediḥ*. So, an altar, especially one prepared for a sacrifice (cf. *iyaṁ vediḥ paro antaḥ pṛthivyā ayaṁ somo vṛṣṇo aśvasya retaḥ*—AV IX.10.14). Measurements and shape of a *vedi* differ according to the type of rite and the texts.

***Vidyā* :** Lit. means knowledge (from the root *vid-* 'to know') learning, lore, science, etc. *Vidyā* is stated to be fourteen, i.e. the four Vedas, six *aṅgas* (Vedāṅgas), Dharmaśāstra, Mīmāṁsā, Tarka or Nyāya and the Purāṇas. As knowledge, *vidyā* is of two kinds, viz. *parāvidyā* (spiritual knowledge) and *aparavidyā* (material knowledge).

***Vihāra* :** A living place of the Buddhist monks. It is also known as a Buddhist monastery.

***Vijñānavāda* :** One of the four Buddhist school of philosophy, also called Yogācāra which holds the theory of subjective idealism.

***Vivartavāda* :** The Vedāntic theory of causation, according to which, change of a cause into its effect is not real and illusory. It is contrasted with the Sāṁkhya theory of causation (*pariṇāmavāda*), which holds the change to be real.

***Vrata* :** Lit. means a religious act of devotion or austerity, a vow in general. It is an observance of pious act like fasting on a particular sacred day. In the sense of religious observance the Āpastamba Śrautasūtra (*vratam upaiti*, IV.2.6), the Kātyāyana Śrautasūtra (*vratopeta*, II.1.11), and the Baudhāyana Śrauta-Sūtra (I.1), which includes abstinence from certain things like: *māṣa*(beans), *māṁsa* (flesh) and sexual intercourse. One has to follow certain prescribed rules while observing a particular *vrata*. *Vrata* also means rituals intended for certain purposes. These are regional and local in character, performed specially by the women folk for averting diseases and calamities, for progeny and prosperity and for other practical purposes of life.

The majority of the *vratas* are supposed to produce tangible results. Their performer is endowed with a beautiful form, and he/she gets immense fortune, subdues the enemy, and is rendered free from all earthly calamities including various diseases. In short, all conceivable temporal Bliss can be obtained through *vratas*.

***Vṛkṣa* :** Lit. means tree. The term is derived from the root *vraśc-* 'to cut down' with the suffix *sa*. In Nirukta, the etymologies of *vṛkṣa* are given as: (1) *vṛkṣa vraścanāt* (Nir II.6; XII.29), here the term is derived from the root *vraśc*—'to cut down'; (2) *vṛtvā kṣāṁ tiṣṭhatīti vā* (Nir II.6)—here the term stands for having covered (√*vṛ-)* the earth (*kṣā*), i.e. *vṛkṣa* = √*vṛ-* 'to cover' + *kṣā* 'earth'; (3) *vṛtakṣaye vā* (Nir XII.29)—it means the chosen dwelling place (root *vṛ-* 'to choose' + *kṣaya* 'to dwell' = *vṛkṣa*).

Vṛkṣa is a symbol of stability, as it is clear from the above explanations. Lord Viṣṇu is called *Vṛkṣa* on account of His stability, as He is known as the sheltering tree of the wise persons (Viṣṇusahasranāma Bhāṣya 72). In the Saṁhitās, the Brahman is treated as the Primordial tree from which the entire creation is manifested *Vṛkṣa* is explained by the scholars as the body or the orb or region of the Sun or the sacrificial post or the world or the mythical world-tree. In the Śvetāsvatara Upaniṣad the cosmic person is treated as an eternal tree rooted in heaven and the entire world is filled by that Supreme Being (*vṛkṣa iva stabdho divi tiṣṭhatyekastenedaṁ pūrṇaṁ puruṣeṇa sarvam*—III.9).

Vṛkṣa has a great importance in Buddhist Literature as different *vṛkṣas* are related with Buddhas or Bodhisattvas. Aśvattha is the tree of enlightenment of Gautama Buddha.

Wheel of Law : The *dhamma* as an ever-rolling chariot Wheel, the symbol of conquering efficacy; the Buddha, being the *dhammacakka-vattin* or Universal Monarch in the domain of Righteousness. The preaching of the first *upadeśa* in Varanasi is called Dharmacakra pravartana Sutta or the discourse of sitting in motion the chariot of Wheel of the holy law.

***Yantra* :** The term *yantra* is derived from the root *yam-*, 'to control'. It has various meanings like: restraint, curb, check, bind, fasten, force, etc. Besides, it also denotes a fetter, band, tie and rain. In the Ṛgveda (X.149.1) it is used in the sense of bend or fetter. In the Aṣṭāṅgahṛdaya (Sūtrasthāna, XXV.3-28), *yantra* is described as different types of instruments. According to the Sūryasiddhānta (XIII.19-24), various *yantras* were used for measuring time, like: *chāyā-yantra, kapāla-yantra, toya-yantra*, etc. The Mayamata, as an archaeological text, used *yantra* in the sense of a device and machine as: *jala-yantra*. In the Tāntric point of view, *yantra* means an amulet, i.e. a mystical or astronomical diagram used as an amulet. This diagram is engraved or drawn on metal, paper, stone, wood or other materials which are worshiped in the same manner as an image. The *yantra* worship is an essential feature of Tantra *sādhanā* and it is also a mystic process of awakening the Divine Power.

Yoni : Lit. means womb, uterus, vulva, the female organ of generation (cf. *jīvo mṛtasya carati svadhābhiramartyor martyenā sayo-niḥ*—Ṛgveda, I.164.30 cd). The term is derived from the root *ya-* 'to unite, to yoke, to push or towards, to worship', etc. Brahman is the *yoni* (main source) of everything. *Yoni* signifies the causal factor that produces a particular class of beings. In the Bhagavad Gītā, Lord Śrī Krişṇa says that His womb is the great sustainer where He places the seed of creation (*mama yonirmahad brahma tasmin garbhaṁ dadhāmyaham*—XIV.3).

Yūpa : It is derived from the root *yu-* 'to bind' is known as the pillar of sacrifice. The sacrificial post is an essential feature of animal sacrifice. There are six synonyms of mulberry: *nūda, yūpa, kramuka, brahmṇya, brahmadāru, and tūla* (Amarakośa II.4.41-42). *Yūpa* is used here as a synonym of Mulberry. Perhaps the sacrificial stake is made from mulberry tree. Besides, *yūpas* are made of *Palāśa*, *Khadira* & *Vilva* wood. The word *yūpa* occurs in the Ṛgveda (I.51.14; I.162.6; IV.33.3; V.2.7, etc.), the Yajurveda (V.43; VI.2,etc.), Atharvaveda (XIII.1.47), Taittirīya Saṁhitā (VI.3.4), Śatapatha Brāhmaṇa (III.6.4.1, V.2. 1.5; XI.7.4.1; XI.7.3.2, etc.), Aitareya Brāhmaṇa (II.1; II.3, etc.), Baudhāyana Śulba Sūtra (I.106, 112-113), Baudhāyana Dharma Sūtra (I.5.11.34; I.6.9.5), Kātyāyana Śrauta Sūtra (I.7.15), Kātyāyana Śulba Sūtra VI.8; VI.10) and other Vedic and non-Vedic texts, generally in the sense of 'sacrificial post'. The number of *yūpa* differs from sacrifice to sacrifice. As the Śatapatha Brāhmaṇa (XIII.4.4.5) says: '*ekaviṁsati yūpām*'—there are twenty one sacrificial stakes. According to Śāṅkhāyana Brāhmaṇa (X.1), *yūpa* is known as thunderbolt (*vajro vā eṣa yūpaḥ*). The Vāstu Sūtra Upaniṣad (IV.21) records '*daivyajñārthaṁ yūpaḥ*'—a *yūpa* is the set up for sacrifices to the gods.

Index (Sanskrit)

A

B

◆ ◆ ◆

Index (English)

D

E

F

M

N

O

P

T

U

V

W

Y

◆ ◆ ◆

SELECT OPINION OF EMINENT SCHOLARS
ON
THE WORK

Blessings

I am very happy to learn that a collection of the scholarly contributions of my learned colleague Dr Narasingha Charan Panda is going to be brought out in the form of a book under the title '**Perspectives of Indian Thought**'. The articles contained in this volume pertain to the various themes of indological disciplines and speak highly of the erudition and painstaking research of Dr Panda. Every article is a brilliant testimony to his original ideas and independent thinking which is supported by a wonderful knowledge of the subject concerned and his wider reading. His analysis of the references and the interpretation of the text passages are logical and findings are all well supported by the textual evidences.

Dr Panda is one of the highly accomplished young scholars whom I know of. I am highly impressed by his knowledge of the various disciplines of Sanskrit ranging from Vedic literature not only to philosophy and Buddhism but also to Āyurveda, German and Computers. Academics is his profession as well as hobby; vocation and avocation at the same time. I am quite sure that this valuable collection of papers shall be received with great enthusiasm by all lovers of Indic Studies. **I congratulate Dr Panda and give all my blessings to the author and to the book.**

—Prof. G.C. Tripathi
Professor & Head (Kalakosha Division)
Indira Gandhi National Centre for the Arts
New Delhi

Blessings

Dr Narasingha Charan Panda is too well-known among scholars of Indology. Basically a student of Indian Philosophy, Dr Panda had devoted himself to illuminate a large number of topics related to the entire gamut of Indological studies, viz. the Vedas, Tantras, Buddhism and other schools of Indian Philosophy, the Epics, Purāṇas and literature. Questions relationg to all these subjects have been subjected to a keen enquiry by Dr Panda and the outcome is the present welcome Volume.

I have known Dr Panda as a sincere student and as a devoted researcher, who combines in him a comprehensive understanding of scholarly issues, impartial judgemeni and an exemplary clarity of expression. All the seventeen articles collected in this book entitled : "**Perspectives of Indian Thought**" will bear me out to prove the author as a sincere and painstaking Indologist.

Dr Panda has covered a diversity of subject matters right from the Vedas down to Kālidāsa, touching inter-alia Buddhism, Tantra and Purāṇa. Philosophy being the *forte* of the author his treatment of the subject matter is marked throughout by clarity of understanding and unambiguity of expression. I am happy to note that Sri Panda has stuck to the Indian motto **"नामूलं लिख्यते किंचित् नानपेक्षितमुच्यते"** and so all his articles are free from avoidable repetition and redundancy. Arguments and conclusions reached at, it is hoped, will satisfy the scholarly world.

Dr Panda has done well to provide a number of illustrations to clarify some of the points raised especially in these articles on ten *bhūmis*, the *avatāras*, and the tantric symbols. Similarly, some sketches have been provided to illustrate the sacrificial utensils used in the Vedic rituals. These illustrations will go a long way to show up the ritual and esoteric pattern of worship in ancient India. Addition of a Glossary of obscure and technical terms is also a notable feature of the volume. While congratulating the author for this *sārasvata śrama* I beg to conclude with the following prayer:

"विदुषा ग्रन्थकारेण शास्त्रतत्त्वनिरूपकाः।
निबन्धा रचिता यत्नाद् भवन्तु सुधियां मुदे॥"

—Prof. Biswanath Battacharya
Former Head, Dept. of Sanskrit,
Banaras Hindu University, Varanasi

KALIDASA SAMSTHANA
[Estd.1986]
28, Mahamanapuri, P.O.-BHU, Varanasi - 5

Blessings

I have gone through all the four layers of Indian wisdom—Vaidika, Paurāṇika, Bauddha and Tāntrika in Dr N.C. Panda's work : **'Perpsectives of Indian Thought'.**

The work, started with Vedic articles, is systematic, lucid and quite informative.

In Philosophy, the Tāntrika view is more or less touched with Buddhist concept, yet they do not give up the Vedic thoughts at all—"वैदिकास्तु वयं बौद्धाः" and therefore, admissible as theists too. Dr Panda has shown his ability to maintain the balance of his mind while talking both the opposite believers simultaneously.

This kind of study in ancient literature is welcome.

I think this work will show the path to the new generation to go through the tradition smoothly.

यद् वै भारतवर्षसीमनि सहस्राब्दीद्वयेनार्जितं
विज्ञानं, चतुरस्रतामुपगतं तद् वीक्ष्यतेऽस्मिन् युगे।
पण्डा-श्रीनरसिंह-वाग्विलसिते ग्रन्थेऽत्र तस्य च्छटा
प्राप्तुं शक्यत इत्यमुं बुधवरं वर्धापयामो हृदा ॥

With best wishes,

Dwivedi. R. Prasad.

—**Mahāmahopādhyāya Prof. Rewaprasada Dwivedi**
Former Dean, Faculty of Sanskrit
Dharmavijñāna Saṅkāya, B.H.U.
Recipient of the Certificate of Honour from President
of India, Sahitya Academy Award

Blessings

I felt delighted to glance through some of the essays written on a variety of subjects within broad spectrum of Indian Philosophy and Religion by Dr Narasingha Charan Panda, **one of my illustrious students of Sanskrit** at Kurukshetra University, Kurukshetra, many years ago. Though he had then specialized in Kashmir Śaivism, studying Sanskrit texts with me on the subject and producing a brilliant dissertation in that field for M.Phil. degree, he did not keep his studies confined to one narrow branch of Indian Philosophical Thought. Forced by his inquisitive mind to know more, his keen intellect and sheer perseverance, he extended the range of his study to cover other branches of knowledge included in Indian Philosophical thought ranging from the Vedas, the contribution of Swami Dayananda to Vedic Studies and Buddhism in which he specialized later on and other schools of orthodox Indian Philosophy from the study of original Sanskrit texts.

His essays, collected and published in this Volume entitled **'Perspectives of Indian Thought'**, bear eloquent testimony to the range of his study of texts on Indian Philosophy. His articles are marked by depth, originality in approach and precision of expression.

As his teacher, my blessings are always with him. I congratulate him heartily for this endeavour which I commend to its readers without any reservation whatsoever.

July 11,2006
Gurupūṇimā,
Kolkata

—Prof. Devavrata Sen Sharma
Research Professor, Sri Rama-krishna Mission, Golpark, Kolkata
Recipient of President's Certificate of Honour
Former Chairman, Dept. of Sanskrit, Pali & Prakrit
Ex-Director, Institute of Sanskrit & Indological Studies
Ex-Dean, Faculty of Indic Studies, Kurukshetra University
Former M.M Gopinath Kaviraj Senior Research Professor,
Asiatic Society, Kolkata

Blessings

It is my pleasure to write a few lines by way of blessings for a work entitled "**Perspectives of Indian Thought**" written by Dr Narasingha Charan Panda, Senior Research Officer of Indira Gandhi National Centre for the Arts, Varanasi. The author is known to me for about 20 years and I am happy to watch him growing in his field of research during these years. Dr Panda is a versatile scholar both in Vedic and Buddhist studies. Many research works written in these fields have brought glory to the author. Besides these, he has also earned good name in Āyurveda, Computer Science and Hindi language. His editing skill has been amply proved from his edited works. **Thus, with his varied experience he has proved himself as an asset to any Research Institution or University he serves.**

The present work "Perspectives of Indian Thought" is a new addition to his publications, although a few of its chapters have been published earlier by way of articles published in different Indological Journals of National and International repute. I am sure, like his other works, this too will be appreciated by the galaxy of scholars and I prey **Lord Jagannatha to Bless the author** for his future undertakings.

—Prof. A.C. Sarangi
Vicc-hancellor
Shri Jagannath Sanskrit Vishvavidyalaya, Shri Vihar,
Puri, Orissa

26 7 2006
Puri

Blessings

It gives me great pleasure and satisfaction in introducing this book, **'Perspectives of Indian Thought'** containing selected research articles related to various aspects of Indian Thought. The author, Dr Narasingha Charan Panda carries with him a wonderful academic record, possessing Research degrees and high record of higher studies. When we take a bird's eye view of these essays we find that the author has dealt different topics of academic interest, starting from Vedic Literature, including the great epic the Mahābhārata, Buddhist studies and an interesting study of the geographical data appearing in the Meghadūta of Kālidāsa. Swami Dayananda was the greatest Vedic scholar of nineteenth century, who had revolutionized in the field of Vedic interpretation and influenced the whole of scholar-world. Dr Panda has thoroughly examined the method of Vedic interpretation deduced by the great Swami and has shown the merits of Yāska's theory of Vedic etymology.

It is a novel idea to throw light on the sacred place like Naimiṣāraṇya which has often been depicted in our mythological literature like Epics and the Purâṇas. It is unfortunate that our younger generation is totally ignorant and unaware about these holy places. It has been mentioned in various Purāṇas that thousands of Ṛṣis of yore used to gather in these forests to discuss the subtle philosophical theories based on sacred writings.

As far as Buddhism is concerned, the author has dealt with many topics which hitherto have not been touched by other scholars. For example, I may mention: Concept of Indriyas, Concept of Bhūmi and the mythology surrounding Māra (Cupid). These have been ably discussed in this book. Last but not the least, I may say that the author has taken great pains in bringing out this volume which will definitely add to the Indological writings of merit. My good wishes and blessings to Dr Panda who had been my student in the Dayananda Chair for Vedic Studies in the Panjab University during years 1986-1991. I hope more useful writing will come down from his pen in future.

Nandanvan, Jodhpur
23 Aug., 2006

—Prof. Bhawani Lal Bhartiya
Editor, Paropkārī Journal
Former Professor & Head
Dayanand Chair for Vedic Studies
Panjab University, Chandigarh

Blessings

I have gone through the book entitled '**Perspectives of Indian Thought**' by Dr N.C. Panda of the Indira Gandhi National Centre for the Arts. The book commands a wide range of Indian wisdom, analyses some baffling issues involving human psyche and ethos. He reflects on the Vedic lore and Purāṇic exegesis, enters into the layers of the Śākta and Śaiva experiences and evaluates socio-religious concepts.

Nature of the Absolute in Kashmir Śaivism, Abhinavagupta on mystical experience and Symbols and Śakti worship are the articles which deal with the fine threads of Indian Philosophical enquiry. Problems pertaining to art and culture present interesting accounts marked by scholarly discussions.

I may safely remark that the main signposts of some absorbing topics have been surveyed with great care. **I hope the work will be widely appreciated by serious students of Indian Philosophy and Culture.**

—Prof. Amar Nath Pandey
Former Professor & Head
Dept. of Sanskrit
Mahatma Gandhi Kashi Vidyapith
Varanasi

My Felicitations

Although infrequently, but whenever I have the occasion of coming across Dr Narasingha Charan Pandaji, I feel gentle touch of a scholarly aura surrounding him. His pronouncements, I feel, are like a silken breeze. Here is an unpretentious young man but with a rich account of study and publications, spanning a variety of Indological rubrics. He specializes in Kashmir Śaivism while he is equally involved in the in-depth of study and researches in Buddhism and especially its thought processes. It is gratifying to find that, besides the above, he holds a "Ratna" degree in Āyurveda. Thus it is a pleasure to know a scholar with multi-faced academic commitments / involvements. Even a cursory look at his publications or paper presentation would convince us for the catholicity of his knowledge. He has participated with great success in various conferences and seminars.

His contribution to the Kalākosha Project of the Indira Gandhi National Centre for the Arts deserves our great admiration. I have gone through the synopsis of his proposed publication, "**Perspectives of Indian Thought**" and am very much impressed by its contents. **It is going to be a reference material or resource publication for both the students and scholars**.

I wish him from success to success and wish him to attain further and further glory.

—Prof. Rai Anand Krishna
Former Dean, Faculty of Arts
& Director,
Bharat Kala Bhawan,
Banaras Hindu University
Varanasi.

Krishna Kutir,
N 1/55, Nagwa
Varanasi-5.

Blessings

Dr Narasingha Ch. Panda is a versatile young scholar and has succeeded to make a mark in the present day scenario of Indological Studies. His dedicated approach towards the Vedic Studies and to the contribution of Dayananda Sarasvatī has brought him a very good name. The present work **'Perspectives of Indian Thought'** speaks itself about his multi-form approach towards Indian thought. He has studied moral and cultural aspects of Vedas and Vedic Literature, and has traced the continuity of Vedic thoughts and rituals in the text of the Mahābhārata along with the evaluation of beliefs and Socio-cultural aspects of Purāṇic literature. He has examined many concepts of Buddhism and Kashmir Śaivism and also taken account of mystical experiences of Abhinavagupta and symbols of Śakti worship and much more. Dr Panda has put in such a variety of topics in this volume that this work looks like a **Panorama of Indian thought**.

I feel personal belonging to this work as it has been dedicated to my Revered Guru Late Prof. Gopikamohan Bhattacharya.

I bestow my hearty blessings to Dr Panda and wish him all success in life.

—Prof. Dr Ranvir Singh
Institute of Sanskrit & Indological Studies
Kurukshetra University
KURUKSHETRA

शुभाशंसा

श्रीमता डॉ० नरसिंहचरणपण्डामहाशयेनोपनिबद्धमाङ्ग्लभाषया **"Perspectives of Indian Thought"** इत्यभिधेयं ग्रन्थं स्थले स्थलेऽधीत्य नितरां प्रसीदति चेतः। अत्र बहूनां भारतीयानां वैदेशिकानुयायिनां विभ्रममपाकर्तुं जिज्ञासुँश्चोपकर्तुं निबद्धेऽस्मिन् ग्रन्थे आवेदादानीतिशास्त्रमाश्रित्य विविधान् विषयान् न्यरूपयद् ग्रन्थकारोऽत्र येनास्य वैदुष्यं प्रमितं भवति। निरूपणं च प्रामाणिकमभिव्यक्तिश्च स्फुटेति हेतोः

भवन्ति ते सभ्यतमा विपश्चितां मनोगतं वाचि निवेशयन्ति ये।
नयन्ति तेष्वप्युपपन्ननैपुणा गभीरमर्थं कतिचित्प्रकाशताम्॥

इति महाकविभारविवचनं (किरातार्जुनीय १४.४) स्मर्यत एव ।

अन्ते च ग्रन्थकारमाशीर्भिर्वर्धयन् मनीषिणोऽध्येतारो निवेद्यन्ते यत्ते निष्पक्षं विवेचयन्तु ग्रन्थेऽत्र कियान् गुणः कियान् वा दोषः - **भावावबोधविहितो न दुनोति दोषः** इति नीतिमनुसृत्य येन ग्रन्थान्तररचने ग्रन्थकारस्योत्साहो वर्धेतेति।

वाराणसी
27.7.2006

–प्रो० श्रीनारायण मिश्रः
पूर्वकलासंकायप्रमुखः,
आचार्यः संस्कृतविभागाध्यक्षचरश्च
काशीहिन्दूविश्वविद्यालयः, वाराणसी

शुभाशंसा

श्रुतिस्मृतिपुराणोक्तसिद्धान्तसरणीकृतम् ।
भारतीयविचाराणां सन्दृश्यं दर्शनोदितम् ॥ १ ॥

प्रकीर्णं बहुधा तत्र ग्रन्थेष्वेतत्पृथक् पृथक् ।
महाविषयसन्दर्भानेकत्रीकर्तुमिच्छुकः ॥ २ ॥

नरसिंहः सुधीः शोधप्रबोधोद्बुधचेतसा ।
प्राणैषीदुक्तसन्दर्भग्रन्थरत्नमनाविलम्॥ ३ ॥

भारतीयविमर्शोच्चपराकाष्ठामधिष्ठितम् ।
यज्ज्ञानं दर्शनप्रख्यं तन्नूनं श्रुतिमूलकम्॥ ४ ॥

विरोधादनुरोधाद् वा नास्तिक्यास्तिक्यभेदभाक्।
कामं भिन्नार्थकं तत्तद्दर्शनं श्रौतसंहितम् ॥ ५ ॥

नवमाधुनिकं तत्त्वानुसन्धाननिदर्शनम् ।
नानाविषयभूयिष्ठं दर्शनं नाम सार्थकम् ॥ ६ ॥

सुधीशोधार्थिविदुषां सर्वेषामुपकारकम् ।
विपश्चिन्नरसिंहेन प्रणीतं पुस्तकं ध्रुवम् ॥ ७ ॥

श्रीनरसिंहबुधोऽयं सदसद्बुद्धिविचक्षणो मनस्वी ।
पण्डापरवरसंज्ञो कीर्तिं प्रीतिं च विन्देत ॥ ८ ॥

–प्रो० शिवजी उपाध्याय
उपकुलपतिचरः एवम् विभागाध्यक्षश्च
साहित्य संगीत कला विभाग
सम्पूर्णानन्द संस्कृत विश्वविद्यालय,
वाराणसी।

शिवसंकल्पः

दर्शनस्य किं स्वरूपम्? तस्य परमं तात्पर्यं कीदृशमिति वेदा एव प्रमाणम्। वेदार्थानुसन्धानपरा गहनाध्ययनपुरःसरमस्य नित्यं नूतनं रहस्यमुद्भावयन्ति। एतेषु पुरीगोवर्धनपीठस्य शंकराचार्याः श्रीभारतीकृष्णमहास्वामिनो गणितसूत्ररहस्यं समुद्घाट्य "वेदिक् मेथमेटिक्स" ग्रन्थरत्नं निर्मायाभिनवां सरणीं दर्शितवन्तो नूतनगवेषकाणां कृते। देशान्तरेष्वपि मैक्समूलर-रोथप्रभृतयः स्वोपज्ञेषु ग्रन्थनिकायेषु शोधमन्दाकिनीमाप्लावयन्ति स्म। भारते स्वामिदयानन्दाऽरविन्द-मधुसूदन-ओझाप्रभृतिभिर्ग्रन्थग्रन्थिविभेदनकर्तृभिर्नवनवोन्मेषशालिन्यो व्याख्याः शास्त्रस्य कृताः। सा एव सरणी ज्यायसी ।

'पुराणपूर्णचन्द्रेण श्रुतिज्योत्स्ना प्रकीर्तिता' इति न्यायेन सरलया तरलया गिरा पुराणकारैः सामाजिकानां कृते निबन्धितानि पुराणानि। वेदार्थास्तत्रापि निरवच्छिन्नाः प्रवहन्तः नैकानि काव्यनाटकानि जनयन्ति समाजोपस्कारकाणि।

तरुणेन बुधवरेण श्रीनरसिंहेन "**Perspectives of Indian Thought**" इति शीर्षकशेखरितग्रन्थमाध्यमेन वेदादारभ्य पुराणानि क्रोडीकृत्यालङ्कारशास्त्रं विचुम्ब्य, बौद्धदर्शनमुल्लिङ्ग्य, भारतीयसंस्कृतिं संपोष्य, प्राच्यपाश्चात्ययोर्मतं निरीक्ष्य जिज्ञासूनां कृते निकषं स्थापितमिति निश्चप्रचं ब्रवीमि। सहृदयस्य डॉ० नरसिंहपण्डामहोदयस्य सर्वविधं शुभं भूयादिति भवानी-जानिमभ्यर्थये।

नरसिंहो गुणी दक्षो विद्याविनयमण्डितः ।
बहुशास्त्रसमालोकी ग्रन्थस्यास्य सुलेखकः॥

–प्रो० गंगाधरपण्डाः

शुभाशंसनम्

समेषां शेमुषीजुषां विदुषां कृतेऽयं परमप्रसन्नताया विषयो वरीवर्ति यदिन्दिरागान्धिराष्ट्रियकलाकेन्द्रे वरिष्ठस्याऽनुसन्धातुः पण्डोपाह्वस्य डॉ० नरसिंहस्य **Perspectives of Indian Thought** इत्याख्यं पुस्तकं प्रकाशते। **इदं खलु स्वनामधन्यानां गुरुवर्याणां स्व० डॉ० गोपिकामोहन भट्टाचार्याणां पुण्यस्मृतौ समर्पितमस्ति।** श्रद्धेयैः गुरुचरणैः सह सम्बद्धं पुस्तकमनुरुध्य कञ्चिल्लेखनं वस्तुतः मत्कृते कमप्यपूर्वमाह्लादं जनयति ।

पण्डामहाभागानां गम्भीरवैदुष्येणाहं बहुतिथात्कालात् परिचितोऽस्मि यस्य पुष्टिर्ह्यस्य पुस्तकस्य पठनेन स्वतः जाजायते। वस्तुतः पुस्तकमिदं केनाप्येकेन विषयेण सह सम्बद्धं न भूत्वा लेखकस्य प्रकाशितानामप्रकाशितानां च शोधलेखानां संग्रहभूतं विद्यते। अनया दृष्ट्या पुस्तकस्यास्य विषयसूची एवास्मिन् तथ्ये पर्याप्तमुपोद्बलकं वर्तते यदेतैः चिन्तनस्य के के आयामाः स्पृष्टाः। तदनुसारेणात्रादौ तावत् वेदा मानवतायाः प्रतीकभूताः प्रतिपादिताः। अनन्तरं महाभारतं पुराणानि बौद्धदर्शनं च वगाह्यान्ते मेघदूतशुक्रनीतिसाराभिनवगुप्तपादानां चापि विचारक्षमा मीमांसा व्यधायि। नेदं वाचनिकं प्रत्युत स्वाभाविकं यदत्र सर्वे निबन्धाः प्रमाणतर्कपुरस्सरत्वेन प्रशस्याश्चकासति। पुस्तकान्ते प्रदत्तया सन्दर्भग्रन्थसूच्या अनुक्रमण्या चास्य महत्त्वमत्यधिकं प्रवृद्धम्। डॉ० पण्डामहोदया विद्याविनयसम्पन्ना युवानश्च सन्ति। भविष्यदृष्ट्या संस्कृतस्यानन्ताः संभावना अत्रानुमातुं शक्यन्ते। अत एव संस्कृतजगद् उद्ग्रीवं सदेतान् प्रत्यन्तमाशापूर्णया दृष्ट्योत्प्रेक्षते। अहमेतेषां दीर्घायुष्यं स्वास्थ्यं च कामयमान इदमपि दृढं विश्वसिति यत्प्रकृतं पुस्तकं विदुषां कण्ठहारत्वेनावश्यं समुचितमादरं प्राप्स्यति, आशासे च यच्छीघ्रमेवाहमेषामन्यत् किमपि पुस्तकमाश्रित्य लेखनस्यावसरं लप्स्य इत्यावेदयते।

–प्रो० डॉ० भीमसिंहः
आचार्योऽध्यक्षश्च
संस्कृत-पालि-प्राकृतविभागे
कुरुक्षेत्र-विश्वविद्यालयः
कुरुक्षेत्रम्

शुभाशंसा वर्धापनञ्च

उत्कलप्रान्तसम्भवेन विविधविश्वविद्यालयाधीतविद्येन विशेषतश्चण्डीगढस्थपंजाबविश्वविद्यालय-विद्यातीर्थकृतस्नानेन वेदादिसच्छास्त्रपारावारपारीणेना-पीतसरस्वतीरससारेण 'पण्डा' इति विश्रुतेन विदुषा श्रीनरसिंहचरणेन **'Perspectives of Indian Thought'** इत्यभिधेयं पुस्तकं विद्वत्समक्षे समुपस्थापितमिति हर्षस्यायं विषयः।

वस्तुतस्त्वयं ग्रन्थः पण्डामहाभागानां प्रकाशिताप्रकाशितशोधलेखानां संग्रहस्वरूप एव। वेदमधिकृत्य लिखितं लेखत्रयं ननु तत्तद्विषयेऽपूर्वमिति पठित्वैव विज्ञास्यन्ति विज्ञाः। महाभारतमहाकाव्यमनुसृत्य लेखद्वयं, पुराणान्यधिकृत्य लेखत्रयं, बौद्धमतमनुकृत्य चत्वारो लेखाः, अन्ये च विविधविषयाधिकृताः पञ्च लेखाः लेखकस्य लेखनवैदुष्यमेव प्रतिपादयन्ति। यतो ह्येते लेखाः शोधलेखाः खल्वसामान्या विशिष्टाश्च। अतः पाठकानां कृते पाथेयात्मका एव ।

षड्भाषाज्ञेन, अष्टलिपिज्ञेन, शोधप्रवीणेन, पञ्चत्रिंशच्छोधपत्रलेखकेन, त्रिंशद्यावद्राष्ट्रीयान्ताराष्ट्रीय-विविधसंस्कृतसंगोष्ठीषु कृतकृत्येन विदुषा लिखितत्वादिमे शोधलेखाः पुस्तकत्वेन संग्राह्या एव। शोधात्मकं पुस्तकमिदं सर्वेषां विदुषां संस्कृतप्रियाणां छात्राणाञ्च कृते पठनीयमेव। ग्रन्थोऽयं पुस्तकालयानां शोभां वर्धयतु। श्रीमान् नरसिंह चरणः पण्डा नैकानेतादृशान् लेखान् लिखित्वा ग्रन्थांश्च विरचय्य संस्कृतजननीचरणशरणभाग् भवत्विति च कामयते ।

–प्रोफेसरः डॉ० विक्रम कुमारः
संस्कृतविभागः,
अध्यक्ष, दयानन्द वैदिक अनुसन्धान पीठ,
पंजाब विश्वविद्यालयः

शुभानुशंसनम्

प्राचीना खलु भारतीया संस्कृतिः स्वगतभेदोपभेदमाबिभ्राणाऽपि शकहूणादिविविधजनजातीय-प्रभावानात्मन्यन्तर्यमयन्त्यप्येकाऽखण्डाऽनादिकालतो निरवच्छिन्नं प्रवहमाना च विराजते। तस्याः सम्यगध्ययनमाकलनं च सुतरामत्यन्तं दुष्करं विस्तृतं समयसाध्यं च, तथापि डॉ० नरसिंहचरणपण्डामहोदयैरस्यां दिशायां किमपि स्तुत्यकार्यमनुष्ठितम्।

अस्मिंस्तावल्लघुकाये ग्रन्थे वैदिक-पौराणिक-शैव-बौद्धपरम्परामधिकृत्य काऽपि परिचयात्मिका दिक् प्रकाशिता। मन्ये, अग्रेऽप्येतैरेतादृशमेव कार्यमनुष्ठाय भारतीयसंस्कृतेर्लोके प्रकाशनं विधास्यत इति।

अनुमोदे चाहमेतत् कार्यं साफल्यं च कामये विद्वद्वराणामेषां पण्डामहोदयानां जीवनस्येत्यलम्।

दि० २३-९-२००६

–प्रो० रामशंकरः त्रिपाठी
शोधाचार्यः
केन्द्रयोच्चतिब्बतीशिक्षासंस्थानम्
सारनाथः, वाराणसी।
(पूर्व आचार्य एवं अध्यक्ष, बौद्धदर्शन विभाग
सम्पूर्णानन्द संस्कृत विश्वविद्यालय)

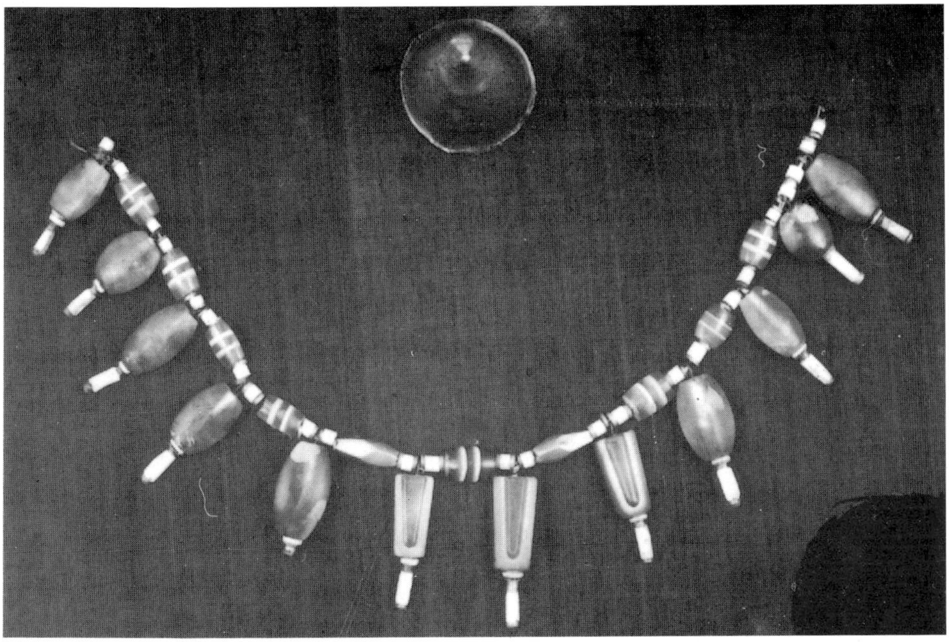

Pl. 2.1 Jade Necklace, Harappa, circa 2700 B.C., Collection : National Museum, New Delhi.

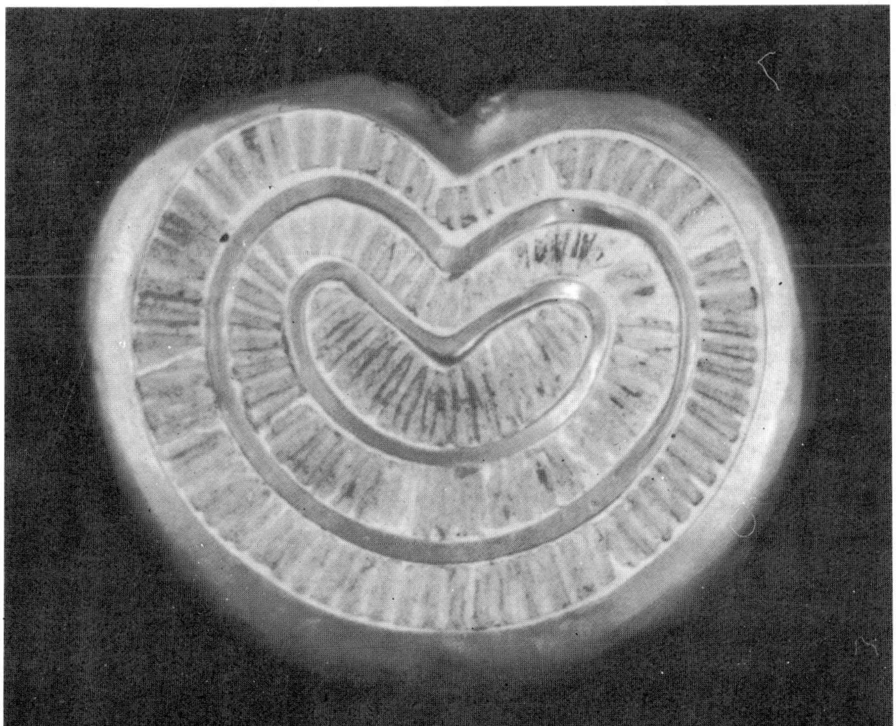

Pl. 2.2 Gold Pendant, Harappa, circa 2700 B.C., Collection : National Museum, New Delhi.

Pl. 11.1 Buddha's First Sermon at Sarnath. (Archaeological Museum, Sarnath)

Pl. 11.2 Buddha in Earth Touching Mudrā. (British Museum)

Pl. 12.1 Dharmacakra Kuṣaṇa period, 2nd century A.D. (Patna Museum)

Pl. 12.2 Buddha's descent from the Tuṣita heaven, Kurkihar, early 9th century A.D. (Patna museum)

Pl. 15.2 Lakshṃī (Kamalā) Painted by Molaram Bharat Kala Bhawan. (B.H.U.)

Pl. 15.3 Śrī Vidyā Painted by Molaram Bharat Kala Bhawan. (B.H.U.)

Pl. 15.4 Devī Ṣoḍṣī Painted by Molaram Bharat Kala Bhawan. (B.H.U.)